I0884559

"Nearly all men can stand adversity,
but if you want to test a man's character, give him power."

— President Abraham Lincoln

Lincoln Takes Command

Steve Norder

The Campaign to Seize Norfolk and the Destruction of the CSS *Virginia*

Savas Beatie
California

© 2020 by Steve Norder

All rights reserved. No part of this publication may be reproduced, stored in a retrieval system, or transmitted, in any form or by any means, electronic, mechanical, photocopying, recording, or otherwise, without the prior written permission of the publisher.

Library of Congress Cataloging-in-Publication Data

Names: Norder, Steve, author.
Title: Lincoln Takes Command: The Campaign to Seize Norfolk and the Ddestruction of the CSS *Virginia* / by Steven Norder.
Description: First edition. | California : Savas Beatie, [2019] | Includes bibliographical references and index. | Summary: "The first study to detail the important week in May 1862 when, for the first and only time in the country's history, a sitting president took direct control of military forces, land and sea, to wage a campaign with wide-ranging consequences. Abraham Lincoln ordered a beach-landing to capture Norfolk, the shelling of major Confederate installations and defenses, and guided naval assets that helped capture two important cities (Norfolk and Portsmouth) and the Gosport Navy Yard, the best of its kind along the entire Atlantic seaboard. Based on extensive primary sources, supported by original maps and photos, footnotes, biblio, appendices, and index." — provided by publisher.
Identifiers: LCCN 2019048055 | ISBN 9781611214574 (hardcover) | ISBN 9781611214581 (ebook)
Subjects: LCSH: Hampton Roads, Battle of, Va., 1862. | Lincoln, Abraham, 1809-1865. | *Virginia* (Ironclad) | United States. Navy—History—Civil War, 1861-1865. | Confederate States of America. Navy—History.
Classification: LCC E473.2 .N67 2019 | DDC 973.7/52—dc23
LC record available at https://lccn.loc.gov/2019048055
ISBN-13: 978-1-611214-57-4

First edition, first printing

SB

Savas Beatie
989 Governor Drive, Suite 102
El Dorado Hills, CA 95762
916-941-6896
sales@savasbeatie.com
www.savasbeatie.com

MIX
Paper from responsible sources
FSC
www.fsc.org
FSC® C011935

Savas Beatie titles are available at special discounts for bulk purchases in the United States. Contact us for additional information.

Printed in the United States of America

For Cleis A. Hahn, Tavik A. Hahn and Mary A. Norder

May you know the past to understand the present and anticipate the future.

Table of Contents

Table of Contents (continued)

List of Maps

List of Photos/Illustrations

List of Photos/Illustrations (continued)

Citation Abbreviations

American Swedish Historical Museum	ASHM
Army Military History Institute, U.S.	AMHI
Battles and Leaders of the Civil War	B&L
[British] National Archives	BNA
Chattahoochee Valley Historical Society	CVHS
Historical Society of Pennsylvania	HSP
Library of Congress	LC
Lincoln Studies Center	LSC
Mariners' Museum	MM
National Archives	NA
National Museum of American History	NMAH
Naval History and Heritage Command	NHHC

Acknowledgments

CRAMMED onto bookshelves in my "den" are almost 1,400 books on the Civil War. It is not a topic of interest as much as a topic of compulsion since my grandparents gave me my first Civil War book for my 12th birthday. That slim volume still is in my collection.

My collection is, of course, just a fraction of the books published since the nation's greatest tragedy. No one could possibly read them all, so why add another to the list? Why undertake years of research and writing about a single week that involved Abraham Lincoln, the most written-about president? There is no simple answer. I hope readers find the endeavor worthwhile. Whatever faults this book may possess, they are solely my own.

No one can research and write a book alone. While the Internet has revolutionized the exciting and often tedious chore of finding 19th century primary sources in all their various forms, technology—at least not yet—has not eliminated the need to visit libraries and archives. Those individuals who devote their time and energy to preserving our past need to be praised and thanked every day.

At the top of my list is Nancy Torres, the tech services clerk at the North Richland Hills Library in North Richland Hills, Texas. Without her help during the early years of research, the need for long hours of traveling from archive to archive, and library to library would have overwhelmed me. Nancy's help with inter-library loan requests proved invaluable and brought the books I needed to me. Thank you.

The Sargeant Memorial Collection at the public library in Norfolk, Virginia, had many valuable documents including the Virginia Gordan scrapbook. Other important help was provided by library staff at Georgia State University, Emory University, and public libraries in Fort Worth, Texas; DeKalb County, Georgia;

and Allen County, Indiana. They all provided materials that allowed me to flesh out the story.

I spent many enjoyable hours at the New York State Library and Archives in Albany, New York, where the John E. Wool Papers are housed, as well as the Philip Corell Papers on the 99th New York regiment. Thanks also to the staff at other research stops, including: the Historical Research Center at Hill College in Hillsborough, Texas; Swedish-American Historical Museum in Philadelphia for the John Ericsson Papers; Historical Society of Pennsylvania, also in Philadelphia; The Library Company of Philadelphia; Virginia Historical Society in Richmond, Virginia; Hampton Roads Naval Museum in Norfolk, Virginia; Mariners' Museum in Newport News, Virginia; and the British National Archives in Kew, Richmond, England.

An incredible amount of quality research can be conducted online, and government sources are especially worthwhile. One invaluable source, what I like to refer to as "history's first draft," is the digitized newspapers provided by the website Chronicling America, which is part of the Library of Congress. These keyword searchable newspapers save endless hours and a lot of eye strain scrolling through microfilm. The National Archives, though not fully digitized, also remains the premier source of original documents.

Once the manuscript was drafted it was time to solicit opinions from others beyond my family. Civil War historian Michael Shaffer and Terry Kingery, past president of the Atlanta Civil War Roundtable, both graciously volunteered to read the draft and provide their critiques. While their comments were important and helped improve the story, it was their encouragement that took the project to the next level.

Happily, Shaffer suggested approaching Savas Beatie with the manuscript. Its managing director, Theodore P. Savas assigned editor Thomas Schott, and both guided the manuscript and me through the long process to the finished book. Thanks also to Joel Manuel and James Epperson for proofing and commenting on the manuscript. They cannot be thanked enough. That thanks also applies to Marketing Director Sarah Keeney. I also must thank Jeff Boyer for producing the original maps. We have the same conviction that a history without maps leaves the reader lost at sea.

While research and writing mostly is a solitary job, family support is most welcome. My oldest daughter, Akum, went beyond just encouragement. Despite working on her own history book of Albany, New York, she took the time to run over to the New York State Archives for a page number I forgot to note or to verify a quote. Of course, there is Lois, my friend, my partner, and my wife. An outstanding newspaper editor, Lois' suggestions on text flow and presentation vastly improved every chapter. I will never tire of our arguments over comma placements.

None of these wonderful and helpful people who contributed so much to this process are responsible for any errors in the history, misspelled words, or misplaced commas. Those are my errors alone.

My hope is that you will enjoy the story of Lincoln's week leading a military campaign as much as I enjoyed researching and writing about it.

Steve Norder

Preface

LINCOLN *Takes Command* is not just another book about the 16th president. Instead, it tells the story about perhaps the most important early week in Lincoln's presidency—seven days that involved ironclad ships, combined operations, and a president who assumed control of land and sea assets to act as a military commander. It was the first and last time an American president has done so.

I presented this week in a day-by-day account (as close as I could construct such a thing) after spending years researching and reading primary sources. From May 5 to 12, 1862, Lincoln was not only the recognized commander in chief of United States forces, but a field commander directing a campaign that he hoped would help bring that war closer to an end.

As strange as it sounds, given all the books written on this president, we simply don't know enough about Lincoln and his presidency. Modern presidents have almost every minute of their lives in office recorded and chronicled. No stenographers or videographers recorded Lincoln's every word or action. Indeed, so much of what he did, from the mundane to the important, passed unrecorded. No one noted when he got up each morning, whom he saw each day, when, and what they talked about, or when he would go for a walk—though that most often led him to the war department's telegraph office. We have snippets of such things, but the record is woefully incomplete.

Most of the insights we do have come from those who met the president and wrote down the conversation—sometimes years later and not always accurately. These accounts often disagree on the important particulars. Vital pieces of information yearned for by historians needed to make sense of what happened, and, more importantly, why something occurred, remain in the shadows.

Lincoln's week in May did not unfold in a vacuum. The Confederates had evacuated the massive Yorktown defenses, George B. McClellan's Army of the Potomac was moving slowly but steadily up the Peninsula toward Williamsburg, and Maj. Gen. Ambrose Burnside's troops threatened Norfolk and its environs from the south. The most momentous events unfolded two months earlier on March 8-9 when the CSS *Virginia* (formerly the wooden frigate USS *Merrimack*) steamed into Hampton Roads and decimated part of the Union fleet, proving that wooden ships did not stand a chance against the new Confederate ironclad. The next day, the *Virginia* met ironclad USS *Monitor* in the same waters and fought to a draw before the antagonists withdrew to their respective corners. In public opinion, and in the imaginations of Americans North and South and European countries, the fight between the *Virginia* and the *Monitor* marked a radical advancement in naval warfare. Many in the North greatly feared the *Virginia* would change the course of the war. Secretary of War Edwin Stanton, who worried she would steam up the Potomac River and shell Washington and the White House, ordered a small fleet of barges sunk to prevent such a calamity. Few realized the *Virginia's* structural and mechanical problems. What was apparent, however, was that the battle of the ironclads made the wooden fleets of the two main European powers—Britain and France—obsolete. The day of iron ships had dawned.

However, the *Virginia* wasn't the first ship made of wood and covered with metal, and the *Monitor* wasn't the first ship made of metal. The British had built one. The French had, too. What they had not done was turn those experimental vessels on each other. No one knew how a battle between metal ships would unfold. Now they had a better idea.

The fact that the clash between iron ships was essentially a draw—neither was sunk or sustained serious material damage—was not expected, but it might have been predicted. The first confrontation pitted unknowns against one another. The *Virginia*, for example, was armed with ordnance designed to sink wooden, not iron-plated, ships. The *Monitor's* new unique turret system was untested, hard to control, and resulted in inaccurate fire. Based on what they learned in that first clash, both sides prepared for the second battle confident they would be able to sink or capture their antagonist.

But the second clash never happened. President Lincoln and many of his high ranking naval officers did not want to risk the *Monitor* in another fight with the *Virginia*. The Union ironclad, after all, was the only true ironclad available that could stand up to the *Virginia*. While that decision grated on the *Monitor's* crew—who were taunted as cowards in the Southern press—the president had a larger picture in mind. The *Virginia* may have shifted the balance of naval power on March 8, but the *Monitor's* appearance that night returned that balance to the Union's favor the following day.

For all its power, the Confederate's hope could never leave Hampton Roads. Her first captain, Flag Officer Franklin Buchanan, knew the heavy iron casemate made the *Virginia* too top-heavy for anything but the calmest of waters, and that her engines were too weak and too unreliable to rely upon. She could not survive in the open sea. His successor, Josiah Tattnall, eventually faced the critical choice of trying to save the *Virginia* by steaming across the Roads and into the James River, or moving out to meet the Federal fleet in an effort to reach a port in the Carolinas or Georgia. He decided upon the former. When it proved impossible to sufficiently lighten her draft to get her upriver, however, his only option was destruction. Hampton Roads, the outlet to the world for the Richmond government up the James River, remained blocked. The Rebels would never find a way to threaten Hampton Roads or the Union fleet again.

Ironically, the same issue that hindered the *Virginia* from becoming a more potent Southern weapon with the ability to break the Union blockade also did in the *Monitor*. She, too, was unstable at sea. The initial confrontation between the two ironclads almost never took place because John Ericsson's invention barely survived the trip from New York to Hampton Roads. Only the quick thinking of her captain, John Worden, and the availability of calmer leeward water kept the *Monitor* afloat or she may have become little more than a footnote in Civil War history. Just nine months after the famous battle, she floundered and sank in rough seas off Cape Hatteras in an attempt to make it to Wilmington, North Carolina.

Just as this book is not a story about just President Lincoln, it also is not just about the *Monitor* and *Virginia*. *Lincoln Takes Command* explains, on a day-to-day basis, how the president assumed command in the field and led a nearly bloodless and very consequential campaign during a single week of what was about to become a prolonged and bloody war. The main chapters, with explanatory footnotes that expand our understanding of events, encompass the day-by-day events of that important week. A timeline of events intended to provide context to Lincoln's week in Hampton Roads follows, beginning with his election and continuing to just before his arrival at Fort Monroe. Three appendices close out the study with a variety of information on personalities and ships involved, as well as the legal documentation for the concluding chapter.

My hope is that readers find it both informative, and satisfying.

President Abraham Lincoln. *Library of Congress*

Timeline

November 1860 – May 1862

1860

November 6 (USA): Abraham Lincoln, Republican from Illinois, is elected U.S. president.

December 20 (CSA): South Carolina becomes the first Southern state to announce its secession from the Union. Six Deep South states soon follow.

1861

February 9 (CSA): The Provisional Confederate Congress selects Jefferson Davis of Mississippi as president of the newly declared Confederate States of America.

February 18 (CSA): Davis takes the oath of office at the Alabama state capitol in Montgomery and nominates Stephen R. Mallory, of Florida, as his secretary of the navy.

February 27 (CSA): The naval affairs committee of the Confederate Congress offers a resolution to investigate the "propriety of constructing . . . two iron-plated frigates and such iron-plated gunboats . . . necessary to protect the commerce and provide for the safety of Confederacy."[1]

1 U.S. Congress, *Journal of the Congress of the Confederate States of America, 1861-1865*, U.S. Senate Document no. 234, 58th Cong., 2nd sess., 7 vols. (Washington, DC, 1904), 1:90.

March 4 (USA): Lincoln takes the oath of office as the country's 16th president.

March 7 (USA): Gideon Welles takes office as U.S. secretary of the navy. Welles, a four-year Navy department veteran in the James K. Polk administration, realizes the American Navy is ill prepared for war with only 69 ships of all types, 42 of which are serviceable.

April 10 (USA): The safety of the Gosport Navy Yard near Norfolk, Virginia, is a concern. Welles orders Commodore Charles S. McCauley to prepare ships under repair, especially the wooden frigate USS *Merrimack*, to sail with as much equipment and government stores as possible.

April 12 (USA): Welles orders the Navy's chief engineer, Benjamin F. Isherwood, to Gosport to prepare *Merrimack* for sailing.

April 12 (CSA): The Confederates fire on Fort Sumter in the harbor of Charleston, South Carolina. Lincoln calls for 75,000 volunteers the next day to suppress the rebellion.

April 16 (USA): Engineer Isherwood reports the *Merrimack* repaired and ready to sail. McCauley, perhaps influenced by junior Southern-born officers, delays her departure three times and then extinguishes ship's boiler fires.

April 17 (USA): Welles dispatches Commodore Hiram Paulding to move the *Merrimack* out of harm's way. Paulding returns to Washington when he discovers the ship still in port.

(CSA): Virginia delegates convene to consider a secession vote to leave Union. Norfolk and Portsmouth's delegates vote with majority "aye," after Lincoln's call to arms.

April 18 (CSA): Virginia's Governor John Letcher orders Maj. Gen. William B. Taliaferro to Norfolk to evaluate the current situation in the Norfolk-Portsmouth area and the Gosport Navy Yard. He also orders Lts. Robert B. Pegram and Catesby ap Roger Jones, of the state's fledgling navy, to take over the yard and organize its defenses if the U.S. Navy vacates.[2]

2 William B. Taliaferro to John Letcher, Apr. 23, 1861, *in Official Records of the Union and Confederate Navies in the War of the Rebellion*, 30 vols. (Washington, DC, 1894-1922), 4:306, hereafter cited as *ORN*; John W. H. Porter, *A Record of Events in Norfolk County, Virginia, from April 19th, 1861, to May 10th, 1862, with a History of the Soldiers and Sailors of Norfolk County, Norfolk City and Portsmouth Who Served in the Confederate States Army and Navy* (Portsmouth, VA, 1892), 11.

The destruction of the Gosport Navy Yard. Virginians tried to stop the destruction of U.S. ships in Norfolk's harbor on the night of April 20-21, 1861. Union marines and sailors both scuttled and burned the ships and set buildings and supplies on fire to prevent Virginia, and the newly created Confederacy, from using the facility. *Naval History & Heritage Command, NH 1059*

April 19 (USA): With Virginia's secession certain, McCauley refuses to sail *Merrimack* out from Gosport. Welles orders Paulding to return to Norfolk, remove ships, and put materials in Federal-held Fort Monroe.

(CSA): Taliaferro doubts he has the men and weapons needed to seize the Gosport Navy Yard, but he does take Fort Norfolk and 2,800 pounds of gunpowder.

April 20 (USA): Most of McCauley's subordinate officers resign to join the Southern cause. He orders U.S. ships in the harbor scuttled. Paulding, aboard USS *Pawnee*, arrives at Gosport and orders the yard's destruction before sailing down the Elizabeth River using the *Pawnee* to tow the *Cumberland* out of danger. He leaves 10 vessels behind: the *Pennsylvania*, *Germantown*, *Raritan*, *Columbia*, *Dolphin*, *Delaware*, *Columbus*, *Plymouth*, *United States*, and *Merrimack*.

April 21 (CSA): Secessionists quickly douse flames and rescue equipment and stores. The destruction proves less extensive than expected, but some buildings were destroyed. One thousand and eighty-five cannon of all calibers, some spiked, are usable, and many are sent across the Confederacy to be used where needed. A large quantity of provisions is seized.[3]

April 27 (USA): Lincoln proclaims an extension of the Southern blockade to include the Virginia and North Carolina coastlines.

May 8 (CSA): Navy Secretary Mallory reports to the Confederate Congress that an "iron-armored ship as a matter of first necessity."[4]

May 21 (CSA): Confederate Congress votes to move its capital from Montgomery, Alabama, to Richmond, Virginia.

May 23 (CSA): Virginia's voters approve secession. Union sentiment remains strong in Portsmouth. Brig. Gen. Benjamin Huger is named commander of the Norfolk district.[5]

May 30 (CSA): Gosport Navy Yard workers, at cost of $6,000, raise the scuttled and burned *Merrimack* from the river bottom and place her in the yard's dry dock.

June 10 (CSA): Naval engineer Lt. John M. Brooke presents Mallory with a rough sketch of a proposed ironclad ship. Both the bow and the stern are submerged, leaving what appears to be a barn-like structure above water. Mallory approves the concept and tasks Brooke with the details of completing the ship.

June 15 (CSA): Gen. Robert E. Lee reported to Governor Letcher on the work done to protect Norfolk, Portsmouth, and the important navy yard. Six batteries were erected to guard the approaches to Norfolk and the Navy Yard, and three batteries were constructed "to prevent the ascent of the Nansemond River and occupation of the railroad from Norfolk to Richmond." Much of the work was done by nearly 900 area slaves contracted out by their owners, along with 650 free blacks from surrounding counties.[6]

June 23 (CSA): John L. Porter, the Gosport Yard's constructor, and William P. Williamson, the chief engineer, visit Mallory and Brooke at Mallory's office in Richmond. The men agree to pattern the new ironclad after Porter's model, adding Brooke's design of a submerged bow and stern. Porter is assigned as its constructor, Williamson takes charge

3 "Burning of the Navy-Yard!," Richmond *Daily Dispatch*, Apr. 23, 1861; Peters, "Norfolk Navy Yard," Aug. 4, 1891, Hampton Roads Naval Museum, NHHC, 2, 5-11.

4 Stephen R. Mallory, "Report to the Confederate Congress," May 8, 1861, in *ORN*, 1/2: 742.

5 Porter, *A Record of Events*, 20-21, 232.

6 Naval History Division, Dept. of the Navy, *Civil War Naval Chronology*, 1861-1865, 6 vols. (Washington, DC, 1971), I:16 to I:17. James Brewer, *The Confederate Negro: Virginia's Craftsman and Military Laborers, 1861-1865* (Durham, NC, 1969), 134-35.

of the ship's machinery, and Brooke is charged with securing the tons of iron needed to finish her.

July 4 (USA): Secretary Welles asks for congressional authorization to appoint a board to study the construction of iron vessels.[7]

July 18 (CSA): Mallory reports to the Confederate Congress that work has begun to convert the former wooden USS *Merrimack* into an ironclad, and asks that body to appropriate $175,523 for the task.

Late July (USA): Late in July, Welles persuades Cornelius S. Bushnell, a Connecticut shipbuilder interested in creating an ironclad, to present authorization legislation to congressmen to spur action.

August 3 (USA): The House and the Senate approve Welles's proposed bill (which Lincoln signs) providing $1.5 million for the construction of an ironclad. Lincoln authorizes Welles to appoint a board to consider ironclad design.

August 6 (CSA): The Confederate Congress approves a bill "to provide for the construction of a newly invented implement of war." [8]

August 8 (USA): The Navy department's advertisements begin to appear in Northern newspapers seeking the designs and cost details and a building timetable for small draft "Iron-Clad Steam Vessels."[9]

August 9 (USA): Welles appoints a three-man board to consider the ironclad plans under chairmanship of Commodore Joseph Smith, who, with Commodore Paulding and Captain Charles H. Davis, constitutes the "Iron-Clad Board."

August 12 (CSA): Mallory orders Lt. Brooke to conduct tests on iron plates they intend to use on the converted *Merrimack*. Tests to check resistance to shot and shell run for several months amid labor issues in the Gosport yard.

August 27 (USA): The Iron-Clad Board evaluates 17 ironclad ideas. Two hold some promise, including one by Cornelius Bushnell, who is urged by a friend to takes his plans to a well-known inventor and ship designer in New York City named John Ericsson.

7 G. Welles, "Report of the Secretary of the Navy," July 4, 1861, in *Congressional Globe*, Appendix, 37th Cong., 1st sess. (1861), 9.

8 U.S. Congress, *Journal of the Congress of the Confederate States,* 1:318. The subject was left vague to prevent the press on both sides from learning any more information.

9 Advertisement as it appeared in the Washington *National Republican*, Aug. 8, 1861, 3.

August 28 (USA): Ericsson shows Bushnell his own plans and model for a radically different iron ship, and allows Bushnell to show the plans to the Iron-Clad Board. Ericsson writes directly to Lincoln and offers his services and ironclad plan. Ericsson stresses the simplicity of building a ship based on his proposal. Lincoln apparently never sees Ericsson's letter, which is redirected to the Navy Department.[10]

August 30 (USA): Bushnell rushes to Hartford, Connecticut, to show the model to Welles, who is impressed by the Ericsson model and its "extraordinary and valuable features." Welles urges Bushnell to take it to Washington.[11]

September 1 (USA): Bushnell arrives in Washington, D.C., and seeks out John F. Winslow and John A. Griswold, owners of a Troy, NY, iron manufacturing company. Bushnell secures their participation for Ericsson's project in return for a half interest. Griswold suggests going to Secretary of State William S. Seward, a former New York governor, to ask for an introduction to meet with President Lincoln.

September 2 (USA): Meeting with Seward, the trio obtains an introduction to see the president. Ericsson's model impresses Lincoln, and he agrees to attend an informal presentation to the board the next day.

September 3 (USA): Bushnell presents the model and outlines Ericsson's design. Many Navy officers ridicule it, but Lincoln allows the project to proceed. Smith and Paulding agree to support the project, but only if Captain Davis agrees; Davis demurs. Welles suggests to Bushnell that Ericsson come to Washington. Bushnell agrees and leaves for New York.[12]

September 4 (USA): Ericsson is excited to hear the Navy's reaction to his design. Bushnell exaggerated their reaction, however, claiming the officers called the ship's design "glorious." Captain Davis, however, desired "a little explanation in details" that he (Bushnell) could not provide. Ericsson leaves for Washington at once.[13]

10 John Ericsson to Lincoln, Aug. 29, 1861, John Ericsson Papers, American Swedish Historical Museum (ASHM).

11 Gideon Welles, "The First Iron-Clad Monitor," in Alexander Kelley McClure, ed., *The Annals of the War Written by Leading Participants North and South* (Philadelphia, 1879), 18-19.

12 Cornelius S. Bushnell speech, June 22, 1894, in William S. Wells, ed., *The Original United States Warship* Monitor*: Copies of Correspondence Between the Late Cornelius S. Bushnell Captain John Ericsson and Gideon Welles* (New Haven, CT, 1899), 27.

13 Ibid.

September 5 (USA): Before the Iron-clad Board and Secretary Welles at 1:00 p.m., Ericsson shows on paper his proof of stability and explains other aspects of his design. He declares the ship could be built in 90 days for $275,000. The board gives its verbal approval. Welles tells Ericsson to return to New York and begin preparations for the work. A contract is to be ready for signatures the following week.[14]

September 16 (USA): In its report to Welles, the Iron-Clad Board declared it considered "iron-clad vessels of light draught, or floating batteries thus shielded . . . very important" for service in "rivers and harbors." Out of the 17 proposals presented to the board, the members recommend construction of three ships: the Philadelphia firm Merrick & Sons' *New Ironsides*, Bushnell's *Galena*—both to be built as wooden ships covered with iron powered initially by both sail and steam—and Ericsson's unnamed, iron-hulled steam vessel. However, only "the Ericsson" (its temporary name) would be built in time to confront the South's rebuilt *Merrimack* in March of 1862. The agreed timetable stipulates 100 days for construction.[15]

September 18 (CSA): With the Union capture of Fort Hatteras, North Carolina, on August 28, Brig. Gen. Huger in Norfolk begins worrying about the safety of his district. He does not expect a direct attack from Fort Monroe.[16]

October 4 (USA): All parties formally sign a government contract for constructing Ericsson's ship. The total price, $275,000, is to be paid in $50,000 installments, minus a 25 percent reservation, as the work progressed. The contract includes a stipulation that the builders guarantee the ironclad will perform satisfactorily.

October 7 (USA): By October, much of the country, including those in the North, are aware the Confederacy is using the *Merrimack* to construct an iron ship, though many details, including when it will be ready, remain sketchy.[17]

October 12 (USA): Although the former *Merrimack* is far from complete, Flag Officer Louis M. Goldsborough, the commander of the Atlantic Blockading Squadron, is already

14 Ibid. 27, 29; John Ericsson, "The Building of the 'Monitor,'" in Robert U. Johnson & Clarence C. Buel, eds., *Battles and Leaders of the Civil War*, 4 vols. (New York, 1956), 1:731.

15 Naval History Division *Chronology*, I:26.

16 Benjamin Huger to W. F. Lynch, Sept. 18, 1861, in *The War of the Rebellion: A Compilation of the Official Records of the Union and Confederate Armies*, 128 vols. (Washington, DC, 1880-1901), Series 1, 4:651. All references are to Series 1 unless otherwise noted. Hereafter cited as *OR*.

17 "The Merrimac Coming," *New York Daily Tribune*, Oct. 10, 1861, 5.

worried about the damage she might inflict against his wooden ships stationed in Hampton Roads.[18]

October 25 (USA): Ericsson begins construction on his ship at Greenpoint, New York.

November 2 (CSA): Tests show that thicker iron than originally called for will be needed, so the outer shell for the proposed *Merrimack* shield is increased from three inches to four. Porter affirms the ship can handle the extra weight. The iron will be affixed with two layers of 1-inch iron and a single 2-inch layer set perpendicular to the first two layers. Brooke designed and has cast the ship's 7-inch rifled bow and stern guns, known as the Brooke Rifle.

November 11 (CSA): Catesby ap Roger Jones meets with Brooke to discuss the new cannons. Jones is named as the ironclad's first lieutenant the next day. When he learns about the Union's ironclad plans, Brooke decides to work on the production of solid shot that can be heated (hot shot), and considers changing the mix of planned guns on the ship to better oppose an iron enemy.

November 27 (CSA): Catesby Jones complains of issues delaying the work on the *Merrimack*, such as "a hitch generally in the transportation," and getting experienced seamen transferred from other ships and gunners from the Army.[19]

1862

January 5 (CSA): According to Jones, "Mr. Porter says the ship will be ready by the 1st of February" Recruiting efforts for experienced seamen is faltering; though the effort would continue for the next few weeks.[20]

January 10 (USA): Persistent rumors of the former *Merrimack's* conversion and new strength circulate. Flag Officer Goldsborough orders two steam tugboats to stand by the USS *Congress* and *Cumberland* in order to maneuver the large sailing ships to better use their guns if and when the Confederate ironclad appears.

18 Naval History Division, *Chronology*, II:5.

19 Catesby ap Rogers Jones to John M. Brooke, Nov. 27, 1861, in George M. Brooke, Jr., ed., *Ironclads and Big Guns of the Confederacy: The Journal and Letters of John M. Brooke* (Columbia, SC, 2002), 50.

20 Ibid., 59.

January 12 (USA): An expedition sets out from Fort Monroe under Flag Officer Goldsborough and Maj. Gen. Ambrose Burnside to capture Roanoke Island, North Carolina.

January 13 (USA): Welles names Lt. John L. Worden to command the "Ericsson Battery," which is under construction near New York City.

January 16 (CSA): The Confederate Congress authorizes a $50 bounty for volunteers to serve in the Confederate Navy.[21]

January 20 (USA): Designer Ericsson suggests the ironclad be called the *Monitor*.[22]

January 21 (CSA): Construction delays continue on the new Southern ironclad. Catesby Jones tells Brooke she is still not ready because the ship does not have a crew, no coal or stores are aboard, and there is not enough gunpowder to safely take the ship into battle.[23]

January 22 (USA): Work on the *Monitor* is progressing, but the two 11-inch Dahlgren guns to be installed in her turret have not yet arrived. Worden begins recruiting volunteer sailors from other naval vessels in New York harbor.

January 30 (USA): The *Monitor* is launched. Assistant Secretary Fox wires Ericsson his congratulations and urges him to "[h]urry her for sea" because she is needed to counter the growing *Merrimack* threat at Norfolk.[24]

February 8 (USA): The U.S. amphibious force under Goldsborough and Burnside captures Roanoke Island, a key to "the rear defenses of Norfolk and the navy yard." Norfolk officials continue to worry about an attack from the south.[25]

(CSA): Franklin Buchanan, the converted *Merrimack's* probable commander complains that his crew is too small. He needs 320 to fully man the ship. A complete lack of experienced seamen forces reliance on Army volunteers.

21 "Register of the Navy of the Confederate States of 1864," in ibid., 61.

22 John Ericsson to Gustavus V. Fox, Jan. 20, 1862, in Ericsson, "The Building of the '*Monitor*,'" in Johnson & Buel, *B&L*, 1:731n.

23 Jones to J. Brooke, Jan. 21, 1862, in Brooke Jr., ed., *Ironclads and Big Guns*, 62.

24 Naval History Division *Chronology*, II:14.

25 Ibid., II:7.

The launch of the USS *Monitor* on January 30, 1862. The ironclad's inventor, John Ericsson, had every confidence his iron ship would float. The fact that it did surprised many skeptics inside and outside the Navy. *Naval History & Heritage Command, NH 604*

February 10 (USA): Capt. John Marston, senior naval officer at Hampton Roads, tells Secretary Welles that the reassignment of some engineering officers would not create problems because "the *Merrimack* is pronounced by the rebels themselves [as] a failure."[26]

February 12 (USA): A Gosport Navy Yard workman gets a message to Maj. Gen. John E. Wool, the Union commander at Fort Monroe, that the Confederates plan to sail the *Merrimack* within a month to attack the U.S. ships *Cumberland* and *Congress* at the mouth of

26 John Marston to Welles, Feb. 10, 1862, *ORN* 6:627.

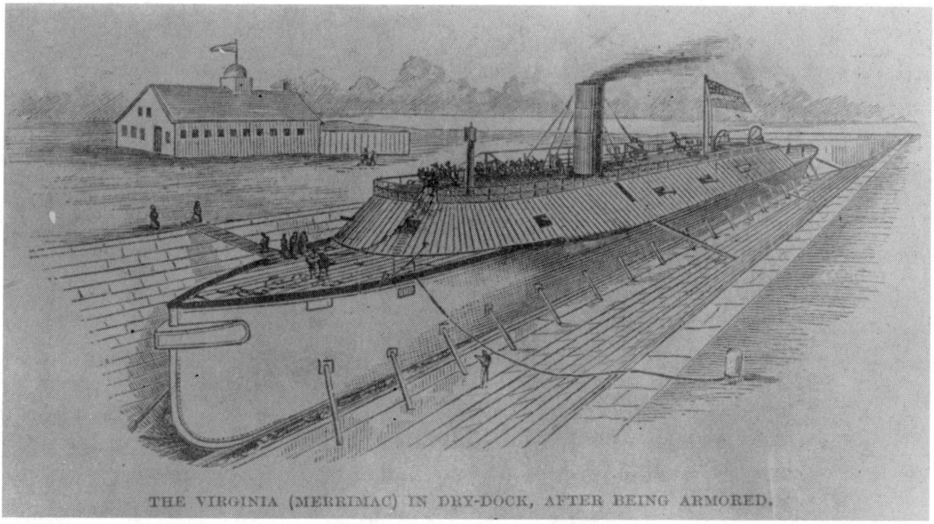

The CSS *Virginia* sits in the Gosport Navy Yard's dry dock waiting for her launch. When finally afloat, the iron-covered casemate sat too high out of the water, exposing her wooden hull. It would take tons of pig iron stacked at both ends plus her full complement of coal to lower the ship to a fighting level. *Naval History & Heritage Command, NH 314*

---

the James River. Wool sends his aide to Washington with the warning, but Fox dismisses it as impossible.[27]

February 17 (CSA): The *Merrimack* conversion into a functional ironclad nears completion. She is taken out of dry dock and officially commissioned the CSS *Virginia.*

February 19 (USA): Lt. Worden and crew take the *Monitor* on her maiden trial run in New York harbor. They find her hard to control and she sluices wildly from side to side.

February 20 (USA): Secretary Welles receives a disturbing report on the *Virginia's* progress from a "Union man," a mechanic working on the ship. Ignorant of the extent of the *Monitor's* steering problems, he orders Worden to sail the "U.S.S. *Monitor* under your command, to Hampton Roads."[28]

27 Le Grand Cannon, *Personal Reminiscences of the Rebellion, 1861-1866* (New York, 1895), 75-79.

28 Welles, "Iron-Clad *Monitor*," in McClure, ed. *Annals*, 20. Reportedly, Mary Touvestre, a Norfolk seamstress or housekeeper and former slave, provided the information to Welles. One story says Touvestre (some sources give her name as Louvestre) worked for an engineer who helped to build the *Virginia.* She overheard talk about the recreated ship and copied the plans. Touvestre then made her way to Washington, D.C., to give those plans to Welles. Public Affairs Central Intelligence Agency, *Intelligence in the Civil War* (Washington, DC, no date), 27, accessed Jan. 20, 2019, https://fas.org/irp/cia/product/civilwar.pdf.

(CSA): The *Virginia* is not nearly as close to beginning her own sea trials. According to reports, she "leaks everywhere. Mechanics are at work at a thousand things which should have been done months ago"[29]

February 21 (USA): Maj. Gen. Wool learns the "iron clad Steamer *Merrimac*, *Yorktown* and *Jamestown* within five days in conjunction with a land force will attack Newport News at night." Wool passes that intelligence on to the Hampton Roads senior naval commander, John Marston, who assures Welles, "we shall do our best."[30]

February 24 (CSA): Secretary Mallory officially appoints Capt. Franklin Buchanan flag officer for the Confederacy's James River fleet and naval defenses, with his flag to be posted on the CSS *Virginia*. Catesby Jones becomes his executive officer. Buchanan's fleet includes five other warships. The naval department will not issue specific attack orders to the new ironclad, an untried "novelty in naval construction" of unknown capabilities. Mallory fancifully suggests that, if possible, Buchanan take the *Virginia* up the Potomac to Washington. "Its effect upon the public mind would be important to our cause."[31]

February 25 (USA): The *Monitor* is officially commissioned into the U.S. Navy.

February 25 (CSA): Problems continue to plague the *Virginia*. Norfolk had no coal for the vessel, tons of which are needed for fuel and for ballast to lower the vessel in the water.[32]

February 27 (USA): Worden delays his departure from New York to take aboard iron shot and powder for the *Monitor's* two 11-inch guns. Once at sea, the ship begins once more to slide wildly from side to side. Worden returns to the harbor.

February 28 (USA): The USS *Minnesota's* captain, Gershom J. van Brunt, reports "all is quiet" in Hampton Roads. No *Merrimack* in sight.[33]

29 Jones to J. Brooke, Feb. 20, 1862, in Brooke Jr., ed., *Ironclads and Big Guns,* 68.

30 Wool to McClellan, Feb. 21, 1862, in Robert Means Thompson and Richard Wainwright, eds., *Confidential Correspondence of Gustavus Vasa Fox, Assistant Secretary of the Navy, 1861-1865.* 2 vols. (New York, 1918), vol. 1, 428; Marston to Welles, February 21, 1862, *ORN* 6:659.

31 Naval History Division *Chronology*, II:26.

32 Jones to J. Brooke, Feb. 25, 1862, in Brooke Jr., ed., *Ironclads and Big Guns*, 69.

33 Gershom J. van Brunt to Louis M. Goldsborough, Feb. 28, 1862, *ORN* 6:672.

Flag Officer Franklin Buchanan orders the CSS *Virginia* to ram the wooden frigate USS *Cumberland* because he believed her guns were a greater danger than those of the USS *Congress*. The *Cumberland* was rapidly filling with water, but her crew continued to fire her remaining guns. *Naval History & Heritage Command, NH 65698*

March 4 (CSA): Despite unresolved issues and high expectations for the *Virginia*, she might fail Catesby Jones writes Brooke. "I can only say for the officers that they are willing and anxious to try."[34]

March 5 (USA): By this time it is no secret that the *Virginia* is ready to sail. By now Northern newspapers have half a dozen correspondents to Fort Monroe to be on hand when she appears.

March 6 (USA): With the steering issue fixed, Lt. Worden reports the *Monitor* on her way about 11:00 a.m., under tow by the tugboat *Seth Low* and accompanied by the USS *Currituck* and USS *Sachem*.

March 7 (USA): The *Monitor* has a tough time in moderately rough seas, and water pours into the ship. Many members of the crew, including the captain, become seasick. The drenched air pumps stop working and engineers and firemen pass out. The air blowers are restored five hours later and the tugboat tows the iron ship into calmer waters.

34 Jones to J. Brooke, Mar. 5, 1862, in Brooke Jr., ed., *Ironclads and Big Guns*, 70-71.

The smaller USS *Monitor* takes on the CSS *Virginia* in this post-battle illustration. The distances to other ships are deceiving because the wooden vessels from both sides stayed well clear of the iron ships. However, the *Virginia's* gunners did throw a few shells at the stranded USS *Minnesota*. *Naval History & Heritage Command, NH 65698*

March 7 (CSA): The workers apply a heavy coating of tallow and animal fat to the *Virginia's* iron sides so enemy cannon balls slide off her sloping walls more easily.

March 8 (USA): Early in the morning the *Monitor* once again hits rough water, and once more the sea pours into the ship through the anchor well, drips from around the turret and down the air blower vents soaking the belts. The wire wheel ropes needed to steer the ship come undone. While still being pulled by the tugboat, she once more sluices side to side. The sea finally calms and the steering is repaired, but the barely working pumps remain a concern.[35]

(CSA): Flag Officer Buchanan is determined to give the new ironclad her shakedown cruise and attack the two Union ships floating off Newport News. Accompanied by the gunboats *Beaufort* and *Raleigh*, the *Virginia* glides downriver to Hampton Roads at 11:00 a.m. By mid-afternoon he has targeted the USS *Congress* and *Cumberland*. He delivers a broadside to the *Congress* as he steams past, and rams the

35 Samuel D. Greene to "mother," Mar. 14, 1862, in Richard S. Collum, *The Description of the Fight Between the Monitor and Merrimac on 9th of March, 1862* (Philadelphia, 1898), 13-15; Alban C. Stimers to Eden P. Dorr, n.d., in Eben P. Dorr, *A Brief Sketch of the First Monitor and Its Inventor* (Buffalo, NY, 1874), 49.

Cumberland. With that ship sinking, Buchanan returns to the *Congress* and sets her ablaze. The USS *Minnesota*, meanwhile, has grounded on a shoal and is helpless. *Virginia* remained impervious to the furious defensive fire that bounces off its iron plating. Buchanan, however, is wounded in the leg by a rifled musket shot from shore and relinquishes command to Catesby Jones, who decides to return to the safety of the Sewell's Point batteries for the night and finish the job of sinking other Union ships in the morning.

(USA): The *Monitor* rounds the Peninsula's Old Point Comfort late in the evening and spots the *Congress* afire—the first inclination that the CSS *Virginia* had come out to fight. The *Monitor* is ordered to post herself next to the grounded USS *Minnesota* and protect her from the Confederate ironclad, which everyone expects will make another appearance in the morning.

March 9 (USA): A telegraphic connection between Fort Monroe and Washington, D.C., was only established late the evening before, so the news of the March 8 disaster does not arrive at the capital until today. Secretary of War Stanton hastily calls all the cabinet secretaries to a meeting at the Executive Mansion. Looking out the window toward the Potomac River, he expects to see the *Virginia* at any moment. According to Capt. John A. Dahlgren, whom the president had consulted regarding the "frightful news," Lincoln is "not at all stunned by the news [but rather] in his usual suggestive mood."[36]

(CSA): Catesby Jones is determined to capture or destroy the *Minnesota*, stuck hard on the rocks of Hampton Roads' shallow Middle Ground the day before trying to help the doomed ships of Newport News. By 5:30 a.m. an estimated 40,000 spectators line the shores of Hampton Roads to witness the expected battle. As the *Virginia* slowly approaches Capt. Worden brings the *Monitor* from around the *Minnesota's* bow and steers directly toward the Confederate ship. At first the *Virginia's* crewmen are unsure what it was, but they soon realize it is the "Ericsson Battery" had arrived. Worden fires first. The *Monitor's* two guns send a pair of 168-pound solid shot hurling toward the *Virginia.* Thus begins the historic four-hour fight, during which neither vessel was able to seriously damage the other. Finally, a shot from the *Virginia* hits and explodes against the *Monitor's* pilothouse just as Capt. Worden is looking out, temporarily blinding him. The *Monitor* moves off into shallow water. Jones believes she is retreating, but by this time is unable to move closer to the *Minnesota* and finish her off. The tide, warns his pilots, will change while he is fighting the warship and he will risk grounding his own vessel. The fight is over, and both sides declare victory.

36 Welles, "Iron-Clad *Monitor,*" in McClure, ed., *Annals*, 24; Madeleine V. Dahlgren, ed. *Memoir of John A. Dahlgren, Rear Admiral, U.S.N.* (Boston, 1882), 358-59.

March 10 (USA): Worried that the *Monitor* might not stand up in a second fight with the *Virginia*, Washington's political leaders restrict her actions. "The president directed that she "be not too much exposed and that in no event shall any attempt be made to proceed with her unattended to Norfolk."

March 11 (USA): Lincoln issues War Order No. 3 relieving Maj. Gen. McClellan of the responsibility for all the U.S. Army forces. McClellan retains departmental command and the Army of the Potomac for his planned assault against Richmond up the Virginia Peninsula from Fort Monroe, but other department commanders are ordered to report to Stanton. In effect, Lincoln, through Stanton, becomes the Army's general in chief, a position he will retain until July.

March 13 (USA): Lt. William N. Jeffers is ordered to take command of the *Monitor*, the iron ship's fourth commander in four days. Lt. Samuel Greene had taken over from the wounded Worden, only to be replaced by Lt. Thomas O. Selfridge, both of whom were considered too young for such an important command.

March 16 (USA): Flag Officer Goldsborough advises Gustavus Fox not to count on the *Monitor* to stop the *Virginia* in another clash. Agreeing with Lincoln's admonishment to not risk the *Monitor*, the cautious Goldsborough declared his determination "to act as strongly on the defensive as possible, & to incur no avoidable risk" [t]o the *Monitor* beyond expending her energies carefully & guardedly against the *Merrimac*."[37]

March 20 (USA): Secretary of War Stanton accepts Cornelius Vanderbilt's offer to use the large paddlewheel steamship *Cornelius Vanderbilt* for Union service and Stanton sends her to Hampton Roads. The secretary gives Vanderbilt "full discretion and authority" to arm, equip, and crew the ship with his own employees, and to give any ship officers he may appoint "instructions as you may deem proper."[38]

March 25 (CSA): With Buchanan down, Confederate Secretary Mallory orders Flag Officer Josiah Tattnall to take command of the Confederacy's little fleet at Norfolk including the CSS *Virginia*, much to the dismay of Catesby Jones.

March 27 (USA): Secretary Stanton is unhappy with Maj. Gen. Wool for turning the *Vanderbilt* over to the Navy upon her arrival at Fort Monroe. Stanton insists the ship remain under Army command. The next day, his assistant, Peter H. Watson, writes from Hampton

37 Goldsborough to Fox, Mar. 16, 1862, in Thompson & Wainwright, eds. *Confidential Correspondence*, 1:248.

38 Stanton to Cornelius Vanderbilt, Mar. 20, 1862, *OR* 11/3:26.

Roads that he and the ship's owner are happy with the Navy's retaining control and the plan for her to run down the *Virginia*, if possible. Stanton acquiesces.[39]

April 2 (USA): Maj. Gen. McClellan personally arrives at Fort Monroe to begin his campaign up the Virginia Peninsula to Richmond. His plans depend upon the Union Navy being able to guard his flanks along the James and York rivers and transport troops around any enemy forces trying to block his way on land. With the *Virginia* lurking nearby, however, Goldsborough's priority is blocking the Confederate ship, not helping McClellan. Goldsborough does not send any vessels up the James, but he does transfer a few ships around the Peninsula to enter the York River.

April 11 (CSA): Under Tattnall's command, the *Virginia* reappears in Hampton Roads ready to fight. Besides her usual escorts, two tugboats with 15 volunteers each accompany the ironclad. The plan is for the volunteers to board the *Monitor* on both sides, throw "lighted tar balls down through the ventilators and wedge up the turret so it would not revolve," explained James Byers, the captain of one of the tugs. Byers, however, is a Northerner by birth and refuses to sail his ship that day.[40] The Union ships, including the *Monitor*, have standing orders not to engage the *Virginia* unless absolutely necessary, and to keep out of her way, leaving the Rebel ironclad to sail around the western end of Hampton Roads unmolested. Two of her consort ships capture three small Union ships. Frustrated by the *Monitor's* refusal to fight him, Tattnall steams the *Virginia* back to the Elizabeth River.

April 28 (CSA): McClellan's army has been confronting Gen. Joseph Johnston's Confederate command at Yorktown. At the last possible hour before McClellan opened with his large siege weapons, Johnston falls back up the Peninsula. His retreat further exposes Norfolk, Portsmouth, and the naval yard to capture. Richmond authorities order the removal of Confederate soldiers from the cities, and Maj. Gen. Huger is directed to hasten the shipment of valuable stores.

April 30 (CSA): Secretaries of the Navy Mallory and Secretary of War George W. Randolph visit the Norfolk area to formulate evacuation plans. Mallory orders the shipyard's removable naval supplies sent to a safe interior location. From this day until May

39 Stanton to Wool & P. H. Watson to Stanton Mar. 27, 28, 1862, *OR* 11/3:43, 46.

40 James Byers to Dorr, n.d., in Eben P Dorr, *A Brief Sketch of the First Monitor and Its Inventor* (Buffalo, 1874), 52.

10, supply shipments out of the area "continued day and night." The unfinished ironclad *Richmond* and two new wooden gunboats were hauled up the James River to Richmond.[41]

May 4 (CSA): The coal-laden CSS *Beauregard*, bound for Norfolk to re-supply the *Virginia*, is captured and burned on her way down the James River. Rumors spread that the Confederate government has decided to abandon Norfolk and Portsmouth. The latter city appoints a city committee to plead with the Gosport Navy Yard commander to spare its destruction.

41 Peters, "Norfolk Navy Yard," Hampton Roads Naval Museum, NHHC, 12; Porter, *Record of Events*, 32.

Introduction

PRESIDENT Abraham Lincoln stood on the deck of the USS *Baltimore* on the clear early Sunday morning of May 11, 1862. He was eager to return to Washington, but keen to see for himself the results of his week in the field as commander in chief. For the first time, the president had taken a direct role in organizing and leading a campaign during the Civil War. He would never do so again.

We can only speculate as to what he felt that morning as the *Baltimore* steamed across Hampton Roads to the mouth of the Elizabeth River. Lincoln sought privacy aboard the ship to read the Bible, but was satisfied enough with his week of campaigning to be jocular during a shipboard breakfast.[1]

Just two days earlier, no Union vessel—not even the revolutionary ironclad *Monitor*—dared sail up that river to Norfolk, Virginia. Fortifications and heavy Confederate artillery positions at Sewell's Point, on Craney Island, and along the river's banks—more than 230 guns, all told—blocked northern traffic on the waterway. Obstructions driven into the river bottom and sunken ships left only a narrow navigable channel. An even greater deterrent was the "Big Thing," as one Union sailor called her: The mighty and feared ironclad CSS *Virginia*, better known as (and always called by Northerners, and by some Southerners) the *Merrimack*.[2]

1 Le Grand B. Cannon, *Personal Reminiscences of the Rebellion, 1861-1866* (New York, 1895), 167-68.

2 Thomas J. Cram, "Report of Colonel T. J. Cram . . . Upon the Taking of Norfolk, by Major Gen. Wool, U.S.A, May 10, 1862," May 31, 1862, John E. Wool Papers, NYSA. I use the official Confederate designation of *Virginia*. In 1876, Gustavus V. Fox, the Union's assistant secretary of war, penned an 1876 article that referenced the ironclad by the ship's former name

The mere existence of the "rebel monster" terrorized Northerners up and down the Atlantic coast. But on the morning of May 11, the *Virginia* was no more. Her captain and crew set her afire off Craney Island, near the entrance to the Elizabeth River, just a handful of hours before Lincoln arrived on the spot where she had exploded and sank. Bits of her smoking remains floated on the water.

As important as the destruction of the *Virginia* was to Lincoln's war effort, it was not as significant as the recapture of Norfolk, Portsmouth, and the Gosport Navy Yard. The facility was the largest in the country before the war. Located across and up the Elizabeth River from Norfolk and less than six miles from Hampton Roads, Gosport offered the largest dry dock in the Americas, and the largest supply depot. It was simply invaluable.

The U.S. Navy suffered a major blow when Gosport was abandoned on April 20, 1861. Federal sailors and marines burned supplies, threw cannons and shells into the river, spiked the large artillery pieces they could not move, and set off explosives in the dry dock. Their efforts destroyed an estimated $50 million worth of government property. Ten naval vessels that could not be sent to Fort Monroe were lost.[3]

Merrimack. Catesby ap R. Jones, the first lieutenant on the *Virginia*, took offense. "As all Confederate accounts called our vessel the '*Virginia*,' it would have been well to have mentioned it, or at the next centennial the two names may be believed to refer to different vessels," chastised the former Southern naval officer. C. Jones to Gustavus V. Fox, June 20, 1876, Gustavus V. Fox Papers, Naval History Society Collection, NYHSL. Many years after the war, William Norris, the former chief of the Confederate Army's Signal Corps, wrote of his contempt for the ship's former name. "And *Virginia* was her name, not *Merrimac*," he emphasized, "which has a nasal twang equally abhorrent to sentiment and to melody, and meanly compares with the sonorous sweetness of '*Virginia*.'" William Norris, "The Story of the Confederate States Ship *Virginia* (Once *Merrimac*): Her Victory over the *Monitor*," *Southern Historical Society Papers*, 52 vols. (Oct. 1917), 42:224, hereafter *SHSP*. Two decades after the war, Norfolk resident Clifford Millard complained to the secretary of the navy that models of the *Virginia* displayed at various naval installations and museums called her the "*Merrimac*." Using that name is of a "Yankee stream," he added, "I . . . can prove that the said 'label' is a LIBEL!" Edward E. Barthell Jr., *The Mystery of the* Merrimack (Muskegon, MI, 1959), 50. Not everyone agreed. John L. Porter, who created the *Virginia* out of the husk of the *Merrimack*, continued to call her by that name. A young and careful teenaged Georgia diarist named LeRoy Gresham referred to the vessel as the "*Merrimac*," a name he read in the various newspapers and magazines he perused. Janet E. Croon, ed., *The War Outside My Window: The Civil War Diary of LeRoy Wiley Gresham, 1860-1865* (Savas Beatie, 2018), 26, 116. Another Southern diarist complained in her journal on March 20, 1862, "The *Merrimac* is now called the *Virginia*. I think these changes of names so confusing and so senseless." Mary Boykin Chesnut, *A Diary from Dixie*, Isabella D. Martin & Myrta L. Avary, eds. (New York, 1905), 148.

3 Bradley S. Osbon, ed., *Hand Book of the United States Navy: Being a Compilation of All the Principal Events in the History of Every Vessel of the United States Navy from April, 1861, to May, 1864* (New York, 1864), 69. The $50 million in 1860s dollars is $1.25 billion in 2019.

The resourceful Confederates, however, found many of the supplies still useful, lifted the artillery and shells out of the water, bored out the spiked guns, and repaired the dry dock. Possession of the best naval facility on the Atlantic coast provided the South with the means, when joined with necessity and innovation, to create an ironclad ship they believed powerful enough to break any hope the Union entertained of blockading Southern ports.

The CSS *Virginia* was built on the remains of the former wooden frigate USS *Merrimack*, a combined sailing and screw-driven steamship burned to the water line and raised from it watery grave. Possession of the naval yard would enable the Confederates to build more ironclads as well as other large warships and smaller gunboats. For more than a year reports seeping northward told of feverish building activity. On April 22, 1862, two weeks before Lincoln arrived at Hampton Roads, Norfolk refugees talked about "a large gang of men working" on the *Virginia* more than a month after her fight with the USS *Monitor*. Five new wooden gunboats had been completed and four more were under construction. More ominously, a second ironclad was "already far advanced toward completion in her woodwork," but not yet sided with iron.[4]

Accompanying Lincoln on the *Baltimore* that morning were Secretary of War Edwin Stanton, Secretary of the Treasury Salmon P. Chase, Flag Officer Louis M. Goldsborough, and brevet Maj. Gen. John E. Wool—each of whom had been principals in the recent events. As the ship drew near, Lincoln could see the battery emplacements along both banks of the Elizabeth. The smoke from the still-smoldering navy yard would have filled his nostrils, but the Rebels were no more successful at destroying the place with fire than the Yankees had been a year before.

Norfolk came into full view on the port side of the *Baltimore*. The occupied city was still standing, though the departing Confederates had tried to burn the government buildings and flood their basements. Smoke rose on the river's left (western) bank, where Lincoln took in the remains of the Gosport Navy Yard in the form of charred wooden buildings, heaps of scattered cannon balls and shells, and dismounted guns. There had simply been too much invaluable war materiel for the Confederates to carry off to Richmond or Petersburg before the fall of the city.

4 Louis M. Goldsborough to Sec. of Navy Gideon Welles, Apr. 22, 1862, in *ORN*, 7:255. The second ironclad was the CSS *Richmond* (sometimes called the *Virginia II*), which was no where close to being completed. She was towed up the James River to Richmond to save her from capture or destruction and finished there.

Treasury Secretary Salmon P. Chase accompanied President Lincoln to Hampton Roads. His letters to his daughter memorialized many of the details that would otherwise have been lost.

Library of Congress

Lincoln may have also set eyes upon the large flooded dry dock, the doors to which the fleeing Southerners had blasted open.

Norfolk's stunned residents remained mostly silent that Sunday morning. Their mayor had surrendered the city to Union troops just 15 hours earlier, and it took most of the night for Brig. Gen. Egbert L. Viele, the new military governor, to post his soldiers here and across the river in Portsmouth. Some residents felt abandoned by their own government, which had withdrawn their troops to help defend Richmond against Maj. Gen. George B. McClellan's Army of the Potomac, which was steadily driving up the Peninsula toward the Southern capital.

The city's residents had no idea the president of the Union they had been trying to leave was standing aboard a ship just 100 yards from the bank of the river. Lincoln did not go ashore.[5] He looked about, taking in the sights as Maj. Gen. Wool debarked to attend to his new responsibilities at Norfolk and Portsmouth, and Goldsborough did the same to inspect the destruction of the Gosport Navy Yard. With the press of official duty awaiting him back in Washington after his six-day absence, Lincoln asked the *Baltimore's* captain to build up steam and head back downriver.

A short time later Lincoln was steaming across the placid Hampton Roads and, after a brief sojourn at Fort Monroe, moving up Chesapeake Bay to the Potomac River. While doing so, he surely reflected on the week-long campaign that capped a

5 Some reports claim the president stepped ashore at Norfolk, but there is no firsthand evidence that he did so.

successful first spring for his, and the Union's, efforts to bring the states of the Confederacy back into the United States.

* * *

President Lincoln had been urging and prodding his military commanders into action since the beginning of the war. Being stuck in the nation's capital limited his firsthand knowledge and ability to control events unfolding across much of the country. He often reached out by telegraph for any information: "What news?" became his constant telegraphic refrain. The responses usually served little more than to fuel his frustration. Lincoln also visited the many camps around Washington to see the improvements his new Eastern Theater commander, George McClellan, had made following the defeat of Maj. Gen. Irvin McDowell's army at Bull Run in northern Virginia in July 1861. Impressed with McClellan's abilities, the president named him general in chief of all the U.S. Armies once Maj. Gen. Winfield Scott retired that October.[6]

Through the fall and well into the winter months, McClellan—dubbed the "Young Napoleon" by his admirers—rebuilt and drilled the growing Army of the Potomac. Lincoln, together with the Northern press, prodded him to act, to no avail. "If General McClellan does not want to use the army," Lincoln quipped to a couple of his generals and cabinet members at a meeting on January 10, 1862, "I would like to borrow it."[7]

In early December 1861, McClellan proposed a bold flanking maneuver by water to avoid Gen. Joseph E. Johnston's Confederate army in northern Virginia at Centreville. The Urbanna Plan called for a water-based move down the Chesapeake to Urbanna and a quick march by land to Richmond some 45 miles distant. By the time the action was approved and the army ready to move, however, word arrived on March 9 that Johnston was withdrawing south. McClellan moved forward a few miles out of his Washington camps and established his headquarters at Fairfax Court House.

6 See Tom Wheeler, *Mr. Lincoln's T-Mails: How Abraham Lincoln Used the Telegraph to Win the Civil War* (New York, 2006). The Army of Northeastern Virginia was constituted under Brig. Gen. Irvin McDowell on July 8, 1861. But with that army's defeat later that month at Manassas Junction, Va. (Bull Run), McDowell was replaced. The new commander, George B. McClellan, not only reorganized the army but also renamed it as the Army of the Potomac (AOP).

7 Secretary of State William H. Seward, Secretary of the Treasury Salmon P. Chase and Major Generals Irvin McDowell and William B. Franklin were present at the council. McClellan was ill and did not attend. Harry Hansen, *The Civil War: A History* (New York, 1961), 174.

With his Urbanna Plan now unfeasible, McClellan held a council of war on March 9 and proposed another flanking maneuver to send his entire army by sea all the way to Fort Monroe at the tip of Virginia's Peninsula between the York and James rivers. His plan was to swiftly land his army, use the fort and surrounding terrain as a staging area, and march against Richmond roughly 80 miles to the northwest before Johnston could react. Lincoln reluctantly agreed to the plan, but insisted McClellan leave sufficient troops behind to protect Washington.[8]

The presence of the CSS *Virginia* in Hampton Roads posed a serious threat to the Peninsula campaign, but the arrival of the USS *Monitor* on the evening of March 8, and her nimble maneuvering the next day as the two ironclads dueled to a standstill, reassured the cautious McClellan that his army could be safely transported to the Peninsula. The transports set off on March 17. McClellan shifted his supply route from the James River to the York on the northern side of the Peninsula, away from the *Virginia's* guns.

Lincoln was pleased the campaign was finally underway, but his patience with his top general was wearing a bit thin. On March 11 the president had issued a new order relieving McClellan as general in chief, but leaving him in charge of the single Department of the Potomac, i.e., command of Washington defenses and the Army of the Potomac. McClellan (and the commanders of the other departments) would henceforth report to Secretary of War Stanton, and thus directly to Lincoln. The president, in effect, became his own general in chief of the Army.[9]

* * *

For all of Lincoln's frustrations, even a reluctant Rebel soldier named Philip Whitlock could see that the war was going badly for the South by the spring of 1862. The 12th Virginia private, who was stationed three miles outside Norfolk at this stage of the war, later wrote that "the Confederate Cause was getting weeker &

8 In a letter to McClellan from Stanton on March 13, 1862, the secretary of war laid out Lincoln's caveats for approving the general's Peninsula plan. First: "Leave such force at Manassas Junction as shall make it entirely certain that the enemy shall not possess himself of that position and line of communication." And secondly: "Leave Washington secure." Finally he urged McClellan to move the rest of the army "in pursuit of the enemy by some route." Roy P. Basler, ed., *The Collected Works of Abraham Lincoln*, 9 vols. (New Brunswick, NJ, 1953), 5:207.

9 President's War Order No. 3, Mar. 11, 1862, *OR* 5:54. The general in chief position remained vacant until that July, when President Lincoln brought in Maj. Gen. Henry A. Halleck from the Department of the Mississippi to fill it.

weeker every day. I could see that there was no chance as we were getting week and the other side was getting stronger as they had the whole world to recruit from."[10]

Confederate President Jefferson Davis recognized the same problems. The forts at Port Royal sound in South Carolina fell in November 1861 following a short naval bombardment. Their capture provided the North with one of the finest harbors on the Atlantic coast, a base for a coaling station, repair shops, and supply depots to be used by the blockading ships, and a jumping-off point for future operations.

Boosted by the success at Port Royal, Brig. Gen. Ambrose E. Burnside suggested that McClellan (as general in chief) follow-up this success by widening Union control of the North Carolina coast. To do this, Burnside planned to create an army "coast division," including men primarily from the northern seacoast, and a fleet of light-draft steamers and sailing vessels. This fleet, with about 10,200 officers and men, entered Pamlico Sound on the North Carolina coast by mid-January. From the fleet's safe shelter behind the barrier islands, Burnside's troops landed on Roanoke Island on February 7. The Confederate defenders, pushed to its northern end, had little choice but to surrender. By mid-March Union soldiers also occupied New Berne, North Carolina, farther south.[11]

Three months after the Port Royal success, and while Burnside was finding success at Roanoke, Brig. Gen. Ulysses S. Grant, with the help of the inland navy, captured two Confederate strongholds: Fort Henry on the Tennessee River, and Fort Donelson on the Cumberland River. The twin victories opened river arteries into the Deep South and earned him a promotion to major general. The Confederate defensive perimeter in Kentucky collapsed, and the entire Western Theater seemed on the verge of imploding.

The Confederates failure at Shiloh in early April was another major setback for the Davis administration and another triumph for Grant. The surprise attack launched by Gen. Albert Sydney Johnston, the commander of the Confederate army, nearly drove the Union army from the field on April 6, but Johnston was killed that afternoon and the drive stalled for a variety of reasons. The overnight arrival of Union reinforcements allowed Grant to take the offensive on April 7 and drive the Rebel army from the field. The victory opened northern Mississippi to

10 Philip Whitlock, "Recollections, 1843-1913," Virginia Historical Society (VHS).

11 Charles D. & E. Kay Gibson, *Assault and Logistics: Union Army Coastal and River Operations, 1861-1866,* 2 vols., The Army's Navy Series (Camden, ME, 1995), 2:24-35. See also, Ambrose E. Burnside, "The Burnside Expedition," in Johnson & Buel, eds., *B&L*, 1:660-69.

Union invasion and eliminated the general that many Southerners (including Jeff Davis) believed was the most able officer fielded by the Confederacy.

Through the month of March, meanwhile, Brig. Gen. John Pope's Union army, along with six river steamers and ten mortar boats under Flag Officer Andrew H. Foote, attacked Confederate-held Island No. 10 below Cairo, Illinois. On April 8, the day after Grant's victory at Shiloh, Pope's soldiers occupied the island, removing the first barricade in the Union's effort to seize control of the Mississippi River. Three days later federal artillery pounded Fort Pulaski, a large masonry bastion guarding one of the approaches to Savannah, Georgia. It fell with its 360-man garrison after 18 hours of continuous bombardment.

At the mouth of the Mississippi River, Flag Officer David Farragut gathered his naval forces at the Head of Passes, where the river delta splits into numerous outlets to the Gulf of Mexico. Farragut's mission was to steam up the Mississippi and capture New Orleans, the South's largest city and an absolutely vital seaport. On the night of April 23-24, Farragut forced his mix of oceangoing and riverine vessels past the lower forts guarding the approach to the Crescent City. New Orleans formally surrendered on April 25. The Confederacy was, piece by piece, falling apart all around its perimeter.

The next prize craved by Union strategists was Elizabeth City, North Carolina, the southern terminus of a direct waterway from Albemarle Sound to Norfolk—the canal through the Dismal Swamp that linked to the Pasquotank River flowing into the sound. Burnside's soldiers, firmly established at Roanoke Island and New Bern, were in position to attack Norfolk's back door from the south.

Norfolk, one of the Confederacy's principal seaports, together with the nearby Gosport Navy Yard, had demonstrated their vulnerability that February when Burnside sent a force to land at Elizabeth City and march north with the intent of destroying the canal's locks at South Mills and eliminating the threat of a Confederate ironclad coming south through the canal to attack his fleet. President Davis and his military advisor, Gen. Robert E. Lee, grasped the threat immediately. The Yankees retreated in the face of Confederates from Norfolk, but the bold attempt to come up the canal even part way confirmed the very real danger facing Norfolk.

Davis and Lee had been expecting a direct attack from Fort Monroe against Norfolk, Portsmouth, and the naval yard—the very operation Lincoln and others had been advocating. Norfolk, the county seat of Norfolk County, was a bustling city with a population of 14,620 people. Portsmouth, directly across the river, was

Norfolk county's second largest community with 9,496. Combined, the two cities made up two-thirds of the county's total population of 36,227.[12]

The tall task of defending the area fell to Maj. Gen. Benjamin Huger, the Confederate commander of the Department of Norfolk. The 56-year-old graduate of West Point and former Mexican War veteran had more than 15,300 officers and men under his command in January 1862, with almost 5,000 of them in Norfolk itself, along with 61 pieces of artillery. Another 4,780 were stationed in Portsmouth and 3,330 more northwest of Norfolk in Smithfield near the James River. The rest manned various garrisons along the shorelines of Hampton Roads and the Atlantic.[13]

Responding to Union threats, the most immediate being Burnside in North Carolina, became more difficult for Huger with each passing week because his forces were being slowly depleted, some to North Carolina "to the extent of his means," directed President Davis, and others elsewhere. Huger was also keeping an eye on threats from Hampton Roads to the north. Nailed into place, he could only do so much. On February 9, he wired Davis that he had sent a shipment of ammunition from Norfolk to Elizabeth City to oppose Burnside's advance. "Should the enemy attack in front I must be re-enforced," he warned.[14]

Not everyone thought the general was doing enough or even what was needed. A committee of the Confederate Congress later investigated Burnside's victories in North Carolina and concluded, "whatever of blame and responsibility is justly attributable to any one for the defeat of our troops at Roanoke Island on February 8, 1862, should attach to Major General B. Huger and the late Secretary of War, J. P. Benjamin."[15]

Huger's was not the only voice sounding the alarm. Many prominent civilians also realized there were problems. On February 17, Robert D. Hart, a North

12 Gibson & Gibson, *Assault and Logistics*, 2:35; Joseph C. G. Kennedy, *Population of the United States in 1860; Compiled from the Original Returns of the Eighth Census*, Bureau of the Census, (Washington, DC, 1864), 514-15, 517, 519.

13 "Abstract from return of the Department of Norfolk, Maj. Gen. Benjamin Huger, commanding, for January, 1862," Jan. 31, 1862, *OR* 9:38.

14 Jefferson Davis to W. W. Avery, Feb. 18, 1862, Huger to Davis, Feb. 9, ibid., 435-36, 429.

15 Porter, *A Record of Events*, 238. Judah Benjamin was no longer secretary of war by this time. Robert M. T. Hunter, a lawyer from Virginia and plantation owner who had served as a U.S. Representative (Speaker of the House) and as a U.S. Senator (and who was an outspoken critic of President Davis) had resigned as Confederate secretary of state in February of 1862. Davis took the opportunity and gave the position to Judah Benjamin, who would hold it until the end of the war.

Carolina Baptist minister, wrote Davis of his fears that the Confederate army around Norfolk wasn't secure and lacked adequate ammunition. Moreover, he did not believe Huger "competent for the current assignment." Davis, however, dismissed Hart's concern and wrote Huger, on February 26, 1862, "my confidence in you has been to me a constant source of hope."[16]

On February 24, Huger reported to the Confederate war department the "reliable information" that Fort Monroe and Newport News had received reinforcements. While the report of additional troops was correct, those reports also included the erroneous news that the Ericsson (the *Monitor*'s early common name) had already arrived at Hampton Roads. "I write this to call the attention to the Government to the probability of this place being severely threatened by powerful forces," Huger wrote Secretary of War Benjamin, "and a general attack may be expected in a week or more."[17]

Just two days after this letter, Norfolk's mayor William W. Lamb asked Davis for 20,000 soldiers to protect the city, assuring him that "[w]ith those soldiers, and a good supply of ammunition, Norfolk, Portsmouth, and the navy-yard will be safe from any attack of the enemy." Lamb argued that since the British could not land near Norfolk during the War of 1812, Union soldiers also would find it difficult, "so great are the natural obstacles to the advance of an enemy." The president should come visit the city, he urged. "If Norfolk, Portsmouth and the navy-yard fall into the hands of the enemy a crushing blow will fall upon our glorious cause." [18]

Davis was aware of the circumstances. On February 28, he wrote Gen. Johnston to warn him of potential trouble from the south of Norfolk and urged him to be prepared to pull his forces and precious equipment and stores back from north-central Virginia. "Threatened as we are by a large force on the South east you must see the hazard of your position by its liability to isolation & attack in rear, should we be beaten on the lines South & East of Richmond," warned Davis.[19]

Davis was receiving advice from many people, much of it contradictory. The same day Huger complained of not having enough soldiers, A. F. Purefoy of

16 Robert D. Hart to Davis, Feb. 17, 1862, in Lynda L. Crist, et al., eds., *The Papers of Jefferson Davis*, 14 vols. (Baton Rouge, LA, 1995), 8:51; Davis to Huger, Feb. 26, 1862, *OR* 9:45.

17 Huger to Judah P. Benjamin, Feb. 24, 1862, *OR* 9:43-44.

18 William W. Lamb to Davis, Feb. 26, ibid. 51/2:481. On the British attempt in the War of 1812, see Egon Hatfield, "War of 1812 Bicentennial: Battle of Craney Island," June 6, 2013, Research, Development and Engineering Command History Office, accessed Feb. 5, 2019, https://www.army.mil/article/104909/war_of_1812_bicentennial_battle_of_craney_island

19 Davis to Joseph Johnston, Feb. 28, 1862, in Crist, et al., eds., *Papers of Jefferson Davis*, 8:68.

Forestville, North Carolina, wrote Davis that the Union would only feint toward Norfolk from the south. Instead, their true object, according to Southerners captured and released on Roanoke Island, was an invasion of the entire state.[20]

On March 3, Huger again complained to Davis of being "much weakened" when the navy called away "experienced artillerists [who] have had charge of the different batteries" protecting the southern shore of Hampton Roads. Huger had no choice but to man the guns with infantry. No official return for this period has been located, but a prominent citizen of Norfolk area wrote the Davis administration a warning. Huger's defenders, he wrote, numbered 12,000-14,000 on March 4 (a reasonable estimate), but they stood "little chance against estimated 70,000 enemy troops." The writer went on to lament "the likely loss of the navy yard and its value to the enemy." The "people here," he continued, "are puzzled by 'inertness' of government." Of Benjamin Huger, he concluded, the people have "little confidence." In a message to the Confederate House that same day, the president recommended expanding the army by another 300,000 soldiers and building 50 new ironclads. The South would never come close to accomplishing either.[21]

Davis did not have enough soldiers to protect every threatened portion of the Confederacy. On February 27, he declared martial law in Norfolk, Portsmouth, and the surrounding countryside for 10 miles and appointed Mayor Lamb as provost marshal. Davis' order included that all males be enrolled for military service, that all women and children be sent "away as rapidly as can be done, without exciting panic," and that "all merchandise, cotton, tobacco, etc." the military did not need be removed. Lamb had the authority to imprison anyone for "whom there is well-grounded suspicion of disloyalty."[22]

The loyalty of Norfolk's citizens also concerned other Confederate leaders and was a factor in deciding where to deploy forces. While Mayor Lamb was seen as "a zealous friend of our cause," Norfolk itself—"an important shipping point for Virginia cotton, rice and other staples"—had strong commercial ties to Northern markets before the war. Norfolk area farmers had supplied many of the crops that

20 A. R. Purefoy to Davis, March 3, 1862, in ibid., 77.

21 Huger to Davis, Mar. 3, 1862 & Davis to "Speaker of the House of Representatives," Mar. 4, 1862, *OR* 51/2:483-84 & 1/4:969-70; Cincinnatus W. Newton to Willoughby Newton, forwarded to R. E. Lee, Mar. 4, 1862, in Crist, et al., eds., *Papers of Jefferson Davis*, 8:79-80.

22 Davis proclamation, Feb. 27, 1862, & Benjamin order, Mar. 5, 1862, in James D. Richardson, ed., *A Compilation of the Messages and Papers of the Confederacy Including Diplomatic Correspondence, 1861-1865*, 2 vols. (Nashville, TN, 1904), 1:219.

fed New York City, and the navy yard had employed a large civilian workforce. Indeed, Norfolk voters, along with their neighbors in nearby counties, voted against secession before the war.[23]

These considerations influenced where Davis, Lee, and the rest of the South's leadership sent soldiers. They understood Norfolk's vulnerability, but Richmond also hung in the balance now that McClellan had landed a large army on the Virginia Peninsula and was marching toward the Confederate capital. The defense of one helped defend the other. Armistead Long, one of Lee's staff officers, described the symbiotic relationship after the war when he wrote, "Norfolk and Yorktown [on the Peninsula] bore a defensive relation to each other, so that the fall of one would necessarily involve the evacuation or capture of the other."

Of the two, however, Richmond took precedence. The people of Norfolk, Portsmouth, and the Gosport Navy Yard would have to hold out as long as they could, and if necessary, fend for themselves. It looked as though McClellan might concentrate his entire effort on the Peninsula and spare Norfolk. But even if it and the surrounding area fell, believed Davis, once McClellan was defeated the cities and navy yard could be recovered.[24]

What the Southern leaders did not know was that Lincoln had plans of his own. The president still had his doubts about whether the Peninsula Campaign was the best way to end the war. McClellan's decision to bring in heavy guns and pound open Yorktown, ending any pell-mell rush to Richmond before the Confederates could react, only served to increase his doubts. Lincoln realized he needed to prod his Army and Navy commanders into action. In his mind, Norfolk, Portsmouth, and the all-important navy yard were ripe for the taking.

All that was needed was someone to kick the operation into action.

23 Ibid.; Marc Egnal, *Clash of Extremes: The Economic Origins of the Civil War* (New York, 2009), 193-94, 294. W. H. Lyon, one of the area's civilians who had opposed secession, wrote Union naval secretary Gideon Welles that the Confederate takeover of Gosport had not ensured everyone a job. A third of Huger's troops and more than half of Norfolk's and Plymouth's citizens, he claimed, were still loyal to the United States. W. H. Lyon to Welles, Dec. 18, 1861, *ORN* 6:482. On May 8, just as Huger's troops were abandoning Norfolk, Richmond's *Daily Dispatch* reported "several hundred Union men whose sentiments were well known," in the city, "and several others, including some of the soldiers, who felt the same way but were keeping quiet." Lucille Madora Stephens, "Historic Norfolk: 'A Child of Mars,'" M.A. thesis, SMU, Aug. 1948, 33-34.

24 Armistead L. Long, *Memoirs of Robert E. Lee: His Military and Personal History* (New York, 1886), 148.

Chapter 1

Monday, May 5, and Tuesday, May 6, 1862

"[I]f there were troops at Fortress Monroe that could be spared, the movement should be made."

— *Brig. Gen. Egbert L. Viele*

EGBERT Ludovicus Viele arrived outside the Washington Navy Yard after dark on May 5, 1862. Thanks to a strong spring shower, few people noticed. He was just another army officer in a city full of soldiers, albeit this officer was a brigadier general. Viele had returned the previous month from the Union's successful capture of Fort Pulaski outside Savannah, Georgia, where the Confederate garrison had surrendered after an 18-hour bombardment.

Secretary of War Edwin M. Stanton had asked the presently unattached brigadier earlier that day to come to the navy yard, but "with somewhat mysterious caution" urged him to tell no one where he was going. Stanton soon showed up and the war secretary and brigadier walked through the yard's stockade down to the wharf, where the Treasury Department's revenue cutter *Miami* was moored. "We went on board and proceeded at once to the cabin, where, to my surprise, I found the President and Mr. [Salmon P.] Chase, who had preceded us," Viele recalled. The general soon learned he would be accompanying Abraham Lincoln, Stanton, and Treasury Secretary Chase on a trip to Fort Monroe, at the tip of the Virginia Peninsula. According to the president's two cabinet secretaries, Lincoln's trip, "so

Brig. Gen. Egbert L. Viele

Library of Congress

far as is known," had the goal "to ascertain by personal observation whether some further vigilance and vigor might not be infused into the operations of the army at that point."[1]

Lincoln needed to prod his overly cautious commander of the Army of the Potomac, Maj. Gen. George B. McClellan, into action along the Warwick River and at Yorktown. He also had to find a way to blunt the threat the CSS *Virginia* posed to that campaign, as well as free up the Union fleet the Rebel ironclad had stymied at Hampton Roads.

The first task had taken care of itself just the day before when Confederate Gen. Joseph E. Johnston, the commander of the Confederate field army on the Virginia Peninsula, finally gave up the strong position at Yorktown that had delayed McClellan's advance for 29 days. On May 5, McClellan wired Stanton that he had advanced up the Peninsula to Williamsburg. Though he complained that his army was "considerably inferior" to Gen. Johnston's opposing force that was standing between him and Richmond, McClellan managed to advance into Williamsburg the next day after fighting a sharp action that drove back the Rebels.[2]

Now the president had to neutralize the CSS *Virginia*. There had been grumblings for some time about why Union forces hadn't struck Norfolk and—

1 John G. Nicolay & John Hay, *Abraham Lincoln: A History*, 10 vols. (New York, 1890), 5:234. Egbert L. Viele, "A Trip with Lincoln, Chase and Stanton," *Scribner's Monthly* (October 1878), 16:813. The general pronounced his name Vee-lee. For more information, see Appendix I: Principal Biographic Vignettes.

2 McClellan to Stanton, May 5, 1862, U.S. Congress, *Report of the Joint Committee on the Conduct of the War*, 3 vols. (Wilmington, NC, 1998), 1:324.

Secretary of War Edwin Stanton

Library of Congress

especially within the U.S. Navy—the Gosport Naval Yard, the *Virginia's* home base. That facility was considered the best of its kind in the country, and its loss on April 21, 1861, hurt both the war effort and the Navy's pride.[3]

On November 11, 1861, a young naval officer stationed on the USS *Cumberland* in Hampton Roads wrote the naval department outlining a plan to retake Norfolk and the naval yard. Lt. Thomas O. Selfridge explained to Assistant Secretary of the Navy Gustavus V. Fox that 3,000 Union troops could be sent across the Roads to Sewell's Point while Federal vessels bombarded Rebel fortifications. From there, he continued, a second attack mounted across the mouth of the Elizabeth River to occupy Craney Island would deny access up the river to Norfolk, which would then fall easily. Selfridge claimed there was "nothing original" in his plan, "nothing which . . . has not been discussed elsewhere . . . I put them on paper from zeal, rather than to commit notoriety."[4]

Some in Congress were also growing impatient for action. At a hearing on December 24, 1861, in front of the Congressional Joint Committee on the Conduct

3 Edward P. Lull, *History of the United States Navy-Yard at Gosport, Virginia* (Washington, DC, 1874), 5, 33.

4 Thomas O. Selfridge to Gustavus V. Fox, November 11, 1861, in Robert Means Thompson & Richard Wainwright, eds., *Confidential Correspondence of Gustavus Vasa Fox, Assistant Secretary of the Navy, 1861-1865*, 2 vols. (New York, 1918), 1:397-400. The Confederate batteries at Sewell's Point and Craney Island would not be easy to storm from the waterside. A few days before Selfridge sent his letter, a *New York Herald* correspondent reported that the Rebels were "very busy at Sewell's Point," having mounted 20 large guns with more to come. "At Craney Island thirty-four bulldogs show their ugly muzzles. . . . With a proper force the rebels might be driven out by shell, but it would cost many lives and some vessels to do it." Richmond *Daily Dispatch*, Oct. 26, 1861, 3.

of the War, Brig. Gen. Samuel P. Heintzelman was asked, "Do you think that 50,000 men could not land near Lynnhaven Bay and pass over to Norfolk and hold that place?" Heintzelman, one of McClellan's division commanders, had no answer to that question.[5]

On February 12, 1862, however, Brig. Gen. John G. Barnard, the Army's chief engineer and designer of some of the capital's fortifications, dismissed landing on the Atlantic Ocean side at Lynnhaven Bay as impractical. Without knowing the circumstances, Barnard reckoned "that the approach from Linnhaven Bay [sic]" had been discussed so widely "that I imagine the rebels' most elaborate defences are on that side; besides the tributaries of 'Turner's Creek,' and the Eastern Branch of the Elizabeth, so interlock that the defensive position is very strong." Barnard also considered other routes to Norfolk: sailing directly up the Elizabeth River—requiring the batteries at Sewell's Point and Craney Island to be taken first—or landing forces up the nearby Nansemond River to seize both Suffolk and Portsmouth to choke Norfolk off. He admitted he lacked the expertise to decide which plan would succeed.[6]

Louis M. Goldsborough, the flag officer commanding the North Atlantic Blockading Squadron based at Hampton Roads, didn't see barriers that would stand in the war of Union success in that quarter. Possibly after talking with Lt. Selfridge, he advocated strong action. "Norfolk ought to be taken forthwith & the Navy Yard there totally destroyed," he wrote Fox. "It can be done, either by starting a large force from here, or the neighborhood of Cape Henry [from the south] which is better, & taking all its defences in reverse." The week before the *Virginia* attacked his ships off Newport News, Goldsborough urged Fox again. Having spent substantial time thinking about an attack on Norfolk, he'd become even more persuaded it would succeed, "& therefore, ought to be undertaken without delay. . . . That dock-yard at Norfolk is an infernally sore thing to us, & have it we must!!" Goldsborough estimated it would take more than 40,000 Federal soldiers to mount an invasion of Hampton Roads' southern shore. Those men,

5 Samuel P. Heintzelman testimony, Dec. 24, 1861, *Report of the Joint Committee,* 1:120. Lynnhaven Bay is some 14 miles down the Virginia coast from Fort Monroe. A landing there would put Union troops about 17 miles due east of Norfolk.

6 John G. Barnard to Gustavus V. Fox, Feb. 12, 1862, in Thompson & Wainwright, eds., *Confidential Correspondence*, 1:422-29. Barnard, a veteran of the Mexican War and West Point graduate, spent his career as an engineering officer in the U.S. Army helping construct numerous forts along the coast. In 1855, he succeeded Robert E. Lee as superintendent of the United States Military Academy. At the start of the war, Barnard was put in charge of constructing the defenses around Washington.

however, were under McClellan's control, and "Little Mac" had other plans for their use on the Peninsula.[7]

The *Virginia's* stunning debut at the battle of Hampton Roads on March 8 increased pressure to act. Iowa Senator James W. Grimes claimed that twice in the months before the *Virginia's* appearance, Navy officers had urged opening the port. At one time, a fleet had been steamed up and ready to go to Norfolk, "but a superior military officer, who undertook to control all offensive operations, refused to let it go," Grimes claimed. On March 14, almost a week after the *Virginia's* exploits and the USS *Monitor's* timely arrival, Navy Secretary Gideon Welles told Stanton that taking Norfolk was "almost indispensable" to deny the Rebel ironclad a home port.[8]

On March 19, Gustavus Fox, Welles's assistant, testified to the Congressional Joint Committee on the Conduct of the War that "taking Norfolk has been talked over a great deal." The goal of Maj. Gen. Benjamin Butler's late May 1861 expedition to take Newport News was "the ultimate possession of Norfolk," Fox explained. The president had endorsed the plan and "believed that it could be done without any difficulty." Butler had written a memo in late May 1861 "setting forth the feasibility of capturing Norfolk."

The committee continued to probe. Fox didn't know why Norfolk had not been seized then, but the "panic" in Washington after the defeat at Bull Run the

7 Louis M. Goldsborough to Fox, Feb. 23 and Mar. 1, 1862, in ibid., 243, 245-246. At the start of the war, captain was the highest official naval rank. To designate officers assigned to command more than one vessel (a fleet), the unofficial ranks of "commodore" or "flag officer" were created. The latter term related to the personal flag the commander would fly from his "headquarters" ship. On Feb. 18, 1862, Congressman Charles B. Sedgwick, chairman of the Committee on Naval Affairs, introduced a bill to recognize all unofficial naval titles and set all officer ranks as equivalent to corresponding U.S. Army ranks. The Senate eventually approved the bill and sent it to the president on July 15. Lincoln signed it the next day. The act replaced "flag officer" with "rear admiral," and recognized the top remaining ranks (in descending order) as commodore, captain, commander, lieutenant commander, and lieutenant. The rank of admiral was added later. The following year, the Confederate Congress also expanded its naval officer rankings to include admiral, vice admiral, rear admiral, commodore, etc. to match the changes made in the Union Navy. *Congressional Globe*, 37th Cong., 2nd sess. (1862), 583-87; U.S. Congress, *Journal of the Congress of the Confederate States of America, 1861-1865*, U.S. Senate Document no. 234, 58th Cong., 2nd sess., 6:131-35.

8 William Salter, *The Life of James W. Grimes, Governor of Iowa, 1854-1858; a Senator of the United States, 1859-1869* (New York, 1876), 171. James Wilson Grimes was first elected to the U.S. Senate as a Whig, but was instrumental in the creation of Iowa's Republican Party. While he was chairman of the Committee on the District of Columbia, Grimes had a strong interest in naval affairs and later became chairman of the Committee on Naval Affairs during the last year of Lincoln's presidency. Gideon Welles to Edwin Stanton, March 14, 1862, Lincoln Papers, Lincoln Studies Center (LSC).

previous July had "blocked this enterprise as it seemed to block every other . . . proposed elsewhere." Butler had amassed some 11,000 troops for the seizure of Norfolk and was receiving more until "this panic here" brought his numbers down to 4,000–5,000. The same panic had "also put off [Flag Officer Samuel F.] Du Pont's expedition two or three months. We could get no soldiers after that for any of our expeditions."[9]

Others recognized the Union occupation of Newport News, where the James River entered Hampton Roads, as just the first step in recovering Norfolk, Portsmouth, and, most importantly, the Gosport Navy Yard. On June 26, *The South-Western* newspaper in far off Shreveport, Louisiana, reprinted a report that Butler had gone to Newport News "to superintend the erection of batteries there, and to survey the surrounding country" for other targets. Speculation arose that Butler meant to land his soldiers at Ocean View, Hampton Roads, ten miles from Norfolk and approach the town with "regular siege movements."[10]

By mid-summer 1861, the Confederate press was reporting that additional Union troops were arriving at Fort Monroe. This could only mean an attack aimed at Gosport Navy Yard alone. The Mobile *Register* speculated that a feint by the Yankees toward Yorktown could induce Confederate troops to concentrate there to protect Richmond, but "the first thing you know [Butler] will be thundering with a powerful army at the gates of the Gosport Navy Yard."[11]

Congress was still considering the issue on February 28, 1863, when the Joint Committee questioned McClellan about why he had not taken Norfolk in late 1861. Could not a force of 30–40,000 "have been concentrated suddenly at Fortress Monroe, and Norfolk captured and the *Merrimack* [*Virginia*] destroyed, without incurring any great hazard to us?" pressed the Committee. Possibly, McClellan responded, but it would have been difficult, plus he didn't "think it would have promoted the general objects of the war." Norfolk would have fallen anyway as "a

9 Gustavus V. Fox testimony, Mar. 19, 1862, *Report of the Joint Committee*, 3:417. Butler sent troops from Fort Monroe to occupy Newport News at the opposite side of the Peninsula on May 27, 1861. Two days later he outlined a plan to send soldiers from Newport News across the mouth of the James River to Pig Point and then to Suffolk, Va., which along with blockading the mouth of the Elizabeth River would render Norfolk "so perfectly hemmed in, that starvation will cause the surrender, without risking an attack on the strongly fortified entrenchments." B. F. Butler, "Expedition to and Occupation of Newport News, Va.," May 27, 1861, *OR* 2:52, 54.

10 Shreveport [LA] *South-Western*, June 26, 1861, 2. It is speculation whether the plan outlined as coming from Maj. Gen. Butler was known to Lincoln, Chase, and others almost a year later.

11 Pickens Court House [SC] *Keowee Courier*, July 20, 1861, 4.

necessary consequence" of his move against Richmond. But would not the destruction of the *"Merrimack"* have made "the movement upon Richmond, by way of the James or York rivers, very much more safe?" McClellan conceded the point, but noted that the formidable Federal vessels "*Congress* and *Cumberland* were [believed] capable of taking care of the *Merrimack*." Taking Norfolk had been discussed after the destruction of those vessels, but it was thought "better not to depart from the direct movement upon Richmond."[12]

By the spring of 1862, given the fear of what the CSS *Virginia* could do, experts predicted any attempt upon Norfolk would require thousands of soldiers and many ships. Fox told the congressional committee in mid-March he believed 15,000 Confederate soldiers to be in and near Norfolk. It would take many more Union troops to accomplish the job. As a result, Norfolk, Portsmouth, and the navy yard remained in Southern hands.[13]

Lincoln hoped to change that with his trip to Hampton Roads. Planning for the trip was left to Chase, a role he seemed to relish. In January his department had purchased the revenue ship to transport everyone, buying it for $25,000 from New York merchant Arthur Leary. Built in Scotland in 1853, the *Lady Le Merchant* was a 115-foot, twin-engine, 213-ton screw steamer with 10 sails on double masts rigged as a schooner. With her teak planking and copper fastenings, the *Lady* sailed the transatlantic crossings with some style.[14]

Chase told his revenue collector in New York City to rename the steamer *Miami* after the Greater and Little Miami rivers in his home state of Ohio. Three guns—a 24-pounder, 12-pounder, and a pivot—were ordered for the ship, plus a new screw, fresh copper fastenings, and a few special amenities. She was carrying important people, after all, not going out on wartime duty. "Provide every particular necessary for comfort," Chase instructed. "Bed, bedding, crockery, glassware, 2 or 3 spare beds and bedding for us if needed." The *Miami's* main cabin, according to Brig. Gen. Viele, "was one of the finest models" afloat. The ship, he admitted, was one of the "most neatly appointed vessels ever owned by the government." He described the new revenue cutter as "neat and cozy [with a] center table, buffet and wash-stand, with four berths, two on each side and some comfortable chairs," as well as a "shaded lamp suspended from the ceiling." Additional comforts were added later—champagne glasses, plus silver or

12 McClellan testimony, Feb. 28, 1863, *Report of the Joint Committee*, 1:425.

13 Fox testimony, Mar. 19, 1862, ibid., 3:420.

14 Florence Kern, *The U.S. Revenue Cutters of the Civil War* (Bethesda, MD, 2010), 88.

An Alfred Waud 1861 sketch of a United States revenue cutter, similar (or even identical) to the *Miami*. *Library of Congress*

silver-plated implements: a coffee urn, two silver teapots, a silver-plated nut-picker, and two silver-plated snuffers. She sported a 24-foot gig fitted with brass oar locks and cushions, a 22-foot launch, and two four-oared rowboats.[15]

Once outfitted and ready, with one of the best captains in the revenue service, Douglass Ottinger, in command, Chase ordered the *Miami* to the capital. She arrived on April 7 and immediately attracted attention from official Washington. Two days later Chase escorted fellow cabinet members Secretary of State William H. Seward and Stanton, as well as Washington Naval Yard commander John A. B. Dahlgren and some "ladies" on a short cruise down the Potomac River past Alexandria and back. The next day, other dignitaries, including Governor William Sprague of Rhode Island, took the same cruise. A couple of days after that, Seward returned with his wife and daughters and was soon joined by President Lincoln, his wife Mary, and their two surviving sons, Robert and Tad.[16]

The president sailed the *Miami* again on April 19 along with Chase, Stanton, Dahlgren, and a handful of Army and Navy officers on an official trip to Army

15 Chase to Hiram Barney, Apr. 3, 1862, in Kern, *Revenue Cutters*, 88; Viele, "A Trip with Lincoln," 813.

16 Kern, *Revenue Cutters*, 88. Lincoln's middle son Willie had died, likely of typhoid, on Feb. 20, 1862.

headquarters at Aquia Creek in Virginia. With the local department commander, Maj. Gen Irvin McDowell unavailable, the dignitaries encountered a *New York Herald* reporter "who knew everything." From him they learned that McDowell had captured Fredericksburg, Virginia. While waiting for McDowell to report, Dahlgren said the group "had a gay evening in the little cabin, and then went to bed." The next day, the general and other officers visited Lincoln on board. On May 2, Ottinger, three lieutenants, two engineers, and a crew of 34 revenue sailors prepared the *Miami* for another cruise. Gossip had it that Lincoln was getting ready to see military operations in person.[17]

Other important government officials were also sailing down the Potomac. The *Miami* made another quick trip on May 3 to Aquia Creek, taking Stanton along with Seward and Chase. They talked with McDowell and were back the following morning. "Notwithstanding this full representation by his Cabinet," a *New York Times* reporter felt "authorized to say . . . that the President is not about to take the field in person." He was wrong. All was in readiness Monday, May 5, for Lincoln to do just that. Amidst an early evening rain, the president, Chase, and Stanton, along with Brig. Gen. Viele boarded the ship.[18]

The *Miami* slipped down the Potomac River under a pouring rain and anchored for the night about 10:00 p.m. a short distance below Mt. Vernon to switch pilots. The president, Chase, Stanton, and Viele, meanwhile, made themselves comfortable with the treasury secretary playing the role of congenial host, displaying "those social amenities for which he was at all times, and under all circumstances, eminently distinguished." Since the steamer belonged to the treasury department, Chase "treated us as if we were in his own house," explained an impressed Viele.[19]

Following supper, the group got down to business. The men discussed the overall situation "long into the night," reviewed the positions of the various armies in the field and the commanders' reports, and voiced their opinions on what should be done. They also discussed "[m]any other topics, relevant and irrelevant . . . interspersed with the usual number of anecdotes from the never-failing supply with which the President's mind was stored."

17 Madeleine Vinton Dahlgren, ed., *Memoir of John A. Dahlgren, Rear-Admiral, U.S.N.* (Boston, 1882), 364. McDowell commanded the Department of the Rappahannock.

18 "News from Washington, Official Toward Yorktown," *New York Times*, May 4, 1862, 8.

19 Viele, "A Trip with Lincoln," 813.

Viele described the evening as an "interesting study" of the country's leaders "relieved for the moment from the surroundings of their onerous official duties." Lincoln, "of course," was at the center of the group:

> kind, genial, thoughtful, tender-hearted, magnanimous Abraham Lincoln! It was difficult to know him without knowing him intimately, for he was as guileless and single-hearted as a child; and no man ever knew him intimately who did not recognize and admire his great abilities, both natural and acquired, his large-heartedness and sincerity of purpose. . . . His inexhaustible stock of anecdotes gave to superficial minds the impression that he was not a thoughtful and reflecting man, whereas the fact was . . . the reverse. These anecdotes . . . came unbidden and like a forced smile were often employed to conceal a depth of anxiety in his own heart and to dissipate the care that weighed upon the minds of his associates.[20]

Lincoln's longtime friend and confidant, Ward Hill Lamon, agreed with Viele. Years after the war, he described the president's humor as "a plaster that heals many a wound," though Lincoln admitted his stories were mostly second-hand. "I remember a good story when I hear it," he said, "but I never invented anything original. I am only a retail-dealer." His stories, Lamon continued, were often told with a well-defined purpose: to cheer the drooping spirits of a friend or to lighten the weight of his own melancholy ("a pinch, as it were, of mental snuff"); to clinch an argument; to expose a fallacy; to disarm an antagonist; but most frequently as simply "labor-saving contrivances."[21]

After some time, the discussion turned to the group's destination: Fort Monroe. Everyone studied a map of the Hampton Roads area spread across the table. Neither Lincoln nor Stanton had been there before, and the "conceptions they had formed of its location and topographical surroundings were quite inaccurate," recalled Viele. Everyone, especially Chase and Viele, thought it reasonable that transporting troops south across the Roads from Fort Monroe would be easy. Norfolk could be taken. "I pointed out what I regarded as a feasible route to the rear of Norfolk from a point near Linn Haven [sic] Bay, opposite

20 Ibid., 813-14.

21 Ward Hill Lamon, *Recollections of Abraham Lincoln*, Dorothy Lamon Teillard, ed. (Washington, 1911), 123-24. Lamon was Lincoln's former law partner, friend, confidant, and protector, and not the only one who understood Lincoln's penchant for humorous stories with himself often the object of the laughter. Wool's aide Col. Le Grand B. Cannon came to know the president during his brief stay at Fort Monroe and concluded that Lincoln "was by nature an intensely sad man, and all his story-telling and humor was a mere shield to cover his real nature." Le Grand B. Cannon, *Personal Reminiscences of the Rebellion, 1861-1866* (New York, 1895), 172.

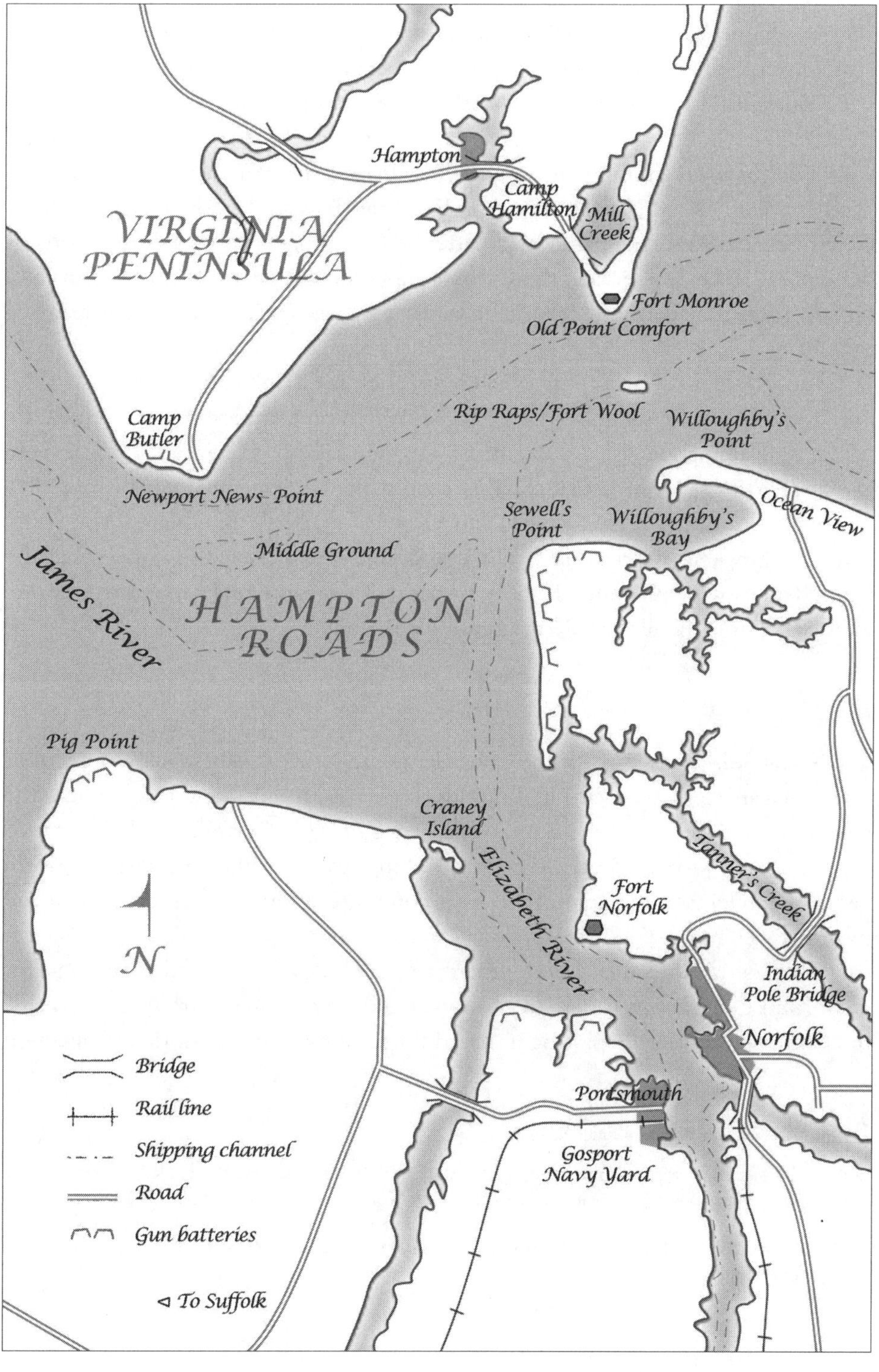
VIRGINIA PENINSULA
Hampton
Camp Hamilton
Mill Creek
Fort Monroe
Old Point Comfort
Rip Raps/Fort Wool
Willoughby's Point
Camp Butler
Newport News Point
Sewell's Point
Willoughby's Bay
Ocean View
Middle Ground
James River
HAMPTON ROADS
Pig Point
Craney Island
Elizabeth River
Tanner's Creek
Fort Norfolk
N
Indian Pole Bridge
Norfolk
Portsmouth
Gosport Navy Yard
Bridge
Rail line
Shipping channel
Road
Gun batteries
To Suffolk

Fortress Monroe," Viele recalled, adding that he had advocated for just such an invasion the previous fall while waiting for the Port Royal expedition to start.[22]

Anticipating Lincoln's wishes, on May 4 Stanton had telegraphed Maj. Gen. John E. Wool, Fort Monroe's commander, asking "whether your force is in condition for a sudden movement if one should be ordered under your command." Wool wired back the next day that his infantry was "ready to march with provisions, etc." He also had a field battery ready along with several squadrons of dragoons. "If for sea service, there would be no delay," wrote Wool. "If for land service, there may be some delay. The want of transportation might delay a day or two."[23]

The presidential party left Washington before Wool's reply arrived, so the question of having enough soldiers nagged the Union planners that evening as the *Miami* rode at anchor. Viele wrote that they eventually decided that, "if there were troops at Fortress Monroe that could be spared, the movement should be made."[24]

Such a move required ships, and they belonged to the Navy. The naval planners, however, feared the *Virginia*, and Union leaders didn't know what the Confederates were planning. Had they known, the group might have rested more easily when they finally decided to retire for the night.

* * *

Not all was going well for the Confederates in Norfolk. Their abandonment of Yorktown and retreat toward Richmond, coupled with calls for soldiers to join the main army to defend the vital capital, threatened to leave Norfolk and the navy yard exposed. Union forces already controlled a long stretch of the James River's north bank, effectively cutting off normal river communication between the capital and Norfolk.

Rumors of Norfolk's abandonment had been floating around Richmond for days. John Beauchamp Jones, an observant and opinionated clerk working inside the Confederate War Department, heard those rumors in late April and again on

22 Viele, "A Trip with Lincoln," 815.

23 Stanton to John E. Wool, May 4, 1862, *OR* 11/3:138; Wool to Stanton, May 5, 1862, John E. Wool Papers, New York State Archives. Maj. Gen. Wool sent two more messages to Secretary Stanton later the same day, both stating his soldiers were ready, except for the lack of transport horses, for which he blamed McClellan, who had taken most of them for the Peninsula campaign.

24 Viele, "A Trip with Lincoln," 815.

May 3. They gradually became more definitive. On May 6 and 7, he confided to his diary, "We have not yet reached the lowest round of the ladder. The [War] Secretary is at Norfolk, and the place is to be evacuated. I would resign first," he added.[25]

In addition to the threat of McClellan's army moving toward Richmond, and its attendant exposure of Norfolk, danger also lurked from the south, with Federal troops under Maj. Gen. Ambrose Burnside only 30 miles away at the southern end of the Chesapeake & Albemarle Canal. Those troops could reach Norfolk by marching up the canal through the Dismal Swamp to the Elizabeth River, or they might swing east and advance northward, marching on land between the swamp and the Atlantic. Still, many Confederates clung to the hope that Norfolk would remain in Southern hands—a hope that rested upon the strength of the *Virginia's* iron sides.

Maj. Gen. John B. Magruder, who had been in command on the lower Virginia Peninsula at Yorktown until superceded by the arrival of Gen. Joe Johnston on April 17, thought that the changed circumstances had released the "*Virginia* . . . from the inaction that she has necessarily remained in for the last month." On May 5, he told Secretary of War George W. Randolph, "[a]ll that the *Virginia* can effect in the Roads is the protection of Norfolk and the James River. The former object is not now a controlling one, as I understand Norfolk is, or is to be, evacuated."[26]

Magruder further opined that the *Virginia's* other job—keeping Union ships from going up the James River—could not be fully accomplished as some boats might slip by at night. Moreover, he added, the Rebel retreat had given the enemy "command of the left bank of the river from the Chickahominy down," which the Confederates couldn't protect to that extent. Keeping "the *Virginia* at the mouth of the James River" wasn't urgent enough "to occupy the attention of the last naval hope we have."

Instead, Magruder suggested—as had others many times since the *Virginia* was first ready for action—that the ironclad be sent past the Union fleet and Fort Monroe to the other side of the Peninsula and up the York River, there to wreak havoc with the Union transports supporting McClellan's Army of the Potomac. Confederate Secretary of the Navy Stephen Mallory had repeatedly rejected this

25 John Beauchamp Jones, *A Rebel War Clerk's Diary at the Confederate States Capital*, 2 vols. (Philadelphia, 1866), 1:123.

26 Mallory to Sydney Smith Lee, Mar. 26, 1862, *ORN* 7:751. Confederate Secretary of the Navy Stephen R. Mallory, back on March 26, had confidentially ordered the navy yard's commander to begin packing up machinery and tools for an evacuation.

suggestion as impractical. Even Randolph thought the *Virginia* needed to stay where she was. Her position "at the mouth of the James River . . . adds materially to the defenses of Richmond," he explained, "besides giving us a chance to move the material from the navy-yard up [the] James River."[27]

Reflecting Randolph's views, and possibly those of Confederate President Jefferson Davis, Mallory wired the *Virginia's* commander, Flag Officer Josiah Tattnall, to reiterate that the ironclad's mission was to protect the entrance to the James River against a Union naval incursion. "We look to the *Virginia* alone to [do this]," he emphasized. "Her presence in the river is of vital importance."[28]

Placing the *Virginia* at the mouth of the James, however, didn't protect Norfolk. That job responsibility rested on Maj. Gen. Benjamin Huger, who was busy organizing the city's military evacuation. Apparently, Huger heard of Mallory's order to Tattnall and complained to Tattnall about it. "[T]he order was imperative," Tattnall responded. "I must execute it." Perhaps Huger should telegraph Mallory "and state the consequences." Mallory soon relented and agreed the *Virginia* also needed to guard the river approach to Norfolk. If not, Craney Island and Sewell's Point would have to be abandoned. In another message the following morning, he reiterated his wish "to afford protection to Norfolk, as well as to [the] James River."[29]

With orders to protect both the James River and Norfolk while taking orders from army commanders whose authority over a naval officer like himself he questioned, Tattnall felt as if he was in an untenable position. His objections soon became widely known. The rumor mill was in full-out operation. "A vague report has been in circulation here for some days . . . that Commodore Tattnall had resigned from the Navy, on the grounds of an attempt to subject him to the orders of General [Joseph E.] Johnston, of the Army," reported the Atlanta *Southern Confederacy* on May 8. The paper went on to discredit the report, since the *Virginia* reported herself "at anchor opposite the Naval Hospital, with a prospect of active service during the present week."[30]

The purpose of keeping the *Virginia* in a position to hold off any Union attempt to take Norfolk, however, was not so the city remained in Confederate

27 Magruder to Randolph, May 5, 1862, and Randolph's endorsement, *OR* 11/3:494-95.

28 Mallory to Josiah Tattnall, May 5, 1862, *ORN* 7:785.

29 Josiah Tattnall, "Report of Flag-Officer Tattnall, C. S. Navy," May 14, 1862, & Mallory to Tattnall, May 6, 1862, *ORN* 7:335, 785.

30 Atlanta *Southern Confederacy*, May 8, 1862, 3.

hands, but to secure the ongoing military evacuation. "General preparing to march, packing up, fixing up tents," wrote a Confederate private on May 6 in describing the scene at Camp Jackson outside Norfolk. "Appeared at dress parade with sack and pack."[31]

The previous day, the *Southern Confederacy* published a report from a "special correspondent from near Norfolk" that the city "is to be evacuated at last . . . Lincoln will soon have control of every city in the Confederate States that can be approached by water." The reporter went on to note that when the secretaries of war and of the navy visited the Norfolk area the previous week, they "examined everything, and, from all appearances . . . decided to give up Norfolk and fall back toward Richmond. They have commenced removing stores and ammunition, and the machinery out of the Navy Yard. Everything is now rearward from Sewell's Point."

The paper's correspondent cited further evidence of the evacuation: "Yesterday a party passed down . . . with axes destroying every boat on the Elizabeth [River] both large and small, to prevent any negro or Unionist from going over to [Fort Monroe], to give the enemy information [about] the evacuation." An imminent attack seemed probable. "A bottle floated ashore here last Friday containing a note, signed, 'Confederate Prisoner at the Rip Raps,' saying the enemy was preparing to attack Norfolk on the 10th with three iron-clad boats," continued the reporter, who concluded, however, that "The darkest hour has not yet come. Do not despair. Daylight, bright and calm, will surely follow."[32]

The pending evacuation also affected the fledgling Confederate navy. Lt. William Harwar Parker, the gunboat *Beaufort's* former commander, watched in frustration as ships were ordered to move up the James River. The gunboat slated to be his new command sat unfinished at the Gosport Naval Yard. Writing after the war, he recalled that he had begun hearing about the "probable evacuation of Norfolk" during the first part of May:

> The *Patrick Henry*, *Jamestown*, *Teaser*, *Beaufort* and *Raleigh* were sent up the James River to operate on the right flank of General Magruder's army, then falling back in the direction of Richmond. The *Nansemond* and *Hampton*, two gunboats built at the navy yard, were completed . . . and sent to Richmond. Rutledge [who also had a new gunboat under

31 Louis Merz, May 6, 1862, "Diary of Private Louis Merz, C.S.A., of the West Point Guards," *Chattahoochee Valley Historical Society Bulletin*, 4 (1959), 35.

32 Atlanta *Southern Confederacy*, May 11, 1862, 3.

> construction] and I did our best to get our vessels ready [to move,] but the engines were not prepared and there was nothing left at the yard to tow us up.[33]

Despite the chaotic evacuation, on May 5 Tattnall defiantly showed the flag to make it clear to the Yankees on the other side of Hampton Roads who still held the southern shore. The *Virginia* steamed "around Sewall's [sic] Point for two hours [and then] returned to Craney Island, without exchanging a shot,"reported the *New York Times.* She was in sight when a Confederate schooner carrying 60 tons of coal for the ironclad ran aground along the southern shore of the James near Newport News. While the schooner's crew took to their boats, several boatloads of Union soldiers tried unsuccessfully to tow the schooner to the northern side of the river, so "[t]hey set her on fire." The *Virginia* made no move to assist the stricken vessel.[34]

* * *

Unaware of any of these events, Lincoln's party aboard the anchored *Miami* prepared to get some sleep. "The driving rain outside only served to make our little cabin seem more cozy," thought Viele. "The President's berth was on the same side of the cabin with mine, and he suggested that, as I had more room than I required and he had not enough, a movable partition would have been a great convenience." He went on to recommend that Secretary Chase should "provide some arrangement of this kind, in case we took another such trip."[35]

When the party woke the next morning the ship was well on her way, having resumed the journey downriver at 3:00 a.m. The *Miami's* captain ordered sails only as the revenue cutter made 10 knots, pushed along by a strong northwest wind.[36]

According to Viele, the time "was spent principally upon the quarter-deck, and the President entertained us with numerous anecdotes and incidents of his life, of the most interesting character." Lincoln also displayed his physical strength:

> While we were sitting on deck, he saw an ax in a socket on the bulwarks, and taking it up, held it at arm's length at the extremity of the helve with his thumb and forefinger, continuing to hold it there for a number of minutes. The most powerful sailors on board

33 William Harwar Parker, *Recollections of a Naval Officer, 1841-1865* (New York, 1883), 278.

34 *New York Times,* May 6, 1862, 1; Philadelphia *Press*, May 7, 1862, 2.

35 Viele, "A Trip with Lincoln," 815.

36 Kern, *Revenue Cutters*, 89.

> tried in vain to imitate him. Mr. Lincoln said he could do this when he was eighteen years of age, and had never seen a day since that time when he could not.[37]

Viele's reading of "an amusing rhyme" from *Harper's Weekly* entertained Lincoln "exceedingly." The president liked it so much he wanted to save it. "Instead of requesting me to cut it out for him," Viele explained, "he borrowed my knife, and extending himself at half length on the deck, spread the paper before him and cut the piece out, remarking at the time that it was not precisely the attitude for the President of the United States to assume, but it was a good position for a man who merely wanted to cut a piece out of a paper."[38]

While still descending the Potomac River, the *Miami* passed a mile-long row of barges laden with stones. Of the barges tied up along the riverbank, Lincoln joked, "Oh! That is Stanton's navy; that is the squadron that Welles would have nothing to do with. . . . It was finally decided, I believe," he continued, "that the War Department might have a fleet of its own to fight the *Merrimac*, and there it is." Secretary Stanton, who was out on the *Miami's* deck with the rest of the party, felt "a little disconcerted by the President's levity" and insisted it was best to prepare for the possibility that the *Virginia* could attempt to come up the Potomac to the capital city.[39]

Lincoln couldn't resist poking additional fun at the ruffled leader of the war department. "Your emergency," he replied,

> reminds me of a circumstance which took place in Illinois. We had on our circuit a respectable lawyer named B—, noted for a remarkable development of his breast, the glands being enormous, more protuberent [sic] than those of many females. In a conversation which took place among the lawyers at one of the hotels, there was a discussion regarding the singular development which, in a man, was almost a deformity, and could be of no possible use. B— controverted this, and said that, supposing he were to be cast away upon an uninhabited island, with no other human being but a nursing infant, for which he would have to provide. In such an emergency, he had no doubt Providence would furnish, through him, nourishment for the child.

He said this, continued the president,

37 Viele, "A Trip with Lincoln," 816.

38 Ibid.

39 Ibid.

> with as much apparent sincerity as Stanton showed when he urged a navy composed of canal boats to stop the *Merrimac*. I think B–'s paps to nurse an infant will be as serviceable, and required about as soon as Stanton's fleet to fight and keep back an iron frigate. The preparation for an anticipated emergency, which is about as likely to occur in one case as the other, is very striking.[40]

By noon the ship had left the Potomac, sailed past Point Lookout, Maryland, and entered the large expanse of Chesapeake Bay. With the cutter "tossing" on the waves, the party returned to the cabin to have something to eat. "It would have amused you to see us take our luncheon," Chase wrote his daughter the next day. "The President gave it up almost as soon as he began, & declaring himself too uncomfortable to eat, stretched himself at length on the locker. The rest of us persisted; but the plates slipped this way and that—the glasses tumbled over & slid and rolled about—& the whole table seemed as topsy-turvy as if some Spiritualist were operating upon it."[41]

Later in the afternoon, when the wind slackened, Capt. Ottinger called all hands to quarters for the firing of the ship's guns. The president and others sat under an awning on deck to watch the exciting event.[42]

The *Miami* eventually reached Old Point Comfort, at the tip of the Virginia Peninsula, between 8:00-9:00 p.m. and sailed around to Fort Monroe on the south side of the Point. The masonry fort was separated from the mainland by a small bay, connected to land by only a thin natural causeway and a narrow bridge.

"The outlines of the grand old fortress were dimly visible along the horizon as we approached," Viele wrote, "surrounded by a cordon of floating vedettes whose thousand lights glimmered like stars in the mirrored surface." The brigadier listed

40 Secretary of the Navy Gideon Welles retold this story many time after the war, adding, "Mr. Chase related to me this incident, which was afterwards, at his request, repeated by the President in the presence of others, to the great annoyance of Mr. Stanton, who never enjoyed the anecdotieal [sic] humors of the President if at his expense." Welles, "The First Iron-Clad *Monitor*," in McClure, ed., *The Annals of the War Written by Leading Participants North and South*, 29-30.

41 Chase to "Nettie," May 7, 1862, in "Diary, July 21-Oct. 12, 1862," Salmon P. Chase Papers, Library of Congress. Chase wrote three letters to his daughter Janet (nicknamed "Nettie") dated May 7, 8, and 11, 1862. The letters, later transcribed in his diary, used many abbreviations, which are spelled out in this text. "The Life of Chase: His Account of the Capture of Norfolk," *New York Times*, Sept. 10, 1874, 4, partially reproduces a couple of the letters. Parts of all three letters also can be found in David Donald, ed., *Inside Lincoln's Cabinet: The Civil War Diaries of Salmon P. Chase* (New York, 1954).

42 Kern, *Revenue Cutters*, 89.

Maj. Gen. John E. Wool, commander of Fort Monroe and vicinity.

Library of Congress

all manner of ships and boats floating in the waters near the fort, including ocean steamers, river steamers, sloops, transports, brigs, canal boats, harbor tugs, men-of-war, gunboats, iron-plated batteries, and "countless smaller craft." Finally, "[t]owering above them all was the *Vanderbilt*, that leviathan of ocean steamers, a million-dollar gift by the owner to the government."[43]

As the *Miami* pulled up to the wharf, Stanton sent a message alerting Maj. Gen. John Wool, the fort's commander, of the president's arrival. Amazingly, the fort had not been informed that Lincoln was coming. Wool's aide, Col. Le Grand B. Cannon, came aboard first and quickly suggested that the party retire to headquarters within the fort. Wool and his staff arrived soon thereafter to escort the distinguished visitors. By this time it was about 10:00 p.m.[44]

Apparently, and while still aboard the *Miami*, Lincoln brought up the prospect of taking Norfolk. Wool readily agreed with the idea, recalled Cannon, but the presence of the formidable *Virginia* lurking in the southern Hampton Roads waters invited disaster for soldiers sent over to do so on wooden transports. The Navy's cooperation would be imperative. It would have to neutralize the *Virginia* first.[45]

43 Viele, "A Trip with Lincoln," 818.

44 Cannon, *Personal Reminiscences*, 153-54; Chase to "Nettie," May 7, 1862, 48.

45 Cannon, *Personal Reminiscences,* 154.

"If you will order the navy to co-operate with me," Wool explained to Lincoln, "I will take Norfolk in three days." There was reason to have faith in Wool's pronouncement. Although at 78 he was the oldest officer in service, Wool (who was still fit enough to ride a horse) had a long record of accomplishments that stretched back to the War of 1812, when as a young attorney he volunteered to fight and never returned to private life.

The president, who was well aware of Wool's storied history, responded by telling the aging general that they needed to talk with the area naval commander, Flag Officer Goldsborough. As it happened, Goldsborough's headquarters was on the USS *Minnesota*, a powerful frigate anchored out in Hampton Roads. Despite the late hour, it was quickly determined that the president, Secretaries Stanton and Chase, and Gens. Wool and Viele should immediately confer with Goldsborough. The party rode a tugboat out to the *Minnesota* and climbed to the ship's main deck via a set of narrow steps flanked by guide ropes. It was, admitted Chase, "very high & a little fearsome."

Goldsborough was hardly enthused about taking on the *Virginia* to secure safe passage for troops. The plan meant risking the *Monitor* in another fight with her nemesis. Lt. Col. Thomas J. Cram of Wool's staff, who created the map Lincoln had studied the night before, also pointed out the dearth of good landing spots on the south side of Hampton Roads. Shallow water prevented transport tugs from getting close enough to disembark troops safely. The plan included a discussion about how to draw the *Virginia* into open water so the *Vanderbilt* or the *Minnesota* could ram her.[46]

Given the late hour (sometime after 1:00 a.m.), it is unclear whether the president and his party remained on the *Minnesota* as Goldsborough's guests or returned to the *Miami*. In all likelihood, the exhausted visitors returned to the comfort of their own ship.

46 Chase to "Nettie," May 7, 1862, 48-49; Cannon, *Personal Reminiscences,* 154. Goldsborough became commander of the North Atlantic Blockading Squadron on Sept. 23, 1861. On Oct. 12, his operational area was divided between northern and southern commands, north and south of the Carolina borders. Goldsborough retained command of the northern squadron, while Samuel F. Du Pont took over the southern one. *Civil War Naval Chronology*, 6:27.

Chapter 2

Wednesday, May 7, 1862

"... the assembled crowd raised hearty cheers of welcome."

— *New York Herald*

ALTHOUGH Abraham Lincoln and his subordinates had devised the rough outlines of a plan for taking Norfolk, it would take time for the various ships to prepare for the operation. The president had a day to fill.

Lincoln often rose before anyone else, but on this morning his shipmates arose about dawn, "for it isn't easy somehow to sleep late on ship-board," observed Chase. Breakfast, as guests of Maj. Gen. Wool, wasn't until 9:00 a.m. In order to avoid wasting the early morning, and probably to satisfy the president's eagerness for activity, Stanton suggested they tour the ocean-going ship *Cornelius Vanderbilt.*[1]

The largest ship at Hampton Roads, the side-wheel steamer measured 340 feet in length and weighed 3,360 tons. The former personal yacht of her namesake, the shipping magnate and richest man in the United States, had set a record for the fastest trip between North America and Europe before the war. In April 1861, with

1 Salmon P. Chase to "Nettie," May 7, 1862, in "Diary, July 21-Oct. 12, 1862," Salmon P. Chase Papers, LC, 49. There is some disagreement between the eyewitnesses (some writing long after the war) about the events and their order on May 7, 1862. For example, Brig. Gen. Viele described an attack on the Sewell's Point batteries on this day, but Secretary Chase does not mention it in his letter. The description of what President Lincoln did on this Wednesday is this author's interpretation after considering all the various statements discovered.

The intent was to ram the large and heavy *Cornelius Vanderbilt* (pictured above) into the CSS *Virginia* and sink her. However, the ship's advantage in weight and size were disadvantages in the mostly shallow Hampton Roads, where there was little room to maneuver the impressive ship. *Naval History & Heritage Command, NH 42188*

war upon the country and the federal government desperate for ships, Vanderbilt offered to charter—or rent—his ship, as well as other company ships, to the U.S. Navy. Deterred by the vessel's prohibitive cost of operation, the Navy turned down the offer. Secretary of the Navy Gideon Welles called the *Vanderbilt* "a white elephant."[2]

2 Gideon Welles, "The First Iron-Clad *Monitor*," in Alexander Kelley McClure, ed., *The Annals of the War Written by Leading Participants North and South* (Philadelphia, 1879), 30. After the war, Welles not only criticized the use of the *Vanderbilt* to ram the *Virginia*, but also the other large ships that were hired for the job, such as the *Baltic* and the *Illinois*. The expense of operating the *Vanderbilt* alone was enormous, and Welles complained that having the *Vanderbilt* and other large steamers under contract to confront the *Virginia* "cost the country more than half a million dollars." Edgar T. Welles, ed., *Diary of Gideon Welles: Secretary of the Navy Under Lincoln and Johnson, Jan. 1, 1867 – June 6, 1869*, 3 vols. (Boston, 1911), 3:474. The *Vanderbilt* was eventually turned over to the navy. "Too large for blockade service," Welles reported, so "the Navy Department sent her off on an unsuccessful cruise for the *Alabama*, under a very capable commander, at a cost . . . of more than one thousand dollars per day [close to $30,000 today] without result."

Undeterred, Vanderbilt renewed his offer to the Lincoln administration the following month. He felt "a great desire" that the government accept the steamer, "as she is acknowledged to be as fine a ship as floats the ocean." Given "her great speed and capacity . . . with proper armament," urged the shipping magnate, "she would be of more efficient service in keeping our coast clear of piratical vessels than any other ship."[3]

Stanton accepted the huge ship on behalf of the War Department, and she was chartered in November 1861 as a transport vessel for the Port Royal expedition. Then, amidst the CSS *Virginia* crisis in March 1862, Stanton either accepted Vanderbilt's offer to donate the ship to the Union cause—at the owner's expense—or agreed to a second charter for the duration of the war. The records about how it all happened are unclear, but what is certain is that Stanton ordered the vessel to Hampton Roads as part of the ramming fleet.[4]

While awaiting transport to the *Vanderbilt*, Lincoln got his first clear view of Hampton Roads in the early morning light. Ships of all types and sizes floated at anchor before Point Comfort protected by the guns of Fort Monroe from the dreaded *Virginia*. Besides the famous *Monitor*, then out in the Roads as "a sort of advance guard for the fleet," the *Galena*, an ironclad of a different design, floated stolidly in the distance. "[S]cattered along at intervals [were] the light draught but heavily armed gun boats of the fleet," wrote one eyewitness. At the harbor's entrance behind the warships bobbed "Steam rams, Frigates, transports & other vessels large & small composing the 'North Atlantic Blockading Squadron.'"[5]

3 Cornelius Vanderbilt to W. O. Bartlett, May 14, 1861, in Frank Moore, ed., *The Rebellion Record: A Diary of American Events, with Documents, Narratives, Illustrative Incidents, Poetry, etc.*, 11 vols. (New York, 1862), 2:152. Besides *Vanderbilt*, the president of the Atlantic & Pacific Steamship Company offered an additional four smaller vessels to the government.

4 Other large ships chartered for ramming duty were the *Illinois*, *Baltic*, *Arago*, and *Ericsson*. Flag Officer Louis Goldsborough instructed the captains of the ramming fleet to "strike [the *Virginia*] with the greatest possible velocity, at right angles to her side or stern, the side to be preferred." Any damage done to the ramming ship "even though it should involve ultimately her entire uselessness, [was] not to be regarded for a moment." Charles Dana Gibson & E. Kay Gibson, *Dictionary of Transports and Combatant Vessels, Steam and Sail, Employed by the Union Army, 1861-1868* (Camden, ME, 1995), 20, 28, 106, 158; Louis M. Goldsborough to D. B. Barton & H. A. Gadsden, Mar. 20, 1862, *ORN* 7:144.

5 William F. Keeler to "Anna," May 7, 1862, in Robert W. Daly, ed., *Aboard the USS* Monitor*: 1862, The Letters of Acting Paymaster William Frederick Keeler, U.S. Navy, to his Wife, Anna* (Annapolis: MD, 1964), 106. Some reports say Lincoln and the others were rowed to the *Vanderbilt*. See Casemate Museum, "Abraham Lincoln's Campaign Against the *Merrimack*," no. 9, *Tales of Old Fort Monroe* (Fort Monroe, VA, n.d.), 2. Others report they took the *Miami*, or her rowboat for the short trip between the ships. Kern, *Revenue Cutters*, 90.

A handful of ships from other countries lolled at anchor: the British ship *Rinaldo* and at least two French observer ships, including the *Gassendi*. The Norwegian corvette *Norvier*—a "sloop of war," according to fleet commander Goldsborough—also arrived. All of these ships had been sent by their governments in hopes of observing another clash between the *Virginia* and the *Monitor*.[6]

No such battle took place between early March and early May, lamented the *New York Herald*, and "in the presence of the English, French, and Norwegian men-of-war, [i]t is a burning shame to have them look upon this fine fleet, and see one solitary vessel keep them all at bay."

Approaching the massive *Vanderbilt* with her large side-wheel housing was an awe-inspiring experience from inside a tiny rowboat. According to the *Herald*, Capt. P. E. LeFevre—who like the rest of the 100-man crew were Vanderbilt employees rather than U.S. military personnel—received Lincoln at the ship's gangway. LeFevre "was in full charge" of the ship, the reporter observed, "and the War Department has allowed [him] to act according to his own discretion. . . . He has all confidence in the successful performance of the duty assigned to his ship." That duty was simple: once the *Virginia* came out to Hampton Roads, the *Vanderbilt* was to steam right over her.[7]

Once aboard the *Vanderbilt*, Lincoln paid close attention to the work at hand of beefing up her prow for her job as a ram. She had been "enormously strengthened about the bow with timbers," Chase related, "so as to be little else from many feet (say 50) from the prow than a mass of solid timber plated outside with iron." He also described visits to other parts of the ship. "We stood a moment on her wheel-house & looked down thro the immense diameter of her wheels, the frame-work of which seemed slight and curiously interlaced; but was in fact of the strongest wrought iron bars & adjusted carefully to the greatest strength. The weight of one wheel was 100 tons and diameter thro which we looked 42 ft."[8]

It was a successful tour, continued the *Herald* reporter. "When the President and his party had been shown all through the ship by Captain Lefevre, they expressed themselves well satisfied with the preparations made on board to destroy the *Merrimac*." Indeed, he continued, the president felt confident that the *Vanderbilt* alone was able to do the job. "The President, Secretaries Stanton and Chase,

6 Goldsborough to Welles, May 7, 1862, *ORN* 7:326. Also see *ORN* 7:87, 176, 220, 227.

7 "Norfolk Is Ours. The Preliminaries of the Capture," *New York Herald,* May 12, 1862, 1.

8 Chase to "Nettie," May 7, 1862, 49-50.

Fort Monroe, on the Virginia Peninsula's Old Point Comfort, dominates the northern shore of Hampton Roads. Named after President James Monroe, the masonry and earthen seven-sided fort remained a Union bastion throughout the war, providing a safe harbor for the navy's ships and a staging area for army expeditions in Virginia and farther south. *Library of Congress*

expressed a hope that some future day they would be able to take a voyage to Europe and back on the *Vanderbilt*."[9]

Nestled at the tip of the Virginia Peninsula, Old Point Comfort encompassed massive Fort Monroe and the village outside the fort's moat. The village "resembles one of those microcosms, which are shown sometimes in a baker's window in London—a town represented in very temporary gingerbread," was how one reporter put it. "The cheap wooden shanties . . . are in all stages of tumbledown-ity," and looked like "the first stiff gale of wind would level it altogether."

The Hygeia Hotel, the largest structure outside the fort, was described as a labyrinth—"a wonderful ant-hill of countless 'accommodations'. . . The mean little door, stained with the leanings of dirty loungers and their tobacco-juice, admitted us to a diminutive dark bar-room, which was, of course, a purgatory of stale

9 "Norfolk is Ours," *New York Herald*, May 12, 1862, 1.

cigar-smoke. Beyond this was a dining-room, with very low ceiling, but horizontally most capacious." [10]

As the *Miami* pulled up to the Old Point Comfort wharf outside Fort Monroe, Maj. Gen. Wool and some of his staff came aboard to formally greet the presidential party and accompany them into the fort. The group walked along the wharf and up to the fort's main sally port, where an honor guard lined both sides of the entrance. Amidst the customary salutes of the guards and the warm congratulations of the departmental personnel, the fortress's cannons fired a 21-gun salute. The president's visit, wrote one onlooker, had caused "a great commotion ashore and in the fleet."[11]

According to the *New York Herald* correspondent, the president appeared careworn, but "his simple and easy manners" belied his position as chief executive of a country of more than 30 million people. Proceeding "to the beautiful parade ground, shaded by umbrageous [live oak] trees," the visitors watched the fort's garrison on morning parade. At Lincoln's appearance the regimental band struck up "Hail to the Chief," the troops presented arms, and "the assembled crowd raised hearty cheers of welcome."[12]

Wool led his guests across the parade ground and on to breakfast at his headquarters, known at Quarters Number One, a three-story "graceful old house just inside the fort's east gate" with wide steps leading up to a broad second-floor veranda. Following the meal, which likely included more discussion of the CSS *Virginia*, Norfolk, and the advance of McClellan's army up the Peninsula, Lincoln made an inspection tour of the fort. The president, who loved all things mechanical, took an interest in the fort's machine shop, especially "the machine for rifling cannon," recorded the reporter. "It was in operation at the time of his visit. The simplicity and efficiency of its movements were highly satisfactory."[13]

The water batteries outside the fort were next on the tour. For the president's "special edification," two Rodman cannons deployed on the beach dubbed the

10 N. P. Willis, "Lookings-on at the War," *The Home Journal* [New York City], May 24, 1862, scrapbook clipping in Wool Papers, NYSA. By contrast to the "flimsy and straggling village of 'Old Point,'" the writer described Fort Monroe as a "solid and well-built citadel . . . a skirt of rags to a jeweled bodice."

11 "The President's Visit to Fortress Monroe," *New York Herald*, May 9, 1862, 5; Daniel L. Boyer to "Sister," May 7, 1862, in David M. Sullivan, *The United States Marine Corps in the Civil War—The Second Year* (Shippensburg, PA, 1997), 24-25.

12 "The President's Visit," *New York Herald*, May 9, 1862, 5.

13 *Tales of Old Fort Monroe*, no. 9, 2; "The President's Visit," *New York Herald*, May 9, 1862, 5.

The Lincoln Gun was one of the largest used during the Civil War. This 1864 image shows the 15-inch Rodman, the first of its kind cast in 1860, with is muzzle cap off. The rifled artillery piece could fire a 300-lb. shell up to four miles. It was named after President Abraham Lincoln in 1862. The gun tube pictured above is today on display on the parade ground at the Fort Monroe National Monument. *Library of Congress*

Lincoln Gun and the Union Gun, were fired. The larger Lincoln Gun, a 15-inch smoothbore cast in 1860, "sent shots clear across Sewell's Point," claimed Daniel L. Boyer, a marine on the USS *St. Lawrence.* The Union Gun was a smaller 12-inch rifled cannon.[14]

About 10:30 a.m., Lincoln and others sailed on the steamer *James A. Stevens* (not to be confused with the warship *E. A. Stevens*) the mile or so to Fort Wool on the artificial island known as the Rip Raps.[15] Fort Monroe was constructed at Old

14 Boyer to "Sister," May 7, 1862, in Sullivan, *Marine Corps in the Civil War*, 24-25.

15 *Philadelphia Inquirer*, May 9, 1862, 1. The fort originally was called Fort Calhoun after South Carolinian John C. Calhoun, a former U.S. representative and senator, secretary of war under President James Monroe, vice president under both John Quincy Adams and Andrew Jackson, and secretary of state under President John Tyler. Calhoun had died in 1850, but Secretary Stanton did not want an important military installation named after a Southern slaveholder who had advocated for states rights, so he had the name changed to Fort Wool on March 18, 1862, in honor of department commander "in recognition of faithful service by a distinguished and gallant officer." *OR* 11/3:13; Richard Edling, contributor/photographer, "Fort Wool,

Point Comfort following the War of 1812 to protect the entrance to Hampton Roads from Chesapeake Bay and the Atlantic Ocean. The war department realized its cannons could not completely cover the 1,800-foot opening. Creating an island on the opposite side of the channel from the shoal of shallow water that extended to the southern shoreline solved the problem. The decades-long project began on the Rip Raps in 1817. Once the artificial island broke water, work on the fort's masonry began. Although guns were much more powerful by 1862, holding the fort on the Rip Raps enabled the Union to not only control the eastern end of Hampton Roads, but also cover the southern shore line, including Willoughby's Point and Willoughby's Bay. Both were within cannon shot of Union and Rebel forces, rendering the area a no man's land.[16]

During the tour of the unfinished fortification, Lincoln also caught sight of a large cannon mounted outside the walls. The Sawyer Gun was an experimental cannon of extreme range, power, and accuracy. Its shells easily reached the Confederate batteries at Sewell's Point three miles distant. Lincoln was naturally curious and asked Lt. R. M. Shurtleff about it. The officer oversaw the gun as part of the 99th New York Volunteer Regiment, also known as the "Naval Brigade" or "Union Coast Guard."[17]

"A fine gun," Shurtleff replied. "I informed [Lincoln] that it was three miles, less an eighth, to Sewall's Point, and that we had no difficulty in hitting the barriers, which were made of railroad iron and protected on top by lids, which opened and shut at will." The soldiers of the Naval Brigade "practiced daily with the Sawyer Gun. Our shots would be generally directed at Sewall's Point, and the Confederates would return fire with shots from their Blakely guns." Lincoln asked for "an exhibition of our skill," he added. The president was keenly interested in the gun and watched intently as it fired several rounds, wrote the *Herald* reporter. The chief executive observed "the modus operandi" of loading the guns, and at the first shot he "watched the curling smoke and listened attentively to the whiz of the burning

---

Hampton, Virginia," Civil War Album, accessed July 6, 2007, civilwaralbum.com/misc7/fort_wool1.htm.

16 Carl D. Park, *Ironclad Down: The USS Merrimack-CSS Virginia From Construction to Destruction* (Annapolis, MD, 2007), 199-200. Reportedly by his own request President Lincoln and his secretaries were "received without the customary salute." *New York Herald,* May 9, 1862, 5.

17 The Sawyer Gun was named after its inventor, Sylvanus Sawyer. The shells for the rifled cannon, patented in 1855, had six rectangular ribs on the side that fit into six spiral groves inside the gun's barrel. When shot out of the cannon, the shell developed a tight spin that gave it more distance. Mark M. Boatner, III, *The Civil War Dictionary* (New York, 1988), 722. See also J. Michael Cobb, *Fort Wool: Star-Spangled Banner Rising* (Charleston, SC, 2009), 86.

This sketch by Alfred R. Waud depicts the Sawyer Gun on Sewell's Point outside the defensive walls of Fort Wool on the Rip Raps. The rifled artillery piece was still in its experimental stage. Developing new ordnance was a high-risk business, and the officers and men observing its fire are dangerously close should the piece explode. *Library of Congress*

fuse as the shell struck directly in the rebel works, exploding with a loud retort, throwing up a cloud of dust and smoke in the air." Firing "such a distance with such accuracy," he thought was "perfectly magnificent."[18]

From the Rip Raps, the president, Secretaries Chase and Stanton, and "other dignitaries attended by Gen. Wool & staff" sailed to the *Monitor*, which they reached about noon. Although everyone else viewed the little "cheese box on a shingle" with awe, William F. Keeler, the ship's paymaster, observed a difference in Lincoln's demeanor. The president "had a sad, care worn & anxious look in strong

18 R. M. Shurtleff & J. B. Mendenhall, in Philip Corell, ed., *History of the Naval Brigade: 99th N.Y. Volunteers, Union Coast Guard, 1861-1865* (New York, 1905), NYSA, np; *New York Herald*, May 9, 1862. Lincoln was taking a chance by asking for the gun's demonstration. Almost three months earlier, a Sawyer Gun at Fort Wool had burst, killing two or three men and wounding a number of others. John A. Dahlgren to Gustavus V. Fox, Feb. 14, 1862, in Robert Means Thompson & Richard Wainwright, eds., *Confidential Correspondence of Gustavus Vasa Fox, Assistant Secretary of the Navy, 1861-1865*, 2 vols. (New York, 1918), 1:423. The Confederate fortifications at Sewall's Point, more properly spelled "Sewell's" Point, along with those on Craney Island, provided the principal defense against Union ships sailing up the Elizabeth River to Norfolk. Occasionally, the name is spelled as "Sowel's Point." I employ the "Sewell's Point" spelling.

Lt. William N. Jeffers poses in front of the *Monitor's* turret on July 9, 1862. He was the fourth commander of the iron ship. *Naval History & Heritage Command, NH 48887*

contrast with the gay cortege by which he was surrounded. As the boat which brought the party came alongside every eye sought the *Monitor* but his own," he said. "He stood with his face averted as if to hide some disagreeable sight. When he turned to us I could see his lip quiver & his frame tremble with strong emotion & imagined that the terrible drama in these waters of the [eighth] & [ninth] of March was passing in review before him."[19]

When the ironclad's commander, Lt. William N. Jeffers, introduced the *Monitor's* officers, Lincoln perked up upon learning the paymaster hailed from his home state. "He was very happy he said to find one from Illinois on board the *Monitor.*" Lincoln was most interested in the *Monitor's* mechanics. Not so many months earlier, the president had held a model of the proposed radical new ship in his hands and remarked upon its unique design: "All I have to say is what the girl said when she stuck her foot into the stocking. It strikes me there's something in it." Now he was on the real thing, a ship that had proven her worth and vindicated his decision. "He examined everything about the vessel with care, manifesting great interest," Keeler observed, "his remarks evidently shewing that he had carefully

19 Keeler to "Anna," in Daly, ed. *Aboard the USS Monitor*, 106-107.

The officers (from left to right) of the USS *Monitor.* Front Row: Robinson W. Hands and Edwin V. Gager; Second Row: Louis N. Stodder, George Frederickson, William Flye, Daniel C. Logue, and Samuel Dana Greene; Standing: Albert B. Campbell, Mark T. Sunstrom, William F. Keeler, and L. Howard Newman (of the USS *Galena*). *Library of Congress*

---

studied what he thought to be our weak points & that he was well acquainted with all the mechanical details of our construction."[20]

According to George Geer, one of the *Monitor's* engineers, Lincoln "was very much pleased with the looks of our craft" and saw the improvements being made to the ship in anticipation of her next encounter with the *Virginia.* "We are putting in a Steam Pump and two Engines to drive it . . . in case we get a hole in our side," Greer told his wife. "It will pump 2500 Gallons pr minnit. It will keep us afloat if the hole was large enough for me to crall through." That pump also would be useful to help remove water that continually seeped into the leaky vessel.[21]

20 Ibid.; James L. Nelson, *Reign of Iron: The Story of the First Battling Ironclads, the* Monitor *and the Merrimack* (New York, 2004), 107, 132.

21 George Geer to his wife, May 7, 1862, in William Marvel, ed., *The* Monitor *Chronicles: One Sailor's Account* (New York, 2000), 62.

Most visitors to the *Monitor*, Keeler explained, came on board "filled with enthusiasm & patriotism ready, like a bottle of soda water, to effervesce the instant the cork is withdrawn," but the president was different. "His few remarks as he accompanied us around the vessel were sound, simple & practical, the points of admiration & exclamation he left in his suite."[22]

The *New York Herald* correspondent who reported Lincoln's visit to both the *Monitor* and the *Galena* agreed with Keeler's description. "He examined these vessels with much care, making the most detailed inquiries as to their construction and operation." Some of that examination involved the dents left from the *Virginia's* balls hitting the *Monitor's* turret. Lincoln also studied the pilothouse, which had taken a direct hit that had temporarily cost the eyesight of Lt. John Worden, the ship's captain during the fight. After the battle the chief engineer modified the pilothouse by reinforcing it with iron and sloping its exterior walls.[23]

At the end of the tour, Lincoln asked that the *Monitor's* crew be mustered on deck for a review. He "passed slowly before them hat in hand." In turn, as the president left, the crew gave him three hearty cheers.

As the president stepped off the *Monitor* about 1:30 p.m. for a short sail to the *Minnesota* and further consultation with Flag Officer Goldsborough, another party of visitors—congressmen and other politicians, "some twenty or more" arrived. Keeler was assigned to lead a couple of senators, "but their sight seeing was suddenly interrupted by the bo'sun's whistle & cry of 'all hands prepare ship for action.'" The *Virginia* had been sighted "slowly coming around Sewall's Point apparently bound straight for us," explained the *Monitor's* paymaster to his wife.[24]

Sailors on the *Minnesota* had also spotted the *Virginia*. "As the officers of that vessel were getting their men ready to man the yards and fire a salute" for the president, explained the *New York Herald* to its readers, "the lookout on the foretop announced that the *Merrimac* was coming out of Norfolk. The men were beat to quarters and the fleet in the harbor signalized to get ready for action."[25]

The firing of various Union guns all morning had caught the attention of Confederate authorities in Norfolk. In addition, recorded one sailor, the side-wheel

22 Keeler to "Anna," May 7, 1862, in Daly, ed., *Aboard the USS* Monitor, 107.

23 "The President's Visit," *New York Herald,* May 9, 1862, 5. There is some disagreement about which ship, besides the *Monitor*, Lincoln visited that day. While the reporter wrote it was the *Galena*, another author claimed it was the *E. A. Stevens*. *Tales of Old Fort Monroe*, no. 9, 2.

24 Keeler to "Anna," May 7, 1862, in Daly, ed., *Aboard the USS* Monitor, 107.

25 "The President's Visit," *New York Herald,* May 9, 1862, 5.

steamer USS *Susquehanna*, with her 18 guns, tried out a couple of new 100-pounder rifled cannon, throwing "a lot of shells into the batteries" also on Sewell's Point. The guns of Fort Wool had joined in. Daniel Boyer aboard the *St. Lawrence* wrote his sister that the *Susquehanna's* new Dahlgren guns "worked beautifully, sending their shots clear across the channel which is about four miles wide."[26]

* * *

The Confederates could do little in response to the Union shelling. The commander of the Department of Norfolk, Maj. Gen. Benjamin Huger, was focused on the pending evacuation. Ordered to protect his troops and not endanger them by trying to save private property, he also had to maintain control of the area as long as possible in order to ship out needed supplies. For the individual Rebel soldier at Camp Jackson outside Norfolk this meant "Baggage and sick men sent to town. Dress parade with knapsack."[27]

The 56-year-old Huger, an 1825 graduate of West Point and Mexican War veteran, was under pressure from all sides. Back on April 12, a congressional committee had voted unanimously to blame him, as well as Secretary of War Judah P. Benjamin, for losing Roanoke Island in North Carolina. The newspapers piled on. The *Raleigh Register* blamed Huger for allowing Yankees on the state's land and called for the general's removal from command of the North Carolina coast and eastern Virginia. Jefferson Davis, continued the paper, had neglected his duty by

26 Alfred L. B. Zerega, "The Last Days of the Rebel Iron-Clad Merrimac and Occupation of Norfolk, as Seen from the USS *Susquehanna*," presented to the Military Order of the Loyal Legion of the United States, Commandery of the District of Columbia, Feb. 3, 1897, in War Papers: Being Papers Read Before the Commandery of the District of Columbia, Military Order of the Loyal Legion of the United States, 60 vols. (Wilmington, NC, 1993), 1:450; Boyer to "Sister," May 7, 1862, in Sullivan, *Marine Corps in the Civil War*, 24-25. Designed by navy Commander John A. Dahlgren in 1850, the series of smoothbore cannons that bore his name were highly reliable weapons employed during the war by both sides on land and at sea. Somewhat bulbous shaped at the breech and tapering down to the muzzle's end, a shape sometimes compared to a soda bottle, provided the greatest strength where needed—where the powder exploded to propel the ball. They came in a variety of sizes, including a 32-pounder, and a 9-inch up to a 20-inch. The Monitor-class ships were armed with 11- and later 15-inch guns. Dahlgren also developed a series of rifled cannons that had been removed from service by February 1862. David S. Heidler & Jeanne T. Heidler, eds., *Encyclopedia of the American Civil War: A Political, Social, and Military History* (New York, 2000), 547-48.

27 *OR* 11/3:490; Louis Merz, May 7, 1862, Diary of Private Louis Merz, *C.S.A., of the West Point Guards*, 35.

not removing Huger, and now it was up to the state, "so seriously injured by his recklessness, to demand his removal."[28]

As word trickled out that Norfolk was to be evacuated, other commentators such as Atlanta's *Southern Confederacy* weighed in against the plan. "It almost made my heart sick within me," one person wrote to the paper. Another paper reported, "There has been some vague talk lately of a possible evacuation of Norfolk, destruction of the Navy Yard, &c. But it would seem incredible that the Government harbored such an idea. If [Norfolk] should be evacuated by one ill judged step, we would lose the finest navy yard in the whole country, and a ship . . . which, besides performing so great a part in the maintenance of Norfolk, &c., protects the James river and Magruder's [Gen. Joseph Johnston's] right flank from the enemy's gunboats." The editor worried that pulling Rebel forces out of Norfolk and Portsmouth for use in the protection of Richmond would only make things worse by permitting a Union attack on the Confederate capital from the south. "He will thus be enabled to resume the first and favorite scheme of his government—an attack on Richmond by the south side of James River—where it is supposed by the North, he will not encounter any of the formidable defences which routes by the Peninsula and Manassas present."[29]

The same day one Richmond paper called the idea of giving up Norfolk and the Gosport Navy Yard "incredible," Gen. Robert E. Lee, President Davis' military advisor, sent a message to Huger again requesting the removal of "all guns that you possibly can, selecting the best first." Overriding Huger's earlier concerns about dismantlement of the advanced batteries, Lee replied that he thought it advisable to save the more valuable guns, "if possible." More of Huger's troops needed to be sent to Richmond, Lee continued, to be reassigned to Joe Johnston's army operating on the Peninsula. As regiments could be spared, they were to be organized into brigades and sent forward. Huger was to report to Richmond once all this had been done.[30]

While the embattled Huger was trying to organize the soldiers into units and send supplies elsewhere, Lee cautioned the Norfolk authorities not to leave

28 U.S. Congress, Journal of the Congress of the Confederate States of America, *1861-1865*, U.S. Senate Document no. 234, 58th Cong., 2nd sess., 7 vols. (Washington, DC, 1904), 5:243; *Daily Columbus* [NC] *Enquirer*, May 8, 1862, 2.

29 Atlanta *Southern Confederacy*, May 11, 1862, 3; see, also, a clipping dated May 7, 1862, from an unnamed newspaper in the "Virginia Gordan Scrapbook," Sargeant Memorial Collection, NPL.

30 Lee to Benjamin Huger, May 7, 1862, *OR* 11/3:497.

precipitously. The South needed as many of the supplies stored there as possible shipped away from the Union's closing grasp. On May 7, Lee told another general that troops shouldn't abandon "Norfolk before the stores, men &c." had been withdrawn. "[T]he outposts must be prepared for evacuation, but not abandoned before the proper time." Non-military supplies also needed to be evacuated: "all the cotton, tobacco, spirits of turpentine, and oil in the district" had to be removed by May 8, the city provost ordered; anyone trying to hide such items would be "arrested and severely punished."[31]

The Southern navy was also busy trying to save as many supplies and all the critical machinery possible. The *Patrick Henry* and *Jamestown* had already made one trip from the navy yard up the James River to Richmond, towing supplies and two unfinished ships: the partially completed ironclad *Richmond* and the gunboat *Hampton.* As the two ships approached Union-held Newport News at the mouth of the James about 2:00 a.m. on May 7 on their return voyage, Commander John R. Tucker, the *Patrick Henry*'s skipper, noted signal lights between Union picket boats and the shore. He decided to postpone the run back to Norfolk.[32]

Roads and rails available for use by the evacuating Rebels were limited, given the uncertainty of the floating transport. Navy Secretary Mallory ordered the commander of the navy yard, Capt. Sydney S. Lee—Robert E. Lee's brother—to "secure immediately a safe place in North Carolina . . . for a laboratory, and to transport all the ordnance stores he can save" to that state as well. Lee was also to confer with Huger about using the railroad to bring off naval stores as well as the army's supplies. Mallory was against shipping supplies to Richmond because McClellan's Army of the Potomac was approaching and whether the capital could be held was an open question. Apart from the unfinished ships and the needed materials (a small navy yard called "Rocketts" was being constructed on the bank of the James River in Richmond.), nothing was to be sent to the capital that could not go to North Carolina.[33]

31 "From Fortress Monroe—the Traitor Steamboat Captain," [Richmond] *Daily Dispatch*, May 15, 1862, accessed Nov. 2, 2010, http://dlxs.richmond.edu.

32 John R. Tucker to Stephen Mallory, May 8, 1862, *ORN* 7:786. Although the partially-built CSS *Richmond* was towed out safely, most of the lumber to complete her was torched at the Gosport Navy Yard, greatly delaying her entry into service. The ironclad wasn't completed until November and saw little action before being scuttled on April 2, 1865. Jefferson Davis to Varina Davis, Jul. 6, 1862, in Lynda Lassell Crist, et al., eds., *The Papers of Jefferson Davis*, 14 vols. (Baton Rouge, LA, 1995), 8:281.

33 William N. Still, Jr., ed., *The Confederate Navy: The Ships, Men, and Organization, 1861-65* (London, 1997), 76. The site of Rocketts Navy Yard was first used in the 18th century as a

Much of this frenetic activity had left Flag Officer Josiah Tattnall, commander of the CSS *Virginia* and all other Confederate combat ships around Norfolk, in a state of limbo. His other ships, especially the *Patrick Henry* and the *Jamestown*, had passed beyond his command by ascending the James. Given the current circumstances, "the best disposition" of the *Virginia* had to be decided upon. On Secretary Mallory's order, Commodore George N. Hollins, a former naval commander in Norfolk, traveled there to consult with Tattnall. The officers agreed to hold a conference of the top military brass the next day, May 8. Heavy and prolonged Union artillery fire, however, attracted Tattnall's attention and he ordered the *Virginia* out to investigate.[34]

* * *

Union lookouts scouring the southern shore of Hampton Roads and the entrance to the Elizabeth River quickly spotted the approach of the *Virginia*. The "Big Thing," what *Monitor* paymaster William Keeler called the "Confederate monster," was on the move. The alarm sounded and signal flags were hoisted. The *Virginia*, "with steam up, and black smoke curling out of her pipe," as the *Herald* correspondent described her, passed by Craney Island near the mouth of the Elizabeth. The Union fleet "formed line of battle, and soon were in readiness to give the rebel monster a hearty reception, should it have the temerity to visit the Roads."

The general Northern point of view was that the *Virginia's* commander was too timid to come out for a real fight. The ship remained near Craney Island, protected by the heavy Rebel guns of the sand and earthen fort. She stayed there for several hours before steaming slowly back up the Elizabeth River to Norfolk.

When it became apparent that no second battle between the ironclads would occur, Lincoln and the secretaries boarded the *Minnesota*. The *Herald* reporter

---

landing for Robert Rocketts's ferry. Rocketts Navy Yard had become a small facility by the mid-1800s. Rocketts, also called Rocketts Landing Navy Yard, was vastly expanded as the loss of Gosport Navy Yard loomed. In the following years the yard would complete the *Richmond*, build the *Fredericksburg* and *Virginia II*, and begin the *Texas*, which was burned when Richmond fell in 1865.

34 Josiah Tattnall's report, May 14, 1862, on the evacuation of Norfolk and the destruction of the *Virginia*, *ORN* 7:336. Commodore George N. Hollins commanded the Confederacy's Mississippi River squadron until mid-April, when he was called to Richmond to be president of the Midshipman Examination Board. He thus missed the debacle that was the loss of New Orleans. See Hollins' testimony before the "joint special committee of the Confederate Congress," in September 1862. *ORN* Series 2, 1:471-80.

gloried in "the old ship" that had taken a beating in early March yet remained afloat to assert U.S. supremacy once more. "The President examined particularly the portions of the ship" that a 10-inch rebel shell had struck, and when the explanation of how four staterooms had been blasted into one by the single shot, Lincoln admitted "his surprise at the terrible effect" it had. Thereafter, added the reporter, he had "a perfect horror of wooden war vessels."[35]

After talking with Flag Officer Goldsborough about the preparations for the attack on Sewell's Point, the president and his party returned to Fort Monroe. Maj. Gen. Wool had scheduled a review of his soldiers for Lincoln, but cancelled it when it appeared there could be a fight with the *Virginia*. Now, according to Chase, when the *Virginia* failed to come out, Wool proposed "that we should ride out to camp and see what was to be seen."[36]

While the president and his party were awaiting their mounts, they visited the telegraph room at Wool's headquarters. A young telegrapher, John Emmet O'Brien, who worked with his brother Richard at the station, was oblivious to the strangers and whistling "Dixie" when he entered the room. "Richard chided me rather sharply," O'Brien recalled. "It was such an unprecedented thing for him to do that I was much confused, and had only time to feel more surprised than hurt when a tall, lank, ungainly man rose up and told my brother that it was all right, that 'Dixie' was his favorite tune. It was Abraham Lincoln!"

O'Brien watched as the party, surrounded by Wool's staff, stood on the porch at headquarters about to start out on a horseback tour. "The most striking figure of that group that I still see in imagination is Mr. Lincoln," explained the telegrapher years later. "There he stands, head and shoulders above the rest, his rugged features illumined by a gleam of humor as the staff searches in vain for gauntlets large enough to fit the firm and honest hand that held the destinies of the nation.[37]

The gloveless president "upon a fine bay steed," along with Chase, Wool and his staff, and Stanton and his assistant, John Tucker, all "forming a most brilliant

35 "The President's Visit," *New York Herald*, May 9, 1862, 5.

36 Chase to "Janet," May 8, 1862, in "The Life of Chase: His Account of the Capture of Norfolk," *New York Times*, Sept. 10, 1874, 4.

37 John Emmet O'Brien, *Telegraphing in Battle: Reminiscences of the Civil War* (Scranton, PA, 1910), 88.

The ruins of St. John's Episcopal Church, built in 1728, upset Salmon Chase. When Maj. Gen. John Magruder's forces destroyed part of Hampton, the church was the oldest in the country. George N. Barnard took this image in July 1862. *Library of Congress*

feature of our cortege," left through Fort Monroe's east gate. It was, O'Brien concluded, a "delightful" day with a "beautiful" northwestern breeze.[38]

Of the two ways off the fortress peninsula, the narrow bridge provided the shortest route to Camp Hamilton, where most of Wool's soldiers were camped.[39] As the party rode past, Wool ordered the regimental commanders to form ranks and prepare for a review when the president returned. The riders crossed another bridge and rode through the village of Hampton. The "insurgent" Magruder had burned the village the previous summer, Chase wrote. "I never saw such a ruin—bare, blackened, and crumbling walls on every side; the Court-house about two

38 "The President's Visit," *New York Herald*, May 9, 1862, 5; Chase to "Janet," May 8, 1862, quoted in *New York Times*, Sept. 10, 1874, 4.

39 Since Fort Monroe could accommodate only about 1,400 soldiers, the rest were sent into camp on the Segar farm across Mill Creek. The encampment was called Camp Hamilton. Charles W. Cowtan, a member of the 10th New York Volunteers (the "National Zouaves"), described Camp Hamilton upon his arrival in 1861 as having a "quiet and imposing and eminently picturesque appearance," with the tents of the various companies and regiments lined up in straight rows. Casemate Museum, "Fort Monroe in the Civil War," no. 6, Tales of Old Fort Monroe (Fort Monroe, VA, n.d.), 1; Charles W. Cowtan, Services of the Tenth New York Volunteers, *National Zouaves, in the War of the Rebellion* (New York, 1882), 33.

hundred years old, but of remarkable beauty for that time . . . The burning was an act of sheer vandalism."[40]

Apparently the riders continued their journey on to Newport News for another five miles. Lincoln visited Brig. Gen. Joseph K. F. Mansfield's headquarters, where the James empties into Hampton Roads six miles across the Roads from the Confederate batteries at Craney Island.[41]

Union forces occupied Newport News in May 1861, where they constructed Camp Butler, an entrenched artillery position named after Maj. Gen. Benjamin Butler, who was at that time the commander at Fort Monroe. The battery's four 8-inch Columbiads guarded the entrance to the James River. Mansfield and Camp Butler's soldiers were part of Wool's command, though when the Peninsula Campaign started, McClellan was officially in command of all of Wool's troops. Wool, who was senior in rank to McClellan, persuaded Lincoln to keep him and his department out of McClellan's control.[42]

If he rode to Newport News, the president would almost certainly have borrowed binoculars to take a closer look at the CSS *Virginia* resting at her mooring off Craney Island. He got "a clear view of the *Merrimac*," reported *New York Times,* which was "preventing our gun boats from running up the James river."[43]

The return trip through Hampton's destruction saddened everyone. Union troops, Chase claimed, would not have committed such outrages. He noted the striking contrast to areas the Rebels had not visited. Union troops had protected "the residence of former president John Tyler, a leader in the rebellion, and others hardly less conspicuous." In fact, the Confederates were involved "in remorseless devastation" of public and private buildings.

Back at Camp Hamilton, the president's party found Wool's soldiers lined up ready to march in review. The "well mounted and well equipped" cavalry regiments led off past the still-mounted Lincoln. Next came the regiments of infantry,

40 Chase to "Janet," May 8, 1862, *New York Times*, Sept. 10, 1874, 4. While Chase describes his views on the burning of Hampton, he does not note how Lincoln felt about it. The Federals occupied Hampton, about three miles from Fort Monroe, on July 1, 1861. When they evacuated the town after the defeat at Bull Run, Magruder's Confederates torched the place on August 7 to prevent its reoccupation. Hampton, which dated from 1610, was almost entirely destroyed. *Tales of Old Fort Monroe*, no. 6, 3.

41 "The Visit of President Lincoln—He Takes a View of the *Merrimac*," *New York Times,* May 9, 1862, 8. Chase does not mention any further riding to Newport News.

42 *Tales of Old Fort Monroe*, no. 6, 1.

43 "The Visit of President Lincoln—He Takes a View of the *Merrimac*," *New York Times,* May 9, 1862, 8.

"looking handsomely," including the 1st Delaware, a volunteer unit renowned locally for its splendiferous public appearance.[44] The display inspired Chase. Lincoln paused to talk with Lt. Col. Francis Weiss, commander of the 20th New York Volunteers. Taking Weiss's arm, the president encouraged both the troops and their commander by promising them that under Weiss's lead, "they would soon be in Norfolk, to which the men responded with three huzzas."[45]

As the Delaware companies formed up and the band commenced the cadence,

> the President, accompanied by a very large escort, all mounted, arrived . . . and, turning his horse's head to the right, followed directly behind the band, with his entire escort . . . following after; but when the band had reached the left of the regimental line and had turned to the right-about to march back to its position, and Drum-Major Dooley . . . had advanced with martial stride through the midst of the musicians, he suddenly came face to face with the President, and all were brought to a dead halt. . . . There sat the President, looking some-what embarrassed, and there stood Dooley, firm as the rock of Gibraltar; the equestrian brigade supporting the President, and the band resolutely backing up the drum-major, "marking time" and playing away. . . . After a few moments of hesitation,

44 Commanded by Col. John W. Andrews, the regiment underwent months of "strict discipline [and] instruction" after its formation to become "one of the best volunteer organizations in the service," according to Capt. William P. Seville. It "inspired each man with a just pride in it . . . a most excellent esprit de corps." Andrews bought the soldiers brass shoulder-scales and white gloves and required the officers to have epaulets and regulation felt hats with plumes. The regiment's drum major, Patrick Dooley, wore "the tallest and most gorgeous shakos, with trimmings to match." Other regiments rescheduled their evening dress parades for the soldiers to come watch the 1st Delaware. Wool and other officers often rode out from Fort Monroe to observe. When they learned President Lincoln would review them, "every man exerted himself to make as imposing a martial appearance as possible." William P. Seville, *History of the First Regiment, Delaware Volunteers: From the Commencement of the Three Months Service to the Final Muster-Out at the Close of the Rebellion* (Wilmington, DE, 1884), 29.

45 Chase to "Janet," May 8, 1862; New York Times, Sept. 10, 1874, 4; Francis Weiss, *Reminiscences of Chevalier Karl de Unter-Schill, Later Known as Colonel Francis Weiss* (Troy, NY, 1903), 118; Seville, *Delaware Volunteers*, 29. The 1st Delaware was originally organized as a 90-day unit on May 28, 1861. However, since the Union high command was leery of a regiment from a slave-holding state, the 1st Delaware was only assigned duty as railroad and bridge guards. The regiment was reorganized in October 1861, and the men sailed to Fort Monroe and continued guard duty. To combat the boredom, two lieutenants created a player's company to build an elaborate theater and put on plays and musicals. The theater contained "a stage, movable curtains, shifting scenery, footlights and an orchestra." The opening night included a ball "at which officers and ladies from other camps and the Fort participated." Though only open for officers and selected privates "reported the cleanest and most soldierly in appearance," Chaplain Thomas Murphey noted that "most of the actors were members of the Regiment, and performing their parts well were frequently applauded by the audience." Thomas G. Murphey, *Four Years in the War: The History of the First Regiment of Delaware Veteran Volunteers* (Philadelphia, 1866), 40.

> which provoked a hearty peal of laughter from all, the President finally realized that he was in the enemy's country, where martial law was supreme, and that, therefore, the civil branch of the government should give way to the military; and, doubtless, recognizing the drum-major's determination to do his duty or die in his tracks, turned out of the way with all his followers, and opened the road for Dooley and the band out of their dilemma.[46]

"[T]he spectators greeted [Lincoln] and General Wool with hearty cheers[,]" reported the *Herald*, and both Lincoln and Stanton complimented the brigade commander, Brig. Gen. Max Weber, on the "fine appearance" of his soldiers.[47]

During the ride back to Fort Monroe, the party encountered another regiment drawn up in line: "The colonel and his troops were made glad by the President, who rode along their line alone, uncovered, and inspiring a great enthusiasm," recalled Secretary Chase, and "it is delightful . . . to observe everywhere the warm affection felt and expressed for the President." The *New York Times* reporter also commented that the trip seemed to afford Lincoln some much-needed relaxation.[48]

As relaxing as it might be for Lincoln to ride through the Virginia countryside and visit with the common soldiers, the stress and toil of war never left him. John Nicolay and John Hay, Lincoln's trusted aides who had not accompanied the president on this trip, suspected that the excursion to review troops must have been "a running council of war" with Wool and his staff. Back at Wool's headquarters, the leaders held another conference, which also included Lt. William Jeffers, the *Monitor's* captain. "I feel confident that Capt. J. with his restless energy," Keeler wrote, "will persuade them to do something," but he feared Goldsborough would veto it. Not so Lincoln, who "evidently respects Capt. J.'s opinions," and would support any "reasonable or feasible" plans. Keeler didn't know that plans for the action he desired had already been hatched the previous evening when Lincoln first arrived at Hampton Roads. Now the commander in chief confirmed the attack on Sewell's Point, scheduled to take place the next morning.[49]

46 Seville, *Delaware Volunteers*, 29-31.

47 "The President's Visit," *New York Herald*, May 9, 1862, 5.

48 Chase to "Janet," May 8, 1862, *New York Times*, Sept. 10, 1874, 4. "The Visit of President Lincoln. He Takes a View of the *Merrimac*," *New York Times*, May, 9, 1862, 8. This regiment might have been additional companies of the 99th New York, which had a company stationed at Fort Wool.

49 Nicolay & Hay, *Abraham Lincoln*, 5:234; Keeler to "Anna," May 7, 1862, in Daly, ed., *Aboard the USS* Monitor, 108.

The president also had other actions in mind. He wanted Goldsborough to send the ironclad *Galena* and two gunboats up the James River. Perhaps seeing the wide entrance to the James River from Newport News convinced Lincoln that the *Virginia* could not stop Union ships from ascending the river. Having the *Galena* in the James also would also bar Confederate ships from coming down to Norfolk, which in turn would help protect McClellan's left flank on the Peninsula.

Although McClellan had succeeded in taking Williamsburg, roughly halfway up the Peninsula, he fretted about an attack along the James River. Lincoln told Goldsborough that the general was again requesting "that gunboats be sent up the James." The president added, "If you have tolerable confidence that you can successfully contend with the *Merrimack* without the help of the *Galena* and two accompanying gunboats, send the *Galena* and two gunboats up the James River at once." Secretary of the Navy Welles added his weight, writing Goldsborough the same day Lincoln ordered the ships up the James that the department wanted him to assist McClellan's advance and harass the retreating Confederates.[50]

Goldsborough balked at the idea. His reluctance to send John Rodgers' *Galena* on a mission wasn't just about depleting his forces with the *Virginia* still lurking off Craney Island. In late April, he told Assistant Secretary of the Navy Gustavus V. Fox that, upon inspection, the *Galena* "is, in my judgment, a most miserable contrivance—entirely beneath Naval criticism."[51]

With the prospect of action and the hope of attacking Richmond from the river, Chase requested that Goldsborough have the ironclad revenue cutter *E. A. Stevens* accompany the *Galena*, "unless you think it really injudicious." The *E. A. Stevens*, which had been converted from the former iron steamer *Naugatuck* into an armored gunboat, employed a unique design that featured a single 100-pound

50 Lincoln to Goldsborough, May 7, 1862, in Roy P. Basler, ed., *The Collected Works of Abraham Lincoln*, 9 vols. (New Brunswick, NJ, 1953), 5:207. Welles to Goldsborough, May 7, 1862, *ORN* 7:326. Although Lincoln signed the message, Stanton wrote it. Later that night, Stanton telegraphed McClellan that the three vessels were headed up the James and asked if he wanted "anything else." *OR* 11/3:147. Lincoln was still hoping to meet with McClellan, but the general begged off, telling Stanton he didn't dare "leave my command in the present state of affairs" to go to the rear for a meeting. *OR* 11/3:146, 147.

51 Goldsborough to Fox, Apr. 24, 1862, in Thompson & Wainwright, eds., *Confidential Correspondence*, 1:263. Despite his order, Lincoln may have had to persuade Goldsborough to issue the command to Cdr. John Rodgers, *Galena's* captain. Senator Orville Hickman Browning, a Lincoln confidant, noted in his diary that Rodgers was sent up the James after Lincoln "had a struggle with Goldsborough on the subject." Theodore Calvin Pease & James G. Randall, eds., *The Diary of Orville Hickman Browning, 1850-1864*, 2 vols. (Springfield, IL, 1925), 1:545.

Parrott rifled cannon that had to be lowered under the deck to be loaded. Goldsborough, however, already knew the two wooden gunboats he would use for the mission. The *Aroostook* was a small screw-driven steamship with two sailing masts armed with one 11-inch and two 24-pounder smoothbore cannon, and two 20-pounder rifled cannons. The second gunboat, the *Port Royal*, was a larger side-wheel steamer that carried a 100-pound rifled cannon, a 10-inch smoothbore, and six 24-pound howitzers. Rodgers's orders received later that evening charged him with "assist[ing] the army" and "endeavor[ing] to harass the retreat of the rebels wherever they can be reached." Moreover, the president wanted the expedition to "start at once, to-night," which didn't happen because pilots for the vessels couldn't be found immediately. They did not head up the James River until early the next morning.[52]

As it turned out, the delay may have been fortuitous, since later that evening, the *Virginia*—possibly in anticipation of the approach of the *Patrick Henry* and *Jamestown* coming down the James from Richmond—appeared after dinner, stopping to moor near Craney Island. If the *Galena* had headed toward the James River entrance that evening, the *Virginia's* lookouts would have spotted her.

Keeler and many others out on Hampton Roads also saw the *Virginia*. Waxing poetic, he penned his wife that the ship was "apparently chewing the bitter end of reflection & ruminating sorrowfully upon the future. She remained there smoking, reflecting & ruminating till nearly sunset," Keeler continued, "when she slowly crawled off nearly concealed in a huge, murky cloud of her own emission, black & repulsive as the perjured hearts of her traitorous crew." The paymaster continued:

> The water hisses & boils with indignation as like some huge slimy reptile she slowly emerges from her loathesome lair with the morning light, vainly seeking with glairing eyes some mode of escape through the meshes of the net which she feels is daily closing her in. Behind her she already hears the hounds of the hunter & before are the ever watchful guards whom it is certain death to pass.[53]

With the night churning with northwest winds and rain squalls, Lincoln and Stanton decided to stay at Wool's headquarters rather than join Chase and Viele back on board the *Miami*. Col. Le Grand B. Cannon, Wool's aide-de-camp, noted that military etiquette required that he serve as the president's "aide-in-waiting." As

52 Chase to Goldsborough & Goldsborough to John Rodgers, both May 7, 1862, *ORN* 7:326-327; Stanton to McClellan, May 7, 1862, *OR* 11/3:147.

53 Keeler to "Anna," May 7, 1862, in Daly, ed., *Aboard the USS* Monitor, 105-106.

a result, Lincoln slept in Cannon's room on the third floor, while the colonel slept on a stretcher in the hallway. During Lincoln's visit, Cannon explained, "I was practically secretary to the President." Stanton slept in Cannon's office.[54]

Cannon had been away before the president's formal arrival, and did not return until near dinner, "a very formal affair" with the presidential party, the top officers, plus admirals of some nearby foreign fleets. As he was changing into his formal dress uniform in his room, Lincoln walked in on him and commented on the "elaborate toilet" the colonel was making. When Cannon responded that such a toilet was pretty much "required, given the company," the president asked to borrow his hair brush to "fix up a little, too." Lincoln found the brush useless. "It wouldn't go through my hair," he explained. "Now, if you have anything you comb your horse's mane with, that might do."

The incident launched Lincoln into a story about his hair. When he was nominated to run for president, "an enterprising fellow" remembered that Lincoln had a picture of himself made a couple of years earlier and bought the negative to make prints. "By the time the news got down to Springfield, where I lived," Lincoln said, "the [news] boys were running through the street crying: 'Here's a likeness of Abe Lincoln. . . . Will look a great deal better when he gets his hair combed.'"

When they finally appeared at dinner, Wool admonished Cannon—but not the president—for being five minutes late. Lincoln watched as Cannon smiled and earned another grumble from Wool for his "unseemly merriment." When Cannon blamed their tardiness on the president, Chase remarked that he had "no doubt but possibly the President has been amusing the Colonel with some of his stories." The French admiral Marquis de Montagnac, who was also present, asked Lincoln to repeat his story, but Cannon suggested it could wait until dessert. The story was finally repeated, recalled Cannon, "to the great amusement of every one at the table."[55]

54 Kern, *Revenue Cutters*, 90; Le Grand B. Cannon, *Personal Reminiscences of the Rebellion, 1861-1866* (New York, 1895), 156-57, 161.

55 Cannon, *Personal Reminiscences*, 168-71.

Chapter 3

Thursday, May 8, 1862

"Smoke curled up over the woods at Sewell's Point, 5 or 6 miles from its termination, & each man, almost, said to the other, 'There comes the *Merrimac*'; &, sure enough it was the *Merrimac*."

— *Secretary Salmon P. Chase*

EARLY on May 8, 1862, Commander John R. Tucker, captain of the Confederate gunboat *Patrick Henry*, waited patiently on the James River. Before dawn the previous morning, Tucker, along with Joseph N. Barney, commander of the smaller gunboat *Jamestown*, tried to run down the James past Union guns at Newport News, past the picket-ship patrols and then up the Elizabeth River to Norfolk and the Gosport Navy Yard. Their task was to secure and transport as much of the navy yard's supplies and materiel as possible before it fell to the Yankees. Getting those supplies to Richmond was paramount. Tucker had canceled his previous attempt after signal-light traffic between enemy ships and the shore make it clear that the Rebel gunboats had been discovered. Instead of risking his ship, he returned upriver and anchored off the Harden's Bluff battery.[1]

Now, on the morning of May 8, the gunboats received word that Union ships were approaching up the James. "At 9:30 o'clock three steamers were reported standing up the river . . . [enemy] gunboats, one of them the iron battery *Galena*,"

1 John R. Tucker to Stephen Mallory, May 8, 1862, *ORN* 7:786.

The USS *Galena,* one of the three early Union ironclads, is strong enough to take on shore batteries. She would have trouble, however, with plunging fire at Drewry's Bluff on the James River below Richmond on May 15, 1862. *Naval History & Heritage Command, NH 53984*

Tucker reported. "After maneuvering about a while the iron battery engaged Day's Point battery, the two wooden vessels remaining out of range."

Tucker sent Barney's *Jamestown* racing upriver to alert naval officials about the approaching enemy ironclad. The *Patrick Henry* soon followed. Tucker was emphatic in his determination to do whatever was necessary to block the James. Though it would be folly to engage the iron vessel, he decided "to ascend the river to the point of obstruction" and help complete a "barricade by sinking this ship or any other ship of the squadron if it became necessary." He knew an "impassible barricade" was now the "only efficient mode of defending Richmond" since the *Galena* could come up at any time to shell the city, and the Confederacy lacked the

Commander John Rodgers, USS *Galena*

Naval History & Heritage Command, NH 66662

means of stopping her. Barney on the *Jamestown* also realized how dire the situation had become.[2]

The *Galena* and wooden gunboats *Aroostook* and *Port Royal* entered the James River without any challenge from the *Virginia*, which could not follow even had she been allowed to leave her post guarding Norfolk.

As the Union ships progressed slowly upriver, Barney heaved to at Drewry's Bluff, the strongest point on the James for stopping any enemy naval ascension to Richmond only eight miles distant. The *Jamestown's* captain urged the commanding officer at Drewry's Bluff to expedite the barrier's completion. He also emphasized that, in addition to Tucker's *Patrick Henry*, three other Confederate gunboats plus the steamer *A. H. Schultz* all needed to escape upriver from the lower James.[3]

* * *

Flag Officer Goldsborough wanted to withdraw more gunboats up the York River and send more than three ships into the James, but Lincoln, at Stanton's urging, vetoed that move. Stanton argued, and Lincoln agreed, that the ships were best used on the north side of the Peninsula, and it would take too much time to quit the York River, steam around the tip of the Peninsula, and enter the James. Lincoln's original order to Goldsborough was to have the *Galena* start out the evening before "at once."[4]

2 Ibid., 786-87.

3 J. N. Barney to "commanding officer or engineer in charge at Drewry's Bluff," May 8, 1862, ibid., 7:787. *A. H. Schultz* was a flag-of-truce vessel often used to exchange prisoners of war.

4 Louis M. Goldsborough to Gustavus V. Fox, May 8, 1862, in Robert Means Thompson & Richard Wainwright, eds., *Confidential Correspondence of Gustavus Vasa Fox, Assistant Secretary of the Navy, 1861-1865*, 2 vols. (New York, 1918), 1:267-68.

Flag Officer Louis M. Goldsborough, commander of the North Atlantic Blockading Squadron.

Library of Congress

Instead of moving immediately, however, the three-ship flotilla didn't get underway until about 6:00 a.m. It entered the James just before 10:00 a.m. when the flotilla reached Day's Point on the river's west (right) bank about 9½ miles above Newport News. The point's Fort Boykin wielded 10 large guns, 42- and 32-pounders, to bar Union ships from proceeding any farther upriver. Their ability to do so was about to be tested.

"[T]he reverberation of heavy cannon up the James river indicates that our gunboats are doing good service," reported the *Baltimore Sun*. "The heavy guns of the *Galena* can be distinctly heard." Norfolk's citizens also heard the cannon fire, and many of them pondered what it meant. A crowd flocked "to Town Point to get the best view they could of anything that might heave in sight," but there was nothing to see. Possibly, speculated *The Norfolk Argus*, the firing meant fighting at Day's Point.[5]

According to his brief report to Goldsborough, Cmdr. John Rodgers had little problem silencing Fort Boykin. Lt. John Watters later reported that the Confederates evacuated the fort following the fight. After first trying and failing to remove their guns, the Rebels spiked them and burned their carriages. However,

5 Alfred L. Rives, "Report on the James River Defenses," Mar. 12, 1862, *OR* 51/2:509-10; *The Baltimore Sun*, May 10, 1862, 1; *The Norfolk Argus*, "The Prelude to the Operations in Hampton Roads on Thursday," in [Richmond] *Daily Dispatch*, May 12, 1862, 1, accessed Nov. 2, 2010, http://dlxs.richmond.edu. The point apparently was also called Day's Neck. After inspecting the river's defenses, Confederate engineer Alfred Rives claimed they were "rapidly improving," and already afforded good protection against wooden, but not ironclad, warships. Rives recommended bringing in bigger guns, for "nothing but the very heaviest ordnance can contend successfully" with ironclads. Without time to improve all the batteries along the James, the Confederates concentrated on Drewry's Bluff farther upstream. Rives' report also appears in *ORN* 7:742.

Fort Huger, the second battery Rodgers encountered farther upriver at Mother Tyne's Bluff, proved more obstinate. This battery reportedly mounted seven well-protected large smoothbore guns: three Columbiads (a 10-inch and two 8-inch), two 8-inch Dahlgrens, plus a half-dozen 32-pound guns capable of throwing hot-shot. Rodgers's cannon were having but little effect. To avoid wasting ammunition, he "put the *Galena* abeam of [Ft. Huger] as close as the pilot could take her" and distracted "the aim of the rebels while the *Aroostook* and *Port Royal* ran by," bypassing the troublesome Rebel battery.[6]

Goldsborough, Stanton, Lincoln, and the others back in Hampton Roads had no clear idea what was happening up the James River. In a pair of telegraphic messages to Washington between mid-day and early afternoon, Stanton twice reported hearing heavy cannonading up the James. Shortly after the second wire, Rodgers ran into trouble. At a tight bend in the river at Hog's Point, the *Galena* ran aground. The commander later complained that "none of the pilots have been up the river within a year; since then the channel marks have been altered." The *Galena*, her engine stopped and pipes clogged with "sand and pieces of wood," was stuck fast. Rodgers blamed the problem on a defect in the ironclad's design. "The injection water is taken from the bottom of the vessel, near the keel, and thus in working the engine while aground, the condenser becomes filled with mud, and the valves choked with whatever composes the bottom."[7]

Rodgers and the *Galena* would be stuck off Hog's Point for the next 36 hours, which was a great relief to the Confederates laboring at Drewry's Bluff to build up their defenses and obstructions. Richmond needed the time as well. The *Galena*'s approach toward the Confederate capital caused great angst, admitted diarist Judith McGuire, a refugee in the city. "Richmond, or the croakers of Richmond, have been in a panic for two days, because of the appearance of gun-boats on James

6 Cmdr. John Rodgers wrote two brief reports to Goldsborough, one on May 9 and the other two days later. In the initial report, he noted the batteries were at Rock Wharf (what the Confederates called "Dey's Point"). The official military map of the river put the batteries near a wharf about three miles farther up the James from the point. See George B. Davis, et al. *Atlas to Accompany the Official Records of the Union and Confederate Armies* (Washington, DC, 1891-1895; reprint New York, 2003), plate 18-1. John Watters, "Report of . . . examination of Confederate defences near Day's Point," May 19, 1862, *ORN* 7:390. Rives, James River Report, Mar. 12, 1862, *OR* 51/2:509; John Rodgers to Goldsborough, May 9, 1862, *ORN* 7:328-29. The bluff also was called Hardy's or Harden's Bluff.

7 Stanton to P. H. Watson, May 8, 1862, *OR* 11/3:153; Rodgers to Goldsborough, May 9, 1862, *ORN* 7:329.

River," she wrote, quickly adding, however, "I believe they will not get nearer than they are now."[8]

Varina Davis, the Confederate president's wife, remembered that the ironclad coming up the river prompted her husband to insist she and their children leave the capital to relieve him "from unnecessary anxiety." The couple was at a reception when a courier, passing on Barney's message, brought the president the news. "As he passed me on his return to the drawing-room I looked a question and he responded, in a whisper, 'The enemy's gun-boats are ascending the river.'" After the guests left, Davis told Varina that, while he hoped the obstructions would stop the Union gunboats, he "preferred we [Varina and the four children] should go the next morning." She convinced her husband to postpone the flight a little longer.[9]

Northerners received the news with elation. The press played up the flotilla's ascent without really knowing its details or significance. The *Philadelphia Inquirer*, for example, wrote that the gunboats' successful passage would lead to "rapid annihilation of the Rebels cutting off as it will, all river communication with the retreating army south of the Chickahominy [River]."[10]

Earlier that morning before the *Galena* had reached the mouth of the James, she encountered a little tugboat back at Hampton Roads spewing "a dense cloud of black smoke," recorded the *Monitor's* paymaster Keeler. "On it came enveloped in its smoky vail which disclosed just enough to allow us free play for our imaginations—every moment we expected to see the *Galena* (who led) open her fire, but no, the cloud drove past the *Galena* apparently unnoticed, then past each of the other two [ships] in succession, still not a shot was fired." The mystery soon revealed itself to be "a little tug" bearing a red-bordered white flag with the vessel's name: *J. B. White.* Its captain, James Byers, the entire crew, and a few Southern civilians were renouncing the Confederate cause.[11]

8 Judith Brockenbrough McQuire, *Diary of a Southern Refugee during the War* (New York, 1868), 111.

9 Varina Davis, *Jefferson Davis, ex-President of the Confederate States of America: A Memoir,* 2 vols. (New York, 1890), 2:268.

10 *Philadelphia Inquirer,* May 9, 1862, 4. The Chickahominy River, which flows into the James, is on the Virginia Peninsula roughly halfway between Fort Monroe and Richmond.

11 William F. Keeler to "Anna," May 8, 1862, in Robert W. Daly, ed., *Aboard the USS* Monitor*: 1862: The Letters of Acting Paymaster William Frederick Keeler, U.S. Navy, to his Wife, Anna,* (Annapolis: MD, 1964), 109; Lucille Madora Stephens, "Historic Norfolk: 'A Child of Mars,'" M.A. thesis, Southern Methodist University, August 1948, 37; "From Fortress Monroe—The Traitor Steamboat Captain," Richmond *Daily Dispatch*, May 15, 1862, 2. An unnamed Union

Byers had been under orders to take the *John B. White* to the outlet of Tanner's Creek, which flowed into the mouth of the Elizabeth River near Sewell's Point. The tug's mission was to pick up a small sailing schooner carrying an 11-inch Columbiad-style cannon, the largest gun in the point's battery, and tow the vessel back to Norfolk. Instead, at 5:00 a.m., Byers quietly sailed past the Confederate batteries on Craney Island and made a beeline across the mouth of the James to Newport News and the safety of Union lines. There, Byers, together with his crew and passengers, surrendered to Brig. Gen. Joseph K. F. Mansfield, the commander at Camp Butler. "The troops in garrison at Newport News viewed the fugitive steamboat with great curiosity, and, as she reached the wharf," reported the Richmond *Daily Dispatch*, "the troops crowded it in order to learn the late news from 'sacessia.'"[12]

Mansfield put his provost marshal plus a few troops on board the tugboat and ordered it to Fort Monroe. "The rebel steam tug *John B. White* has just come in to deliver herself up," Mansfield informed his boss, Maj. Gen. Wool. "I sent her in charge of a guard to you immediately."[13]

As the *John B. White* approached Fort Monroe, "there was a great rush to the wharf to know the tidings she brought, including Wool, Stanton, and other officials," wrote one reporter. Byers was soon confirming a Confederate evacuation of Norfolk to not just Wool and Stanton, but also to the president. The defecting captain reported "great excitement" there and the hasty withdrawal of Rebel troops. Preparations were underway "to destroy the Navy Yard and other public property." Moreover, he added, "a panic has taken possession of the inhabitants of Norfolk."[14]

An unnamed Union writer quoted in the *Daily Dispatch* further recorded that "the passengers from Norfolk report that Sewell's Point has been abandoned by the rebels, they are taking away with them all the ammunition except ten charges for each gun. Craney Island has been partly abandoned," he continued, "and some of the guns have been sent to Richmond, and all the powder, with the exception of

---

writer said that besides Capt. Byers, an engineer, a deck hand, and two—some sources say as many as four—passengers were also on board.

12 "From Fortress Monroe—The Traitor Steamboat Captain," [Richmond] *Daily Dispatch*, May 15, 1862, 2.

13 Joseph K. F. Mansfield to John E. Wool, May 8, 1862, *ORN* 7:330.

14 *Baltimore Sun* and *Philadelphia Inquirer*, May 10, 1862; "Norfolk is Ours: Fortress Monroe, May 8, 1862," *New York Herald*, May 12, 1862, 1.

ten rounds to each gun. Norfolk is being evacuated. Great many citizens remain." Other reports from Byers seem to have been exaggerated, however, such as the one that Ambrose Burnside was marching his troops northward to take Norfolk from the rear.[15]

A few days after Byers's dash to the northern side of Hampton Roads, Richmond diarist Judith Brockenbrough McGuire told her journal that a committee of the Confederate Congress met with Jefferson Davis to learn plans about how the capital would be defended. "Those traitors at Norfolk, I fear, have defeated our plans," was the president's reply. Byers and the others aboard the *John B. White* were disclosing "full information as to the unfinished condition of the works" at Drewry's Bluff and the evacuation of Norfolk, he explained. Everything that could be done to counteract this would be done, Davis assured them, but he refused to reveal details, quoting John Brown, of all people: "A man who is not capable of keeping his own secrets is not fit to be trusted with the business of other people."[16]

Lt. William H. Parker, in his postwar reminiscence as commander of the Confederate gunboat *Beaufort*, claimed the desertion of the *John B. White* and her crew "precipitated matters" leading to the day's attack on the Sewell's Point batteries. However, with the *Galena* and her consorts safely on their way—and cannon fire coming from the direction of the James River—Lincoln was anxious to get the rest of the Federal fleet moving on the earlier plan. With fresh evidence that Norfolk and the various batteries protecting the city might be abandoned, he called for another conference to reiterate his orders to take the city.[17]

Given the intelligence gleaned from the tugboat captain, the first order of business was whether to land Union soldiers near Sewell's Point. Lt. Col. Thomas J. Cram, the department's chief topographical engineer, addressed the question while Lincoln, Stanton, and others listened. His answer was generally disappointing. Although troops could be put on some old canal boats and towed near the Southern shore, Cram explained, they would be jumping off into water about 3½ feet deep, about one-half to three-quarters of a mile from dry land. Infantry could do it, he continued, but not cavalry or artillery. Once those soggy troops made it to

15 "From Fortress Monroe—The Traitor Steamboat Captain," Richmond *Daily Dispatch,* May 15, 1862, 1; Baltimore *Sun*, May 10, 1862, 2.

16 McQuire, *Diary*, 113-15. McQuire wrote about this exchange on May 14, 1862, after Norfolk had fallen. According to a note by James I. Robertson, Jr., the "near connection" to her might have been John White Brockenbrough, a member of the Confederate Congress.

17 William Harwar Parker, *Recollections of a Naval Officer, 1841-1865* (New York, 1883), 278.

dry land, they would be in no condition to fight. "To my mind," Cram added, "it was a discouraging mode of debarkation, especially with the prospect of the troops, while wading, being brought under fire from the enemy's batteries on either flank, to say nothing of a fire in front." Lincoln wasn't discouraged by Cram's report, and Maj. Gen. Wool, Cram's commander, "believed he could do the job with infantry, inasmuch as he was well satisfied the enemy of late had been materially lessening his force in that direction, if not evacuating his positions."[18]

Flag Officer Goldsborough, who was already at Fort Monroe, was brought into the conference, along with Secretary Chase. According to Cram, Lincoln asked if Goldsborough's ships could support Union soldiers wading ashore. The naval commander gave "little encouragement" about the debarkation place, but promised to "do all in his power to cover the landing."[19]

Shortly thereafter, Lincoln and Goldsborough asked the *Monitor's* commander, Lt. William Jeffers, to join the meeting. Capt. James L. Lardner, of the USS *Susquehanna*, apparently also attended, as he later led the attacking fleet. The president verbally ordered Goldsborough to attack Sewell's Point "to ascertain the practicability of landing a body of troops thereabouts and to reduce the works if it could be done." Wool was ordered to have his soldiers board the canal boats, ready to cross Hampton Roads.[20]

With the decision made, Lincoln, Chase, Stanton, and a handful of other officials and officers took a tugboat to Fort Wool to get a better view of the upcoming action. Goldsborough returned to his flagship, the *Minnesota*. He apparently told a Philadelphia reporter that he wanted the whole fleet to make the attack, and if the *Virginia* did not come out of her own volition, "he would bring her out."[21]

Alfred L. B. Zerega, who served on the *Susquehanna*, said in a speech long after the war that the crews of the ships had already been turned out for battle. Earlier

18 Thomas J. Cram, "Report of Colonel T. J. Cram . . . Upon the Taking of Norfolk, by Major Gen. Wool, U.S.A, May 10, 1862," John E. Wool Papers, NYSA.

19 Kern, *Revenue Cutters*, 90; Cram, "Report," Wool papers, NYSA.

20 Keeler to "Anna," May 7, 1862, in Daly, ed., *Aboard the USS* Monitor, 109; *ORN* 7:330-31; Cram, "Report," Wool papers, NYSA. The navy's ship *Thomas Freeborn,* under James H. Ward, had tested the newly constructed Sewell's Point batteries almost a year earlier and found them formidable. Bradley S. Osbon, ed., *Hand Book of the United States Navy: Being a Compilation of All the Principal Events in the History of Every Vessel of the United States Navy from April, 1861, to May, 1864* (New York, 1864), 255.

21 "Letter from Fortress Monroe," Philadelphia *Press*, May 10, 1862, 2.

Alfred R. Waud's drawing (above and on facing page) depicts the strong Confederate defenses on Craney Island. *Library of Congress*

that morning, "we received signal orders to prepare for action," and they were ready and awaiting orders with "hardly expressible" alacrity. But the morning dragged on, so by 11:00 a.m. the *Susquehanna*'s men were fed a snack, "which we were very thankful to get." Capt. Lardner came back on board at 11:45 a.m., continued Zerega. At noon he beat to quarters, cleared his ship for action, and stood toward Sewell's Point.[22]

Other ships also prepared for battle. About 11:00 a.m., reported a newspaper, the *E. A. Stevens* raised steam "and about 12 o'clock . . . moved out by the side of the *Monitor*, which vessel had also cleared her deck for action, taken down her awning and pipes and stood forth in fighting trim." The wooden gunboat *Dacotah* also came up, continued the reporter, "followed by the sloop-of-war *Seminole* and the *San Jacinto*." Flag Officer Goldsborough's *Minnesota* prepared for action by raising

22 Alfred L. B. Zerega. "The Last Days of the Rebel Iron-Clad *Merrimac* and Occupation of Norfolk, as Seen from the U.S.S. *Susquehanna*," in *War Papers: Being Papers Read Before the Commandery of the District of Columbia, Military Order of the Loyal Legion of the United States*, 60 vols. (Wilmington, NC, 1993), 1:450-51; "Abstract Log of the U.S.S. *Susquehanna*," May 8, 1862, *ORN* 7:335.

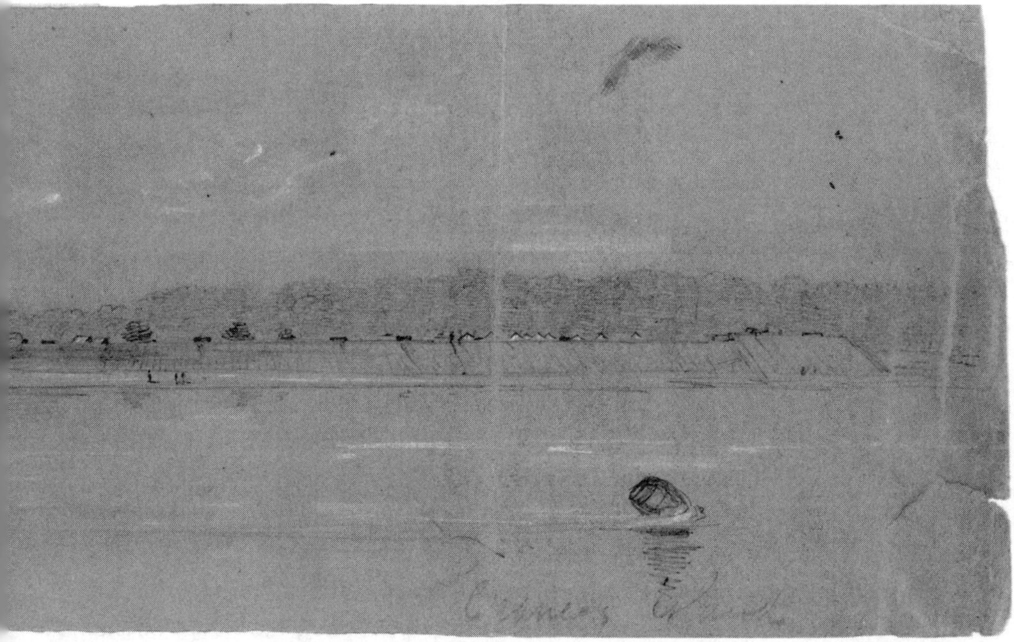

steam, and the side-wheel steamer *Susquehanna* also sailed forward. Meanwhile "the *Dacotah*, *Monitor* and *Naugatuck* [*E. A. Stevens*] had reached the channel and taken a position off Sewall's Point."[23]

By 12:30 p.m., the *Susquehanna* had assumed the lead over *San Jacinto* and *Seminole* while the *E. A. Stevens* was

> lying off toward the mouth of the James River. Presently, the *Dacotah* and *Monitor* approach Craney Island and Sewall's Point. The *Dacotah* fires every few minutes alternately at Sewall's Point and Craney Island, the enemy making no reply. . . . The *Monitor* is now taking the lead, but has not fired. In the meantime, the *Seminole* and *Susquehanna* open on Sewall's Point and two shots are fired from the Point, the latter falling short of the *Monitor*, which is now a mile above the other vessels.[24]

23 "News From Fortress Monroe, Highly Important Movements in Progress, A More Detailed Account," *New York Times*, May 10, 1862, 1; also in Frank Moore, ed., *The Rebellion Record: A Diary of American Events, with Documents, Narratives, Illustrative Incidents, Poetry, etc.*, 11 vols. (New York, 1863), 5:121. The U.S.S. *San Jacinto* is best known for her role in the 1861 Trent Affair.

24 *Baltimore American,* May 9, 1862, quoted in *New York Times*, May 10, 1862, 1.

According to Secretary Chase, when the *Seminole* reached its assigned position, he saw "a belch of smoke, followed in a few seconds by a report like distant thunder" announcing the start of the bombardment. Shortly afterwards the guns of Fort Wool on the Rip Raps, where Chase, Lincoln, and Stanton were gathered, joined in the shelling. Once in range, the *Susquehanna* also opened fire. The ship's gunners "poured in shell as fast as able to load and fire, [and] the return fire was very poor and did little or no damage, as nearly all the rebel shot and shell either fell short or passed over us." The *Monitor*, though not yet firing, drew closer to the Confederate's earthworks, "as close in as the water would allow," according to Keeler. She continued to absorb a consistent hot fire from Sewell's Point while the *Susquehanna*, *Dacotah*, *Seminole*, and *San Jacinto* answered in kind, broadside after broadside. According to Northern accounts, the bombardment almost immediately silenced a small Confederate battery operating near the water's edge. The ships shifted their shelling to the batteries inside the point's fort "a half-mile or a mile nearer Norfolk," explained Chase.[25]

Capt. William H. Stewart of Company A (Jackson Grays), part of the 7th Battalion Virginia Reserves, was in that small battery when the Union ships opened fire. Stewart disagreed that his guns had been "silenced." The pieces simply had no targets at which to shoot. "Our battery could only get [off] a few shots before the Federal squadron had passed too far to our left and were out of range," he wrote. "The whole squadron concentrated its fire on . . . Sewell's Point Fort, and made it too hot for the gunners to work the parapet guns." Unable to return fire, all Stewart and his men could do was stay under cover and wait out the iron storm.[26]

Union onlookers enjoyed the show. Aboard the *St. Lawrence*, which was not taking part in the bombardment, a marine named Daniel Boyer described the scene as "glorious. The shells are exploding . . . over the deviled heads of the 'sesech'," he wrote, and made "a most indescribable but pleasant music to my ears."[27]

Some Union officers of the fleet later complained that they were too far from Sewell's Point to participate in the fight. They "felt much chagrined at not being

25 Salmon P. Chase to "Nettie," May 8, 1862, in "Diary, July 21–Oct. 12, 1862," Salmon P. Chase Papers, LC; Zerega, "Last Days," 451; Keeler to "Anna," May 8, 1862, in Daly, ed., *Aboard the USS* Monitor, 110; *Baltimore American*, May 9, 1862, quoted in *New York Times*, May 10, 1862, 1.

26 William H. Stewart, *A Pair of Blankets: War-Time History in Letters to the Young People of the South*, Benjamin H. Trask, ed. (Wilmington, NC, 1990), 58.

27 Daniel L. Boyer to "Sister," May 7, 1862, in David M. Sullivan, *The United States Marine Corps in the Civil War—The Second Year* (Shippensburg, PA, 1997), 26.

permitted to close in on the rebels and capture their guns," reported the *New York Herald*. Some accounts called Goldsborough's leadership into question. The flag officer took no part in the engagement, choosing instead to observe the bombardment from the deck of the *Minnesota* four miles from the action. According to a reporter, he sent orders "from time to time" during the engagement by steam tugboats, but did little else.[28]

While the focus of the bombardment continued to be the Sewell's Point fort, the Federal ships directed occasional blasts toward Craney Island, across the mouth of the Elizabeth, and other smaller waterfront batteries. By 1:00 p.m., the *Monitor* was "within a mile of Sewall's Point." The ironclad withheld her fire until Lt. Jeffers—after a period of "deathlike silence" aboard the ship—ordered his executive officer, Lt. Samuel D. Greene, to load the two 11-inch smoothbore Dahlgrens in the turret with incendiary shells, set the range for 400 yards, aim, and fire. Once the guns fired, the *Monitor* steamed 100 yards closer and her two cannons boomed again.[29]

Still creeping forward, the *Monitor* continued firing her guns and received heavy return fire from Sewell's Point. A shell from Craney Island exploded "directly over her," reported Keeler, but the iron ship "moved steadily forward," occasionally firing short-fused incendiary shells. The ironclad received return fire from the Confederate batteries with perfect indifference, continued her paymaster, and within about 300 yards of the entrenchments Jeffers increased his rate of fire "as rapidly as possible using Birney [incendiary] shells with five second fuses." One onlooker adjudged the Union fire so effective that the Rebels abandoned Sewell's Point.[30]

The *Monitor*, recalled George Geer, an engineer and fireman aboard the vessel, fired 18 incendiary shells before falling back to join the other ships. Jeffers told Keeler he could go up on deck "if I was good at dodging" enemy shells. Keeler "gladly" took him up on the offer and was struck by what he found there. "[I]n front of us was the battery with the flag still bidding us defiance," he penned in a letter home. "On the other side, four of our gun boats drawn up in a half circle were sending an almost uninterrupted storm of iron over our heads & into the rebel

28 "Norfolk Is Ours. Fortress Monroe, May 9, 1862," *New York Herald,* May 12, 1862, 1.

29 Keeler to "Anna," May 8, 1862, in Daly, ed., *Aboard the USS* Monitor, 110.

30 *Baltimore American,* May 9, 1862, quoted in *New York Times* on May 10, 1862, 1; Keeler to "Anna," May 8, 1862, in Daly, ed., *Aboard the USS* Monitor, 110; Samuel S. Thompson, *Some Personal Experiences at Fortress Monroe in 1862* (Philadelphia, 1915), Historical Society of Pennsylvania (HSP), 15.

The little iron gunboat *E. A. Stevens,* on loan from the Treasury Department to the U.S Navy, was a unique design. With an open deck, her main gun had to be lowered to load. This engraving appeared in *Harper's Weekly,* April 26, 1862. *Naval History & Heritage Command, NH 53984*

defences." The "redoubtable" *E. A. Stevens*, however, stood "as far out of harm's way as she could well get . . . under the Newport News shore." Her position might have been fine had the *E. A. Stevens* not fired a shell that burst prematurely above the *Monitor.* "Why the beggar," Jeffries exclaimed, "we are in more danger from him than the enemy."[31]

The *Monitor* wasn't the only Union ship threatened by the *Stevens.* Keeler recorded another "shot through the *Susquehanna*'s Spanker." Zerega, on board the *Susquehanna*, confirmed the shot. "During the firing," he later wrote, "sabots and pieces of shell from the *Naugatuck* [*Stevens*], which was anchored outside of us, were falling on our deck." Captain Lardner addressed the problem by moving the *E. A. Stevens* away.[32]

As the *Monitor* and *Dacotah* once again steamed slowly up to the mouth of the Elizabeth River, reported the *Baltimore American*, dense black smoke rose from Sewell's Point. Keeler claimed one of the incendiary shells from the *Monitor* set the fort's buildings on fire. Shells "were bursting in, around, overhead & on all sides,

31 George Geer to wife, May 11, 1862, in William Marvel, ed., *The* Monitor *Chronicles: One Sailor's Account* (New York, 2000), 64; Keeler to "Anna," May 8, 1862, in Daly, ed., *Aboard the USS* Monitor, 110, 112.

32 Zerega, "Last Days," 451-52. "Captain Lardner, turning to Mr. Weaver, asked, 'Who commands the *Naugatuck*?' Without thinking . . . I replied, ***," reported Zerega. "'What do you mean, sir?' 'I beg your pardon, Captain, but that is the only name any of us know him by. In the wardroom we had given him this nick-name owing because of an incident which occurred when he was the first lieutenant of the revenue cutter *Harriet Lane.* Lardner with a smile turned to Mr. Churchill, ordered him to take a boat, and go on board the *Naugatuck*, give Captain *** his compliments, and say to Captain *** that if he did not cease firing over us the *Susquehanna* would give the *Naugatuck* a broadside and sink her."

some ricocheting in the water in front then plunging full into the defences, others bursting in the air & sending their fragments in a deadly shower below." As the Union ships continued shelling the Point, Confederate return fire largely fell short of the enemy vessels. The Baltimore reporter conceded the Rebels were "making quite a determined fight," however, and the barracks fire on the Point caused no injuries. In fact, the soldiers had enough time to rescue their personal possessions before the flames took over.[33]

About this time a lucky shot from the *Seminole* hit the Confederate flagpole. "Down comes the emblem of rebellion with three hearty cheers from all our vessels," rejoiced Keeler. The Confederates managed to raise the flag once more "though some lives must have been lost in doing it." Despite the fierce bombardment, Pvt. John Walters, a member of the Norfolk Light Artillery Blues, recalled that the Rebels on Sewall's Point suffered only "three wounded, two slightly and one severely."[34]

With the Confederate defenders now "seldom" firing back because of the risk, they nevertheless "made some good shots, some of their shells but a few feet above our heads," missing the ships altogether. "I could not but admire their pluck," admitted Keeler, "rebels though they were, in putting up their fallen flag amid the burning of their buildings & the iron storm we were raining down upon them." According to Pvt. Walters, the Union shelling lasted about four hours. The Rebel estimated that the enemy fleet and the guns of Fort Wool fired 800-1,000 shots at Sewell's Point "to which we replied by sixty or eighty shot and shell."[35]

Sometime after 2:00 p.m., Lincoln decided to take a closer view of the action. Boarding his tugboat at the Rip Raps wharf, he ordered the captain to sail toward

33 *Baltimore American,* May 9, 1862, quoted in *New York Times*, May 10, 1862; Keeler to "Anna," May 8, 1862, in Daly, ed., *Aboard the USS* Monitor, 112. Capt. William Stewart of the Jackson Grays later described the bombardment as "the most terrific I ever experienced, even more dreadful than the famous Gettysburg, when I was on Seminary ridge, July 3d, 1863." An after-action report noted that only two companies of soldiers under the command of Lt. Col. Samuel M. Wilson manned the Sewell's Point batteries "to keep up appearance" following an earlier partial evacuation. Stewart, *A Pair of Blankets*, 57, 58.

34 Keeler to "Anna," May 8, 1862, in Daly, ed., *Aboard the USS* Monitor*,* 112-13; John Walters, *Norfolk Blues: The Civil War Diary of the Norfolk Light Artillery Blues*, Kenneth Wiley, ed. (Shippensburg, PA, 1997), 19. Geer delighted in seeing "the Shell explode in and around the Works. One Shot from the *Semanole* cared [carried] their Flag away and we could see several Rebels trying to put one up again when another shell struck them and they disapiered very soon—probably not to serve Jef [Davis] any longer." Geer, Marvel, ed., *Monitor Chronicles*, 64.

35 Keeler to "Anna," May 8, 1862, in Daly, ed., *Aboard the USS* Monitor*,* 113; Walters, *Norfolk Blues*, 18-19.

the Union ships. Capt. Bradley S. Osbon found the president on the tug during the bombardment. He and two other officers had just arrived aboard the USS *Cayuga* from New Orleans with Flag Officer David Farragut's official dispatches on the capture of that important port city. Osbon, who had met Lincoln before his trip to join Farragut, together with two of his officers, joined the president aboard the tugboat. "The fleet was then in full play, and we stood ready with the *Cayuga* to enter the fight, if invited," he recalled, but the president was far more eager to learn about New Orleans, information about which he desired in detail.

During the conversation, Capt. Osbon noticed a signal from Goldsborough's *Minnesota* to withdraw from action. "Naturally, my blood began to boil," he explained, "and I freely expressed my opinion of Goldsborough's fighting." When Lincoln inquired how he knew what the flag officer had ordered, the captain explained that, as a signal officer, he could read flags. He picked up a nearby signal book to show the president "just what was going on, and did not hesitate to add that if Farragut were only in Hampton Roads the victory would be ours in thirty minutes." The president, wrote Osbon, "looked puzzled and distressed."[36]

"The rebel monster *Merrimac* now makes her appearance on the scene," reported the *Baltimore Sun*. Goldsborough had gotten his wish: the CSS *Virginia* was steaming out of the Elizabeth River. It was about 2:45 p.m.[37]

Secretary Chase, who was still at Fort Wool, described how the "smoke curled up over the woods at Sewell's Point, 5 or 6 miles from its termination, & each man, almost, said to the other, 'There comes the *Merrimac*'; &, sure enough it was the *Merrimac*." According to Keeler, "The *Merrimac* made her entree upon the stage about this time & our orders being not to bring on an engagement of the vessels at this time & having accomplished our object, we obeyed the Commodore's signal to 'resume moorings.'"[38]

36 Stanton to Watson, May 8, 1862, *OR* 11/3:153; Albert Bigelow Paine, ed., *A Sailor of Fortune: Personal Memoirs of Captain B.S. Osbon* (London, 1906), 212-13.

37 *Baltimore Sun*, May 10, 1862, 2. The exact time the *Virginia* made her appearance is hard to pin down. The abstract log of the USS *Jamestown* agrees with *Baltimore Sun* that it was 2:45 p.m., but *Minnesota's* log records the time as 2:15 p.m. and the *St. Lawrence*'s log notes the Union ships continued firing until 3:00 p.m., which is the same time given in the log for the British observer ship HMS *Rinaldo*. The commander of the *Seminole* wrote that firing ceased at 3:30 p.m.. The heavy black smoke coming from the *Virginia's* stack, the result of burning inferior coal, could be seen long before she entered Hampton Roads. *ORN* 7:332, 334-335; HMS *Rinaldo* ship's log, Jan. 1862-Sept. 1862, May 8, 1862, British National Archives (BNA).

38 Chase to "Nettie," May 8, 1862, Chase Papers, LC; Keeler to "Anna," May 8, 1862, in Daly, ed., *Aboard the USS* Monitor, 113.

Goldsborough ordered the *Minnesota's* signal gun fired and a long drum roll in Fort Monroe called the soldiers to arms. Based on the plan worked out that morning, Goldsborough's signal ordered the bombardment fleet to back away as the *Virginia* approached—but not too fast. Lt. David C. Constable of the *E. A. Stevens* reported that his orders from Goldsborough were to take a position to fire on Sewell's Point "and engage the battery, and if the *Merrimack* [appeared] to fall back out of the way to induce her to come out into the roads, so that she could be attacked by the large steamers" anchored below the fortress.[39]

The Rebel ironclad emerged from behind Sewell's Point about 2:45 p.m. and lumbered toward the Union fleet. "Her black hull [could] be seen moving slowly along shore, in front of Craney Island batteries," wrote one reporter. Initially, the *Monitor* did not back down, choosing instead to come "up from behind the wooden vessels, and moved to meet" the *Virginia.* The larger ships slowly pulled back as ordered. "The *Monitor* and the *Naugatuck* are now in the approaching path of the *Merrimac*," continued the newspaperman. The enemy ships were still about two miles apart.[40]

Confederate soldiers sheltered within the fort at Sewell's Point and in the water batteries were thrilled to see the *Virginia* appear. She had chased all the Yankee ships to Fort Monroe, "much to our relief, for we had prayed for . . . more than two long agonizing hours, and oh, what a relief was her coming!" wrote one of the Jackson Grays.[41]

When the Union fleet began bombarding Sewell's Point, the *Virginia* was at the Gosport Naval Yard above Norfolk. Her commander, Flag Officer Josiah Tattnall, was preparing for a high-level conference on how to use the ironclad once the Rebels abandoned Norfolk when the bombardment caught his attention. The heavy cannonading was followed by a telegraphed message explaining the noisy gunnery. Tattnall, excited by the possibility of action, promptly cancelled the meeting and ordered the *Virginia* to prepare for action. Getting her ready was not an easy task. Yard workers were crawling all over the ironclad making repairs and trying to improve her armament when the news arrived. "[K]nocked off from their work," they got "sent to wind our ship"—i.e., use cables and winches to turn her around—reported Richard Curtis, one of *Virginia's* gunners. The *Virginia* was

39 David C. Constable, "Report of Lieutenant Constable, U.S. Revenue Marine, Commanding U.S. Revenue Steamer *E. A. Stevens* (*Naugatuck*)" to Chase, May 9, 1862, *ORN* 7:332.

40 *Baltimore American*, May 9, 1862, quoted in *New York Times*, May 10, 1862, 1.

41 Stewart, *A Pair of Blankets,* 58.

Flag Officer Josiah Tattnall commanded the James River Squadron (March 29 - May 19, 1862), as well as ironclad CSS *Virginia.*

Naval History & Heritage Command, NH 66595

floating with her bow pointing up the Elizabeth River, but she needed to steam in the opposite direction. "It took some little time to do this," explained Curtis, because the iron "ship was very heavy."[42]

The men aboard the *Virginia* buckled on their side arms and expected "a lively tussle," thought Curtis. Crewman Eugenius Jack agreed and observed that Tattnall was excited by the prospect of a fight. "Before we were called to quarters I heard [him] say to the chief pilot . . . 'we will go through them giving them our broadsides right and left, and return and go at them like a bull in a narrow road.'"[43]

Tattnall's official report was a trifle less braggadocious. Once underway, he reported, the *Virginia* "stood directly for the enemy to engage him." But before "we got within gunshot the enemy ceased firing and retired with all speed under the protection of the guns of the fortress." Long after the war, another witness claimed that "the whole [Yankee] fleet, like a flushed covey of birds, flutters off into shoal water and under the guns of the forts. Every vessel runs, and we cannot fire a single

42 Richard Curtis, *History of the Famous Battle Between the Iron-Clad Merrimac, C.S.N., and the Iron-Clad* Monitor *and the* Cumberland *and* Congress, *of the U.S. Navy*, 1907, Mariners' Museum, accessed May 5, 2019, catalogs.marinersmuseum.org/search?query="Richard Curtis", 16.

43 Ibid., 16; Alan B. Flanders & Neale O. Westfall, eds., *Memoirs of E.A. Jack, Steam Engineer, CSS Virginia* (Portsmouth Naval Shipyard Museum, 1998), 20. Some reports claim the *Virginia* was prepared in other ways to take on the *Monitor* again. For example, this time the ironclad had on board metal-piercing conical shells instead of round explosive balls, plus 1,800 pounds of gunpowder. See Park, *Ironclad Down: The USS Merrimack-CSS Virginia From Construction to Destruction*, 199-200.

shot." A lieutenant, he added, had heard "at the time that [the bombardment] was by way of entertaining Mr. Lincoln, who was at Fortress Monroe."[44]

Goldsborough's report to Gideon Welles contradicted Tattnall's version of events. The *Monitor*, explained the flag officer, "kept well in advance . . . the *Merrimack* could have engaged her without difficulty had she been so disposed, but she declined."[45] Just as it was with the original clash between the two ironclads on March 9, each side held different views on the motivations and intents of the other.

Throngs of sailors and soldiers on the ships and shoreline anticipated another battle. Fort Monroe's walls were lined "black with anxious spectators," reported the *New York Times*. "Every eye was fixed on the *Monitor*" as the *Virginia* approached, continued the paper, "the David for this Rebel Goliath." As she approached, the crowd watched "with humiliation" as the fleet retired to the shelter of the fort. The *Virginia* steamed "in front of the line of vessels with her old saucy air, taking care, however, to keep aloof from the *Monitor*." The strategy to lure the *Virginia* deeper into the harbor had failed.[46]

The slow retreat of the Union flotilla halted once the ships got beyond the deeper channel passing through Hampton Roads. The *Virginia* also stopped about a mile and half away. According to the *Baltimore American*, "The *Minnesota* also steamed up in front of the fortress wharf, followed slowly by the *Vanderbilt*, and both stopped, along with all the guns." They were soon joined by three other "large steamers."[47]

44 Josiah Tattnall, "Report of Flag-Officer Tattnall, C. S. Navy," May 14, 1862, *ORN* 7:336; William Norris, "The Story of the Confederate States Ship *Virginia* (Once *Merrimac*): Her Victory over the Monitor," in *Southern Historical Society Papers*, 52 vols. (Richmond, 1876-1959), vol. 42, 231.

45 Goldsborough to Gideon Welles, May 9, 1862, *ORN* 7:331.

46 "Our Fortress Monroe Correspondence, Bombardment of Rebel Batteries," *New York Times*, May 10, 1862, 1. Drawing the *Virginia* out into deep water was exactly the plan devised by Lincoln and his advisors during the morning conference. Geer, aboard the *Monitor*, wrote: "After we had silenced all their Baterys the *Merimack* was seen coming down. All the other Ships started at once, and I thought we would shurly have a fight with her, but as she came towards us we kept going towards the Fort. Our Captain [Jeffers] said his orders were not to fight her alone, but get her out in Hampton Roads. She was to smart for us, and only came down as far as Crany Island and laid there, so we went back to our old anchorage." Geer, in Marvel, ed., *Monitor Chronicles*, 65.

47 *Baltimore American*, May 9, 1862, quoted in *New York Times*, May 10, 1862, 1. Commander Hewett's May 10 report stated "four large steamers" joined the *Minnesota* for the purpose of ramming the *Virginia*. However, the *Rinaldo's* own log says the "U.S. Frigate *Minnesota* & 3 large paddle steamers intended to act as rams join squadron near Fort Monroe." William N. Hewett,

"Men-of-war from below the forts, and vessels expressly fitted for running us down," reported Catesby ap R. Jones, the *Virginia's* first lieutenant and ordnance officer, "joined the other vessels between the forts [Fort Monroe and Fort Wool]. It looked as if the fleet was about to make a fierce onslaught upon us. But we were again disappointed. The *Monitor* and the other vessels did not venture to meet us."[48]

The Northern fleet's timidity thoroughly disgusted Tattnall. To demonstrate his disdain, he ordered one of the *Virginia's* guns fired windward before steaming slowly back to the Sewell's Point mooring. Among navies, firing windward was a sign of contempt for the enemy.[49]

Despite all the anticipation, by 3:40 p.m. it was clear there would be no confrontation. Twenty minutes later, after some fruitless Union machinations to lure *Virginia* to battle, "with an impudence truly refreshing," wrote a reporter for the *Baltimore American*, "the *Merrimac* has turned and headed for Craney Island. The fleet is taking its former position at the entrance of the Norfolk channel, while a few excellent shots from the Rip Raps are paying parting respects to the *Merrimac*." The Union "expectations of the day"—the destruction of the *Virginia*—had "hardly been sustained, as we had confidently hoped that this would be the last day for the *Merrimac*. Why our vessels did not move on her, Commander Goldsborough alone knows."[50]

In a private letter to Assistant Secretary Fox written on the day of the event, Goldsborough blamed the lack of engagement on the enemy. The *Virginia* "had a fair chance to engage the *Monitor*, but she was extremely cautious, & took good care not to expose herself to even half a chance in the way of a dash by [Goldsborough's *Minnesota*] & the merchant rams to run her down. After remaining outside the point for, comparatively, a little while," he added, "she returned & anchored under Sewall's Point, & there she now lies."[51]

"Extract from letter from Commander W. N. W. Hewett," May 10, 1862, *ORN* 7:338; *Rinaldo* ship's log, May 8, 1862, BNA.

48 Catesby ap R. Jones, "Services of the '*Virginia*' (*Merrimac*)," *SHSP*, 11:73-74. Jones originally wrote the article in 1874 for *Southern Magazine*.

49 John Taylor Wood, "The First Fight of Iron-Clads," in Robert Underwood Johnson & Clarence Clough Buel, eds., *Battles and Leaders of the Civil War*, 4 vols. (New York, 1956), 1:709.

50 *Baltimore American*, May 9, 1862, & "Our Fortress Monroe Correspondence, Bombardment of Rebel Batteries," *New York Times*, May 10, 1862, 1.

51 Goldsborough to Fox, May 8, 1862, in Thompson & Wainwright, eds., *Confidential Correspondence*, 1:267-68.

Once he returned *Virginia* to her moorings, explained Tattnall, "I returned to Norfolk to hold the conference." Catesby Jones boasted about the near-encounter with the Union ships. "Our object . . . was accomplished," he declared. "[W]e had put an end to the bombardment, and we returned to our buoy." To the relief of the *Virginia's* crew, they learned the men at the Sewell's Point batteries had endured the heavy bombardment well. "We anchored off our battery shore and communicated with them, to learn the amount of damage that had been done them, and were glad, as well as surprised, that after so much firing no damage had been done at all," wrote one member.[52]

According to Curtis, the *Monitor* later made a move toward the *Virginia* and even fired a shot, but by this time Tattnall was no longer aboard the ironclad. He had a conference awaiting him, and had taken a small boat back to Norfolk. When Jones signaled his commander about the *Monitor's* seeming invitation to battle, he replied, "don't fight unless you are pressed." The *Monitor* made no further move, and nothing more came of it.[53]

* * *

While the Union navy engaged the Confederate shore batteries, the land forces stirred into action. Some 4,500 of Wool's soldiers from Camp Hamilton marched to Fort Monroe's wharves, where they waited their turn to board a variety of small craft for their intended landing on Hampton Roads' south shore. The force constituted the second phase of President Lincoln's plan to capture Norfolk.[54]

"Thursday, May 8th," penned a 1st Delaware volunteer, "we received an order to prepare immediately for embarking, and to march as soon as we were ready, to the wharf." The soldiers had been "stowed away on steamboats and barges, in very close order, which occupied us till night." Another Delaware soldier described the vessels they had embarked upon as "a lot of filthy canal boats." Others, like former school teacher Eugene Goodwin of the 99th New York Infantry, endured the same exhausting experience. "Made a start today," he wrote in his diary. "After a great

52 Tattnall, "Report," *ORN* 7:336; Jones, "Services of the *Virginia*," 74; Jack, *Memoirs*, 20.

53 Curtis, *Famous Battle*, 16.

54 Cram, "Report," Wool Papers, NYSA; *Baltimore American,* May 9, 1862, quoted in *New York Times*, May 10, 1862, 1.

many halts got to the fort, and about dark embarked on board a canal propeller and canal schooner. Staid on board all night."[55]

Some of Wool's men, including the 10th New York Volunteers (the "National Zouaves"), waited by the shore. They, along with the other Camp Hamilton regiments, "struck tents on the 8th, packed their knapsacks, and, with two days rations and double amount of ammunition, marched a short distance from camp and remained under orders all night."[56]

Lt. Col. Cram continued to have doubts about safely landing on an enemy beach. The topographical engineer shared his concern with Wool's aide, Col. Le Grand B. Cannon, who had already expressed his own misgivings to the general the previous evening. Wool remained determined to advance on Norfolk and had secured many large canal-boats that had previously been used by McClellan to transport horses and mules for his Peninsula Campaign. Wool, explained his aide, planned "to embark about 10,000 men and land them at . . . Pleasure House Beach . . . the most accessible point to the eastward of Norfolk, and take the rebel works."

Col. Cannon pointed out, however, that as garrison troops at Camp Hamilton, the regiments were not organized into brigades and had never seen action, which would make command control difficult for a march, let alone a water-crossing operation and attack like the one Wool had planned. The aide sat up "all night" with Wool organizing regimental assignments. According to their intelligence, "[Confederate Gen.] Huger had about 20,000 men in Norfolk, inside defences." Given the lack of experience, no brigade organization, insufficient artillery, Cannon added, "I suggested to General Wool . . . our chances of success seemed very remote. It seemed to me the attempt would result in inevitable disaster."[57]

The general, however, remained confident. "If I land, General Huger will run," he declared. "Huger has been on my staff, and he knows I will never wet my feet." Wool refused even to entertain the possibility that Huger would stand his ground, lamented Cannon, claiming instead, "General Huger will evacuate."[58]

55 A "volunteer" to "friend Eckel," May 11, 1862, *Delaware State Journal and Statesman*, May 20, 1862, 2; "Dido" to the "Times," May 11, 1862, in Jeffrey R. Biggs, *They Fought for the Union: A History of the First Delaware Volunteers in the Army of the Potomac* (Belli Civilis, 2016), accessed Aug. 15, 2016, bellicivilis.com/letters-from-camp-hamilton. Eugene Goodwin's Civil War diary, May 8, 1862, accessed June 5, 2011, www.ioweb.com/civilwar/goodwin_diary/.

56 Charles W. Cowtan, *Services of the Tenth New York Volunteers, National Zouaves, in the War of the Rebellion* (New York, 1882), 76.

57 Cannon, *Personal Reminiscences of the Rebellion, 1861-1866*, 155-56.

58 Ibid. 156.

Wool would not have the chance to prove whether he was correct. Many of his troops were already aboard the canal boats and other vessels when the *Virginia* made her appearance, which persuaded the general to rethink the idea of sending unarmed transports across Hampton Roads, especially if they had to wade ashore. "The *Merrimac*," Lt. Col. Cram recorded in his final report that week, "deliberately took a position from which she could do the troops infinite harm should they attempt to land at the proposed place, and even shell us out, had we taken possession of the batteries."[59]

The suffering infantry remained crammed onto the bobbing transports all night—"tugs, steamers, barges, canal boats & in fact everything that could carry a soldier crowded with them"—recalled Keeler, who explained to his wife that he expected a landing the next day. "[T]omorrow night is to see us in Norfolk."[60]

The soldiers, ashore or afloat, simply endured the wait. The main concern for those stuck on land was finding "a spot in which to spread our blankets." A Delaware soldier described checking on the nearby boats and walking along the wharf to discover "a novel spectacle" of men sleeping everywhere they could find room. "The decks were literally paved with soldiers, packed like . . . herrings, with no roof over them but the starry vault of heaven." Ashore, the troops slumbered in vast numbers under or on canvas, with blankets or without.[61]

Any optimism about a landing the next day quickly faded. In his postwar narrative, Brig. Gen. Viele described the entire effort a "fiasco [that] had been clearly foreseen by more than one of our party." The option of landing troops had been decided upon when the president's party sailed south a few days earlier, but even then some officers were asserting such a thing could not be done. "For these reasons, so decidedly and authoritatively put forth, the plan which had been determined upon the first evening of our trip had been set aside for the one that had been brought to a most ridiculous termination," wrote Viele. "It was so evident that the *Merrimac* intended to act only on the defensive, and that so long as she remained where she was, no troops could be landed in that vicinity."[62]

"We had left the Rip Raps & had reached the landing on our way to Head-Quarters. Just as we were going ashore, the Monster came slowly about from

59 Cram, "Report," in Wool Papers, NYSA.

60 Keeler to "Anna," May 8, 1862, in Daly, ed., *Aboard the USS* Monitor, 113.

61 "Volunteer," May 11, 1862, *Delaware State Journal and Statesman*, May 20, 1862, 2.

62 Egbert L. Viele, "A Trip with Lincoln, Chase and Stanton," *Scribner's Monthly*, Oct. 1878, 818-19.

behind the Point," lamented Secretary Chase. With the sighting of the *Virginia*, he, and presumably Secretary Stanton and other accompanying dignitaries, beat a hasty retreat themselves. Likely, Lincoln's little tug fled the approaching ironclad.[63]

Around 5:00 p.m., President Lincoln sailed up to wharf at Fort Monroe. "He had just returned," the *Baltimore Sun* reported, "and as he passed up the wharf was vociferously cheered by the troops." The accolades notwithstanding, the day's events discouraged Lincoln. Still, even though the efforts to test the Sewell's Point fortifications and land troops had been blocked by the *Virginia's* untimely appearance, the day was not a total waste. First, it appeared that Sewell's Point was defended by fewer guns than originally thought. Second, to the president at least, it appeared that the *Virginia* was less of a threat than many believed. If the *Monitor* and *E. A. Stevens* worked together to neutralize the Confederate ironclad, she would not advance into the open water of Hampton Roads like she had the previous March.[64]

"Its results were, on one side nobody and nothing hurt," wrote a relieved Secretary Chase. "The results on the rebel side we can't tell but only know that their barracks were burnt by our shells. Another certainty is that the rebel Monster don't *want* to fight & *won't* fight if she can help it," he concluded, "except with more advantage than she is likely to have."[65]

The Confederates drew their own conclusions. Maj. Gen. Huger and Capt. Sydney S. Lee, the navy yard commander, were already evacuating important property, especially gunpowder, guns, horses, and wagons from Norfolk and the yard—a task begun on May 3 under orders from Secretary Mallory. With the very real threat of an invasion at any hour, Huger had to expedite the sending of his soldiers to Richmond. The dispatch of supplies and troops, however, left Tattnall with the weighty question of what to do with the *Virginia*.[66]

Since taking command of the *Virginia* and the small fleet in the Norfolk area, Tattnall had resisted all calls to steam out of Hampton Roads and around to the other side of the Peninsula to the York River. Gen. Robert E. Lee, Davis' military advisor, suggested Tattnall do so in a letter to Gen. Joe Johnston, who was facing McClellan's Army of the Potomac east of Richmond. Such a move, argued Lee,

63 Chase to "Nettie," May 8, 1862, in "Diary," Chase Papers, LC.

64 Baltimore *Sun*, May 10, 1862, 1; Goldsborough to Lincoln, May 9, 1862, *ORN* 7:330-31.

65 Chase to "Nettie," May 8, 1862, in "Diary," Chase papers, LC. Goldsborough did say the *Seminole* "was hit once about the bows," but reported no damage to any other ship. Goldsborough to Fox, May 8, 1862, in Thompson & Wainwright, eds., *Confidential Correspondence*, 1:268.

66 Mallory to Sydney S. Lee, May 3, 1862, *ORN* 7:783.

"would greatly cripple [the Union's] present and future movements, relieve your army from pursuit, and prevent its meeting the same Army in Northern Virginia."[67]

Tattnall was under no illusions about how such a move would end given the *Virginia's* engine problems and other issues. He would make the journey, he told his superiors, only if ordered to do so. He "was mortified beyond measure" by frequent suggestions from "unofficial [to] high official sources" alike of missions the *Virginia* might undertake. These ideas, he believed, were "founded on the most exaggerated ideas of her qualities, among them the feasibility of passing the forts and going into York River to assist the military operations at the peninsulas." As a last resort, he had orders to blow up his ship if he could not save her.[68]

On May 8, Gen. Lee wrote Huger of "the utmost importance that [the *Virginia*] guard the entrance to James River, to prevent its ascent by the gunboats of the enemy." Lee was apparently unaware that the USS *Galena* and two wooden gunboats were already operating on the James. "I am aware of the aid she can render in the evacuation of the batteries at Sewell's Point and Craney Island," Lee continued, but he thought she could "effectually" do this while stationed at the mouth of James River as if in Hampton Roads.[69]

At least Lee was aware of some of the events unfolding at Norfolk. Richmond's citizens, however, remained mostly clueless about them, leaving rumors to ripple through the capital city. War Department clerk John Jones had direct access to what was taking place and even he was confused about what was happening. "Norfolk and Portsmouth are evacuated! Our army falling back!" he recorded in his diary on May 8. "The *Merrimac* is to be, or has been, blown up!" Nothing of the sort had yet taken place.[70]

According to Flag Officer Goldsborough, the day's events had left "the people of Norfolk . . . shaking in their shoes." Wool agreed, and believed its citizenry had good reason to be afraid. His troops were now waiting, if uncomfortably, on boats to invade the city. The old and confident general confided to his son, "I [am] preparing for a movement which I have no doubt will be successful."[71]

67 Robert E. Lee, *The Wartime Papers*, 2 vols. (New York, 1996), 1:164.

68 "Extracts from a General Court-Martial at the City of Richmond, Va., on the 5th day of July, 1862, for the Trial of Flag-Officer Josiah Tattnall, C.S. Navy," *ORN* 7:793.

69 R. E. Lee to Benjamin Huger, May 8, 1862, *OR* 11:499.

70 Jones, *A Rebel War Clerk's Diary*, 1:123.

71 Goldsborough to Fox, May 8, 1862, in Thompson & Wainwright, eds., *Confidential Correspondence*, 1:267-68; John E. Wool to Jacob Wool, May 8, 1862, Wool Papers, NYSA.

Chapter 4

Friday, May 9, 1862

"If you stay here forty-eight hours, I will present Norfolk to you."

— *Maj. Gen. John Wool to President Abraham Lincoln*

At the break of day, reported Lt. Col. Cram to Maj. Gen. Wool on May 9, the CSS *Virginia* "was still in position to dispute the landing" of Union soldiers. It was discouraging news.

Wool had no choice but to order his soldiers off the transports, tugs, and canal boats and back to their tents at Camp Hamilton. Brig. Gen. Viele likened Wool to the King of Yvetot in Pierre-Jean de Beranger's poem: a man of great pretensions but little accomplishment. "The failure of the proposed attack upon Sewall's Point and the disembarkation of the troops that had been hastily crowded into everything in the way of a transport that could be made available was not a very inspiriting spectacle," lamented Viele.[1]

1 Thomas J. Cram, "Report of Colonel T. J. Cram, Aide-de-Camp, Chief Topographical Engineer and Inspector General, Military Department, Va., in Detail, Upon the Taking of Norfolk, by Major Gen. Wool, U.S.A, May 10, 1862," May 31, 1862, John E. Wool Papers, NYSA; Egbert L. Viele, "A Trip with Lincoln, Chase and Stanton," *Scribner's Monthly*, Oct. 1878, 819. Viele was referring to a poetic translation by British author William Thackeray of Pierre-Jean de Beranger's "Le Roi d'Yvetot" (ca. 1813) or "King of Yvetot," which recounted an excessive king of a small kingdom in Normandy, France. Of little "renown," the king "let all thoughts of glory go, And dawdled half his days a-bed," eating four meals a day and drinking heavily, but still once a year he called his soldiers together to march a league only to turn them around to march them back. He was called a man of mighty pretensions, but small merits.

Wool was not the only one dispirited by the latest turn of events. Sgt. William Lancaster of the 11th Pennsylvania Cavalry informed his wife that his regiment was back in camp and wouldn't leave "after we had packed our saddles and tyed up our tents and sleeped out all night." William Keeler aboard the USS *Monitor* was a little more generous toward the Union leaders. "No doubt [for good reason] the plans were changed or at least delayed, so that everything . . . was just as I left it last night," wrote the ironclad's paymaster, "except that the blue coated soldiers had disappeared from the boats, seeking & I hope not vainly for a comfortable spot to spend the night."[2]

An impatient Abraham Lincoln, meanwhile, continued to focus on the capture of Norfolk, the nearby naval yard, and the destruction of the *Virginia*, whose presence delayed any Union advance. Aggressive by nature, Lincoln wanted action. After breakfast, he and Secretary Stanton took a tugboat out to the *Monitor*. Lincoln wanted the ironclad to steam over to Sewell's Point to assess and report back any enemy presence there. Lincoln cautioned her captain, Lt. Jeffers, "not to violate . . . instructions relative to engaging the *Merrimack*."

The president couched his order to Jeffers as a request, for he was aware that Jeffers' superior, Flag Officer Goldsborough, scrupulously observed the Navy's tradition of command authority. Jeffers later reported to Goldsborough that the president had inquired about any possible "military impropriety in my getting underway without your previous order" when he pulled alongside that morning in a tugboat. Jeffers had informed the president "that it was necessary and proper that you [Goldsborough] should be informed" so it would be clear "I had not acted without authority." Lincoln's polite request for action pleased Keeler, who was a wartime volunteer and not a regular naval officer. The president knew, as Keeler put it, that he was "stirring up the dry bones" of the naval commanders, especially Goldsborough.

Following his brief encounter with the *Monitor*, Lincoln directed the tugboat to the USS *Minnesota*. Jeffers understood the president would inform Goldsborough of the assignment and that the *Monitor* should carry it out "if not forbidden by signal" from doing so.[3]

2 William Lancaster to "Maggie," May 10, 1862, Sims Trust, 2002, accessed Aug. 12, 2004, captlancaster.org/home.htm; William F. Keeler to "Anna," May 9, 1862, in Daly, ed., *Aboard the USS* Monitor, 114.

3 William Jeffers to Louis Goldsborough, May 9, 1862, *ORN* 7:340; Keeler to "Anna," May 8, 1862, in Daly, ed., *Aboard the USS* Monitor, 113.

The *Monitor* raised steam about 9:00 or 10:00 a.m. (sources differ on the exact hour) and eased her way slowly toward Sewell's Point and the Elizabeth River. About the same time, the *Virginia* got up steam and moved from her nighttime shelter under the guns of Craney Island. Keeler and others on the *Monitor*, as well as observers on shore, expected another confrontation between the two ironclads.[4]

The *Virginia* was creeping slowly toward the approaching *Monitor*, explained a reporter, and "had proceeded but a few lengths when she apparently brought upon a sand bar, as it was but ebb tide at the time. As soon as she stopped the heavy clouds of steam issuing from her steam pipe indicated that she had a good head or force of steam on."[5]

By 11:00 a.m., "the saucy little *Monitor* has steamed steadily up to the mouth of the Elizabeth river," reported another newspaper. "She has gone up alone, there being no vessels within five miles of her, and in the distance looks no larger than a black beaver hat floating in the water." The *Monitor* continued until within range of Sewell's Point. "There! she fires her first shell, which explodes with a loud report." Still moving closer to the *Virginia*, the *Monitor* fired once again, this time directly at her nemesis. The Rebel ironclad neither responded nor moved.[6]

Rather than keeping her guns on the *Virginia*, the *Monitor* fired a third time at Sewell's Point, with "[t]he report of the gun . . . like a clap of thunder." Sailing within a mile of the point's fortifications, Jeffers had a good look at the enemy location. According to the *New York Herald's* reporter, "Several guns were seen in position: the rebel flag was flaunting defiantly to the breeze, yet but few rebel soldiers were seen."

When the *Monitor's* probing of the Sewell's Point defenses garnered no response, other Union guns—including the Sawyer Gun at Fort Wool on the Rip Raps—joined in. "The very first shell went directly into the rebel camp," wrote an

4 "Our Fortress Monroe Letter," *Philadelphia Inquirer*, May 12, 1862, 4. The abstract log of the USS *Jamestown* made note of the Monitor underway at 9 a.m., but the USS *Dacotah's* log said 10 a.m., as do the reports in the *Philadelphia Inquirer* and *New York Herald*. *ORN* 7:333, 334; report of the *Baltimore American*, May 9, 1862, in "From Fortress Monroe, Operations of the *Merrimac*," *Philadelphia Inquirer*, May 12, 1862, 1, and "Our Fortress Monroe Letter"; "Norfolk Is Ours. Fortress Monroe, May 9, 1862," *New York Herald*, May 12, 1862. The two newspapers speculated that the reason the *Monitor* was underway was to protect the *Galena*, which they said was coming down the James River. In fact, the *Galena*, along with the *Arostook* and *Port Royal*, were still up the James with the mission of protecting the army's left flank on the Peninsula. But at the time, the *Galena* was stuck in the river mud off of Hog's Point.

5 "Norfolk is Ours," *New York Herald*, May 12, 1862, 1.

6 *Baltimore American*, May 9, 1862, in "From Fortress Monroe," *Philadelphia Inquirer*, May 12, 1862, 1.

excited New York reporter. Many more shots followed, "and for upwards of two hours there were fifty shells thrown at the rebels with an accuracy of range, amid effectiveness not to be surpassed."[7]

John Walters, who was manning one of the Confederate guns at Sewell's Point and thus on the receiving end of the Union barrage, described the event differently. "During the morning an old acquaintance, the old Sawyer Gun, threw a number of shells on the point without damage," wrote the artilleryman. "The *Monitor* also appeared off our battery and threw a couple of shells at us without effect." Walters did not record whether the Rebel guns returned fire.[8]

Eventually, according to the *Philadelphia Inquirer*, the *Monitor* and the *Virginia* backed away from one another. The Southern warship returned to her shelter under the Craney Island batteries, while the *Monitor* remained in the area into the early afternoon, continuing "to steam about the Roads between [near Sewell's Point] and Newport News."[9]

The *Monitor's* "reconorter," as one of the ship's sailors called it, was deemed a success. "We threw a couple of shells into the works without eliciting a reply," Keeler confirmed, "sounded out the channel and steamed about awhile & returned to our moorings about two o'clock." Only a few of the enemy were spotted "about the batteries which presented the same appearance they did yesterday."

In truth, Keeler and the rest of the *Monitor's* crew were disappointed at not having another go at the *Virginia.* The ship's officers criticized Lt. Jeffers for "not attacking . . . as we had her in a very favourable spot that would have given us every advantage." Jeffers "has always complained that he could not get permission to attack her from [Goldsborough]," observed Keeler, "but we have reason to think that he had the consent of the President to 'pitch into her' if a favourable opportunity offered." If he had been ordered simply "to discover if the batteries had been strengthened or reinforced with men or guns, he accomplished his object." The *Monitor's* crew considered the *Virginia* "our game," Keeler continued, and they were anxious to get another chance at sinking her. "The *Galena* & our other gun boats have the [Confederate ships] *Jamestown*, *Yorktown*, *Teazer* & one or two other vessels penned up in James river, so that now we could try the 'Big Thing'

7 "Norfolk is Ours," *New York Herald*, May 12, 1862, 1.

8 John Walters, *Norfolk Blues*, 19.

9 *Baltimore American*, May 9, 1862, in "From Fortress Monroe, Operations of the *Merrimac*," *Philadelphia Inquirer*, May 12, 1862, 1; "Norfolk Is Ours," *New York Herald*, May 12, 1862, 1. Jeffers's report to Goldsborough of his reconnaissance is given as "not found" in the Navy's official records, *ORN* 7:340n.

single handed which is all we ask—we want it as a crowning glory to our career so finely commenced."[10]

* * *

What Keeler and his comrades did not know was that the *Virginia* had ignored the *Monitor's* provocation because neither Tattnall nor his executive officer, Lt. Catesby ap Roger Jones, were aboard. Both were in Norfolk to discuss the evacuation, a meeting that had been postponed the day before. Tattnall would later report that the council included Commodore George N. Hollins (who represented Secretary of the Navy Mallory), Capt. Isaac S. Sterrett (who had overseen the construction of the Elizabeth River obstructions), Capt. Sydney S. Lee (who was in charge of the naval yard), and Cmdr. Richard L. Page and Lt. John Pembroke Jones. The Confederate Army was represented by Lt. Col. Samuel S. Anderson (assistant adjutant general to district commander Maj. Gen. Huger) and an unnamed captain who represented Huger, who "was too unwell" to attend.[11]

Eight months later in January 1863, Capt. Lee told the Joint Special Committee of the Confederate Congress that he had opposed Norfolk's evacuation. Everyone had considered Norfolk's capacity for resistance "very strong," Lee testified. Given her "very perfect" defenses and the *Virginia's* availability to cooperate with them, "[w]e considered ourselves very strong and safe from the water and Norfolk defenses." The only danger, he thought, would come from Norfolk's land side, with Union troops coming up behind the city from either Suffolk or farther south.[12]

Others believed that with the soldiers garrisoning Norfolk—1,100 naval yard workers acting as militia—and the *Virginia* sitting in the Elizabeth River, the city was safe. Confederate authorities in Richmond thought otherwise. According to Secretary of War George W. Randolph, they believed Norfolk was vulnerable by land, especially in light of the retreat of Joe Johnston's Confederate army on the Peninsula toward Richmond. Randolph told the Joint Committee in February 1863 that, during a high-level meeting he attended in April 1862 with President Davis

10 Keeler to "Anna," May 9, 1862, in Daly, ed., *Aboard the USS* Monitor, 114.

11 "Report of Flag-Officer [Josiah] Tattnall, C.S. Navy" to Stephen Mallory, May 14, 1862, *ORN* 7:336. *ORN* 5:804-806, lists defensive batteries and their ordnance built in 1861 to protect Norfolk and the entrance to the Elizabeth River.

12 Sydney S. Lee, testimony before the Confederate "Joint Special Committee of Both Houses to Investigate the Affairs of the Navy Department," Jan. 31, 1863, *ORN* 2/1:635.

and several of the army's top generals, everyone agreed "it would be impossible to defend Norfolk if the Peninsula was evacuated." Once Northern forces gained control of the north bank of the James River, they could throw a pontoon bridge across the river and march to Suffolk, cutting off Norfolk. The authorities didn't want Southern soldiers captured, or "starved out," as Randolph put it, nor vital supplies lost.[13]

When Gen. Johnston decided on May 1 to abandon the defenses at Yorktown, he told Tattnall the "evacuation of Norfolk" would be a necessary consequence of that measure, and that he had directed Maj. Gen. Huger to withdraw his forces to Richmond. Johnston also ordered Sydney Lee to abandon the navy yard after saving as much material as he could, and destroying what could not be carried off. Johnston asked Tattnall if "the *Virginia* may cover these operations, and by holding Hampton Roads, prevent the enemy from Norfolk, from James River." Once that mighty vessel had "performed all the service that can be required of her," Johnston trusted Tattnall would see to her "disposal. . . . The enemy will never have possession of her."[14]

Sometime between receipt of that message on May 1 and the eight days that followed, Tattnall considered the possibility of moving the *Virginia* south into Georgia's coastal waters. Until now, both Tattnall and his predecessor, Franklin Buchanan, had rejected calls by higher authorities and the press to run the ship through the Fort Monroe–Fort Wool gauntlet to the open sea as too risky. Now with his options narrowing, Tattnall thought the idea was at least possible, and ordered John L. Porter, the ship's constructor, "to have a set of wooden port bucklers made for her to keep the water from coming in her portholes. . . . He knew a port in Georgia deep enough for her, and he intended taking her there." The attempt was never made. Porter constructed the bucklers as directed, but they never left "the carpenter shop at the yard." The "fear of torpedoes [underwater mines] at Fortress Monroe," coupled with the *Virginia's* general lack of seaworthiness "in stormy weather, when the waves would be liable to wash over

13 Testimony before Joint Committee of: French Forrest, Jan. 31, Robert B. Pegram, Jan. 29, George Randolph, Feb. 5, 1863, ORN, 2/1:626, 629, 632, 716, 718. Confederate fears of an overland attack on Norfolk from Suffolk were overblown, and there is no evidence that either McClellan or Lincoln seriously contemplated such an attack. On June 14, 1864, the Army of the Potomac crossed the James River by erecting a 2,170-foot pontoon bridge from Windmill Point to Fort Powhatan, proving that such a construction feat was easily accomplished.

14 Joseph E. Johnston to Josiah Tattnall, May 1, 1862, *ORN*, 2/1:633.

her," convinced the commodore "to change his mind" about making a voyage to Georgia.[15]

Tattnall's dilemma remained unresolved when the May 9 morning conference convened. Troops were already evacuating Norfolk. Early that morning, the Richmond Grays left the so-called "intrenched camp" that protected the city on its eastern side. While most of the Grays had been posted as guards within Norfolk, a small four-man contingent accompanied a ship down to Craney Island to retrieve baggage, stores, and gunpowder. By the time they returned, the rest of their unit had already left amid swirling rumors of advancing Yankees. Although "the public mind," continued a Richmond newspaper, had been prepared for the news, their evacuation produced "great excitement." All the rolling stock in town was arranged into trains behind the few remaining engines, and the stranded quartet of Grays climbed aboard one of the cars and rode the rails to Petersburg.[16]

Under these conditions, and with three Union gunboats operating up the James River, Tattnall had no way of sending any more supplies or the nearly finished wooden gunboats out of harm's way. The heavy bombardment of Sewell's Point the day before, coupled with that morning's lighter shelling, only increased the pressure. Surely the Northern army would soon be on its way. "The opinion was unanimous," reported Tattnall, referencing the May 9 conference, "that the *Virginia* was then employed to the best advantage and that she should continue for the present to protect Norfolk, and thus afford time to remove the public property." The ironclad's captain "arranged with the general [Huger] that he should notify me when his preparations for the evacuation of Norfolk were sufficiently advanced to enable me to act independently." When that time came, Tattnall and his crew would be on their own.[17]

* * *

15 John W. H. Porter, "Origin of an Ironclad: How the *Merrimac* Came to be Transformed," *Confederate Veteran*, May 1915, 219-21. John W. H. Porter, John L. Porter's son, was in college when the war broke out. He joined the Confederate army and became a lieutenant. Some evidence indicates he helped his father design some of the later *Virginia*-style ironclads. Given the guns at Fort Monroe plus the continued problems with the *Virginia's* underpowered engines, it seems highly unlikely that the commodore gave serious consideration to a breakout from Hampton Roads. It could have been his way of seeking options. Tattnall knew the waters off the Georgia coast very well because he was a native of Savannah.

16 Richmond *Whig*, May 12, 1862, 3.

17 Tattnall, "Report," May 14, 1862, *ORN* 7:336.

Col. LeGrand B. Cannon (postwar image)

United States Army Heritage and Education Command Center

Back on the other side of Hampton Roads, paymaster Keeler and the rest of the *Monitor's* officers and men longed for a chance to help "dispose" of the *Virginia* in a one-on-one battle royale. Lincoln, however, aimed to end the ironclad's threat by depriving her of a home. Such initiative shown by someone in authority was new to Keeler. "It is extremely fortunate that the President came down as he did—he seems to have infused new life into everything, even the superannuated old fogies begin to shew some signs of life & animation. He has been busy today visiting different points," he continued, "not a place has escaped him where he thought his presence could do any good." Lincoln had also made a stop at Fort Wool on the Rip Raps before returning to Fort Monroe.[18]

Once back, Lincoln settled down at Quarters No. 1 to await Lt. Jeffers's reconnaissance report. He passed the time by reading some Shakespeare from Wool's library given to him by an aide the night before. As the president sat close to a window reading, Col. Cannon plowed through paperwork. After two or three hours Lincoln took notice of how busy Wool's aide was and invited Cannon to "come in here and sit with me and rest, I will read you some passages from Shakespeare." Cannon was surprised at how well the president rendered various lines from Macbeth, King Lear, and King John. As he read a section from King John about the loss of a son, Cannon noticed "that his voice became tremulous, and he seemed to be deeply moved."

The president closed the book and inquired of Cannon, "Did you ever dream of some lost friend, and feel that you were having a sweet communion with him, and yet have a consciousness that it was not a reality?" Almost everyone had such

18 Keeler to "Anna," May 9, 1862, in Daly, ed., *Aboard the USS* Monitor, 115.

dreams, Cannon assured him. Lincoln, whose 11-year-old son had died on February 20, replied, "That is the way I dream of my lost boy Willie." At that moment the president "broke down in most convulsive weeping. It was most grievous and distressing to see this great, strong man give way to such emotion," recalled the officer, "and I was so sympathetically moved that I, too, broke down utterly. He sat there with his head bowed down on the table, and I quietly left the room."[19]

Despite his continuing grief, Lincoln never flinched from his responsibilities as president and commander in chief. It mattered not that he was away from the executive mansion. Wherever he was, one newspaper explained, "the business of the government pro tempore appears to have been transferred here." Military matters other than those surrounding the affairs at Norfolk concerned the president, particularly his frustration with Maj. Gen. McClellan. One of the reasons he had gone to Fort Monroe was to consult with his recalcitrant army commander, though thus far McClellan had managed to dodge his superior.

As his forces crept up the Peninsula closer to Richmond, however, the general requested permission to reorganize the Army of the Potomac. In the morning, Secretary Stanton transmitted Lincoln's desires: "The President is unwilling to have the army corps organization broken up, [or] that the commanding general shall be trammeled and embarrassed in actual skirmishing collision with the enemy and on the eve of an expected great battle." Lincoln "also writes you privately," added the war secretary.[20]

Salmon Chase was as anxious as the president to take Norfolk, and was mortified the Union soldiers had left their transports and marched back to camp. The treasury secretary "was keenly alive" to what was required, wrote Brig. Gen. Viele, "and so sensitive to the least thing that savored of defeat that he fairly chafed [with] disappointment." Chase proposed using the *Miami* to reconnoiter "the place

19 Le Grand B. Cannon, *Personal Reminiscences of the Rebellion, 1861-1866* (New York, 1895), 78-79, 172-74. The president and Cannon had met a few months before Lincoln's trip to Fort Monroe. In mid-February, Wool sent his aide to Washington bearing a note written by a Gosport Navy Yard workman outlining the *Virginia's* progress and proposed plans for her attack on the Federal fleet.

20 "Norfolk is Ours," *New York Herald*, May 12, 1862, 1; Stanton to McClellan, Dec. 24, 1861, U.S. Congress, *Report of the Joint Committee on the Conduct of the War*, 3 vols. (Wilmington, NC, 1998), 1:325. Lincoln's private letter expressed his, and others', concern that McClellan's motivation for the reorganization was "merely an effort to pamper one or two pets and to persecute and degrade their supposed rivals." *OR* 11/1:154.

Col. Thomas J. Cram
(postwar image)

United States Army Heritage and Education Command Center

you suggested for a landing," a plan discussed by members of the presidential party some days earlier on the way to Fort Monroe.[21]

Chase could think of only three moves to break the impasse imposed by the *Virginia's* presence: send Wool's soldiers to Ambrose Burnside in Roanoke to assist him in attacking Norfolk from the south; transport the soldiers up the James River to join McClellan in advancing on Richmond; or find another site for landing the soldiers that the Confederate ironclad could not reach. Viele liked the idea of seeking another landing site, "and we started at once. General Wool was sitting at the door of his quarters as we passed, and learning of our design, volunteered to accompany us, and sent his orderly for the very officer (Lt. Col. Cram) who had pronounced the plan impracticable."[22]

The group set out about 9:30 a.m. on Chase's revenue cutter *Miami*, accompanied by the small tugboat *Lioness*, which would be used to check the water depth. The plan envisioned taking the ship and the tug to Lynnhaven Bay, about 16 miles from Fort Monroe. On the way, they rounded Willoughby's Point about seven miles from the fort and arrived off a little summer resort village of "some ten houses hidden over behind a high sand ridge, called Ocean View." From the deck of the *Miami*, "[it] appeared too favorable for our purposes to be passed without examination," observed Cram.[23]

21 Viele, "A Trip with Lincoln," 819.

22 Salmon P. Chase to "Nettie," May 11, 1862, in "Diary, July 21-Oct. 12, 1862," Salmon P. Chase Papers, LC; ibid.

23 Cram, "Report," Wool Papers, NYSA.

Wool's aide still insisted the water was too shallow for the *Miami* to approach the shore. "We anchored in six fathoms of water and betook ourselves to the tug," wrote Cram, "which was in its turn anchored quite a distance from the shore." A rowboat with armed soldiers, Cram, and another officer, moved in for a closer look. The tugboat remained 100 yards out to await the result of the reconnaissance.

Before they had made it halfway to shore the little boat turned quickly about and rowed with speed back to the tugboat "with a breathless account of a large body of men on shore." The boat's occupants reported seeing a Confederate soldier on horseback gesturing as if to others hidden among the tall sea grasses. Chase raised his "powerful field glasses" and scanned the shoreline, but couldn't see any sign of Confederates. Instead, he "saw some people waving a white sheet as a flag of truce." The threatening Rebel force turned out to be two women, one black and one white, a child, and a dog. Accompanied by a second boatload of armed soldiers, Cram returned to the shore.[24]

The location appeared to offer everything Chase hoped it might. The secretary was pleased with the group's "important discovery, a good & convenient landing place, some 5 or 6 miles from Fortress Monroe, capable of receiving any number of troops, & communicating with Norfolk by quite passable roads, with a distance, by one route, of 8 or 9 & by another of 12 or 13 miles."[25]

Cram also reported the site satisfactory, and told Maj. Gen. Wool "that he need seek no farther for a landing place, that his troops could disembark here without wading much, if any, and without being brought under fire of heavy batteries, and that the cavalry and artillery, as well as the infantry, could be disembarked here, provided it was done before the wind, then from the south-west, should change to the north-east." The matter of the wind concerned Cram, for if it blew the top of the water, it might lower the depth enough to prevent the transport boats from getting close to shore. Despite his concerns, Cram explained, the "General decided at once to adopt Ocean View as the point of debarkation." Wool and Secretary Chase agreed "that this was the best point that could be selected under all the circumstances."[26]

24 Ibid.; Chase to Janet, May 11, 1862, in "The Life of Chase: His Account of the Capture of Norfolk," *New York Times*, Sept. 10, 1874, 4.

25 Chase to "Nettie," May 11, 1862, Chase Papers, LC.

26 Cram, "Report," Wool Papers, NYSA. The prospect of strong wind was one of the reasons the CSS *Virginia* pilots would soon bring up to Tattnall as to why the ironclad could not successfully make the journey up the James River past the shoals.

While Chase, Wool, Viele, and Cram were out scouting possible landing sites on Confederate-held beaches, Lincoln and Secretary Stanton used the early afternoon to visit the area's military hospital, where 800-900 wounded soldiers had just arrived following the May 5 battle outside Williamsburg on Virginia's Peninsula. Most were Union men, but about one-third were Rebels who, according to a rumor published in the *Philadelphia Inquirer*, did not want to "remain in the hospital at Williamsburg exposed to the tender mercy of Secession nurses. The women of Williamsburg refused to attend even the Rebel wounded unless a Rebel flag was placed over the hospital." Some of the wounded, continued the *Inquirer*, were sent farther north on the evening of May 9, but a substantial number remained at the Hygeia and Seminary hospitals just outside Fort Monroe. "The President visited each ward, shook hands and conversed with every soldier," to their tremendous gratification.[27]

After his hospital visit, Lincoln returned to Wool's headquarters more determined than ever to seize Norfolk. He decided not to wait for Lt. Jeffers's report on conditions at Sewell's Point, and consider other options instead.

The *Miami*, meanwhile, arrived back at Fort Monroe with her "scouts" about 2:30 p.m. While Lt. Col. Cram "immediately" began planning the invasion, Secretary Chase left to report to Lincoln. "I found the President had been listening to a Pilot & studying a chart," recalled Chase, "& had become [convinced] that there was a nearer landing, & wished to go & see about it on the spot."[28]

Chase, Lincoln, and Stanton once again boarded the *Miami* to inspect the Confederate shoreline. They first stopped at the Rip Raps to pick up a tugboat and 20 soldiers, probably men from the 99th New York contingent garrisoning Fort Wool. Lincoln and Stanton climbed aboard the tug, which "was, of course, nearest shore" and soon stymied by shallow water, and "the Rip Raps [row] boat was manned & sent in."

27 "Arrival of Wounded," *Philadelphia Inquirer*, May 12, 1862, 1. Somewhere between Halfway House and Williamsburg on May 5, part of the Union army under Brig. Gen. Joseph Hooker caught up with the rear guard of the Johnston's retreating Confederate army. Both sides contended with muddy roads and heavy terrain, but managed to throw considerable forces into the battle. By the time it ended nearly 41,000 Union soldiers participated and some 2,200 became casualties (including about 450 killed, 1,400 wounded, and 375 missing). About 32,000 Confederate soldiers were commanded by Maj. Gen. James Longstreet, with about 1,600 killed or wounded. The Rebels continued retreating after the sharp fight.

28 Cram, "Report," Wool Papers, NYSA. Lt. Jeffers's eventual report to the president may have been verbally delivered, for there is no written record of it. As noted earlier, he wrote a report to Goldsborough, but it has not been found. Jeffers to Goldsborough, May 9, 1862, *ORN* 7:340; Chase to "Nettie," May 11, 1862, Chase Papers, LC.

(Above and on facing page) Union forces under Maj. Gen. John E. Wool embark on various ships and barges for the short trip to Ocean View on the Virginia shore to capture Norfolk. *Artist, G. Kaiser, Courtesy of The Mariners' Museum, Newport News, VA*

Fearing for President Lincoln's safety, Secretary Chase ordered the *Miami's* crew to train "her long-range gun . . . on shore, with her other pieces ready for support and directed the Captain [Douglass Ottinger] to land with both boats and all the men they could take fully armed." When several horsemen suddenly appeared on the beach, Chase, believing them to be Confederates, asked Lincoln if the *Miami's* guns should open on them and clear them out, to which the president, noted the secretary, "replied negatively." Apparently, the enemy horsemen rode away a short time later without incident. With the landing site now clear, the president took the opportunity to board one of the rowboats along with some of the soldiers. About 6:00 p.m., with the sun just beginning to set, the American president, "by the light of moon landed on the beach and walked up and down a considerable distance to assure himself that there could be no mistake in the

matter. How little the Confederacy dreamed what a visitor it had that night to the 'sacred soil'!"[29]

The North learned soon enough of Lincoln's exploits. Keeler mentioned it in a May 9 letter to his wife, Anna. The *Philadelphia Inquirer* reported on May 12 that Lincoln "was the first to step on shore." When the president got back to the Fort Monroe wharf, continued the *Inquirer*, the troops received him "with enthusiastic cheering." The *New York Herald* praised Lincoln for taking "an important and dangerous reconnaissance." Not only was he "a calm, dispassionate, honest statesman, but a naval and military commander of no mean pretensions."[30]

29 Chase to "Nettie," May 11, 1862, Chase Papers, LC; Chase to Janet, May 11, 1862, *New York Times*, Sept. 10, 1874, 4; Viele, "A Trip with Lincoln," 819.

30 "Details of Advance on Norfolk, President Lincoln in the Field," *Philadelphia Inquirer*, May 12, 1862, 1; "Norfolk Is Ours," *New York Herald*, May 12, 1862. Chase said the landing site appeared to be as good as the one found earlier in the day. "I supposed [it] to be between 2 and

Despite the president's best efforts, Wool insisted on using the original beach selection as the landing site. "I think the President's examination, however," observed Cram, "may have had the good effect of bewildering the enemy a little, as to the real point of debarkation." In any case, Wool had begun planning long before Lincoln returned from his own scout. He favored the initial site because of a "reported tolerably good" road leading from there to Norfolk, nine miles off, even though the route included a bridge over the broad Tanner's Creek. The site also offered an alternative 12-13 mile route to Norfolk by going around the head of the creek. With the water deep enough for barges almost up to the shoreline, Cram planned to construct a temporary "barge wharf" that horses, artillery, and troops could employ "without wading." He also noted the further advantages of proximity to Fort Monroe, a small brook of fresh water, no expected Confederate resistance, and the complete absence of any "annoyance from the *Merrimac*."

Wool put Cram (his top engineer) in charge of loading Brig. Gen. Max Weber's soldiers onto the transports and disembarking them onto the beach. Once ashore, Weber was to rapidly march his men for the Indian Pole Bridge over Tanner's Creek and secure it. If the Confederates prevented that, the longer alternate route to Norfolk was to be used. That route, however, passed an entrenched Rebel camp armed with as many as 30 artillery pieces. No one knew whether it was manned.

Cram rode out to Camp Hamilton to explain the plan to Weber. Wool scribbled across Cram's report that the "order collecting and embarking the troops was opened . . . at 3 o'clock p.m." According to a member of the 10th New York, troops were marching back to the Fort Monroe wharves an hour later.[31]

The 99th New York companies received their initial order at 5:00 p.m. "to pack knapsacks and break camp" for an unknown destination, recalled a company drummer. "About 9 p.m . . . the regiment fell in line and marched to Fort Monroe, where we embarked on transports." The accommodations of the 1st Delaware improved significantly compared to the previous night's "filthy canal boats" when the men "were soon safely and snugly ensconced on board the large and commodious steamer *George Washington*."[32]

---

3 miles nearer Fortress Monroe but which proved to be only about 1/2 or 3/4 of mile nearer." Chase to "Nettie," May 11, 1862, Chase Papers, LC.

31 Cram, "Report," Wool Papers, NYSA, including Wool's handwritten cover note; Charles W. Cowtan, *Services of the Tenth New York Volunteers*, 76.

32 F. W. Ritschy, quoted in Philip Corell, ed., *History of the Naval Brigade: 99th N.Y. Volunteers, Union Coast Guard, 1861-1865* (New York, 1905), NYSA, n.p.

The men of the 16th Massachusetts were also ordered back to the wharves to re-embark on the steamship *Nellie Baker*, the same ship they had been on the previous night. In a letter written a couple days later, Charles Robinson Johnson, captain of the regiment's Company F, explained that once the men were loaded aboard, the ship "lay in the roads until early in the morning." Some of the soldiers tasked with making the crossing arrived from Camp Butler at Newport News, about eight miles away. The boarding effort continued into the evening by moon and torchlight.[33]

The designated regiments for the mission were the 10th, 20th, and part of the 99th New York, 1st Delaware, 16th Massachusetts, 58th Pennsylvania, 1st battalion of New York Mounted Rifles, a contingent of cavalry, and three batteries of light artillery. Initially, these troops were under the command of Brig. Gen. Weber, a German military school graduate who had organized and led the 20th New York.[34]

Keeler watched the embarkation from the deck of the *Monitor*. "It was a beautiful sight to see them this evening as the long files marched down to the boats to embark," he told his wife. A *New York Times* correspondent described the scene as "highly picturesque. We stood upon the beach—the sea perfectly smooth and reflecting . . . the hundreds of lights that glanced fitfully along from the vessels gliding to and fro, as well as the moon and stars." The steamboats "lying at the wharf on our right," added the reporter, "were all alive with the songs and cheers of the embarking troops."[35]

In the midst of all those soldiers preparing for action that evening was the president of the United States. He was, according to a Philadelphia reporter, "the busiest and hardest working man on the wharf during the embarkation." Lincoln happily noticed the many canal boats that "reminded him of his youth" when he led "the happy life of a 'jolly flat boatman.'"[36]

33 Charles R. Johnson to "Nellie," May 11, 1862, in Albert C. Eisenberg & Michael Hammerson, eds., *"If I Am Alive Next Summer": The Civil War Letters of Captain Charles Robinson Johnson of the 16th Massachusetts Infantry, "The Iron Sixteenth"* (Berwyn Heights, MD, 2015), 67; "Details of Advance on Norfolk," *Philadelphia Inquirer*, May 12, 1862, 1.

34 Cram, "Report," Wool Papers, NYSA; Ezra J. Warner, *Generals in Blue: Lives of the Union Commanders* (Baton Rouge, LA, 1964), 545-46.

35 Keeler to "Anna," May 9, 1862, in Daly, ed., *Aboard the USS* Monitor, 114; "The Preparations for the Advance on Norfolk," *New York Times*, May 14, 1862, 8.

36 "Capture of the City of Norfolk, The New Order to Move," *Philadelphia Inquirer*, May 13, 1862, 1. A historian of the 58th Pennsylvania stated that the regiment passed President Lincoln

The Army had commandeered everything afloat that the Navy didn't own. "The steamer *Adelaide* . . . filled with freight and passengers for Baltimore, was stopped half an hour before her time of sailing, with half a dozen" other vessels," reported the *New York Times.* Infantry and artillery detailed for the expedition "immediately occupied them." At least one Baltimore-bound passenger griped that he "had to trundle ashore, bag and baggage," while the soldiers displaced the passengers. His wasn't a solitary complaint.[37]

Cram, who was shouldering a significant amount of responsibility for the operation, detailed his apprehensions and worries about the formidable and risky task before him. Anybody who'd experienced such an operation, he explained in his later report, could

> appreciate the difficulty, risk and anxiety of suddenly calling out five thousand troops—artillery, infantry and cavalry—and embarking them on board canal boats and all manner of light and heavy steamers and schooners for a movement requiring the utmost celerity, [then] piloting them in the night for seven or eight miles at sea, and . . . disembarking them over a temporary wharf, to be quickly made by running old canal barges aground near the beach, on an open coast, liable at any moment to a change of wind, which in all probability would destroy the barges, drive every steamer and schooner ashore and swamp the men.[38]

A delay cropped up around 10:00 p.m. that potentially threatened the ongoing operation when artillery horses balked at the idea of being loaded aboard the *Adelaide.* The uncooperative beasts created quite a stir before the uncomfortable situation was eventually sorted out and the horses cooperated with the loading process. An hour and a half later, the expedition was finally set to begin crossing Hampton Roads and move out into Chesapeake Bay to Ocean View. Another slight delay ensued to rearrange some of the barges because one of the ships was pulling too heavy a load. Cram, meanwhile, had gratefully accepted Secretary Chase's offer of the *Miami's* services to help cover the landing, "to be able to scour

---

for review before boarding their assigned transport boat. Based on the *Inquirer's* report, however, it appears the president was more likely encouraging the various units as they embarked on the transports rather than conducting a formal review. Samuel P. Bates, *History of* Pennsylvania Volunteers*, 1861-5*, 5 vols. (Harrisburg, PA, 1869), 2:285.

37 "The Capture of Norfolk," *New York Times*, May 13, 1862, 1; "The Preparations for the Advance on Norfolk," *New York Times*, May 14, 1862, 8.

38 Cram, "Report," Wool Papers, NYSA.

the beach, sand ridge and reach beyond with her guns into the woods and over the village."[39]

Charles W. Cowtan and his comrades of the 10th New York were in a good mood as the expedition pushed off. After leaving about midnight, he recalled, both "officers and men . . . being in high spirits . . . [were] full of the novelty of the situation and the expectation of . . . active work."[40]

The *New York Times* reporter had watched the New Yorkers and others board and fully expected Norfolk to fall "before to-morrow night." So did President Lincoln and everyone else who dined that evening at Wool's headquarters. During the meal, Wool, responding to Lincoln's query about how many soldiers he intended to send across Hampton Roads, answered "[a]bout 10,000." Col. Cannon knew Wool didn't command that many men, but he remained silent while his boss brimmed with extravagant confidence. Lincoln next asked Wool whether that number would be sufficient, given that Maj. Gen. Huger might have more men waiting behind defensive works. "Well, possibly," answered Wool. "But that is of no consequence. He is not going to fight. He will run if I land."

Lincoln was well aware that Wool did not expect any opposition taking Norfolk, but remained worried that the country could not withstand a disaster if Wool's effort was bloodily repulsed. "Mr. President," Wool assured Lincoln, "you are not a military man, and do not understand the situation. If you stay here forty-eight hours, I will present Norfolk to you." Cannon didn't record how Lincoln reacted to that patronizing statement. Despite his outward confidence, Wool had never crossed Hampton Roads to take Norfolk, let alone conducted an operation of this size.[41]

As the expedition's leaders ate their supper, Fort Wool's guns once again shelled Sewell's Point. "We have amused ourselves all the evening watching the bursting of the shells around the battery," Keeler penned his wife with delight, "& now the heavy boom of the guns & hoarse howl of the shells are the music to which I write." Sources disagree about the exact time the firing began. The USS *Jamestown's* log noted the time as 5:30 p.m., the *Dacotah's* 6:45 p.m., and the *Minnesota's* 7:25 p.m. Some reports stated that the Confederates started the shelling by firing one of their larger guns, but only one shot came from their direction.

39 "Details of Advance on Norfolk," *Philadelphia Inquirer*, May 12, 1862, 1; ibid.

40 Cowtan, *National Zouaves*, 76.

41 "Dispatches to the Associated Press," *New York Times*, May 12, 1862, 1; Cannon, *Personal Reminiscences*, 158-59.

According to the *Minnesota's* log, the guns at Fort Wool "continued firing rapidly; no response from the enemy."[42]

A *New York Times* reporter thought the expenditure of iron and powder foolish, the shelling "wasted upon deserted works and abandoned barracks. The single rebel gun fired at 7 o'clock was probably a parting salute—and I have no doubt that as our troops advance to-day [May 10], they will enter Sewall's Point and Norfolk without the slightest opposition."[43]

* * *

The reporter proved prescient. The Confederates evacuated Sewell's Point that evening and had indeed fired off a single shot—probably as a goodbye salute when the Norfolk Light Artillery Blues marched away. John Walters, a member of the Blues, told his diary that his section was ordered from the Point to Norfolk that afternoon. Before marching off, the Southerners left a parting gift of "fully one hundred letters" for the enemy soldiers who would soon be taking their places. Without giving any specific examples, the Richmond *Whig* explained that the "letters conveyed, in taunting language, the intelligence that the whole naval and land force of the great Yankee nation at Fort Monroe had been kept at bay for . . . twelve months by a few hundred men. We should like to see the Yankees when they read these epistles."[44]

Because Walters and his unit were on foot, the Blues did not reach their home city from Sewell's Point until around 10:00 p.m. "Shortly after," the artilleryman explained, "I retired to the luxury of an elegant feather bed with the rather uncomfortable conviction that it was to be perhaps the last time for months that I should be able to enjoy that luxury." Before abandoning the Sewell's Point fortifications, the Blues "fired and destroyed all their barracks . . . and blew up their magazine. Of the twenty-two guns formerly mounted at this place, but seven now remain, the balance having been carried to Richmond."[45]

42 Keeler to "Anna," May 9, 1862, in Daly, ed., *Aboard the USS* Monitor, 114-15; Abstract logs of the *Dacotah*, *Jamestown*, and *Minnesota*, May 9, 1862, *ORN* 7:333-34.

43 "The Preparations for the Advance on Norfolk," *New York Times*, May 14, 1862, 8.

44 Walters, *Norfolk Blues*, 19; Richmond *Whig*, May 15, 1862, 3.

45 Walters, *Norfolk Blues*, 19; "From Fortress Monroe, Signs of Evacuation," *Philadelphia Inquirer*, May 12, 1862, 1.

Maj. Gen. Benjamin Huger

Library of Congress

Salvaging all the materiel and supplies possible was an overriding objective during the evacuation. Robert E. Lee had consistently urged Huger "to remove everything of value." Given the difficulties at hand, the evacuation went relatively well. The same could not be said for the Confederate Navy. Lt. William H. Parker, former commander of the gunboat *Beaufort* and, he hoped, future commander of the *Dixie*, a gunboat then under construction, heard firing from the north and east that evening. "Some of the midshipmen went aloft into the main top and saw shells bursting in the direction of Willoughby's Point, about 7 miles distant," Parker later wrote. The naval officer concluded "that the enemy were shelling the beach preparatory to landing a force," and hurried to the house of Sydney S. Lee, the navy yard commander, to report his conclusion. Lee, who was about to retire for the evening, "said he did not think it probable; that he had heard nothing from General Huger, &c—he rather laughed at the idea." The manner in which Lee brushed aside his concern frustrated Parker, who "left about 11 o'clock" convinced that he was correct. Thinking he would be summoned before daybreak, Parker "threw myself on my bed without undressing." The episode signaled the first major breakdown of communication between the two branches of the Confederate military. Another, more costly one, was yet to come.[46]

Back on Norfolk's streets, meanwhile, James Morris Morgan, who had just arrived from New Orleans after a long slow train ride, witnessed a roiling mixture of confusion and order. Morgan had served on the CSS *McRae*, which had been

46 William Harwar Parker, *Recollections of a Naval Officer, 1841-1865* (New York, 1883), 278-79. No reports of Union forces shelling their proposed landing site have been discovered, so the midshipmen may have confused the direction of the bomb bursts with the firing on Sewell's Point.

severely damaged by the Federal fleet during the battle for New Orleans. Capt. Lee issued a pass for him to leave town right away. Morgan's postwar memoirs offers a vivid picture of the "many queer sights" he saw on his way to the train station. "There were orderly commands marching out of the place and disorganized mobs of men in uniform . . . free from all restraint and discipline," he began. "At one place," continued the sailor,

> a gang of men were trying to put a heavy piece of artillery on a light spring wagon drawn by one horse! I don't think they succeeded in doing it, but I did not wait to see the result of their labors. At the station there was a crowd of civilians, and piles of household goods; also many pretty and jolly girls who seemed to regard the matter as a picnic devised to amuse them. Government mules were being driven by in droves scattering the crowd in every direction. There were crates containing pigs and chickens blocking the way, and everything seemed to be in inconceivable confusion—infantrymen with arms, and infants in arms, jostling each other. One poor old stout woman carrying her baby was anxiously searching for her baggage and only found some body else's lost four-year-old boy who clung to her skirts with such a grip that she could not shake him off. Every body was in a hurry to get to some place, but few seemed to know what the name of the place was.[47]

As it turned out, few civilians escaped the advancing Yankees that night or the next day. "[T]he few civilians who did get off [believed] that not more than one hundred males outside of the army, have left Norfolk," reported the Richmond *Whig* a few days later. "Many females have left since it became known that the city was to be abandoned to the tender mercies of the Lincolnites, and a large number who decided to leave, remained because of their inability to get away. Soldiers inform us that when they passed through Norfolk, Saturday morning, they were everywhere met by groups of ladies, who, with tears in their eyes, implored their protection."[48]

The spreading panic reached the streets of Richmond. As noted earlier, President Davis had urged his family to leave the city as soon as word arrived that the Union ironclad *Galena* was steaming up the James River. McClellan's soldiers were continuing their slow but methodical advance up the Peninsula toward the capital's outskirts. Varina Davis, the president's wife, had persuaded her husband to let her stay a couple more days before finally taking leave of the capital on May

47 James Morris Morgan, *Recollections of a Rebel Reefer* (Boston, 1917), 78-79.

48 Richmond *Whig*, May 13, 1862, 3.

10. Many others aware of the dire situation and with the wherewithal to do so, also fled the city.[49]

Except for one son, war clerk John Jones sent his family south to Raleigh, North Carolina. "[I]t is in reality another flight from the enemy," he scribbled, revealing a bit of panic. "No one, scarcely, supposes that Richmond will be defended. But it must be!" Jones was overstating his case. Although Joe Johnston was still retreating up the Peninsula, his army was intact and Southern morale remained high. In addition, infantry, with naval support, was busy fortifying Drewry's Bluff to keep the *Galena* and other Union warships away from the capital. Jeff Davis would never abandon Richmond without fighting.[50]

The evacuation of Norfolk "is doubtless considered a military necessity," observed the *Charleston Mercury* a few days later, "the grounds whereof, as we do not know, we shall not undertake to criticize. If a necessity, it is a very sad and humiliating one—the loss of the only great navy yard in the Confederate States." Endeavoring to maintain an optimistic tone for its readers, the paper concluded, "We trust, however, we shall soon see the good results gained by this important step. If it indicates the sagacity of seizing the most important of two incompatible objects, and sacrificing the other, it may be a great resolve."[51]

The Richmond *Whig's* editor was anything but forgiving or hopeful and admonished the Davis administration and professional class of soldiers for their poor planning. "Very strange to say," he began,

> our authorities decided very suddenly to evacuate the place, but gave the people no information of the fact; and stranger still, they first sent the greater portion of the troops away, and then commenced to remove the valuables. Common sense would have suggested that our troops be retained to hold and defend the place until every article of value had been removed. 'West Point' thought differently, however, and hence the brilliant, but very precipitate departure.

The unhappy editor was appalled Norfolk was abandoned at all. "[N]ine out of every ten men of ordinary mind [believed] that Norfolk could have been held for twelve months longer with as much ease as it has been since the war commenced,"

49 Varina Davis, *Jefferson Davis*, 2:268-69. See also Joan E. Cahin, *First Lady of the Confederacy: Varina Davis's Civil War* (Cambridge, MA, 2006), 125.

50 Jones, *A Rebel War Clerk's Diary*, 1:123.

51 "The Situation of Affairs," *Charleston Mercury*, May 12, 1862, Accessible Archives, accessed Aug. 28, 2009, accessible.com.dbgateway.nysed.gov/accessible.

he argued. This could have been done by placing "the *Virginia* at the entrance of the Elizabeth and James rivers; send[ing] a new ironclad, the *City of Richmond*, south to Albemarle Sound to deal with the Union threat from that quarter; and let the 'gallant boys' at Sewell's Point and Ocean View, 'watch and vigil.'" Instead, Southerners witnessed only abandonment "to the depredations and outrages of a foe more unscrupulous and relentless than were the 'Goths and Vandals.' Military 'science' has thought otherwise, and as 'military science' is supreme, common sense must hide its diminished head, and submit without the expressions of an opinion."[52]

By this time it was clear to just about everyone that Norfolk's evacuation was underway. From 5:00 p.m., when the soldiers in blue began boarding their transports, and all through that evening "a bright light was visible" in Norfolk's direction, wrote a correspondent for the *New York Times*. "[D]ense clouds of smoke showed clearly enough that all the barracks and works of every kind, all along the [southern] shore from Sewall's Point, were being burned."[53]

It looked as though Maj. Gen. Wool's prediction was accurate. The Confederates would not fight for Norfolk.

52 Richmond *Whig*, May 13, 1862.

53 "The Preparations for the Advance on Norfolk," *New York Times*, May 14, 1862, 8.

Chapter 5

Saturday, May 10, 1862

"No time for ceremony, Mr. President, Norfolk is ours!"

— *Maj. Gen. John Wool to President Lincoln*

By 12:30 a.m., the fleet of army transports, commandeered civilian vessels, and canal boats were sailing southeast from Fort Monroe toward the invasion beach. Maj. Gen. John Wool had ordered complete silence—"no cheering or noise of any kind . . . by the troops on landing." A reporter aboard the steamship *George Washington* with Brig. Gen. Max Weber and his staff saw a religious omen in the grand event: In the "clear and beautiful" night, with "the moon and stars . . . shining brightly . . . evidence of the blessing of Divine Providence is with the fleet thus far." The pilot boat ahead of them signaled that all was going well, and in another 30 minutes the invasion fleet arrived at Ocean View.[1]

Lt. Col. Cram reported their arrival off the beach about 1:30 a.m. Most of the transport fleet plus the treasury revenue cutter *Miami* awaited offshore. Secretary Chase had offered the *Miami* to Cram the night before to help protect the landing site, an offer Cram readily accepted since it didn't involve cooperation from the Navy. Cram credited the *Miami's* presence for the unopposed landing, although

1 "Capture of the City of Norfolk, Personal Matters," *Philadelphia Inquirer*, May 13, 1862, 1. The village of Ocean View, where Norfolk's elite summered, was a small resort community of about a dozen dwellings.

some Confederate cavalry pickets had been spotted. When the cutter's captain reported everything "quiet on the beach," Cram directed the barges to move in. The first one carried Capt. Phineas A. Davis's company of the 7th Independent Battery, Massachusetts Light Artillery.[2]

While the landing presented challenges, Cram's assessment that the beach was the right place to drop troops ashore proved accurate. A *New York Times* reporter described the shore as "a smooth sandy beach—the sand being very deep as you leave the water, and suddenly rising into long mounds ten or fifteen feet high . . . forming a complete breastwork." The water was shallow at the shoreline and gradually deepened, such that only "fifty feet out [was] deep [enough] for vessels drawing five or six feet of water."[3]

Cram brought the first barge with Davis's company in "left side on" as the tide began falling. "Two more were next towed in," he explained, "having aboard some of the 20th New York, and placed lengthwise—the head of one barge against the stern of the other, and as near as could be at right angles to the first barge, &c.—thus forming a 'barge wharf,' which reached out into water deep enough for the lightest draft steamers to come up to."

With an anchor from the *Miami* keeping the outermost barge from drifting, Cram had a carpenter and several soldiers lay planking over the connected barges and a gangplank to dry sand. "Men, horses and guns were . . . put ashore . . . safe and dry," he boasted. Although he had worried that a change in the wind might disrupt the barge placement, everything went smoothly.[4]

2 Cram, "Report," May 31, 1862, Wool Papers, NYSA. The battery was also known as Richardson's Light Guard. The Massachusetts unit organized in May 1861 as infantry, and was designated the 7th Massachusetts Battery on March 17, 1862. On May 10, 1862, Davis' company served as infantry. Cram's report also referred to it as the Independent Lowell Artillery since it had been raised in Lowell, Massachusetts.

3 "The Capture of Norfolk," *New York Times*, May 13, 1862, 1.

4 Cram, "Report," May 31, 1862, Wool Papers, NYSA. Cram wasn't the first Union engineer to use barges to create a makeshift wharf for an over-beach landing. In April of 1862, Lt. Col. Barton S. Alexander, an engineering officer with George McClellan's Army of the Potomac, was presented the problem of landing a complete division, including artillery and attached cavalry, from the York River onto the Peninsula above Yorktown. When the Confederates abandoned Yorktown, the landing site was moved farther upriver and the operation carried out on May 6. Alexander connected two canal barges, 70-80 feet long, with planking, so the barges were 12 feet apart and ran them bow first onto the shore. Other shallow draft boats could then pull up at the water end of the barge wharf to unload, crossing over and then down a gangplank to dry land. Later in the day Alexander extended his wharf into deeper water with more barges and canal boats and more planking. He had also solved the problem of transferring soldiers from the transports onto the shallow draft barges and pontoons. Rather than have them climb

Cram sent Davis' company "along and over the sand ridge, hoisting the United States Flag on the very staff which had borne the rebel flag, and posting guards at every house, the rebel cavalry pickets" swiftly retiring. Before six in the morning, Lt. Col. Francis Weiss's 20th New York was heading down the road as Wool's "advance guard" toward Indian Pole Bridge, which crossed Tanner's Creek about seven miles away.[5]

Debarking the rest of the little army proceeded smoothly, each regiment and contingent taking their turn at the makeshift wharf. According to Cram, once each unit assembled itself, he ordered it on its way to catch up with the marching 20th New York. In a letter to a friend, however, a 1st Delaware volunteer complained that his regiment "tumbled out of the boats and instantly commenced the important duty of breakfast." The effort to enjoy an early repast ended quickly. "They were in the midst of ham and coffee, when the ceremony was cut short by an order from General Wool . . . to follow and overtake the advance."[6]

Artillery units followed the infantry, off-loading their guns and horses. Cavalry brought up the rear. The artillery consisted of Company D, 4th Regular Artillery, six guns under Capt. F. M. Follett and, possibly, Howard's four-gun battery. Wool would report that his force totaled fewer than 6,000 men—far short of the 10,000 he had promised the president.[7]

---

singly down the ship's side on rope ladders, the engineer devised gangplanks on both sides of the ship and the soldiers simply walked down onto the barge. Barton S. Alexander, "Reports of Lieut. Col. Barton S. Alexander, U.S. Army, Engineer Officer, of operations from April 20 to July 12," Jan. 28, 1863, *OR* 11/1:134-36.

5 Cram, "Report," May 31, 1862, Wool Papers, NYSA; Janet B. Hewett, ed., *Supplement to the Official Record of the Union and Confederate Armies*, 100 vols. (Wilmington, NC, 1997), 43/2:272. The 20th New York Infantry was organized on May 6, 1861, in New York City with men from the city's boroughs, Newark, N.J., and other nearby communities. The companies included German-born volunteers from various Turner societies, which were German-American gymnastic and social clubs (hence the unit's alternate name of "United Turner Rifles"). Its first colonel was Max Weber, a graduate of the Karlsruhe Military Academy and former lieutenant in a provincial German army. Weber had been promoted to brigadier general that April and put in command of Camp Hamilton, which left Lt. Col. Weiss in charge of the regiment. Frederick Phisterer, *New York in the War of the Rebellion, 1861-1865* (Albany, NY, 1890), 389.

6 "Volunteer" to "friend Eckel," May 11, 1862, *Delaware State Journal and Statesman*, May 20, 1862, 2. The order of debarkation was as follows: 20th New York (Lt. Col. Francis Weiss), 1st Delaware (Col. John W. Andrews), 16th Massachusetts (Col. Powell T. Wyman), 10th New York (Col. John E. Bendix), First Battalion, New York Mounted Rifles (Maj. Charles C. Dodge), four companies of the 99th New York (Col. David W. Wardrop), and 58th Pennsylvania (Col. J. Richter Jones).

7 Cram, "Report," May 31, 1862, Wool Papers, NYSA; *Baltimore American,* May 10, 1862 & Wool to unk., n.d., both in Moore, ed., *Rebellion Record*, 5:43-44, 45.

William Keeler wrote his wife that by 6:00 a.m., he could see the soldiers trudging onto the beach from his position on the deck of the *Monitor*. Everything seemed "auspicious [this] clear beautiful morning [with its] cool westerly wind." Keeler expected the soldiers to attack the Sewell's Point batteries from the rear, and had no idea the plan was to head directly to Norfolk.[8]

While the landing was underway, Secretary Chase, presumably with the president, Stanton, Wool, and Viele, rose early and had breakfast at 6:00 a.m. Either then or before, Stanton told Wool that he "had decided to relieve him of the command of the expedition on account of his advanced age." Whether Wool's 78 years or some other reason (perhaps his condescending boasting at dinner the evening before) prompted Stanton's decision, the news devastated the old general. "[W]ith much emotion, [Wool] begged the Secretary to allow him to command the troops," Viele recalled. Stanton "finally reversed his decision [remarking] that he could not inflict sorrow upon gray hairs."[9]

With the last-minute command decision settled, Lincoln and his party prepared for the boat ride across Hampton Roads. Before boarding, Wool discovered his aide-de-camp Col. Cannon at Fort Monroe's wharf with his horse and an orderly. Wool, who was still simmering over his near-removal from command by Stanton, confronted Cannon who—partially because of the general's boasting— had expressed doubts about the project's success to both Wool and the president.

"What are you doing here, sir?" Wool demanded. Shocked by the tone of his superior's question, the aide replied that he was going with the troops. "I will take nobody with me who has any doubt of my success," shot back the general. Taken aback, Cannon inquired whether he was to be humiliated "in consequence of my confidential relations to you? If so, I shall resign from the service." Wool waved off the threat of resignation. "No," he declared, "you are left in command of the reserves and of this fort, and I will not trust any one else." Cannon later wrote that he considered the order designed to leave him behind "more monstrous than

8 Keeler to "Anna," May 9, 1862, in Daly, ed., *Aboard the USS* Monitor, 116. Keeler often began a letter one evening and continued it the next morning before sending it to his wife. In order for Keeler to have seen the landing site, the *Monitor* must have followed the troop transports around Willoughby's Point. That would have taken her away from the *Virginia*, which continued to float at the other end of Hampton Roads.

9 Salmon P. Chase to "Janet," May 11, 1862, in "The Life of Chase: His Account of the Capture of Norfolk," *New York Times*, Sept. 10, 1874, 4; Viele, "A Trip with Lincoln," 819.

anything else," and he asked that Wool's adjutant general also be left behind. Wool agreed with the request.[10]

With Cannon left standing on Fort Monroe's wharf, everyone else boarded two ships for the trip around Willoughby's Point to the Ocean View landing site. Lincoln, Chase, and Stanton sailed on the *Baltimore* and took a slight detour to consult with Flag Officer Goldsborough. Wool, along with generals Viele and Joseph K. F. Mansfield, troop commander from Fort Butler at Newport News, made the short journey on the steamer *Kansas*.[11]

Aboard the USS *Susquehanna*, Alfred Zerega confirmed Lincoln's visit to the flagship and his subsequent move "to the transport fleet." The president, he wrote, was "very active among the landing party," and he even claimed Lincoln helped "superintend the building of the temporary pier"—which was something of an overstatement since the wharf was built before Lincoln arrived.[12]

Lt. Thomas O. Selfridge, a flag lieutenant working for Goldsborough and Lincoln's temporary aide aboard the *Baltimore*, recalled something altogether different. According to Selfridge, the president didn't go ashore that morning at Ocean View. The lieutenant accompanied Lincoln "while he witnessed this landing and inspected the general vicinity," wrote Selfridge. "He was very much preoccupied. He sat out on deck, aloof from everyone else, and appeared extremely tired, careworn, and weighted down with responsibility. Naturally I stood somewhat in awe of him and was reluctant to engage him in conversation, except to answer his enquiries and explain the situation."[13]

By the time both sets of leaders arrived at Ocean View about 8:00 a.m., "a considerable body of troops had already gone forward," explained Secretary Chase. Before going ashore, the treasury official took a side trip on a small tugboat to find the spot where President Lincoln had landed the evening before, only to discover it was about three-quarters of a mile farther down the beach. Sailing back to the ships off the landing site, Chase found that Brig. Gen. Viele had already gone ashore, so he followed in his wake. Chase found the general and his orderly, whose horse Viele had commandeered so the secretary could ride up the sand dunes to examine

10 Cannon, *Personal Reminiscences*, 159-60.

11 Chase to "Janet," May 11, 1862, *New York Times*, Sept. 10, 1874, 4; Louis Goldsborough to Gideon Welles, May 10, 1862, *ORN* 7:341, and "Dispatches to the Associated Press, Later," *New York Times*, May 12, 1862, 1.

12 Zerega, "The Last Days," 1:454. Like Keeler, Zerega also stated he could see what was happening during the landing at Ocean View.

13 Thomas O. Selfridge Jr., *What Finer Tradition*, 65.

the spot where Viele had seen a Confederate picket the previous day. The small party soon discovered "a shed where the pickets had staid & fresh horse-tracks in many places, showing that the enemy had only withdrawn but a few hours [earlier]."[14]

In the meantime, Secretary Stanton, but not the president, had also gone ashore. The secretary of war had asked Chase to accompany the soldiers on the march to Norfolk, and after some hesitation he agreed to do so. Stanton rejoined Lincoln on the *Baltimore.* Once most of the troops had landed and begun their march, Lincoln and Stanton left the area for the short return trip to Fort Monroe to await news of the operation's results. According to Zerega, the president sailed past the *Susquehanna* on his way back to the fort. The ship's band struck up "Hail Columbia" and the sailors "gave him three cheers."[15]

The landings proceeded according to plan. The 1st Delaware, the second regiment ashore after Weiss' 20th New York, set off down the road in the direction of Norfolk by 9:00 a.m. It did so with the "sacrifice of provisions and severe reproof to clamoring appetites," grumbled the regiment's volunteer reporter. "Kettles of coffee, just made, were thrown away," he complained, "boxes of biscuits left on the ground, every [item] calculated to impede the progress of the regiment was set aside, and we took up our line of march." Not until nearly an hour later did another regiment, the 16th Massachusetts, begin its march. By that time speed was of the essence, and the Bay State troops were "obliged to strike to

14 Chase to "Nettie," May 11, 1862, in "Diary," Chase Papers, LC. Sources dispute when the leaders left Fort Monroe and the time of their arrival at Ocean View. In his postwar reminiscences, Le Grand Cannon claimed Chase and Wool left the fort at 4:00 a.m. Cannon, *Personal Reminiscences*, 158-59. However, a *New York Times* reporter who accompanied the two on the ship put the time at 6:00 a.m. "Preparations for the Advance on Norfolk," *New York Times*, May 14, 1862, 8. As noted earlier, Chase wrote his daughter on May 11 that they were eating breakfast at 6:00 a.m. and left afterward. That timing agreed with Cram's report of late May that Wool arrived at Ocean View "a little before 8 o'clock," Cram, "Report," May 31, 1862, Wool Papers, NYSA, and with the *Miami's* journal of an appearance at 8:00 a.m. Kern, *Revenue Cutters*, 91. Note that about an hour and half later, with most of the *Miami's* crew on shore helping with the debarkation, the ship's engine experienced a serious mechanical failure when "a piece of the boiler blew out causing us to blow off steam and put the fires out." The *Miami* lay at anchor off Ocean View the rest of that day and night until towed back to Fort Monroe for repairs, which weren't completed in time to return the president to Washington. Kern, *Revenue Cutters*, 92.

15 Chase to "Nettie," May 11, 1862, in "Diary," Chase Papers, LC. According to Selfridge, Stanton did not go to the beach that morning, which contradicts Chase's letter written immediately after the event. Zerega, "Last Days," 1:454.

overtake the foremost regiment a fearful gait, which with the dust and heat of the sun wilted the men."[16]

The 1st Delaware and 16th Massachusetts followed Weiss's 20th New York toward the bridge spanning Tanner's Creek. Wool apparently assumed that Brig. Gen. Weber would act as overall commander of the first wave of regiments, though it is unclear whether Wool gave a direct order outlining Weber's role. Mansfield's commission as brigadier predated Weber's by nearly a full year. If the two officers found themselves in proximity without clear authority over who was to lead what body of troops, command confusion was sure to be the result.

In fact, Wool's only orders for the landing were concerned with how his soldiers would treat the civilian population. His general order to the men consisted of two sentences: "The troops of this Command being about to march into the country occupied by the enemy, they are warned that plundering and depredating upon private property, will not be tolerated for a moment. The penalty of death will be executed upon any soldier found violating this order." Wool's second order, this one to his officers, held them responsible for ensuring their commands followed the general order.[17]

Brig. Gens. Mansfield and Viele, their staffs, and Secretary Chase accompanied the 1st Delaware as it marched along the Princess Anne Road road. Wool and those of his staff who accompanied him remained behind to oversee the balance of the troop landings.[18]

The road leading away from the beach ran southeast about one mile before angling south toward what was known as the Half-Way Cross Roads. The Princess Anne Road continued south, but a different road turned to the southwest toward the bridge over Tanner's Creek—the shortest route and the one Wool intended his

16 "Volunteer" to "friend Eckel," May 11, 1862, *Delaware State Journal and Statesman*, May 20, 1862, 2; Johnson to "Nellie," May 11, 1862, in Eisenberg & Hammerson, eds., *"If I Am Alive Next Summer,"* 67-68.

17 General Order No. 40, May 9, 1862, & Special Order No. 121, May 10, 1862, both in Wool Papers, NYSA.

18 "Glorious News," *New York Times*, May 12, 1862, 1. Since they did not see any action in the capture of Norfolk and thereafter only occupation duty at Suffolk, Virginia, the men of 1st Delaware asked to be assigned to an active brigade. They got their wish when Brig. Gen. Joseph Mansfield took them as part of his brigade that joined the Army of the Potomac in the late summer of 1862. The regiment saw plenty of action at Antietam (where Mansfield was killed) and again at Fredericksburg. At Gettysburg on July 3, 1863, the 1st Delaware held the far right side of the line on Cemetery Ridge and helped repel Pickett's Charge. By the fall of 1864, the remnants of the 1st and 2nd Delaware regiments were combined to form the 1st Delaware Veteran Volunteer Infantry. See generally, Seville, *Delaware Volunteers*.

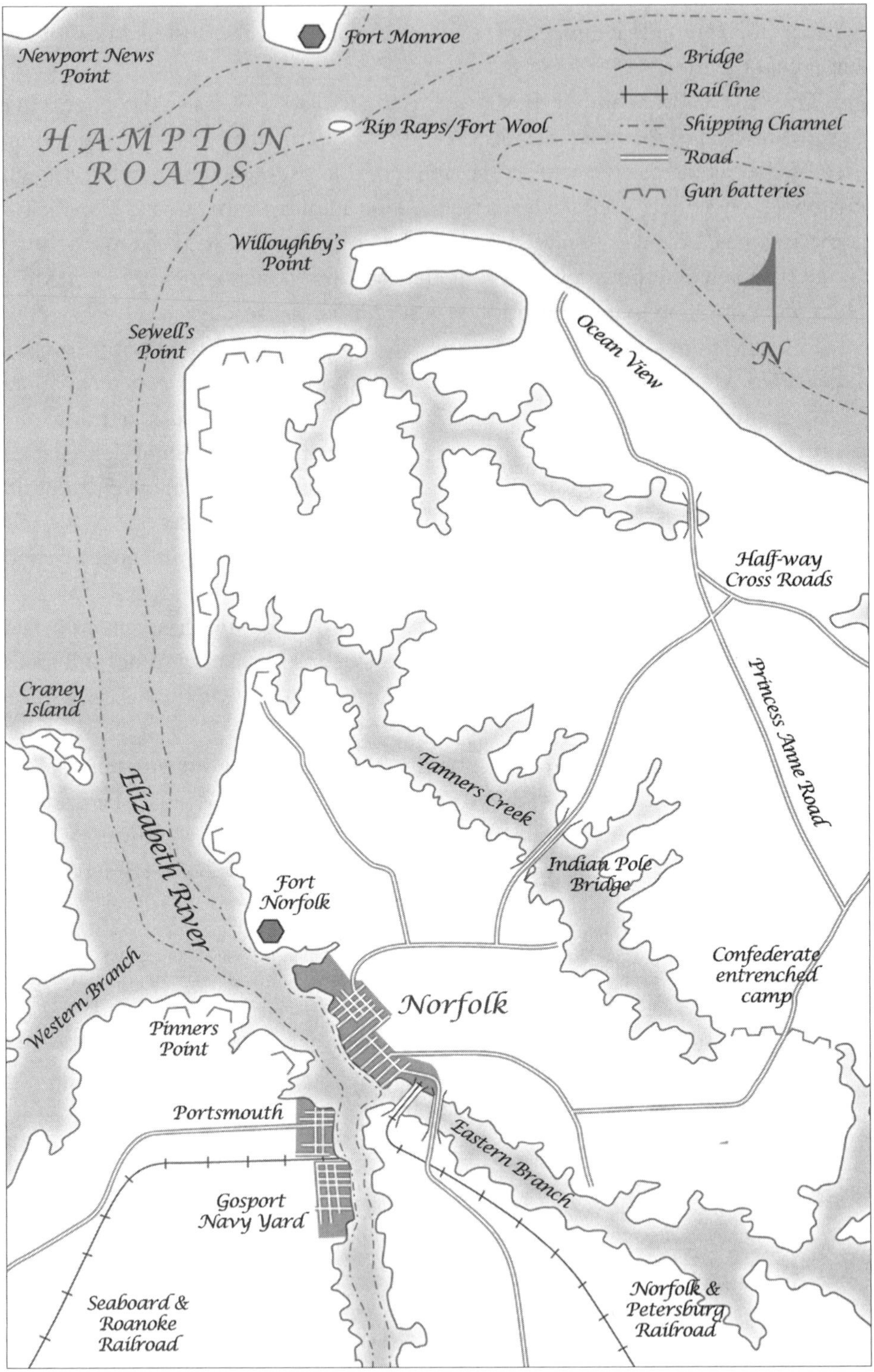
Fort Monroe
Newport News Point
Bridge
Rail line
Shipping Channel
Road
Gun batteries
HAMPTON ROADS
Rip Raps/Fort Wool
Willoughby's Point
Sewell's Point
Ocean View
N
Half-way Cross Roads
Princess Anne Road
Craney Island
Tanners Creek
Indian Pole Bridge
Elizabeth River
Fort Norfolk
Confederate entrenched camp
Western Branch
Norfolk
Pinners Point
Portsmouth
Eastern Branch
Gosport Navy Yard
Norfolk & Petersburg Railroad
Seaboard & Roanoke Railroad

advance to take. The task of securing the wooden Indian Pole Bridge, which shortened the route to Norfolk by at least five miles, would fall to the 20th New York because that regiment was marching in the front of the column.

The route was not without it perils. The narrow road thick with soft sand and "in only tolerable condition" ran through pine woods, explained a *New York Times* reporter accompanying the Union troops. As the sun climbed higher so did the temperature. The heat began taking a toll on the soldiers, who had spent months performing garrison duty and little else. "The [march] over dusty roads," wrote William Seville, a captain in the 1st Delaware, "was a severe trial to the men, encumbered with heavy knapsacks, blankets, overcoats and cartridge boxes, sweltering with the heat and stifled with dust." One of the New Yorkers of the 99th regiment, marching as part of the rear guard, observed "strewn along the road all kinds of clothing and camp material" discarded by the troops who had preceded them.[19]

Around 1:00 p.m. soldiers of the 20th New York encountered a contingent of Rebels near the Half-way Cross Roads within about three miles of the bridge. Some of these troops were the Jackson Grays, who had been taking a beating from naval batteries and the guns of Fort Wool all week at Sewell's Point. While many of their comrades had already been ordered back to Norfolk for evacuation, a few had remained until they heard Northern troops had landed at Ocean View. "This unexpected maneuver forced the hasty evacuation of all the fortifications at Sewell's Point," William H. Stewart, a member the Grays, wrote after the war. "The garrisons at once took up small arms to throw themselves in the path of the enemy at Denby's Church" at the crossroads. They got there in good time and formed a line of battle, but "we were soon ordered to continue the retreat to Norfolk." Most of the Grays hastened back and re-crossed the bridge along with an estimated 1,500 other Confederate soldiers in danger of being cut off. The bridge was to be burned once most of these men crossed.[20]

Once the New Yorkers occupied the crossroads, they found that Confederate cavalry had used Denby's, a Methodist church, as a barracks. The Rebels had departed in some haste, leaving food "lying around, [some] quite fresh yet. The marble-top table at the altar" had become "the officer's mess, with half a dozen handsome stuffed chairs around it," penned a reporter. "The Holy Bible lies upon

19 "The Capture of Norfolk," *New York Times*, May 13, 1862, 1; Seville, *Delaware Volunteers*, 41.

20 Stewart, *A Pair of Blankets*, 64; "Norfolk Repossessed," *Harper's Weekly*, May 24, 1862, 327; Cram, "Report," May 31, 1862, Wool Papers, NYSA.

Brig. Gen. Joseph K. F. Mansfield

National Archives

the pulpit, the only article left undisturbed by the Rebels. I looked at it," he added, "and found it was opened at the account given of Absalom's treason."[21]

Gens. Weber and Mansfield pondered the capture of Tanner's Creek bridge and how best to accomplish it. "General Weber," suggested Mansfield, "I will take these German riflemen of yours [the 20th New York] and try and save the bridge. Send on reinforcements as rapidly as possible." That plan, of course, would subordinate the German general to Mansfield, which Weber had no intention of doing. "I will bring them myself, sir, instantly," he shot back.

The officers rode for another two miles and spotted smoke rising from the bridge. If they hurried, the structure might yet be saved. The regiment's skirmish line came within 800 yards of the span when they spotted Confederates around the burning bridge. The troops leveled their rifled muskets and fired a volley. The enemy, however, were too far away and the creek too wide—three-quarters of a mile at that point—for it to be effective.

With the bridge "enveloped in flames" and a strong Rebel presence, including artillery, holding the far bank, neither Weber nor Mansfield could do anything to

21 "Capture of the City of Norfolk, Affair at Tanner's Creek—The Bridge Burned," *Philadelphia Inquirer*, May 13, 1862, 1. The biblical story of King David's third son, Absalom, is related in 2 Samuel 13-19. The tale involves Absalom killing one of his brothers in revenge for the rape of a sister, a self-imposed exile, partial reconciliation between father and son, Absalom's assumption of some of the king's powers, and his usurpation of the throne. Whether the *Inquirer's* reporter actually found the Bible open to that section is moot. The account took a swipe at the departed Confederates for their rebellion against legitimate (Union/federal) authority.

save the structure or gain the far bank. "At precisely eleven o'clock they [fired] upon us with a howitzer and rifled brass piece, but their shells exploded without doing the slightest harm" wrote one Union eyewitness. Captain Seville of the 1st Delaware, which was now stacked up behind the New Yorkers, reported that his soldiers enjoyed the break from hard marching and headed for whatever cover they could find to get out from under the hot early afternoon sun. What he later described as "slight opposition" was a "welcome relief" for his tired men, and they "enjoyed an hour's rest in the shade" while someone else dealt with enemy.

Without artillery of their own, however, Mansfield and Weber had little chance to dislodge the Confederates. An order, reluctantly issued, instructed the men to fall in and march back to Half-Way Cross Roads. According to Lt. Col. Cram, the Rebels fired about 13 artillery rounds from the far side of the creek.[22]

While Mansfield and Weber were dealing with a blocked creek crossing, Secretary Chase and Brig. Gen. Viele were riding in their direction. It did not take them long to discover that something was amiss. According to Chase, they had ridden about five miles before encountering what he called the "rear of the advance." As Viele later put it, "We had not gone very far before it became evident that a great deal of confusion existed in the command . . . no organization, and an utter absence of definite instructions or orders of any kind." He continued:

> Overtaking a regiment that was scattered along the road . . . Mr. Chase inquired of the colonel to whose command he belonged and what his orders were. He replied that he had no idea who was his commander; that some said Weber and some said Mansfield. He had received no orders, except that when he landed he was told to take a certain road, and he thought he would wait to see what was to be done next.[23]

Within a few miles, Chase and Viele encountered two more regiments without orders or any idea of what to do or where to go. They also encountered Gen.

22 "Capture of the City of Norfolk, Affair at Tanner's Creek—The Bridge Burned," *Philadelphia Inquirer*, May 13, 1862, 1; "Evacuation and Occupation of Norfolk," Philadelphia *Press*, May 13, 1862, 1; Seville, *Delaware Volunteers*, 41; Cram, "Report," May 31, 1862, Wool Papers, NYSA. Captain Johnson of the 16th Massachusetts described the bridge as made of stone. The bridge supports likely were, but the main structure was made of wood. Johnson to "Nellie," May 11, 1862, in Eisenberg & Hammerson, eds., *"If I Am Alive,"* 68. The Beauregard Artillery, of Lynchburg, Virginia, fired the shots at the advancing Northerners. The Confederate account claimed the Union soldiers were cavalry rather than infantry from the 20th New York. Petersburg *Daily Express*, May 12, 1862, in Richmond *Whig*, May 13, 1862, 3.

23 Chase to "Nettie," May 11, 1862, in "Diary," Chase Papers, LC; Viele, "A Trip with Lincoln," 819-20.

Mansfield and his staff resting along the way. About that time cannon boomed ahead of them, and the pair knew it meant trouble. It had to be enemy fire, explained Viele, because the Federal artillery was still at the beach. Soldiers came running back down the road "with exaggerated rumors of the enemy being in force, burning the bridges and contesting with artillery the passage of the streams that crossed the road."[24]

According to the *New York Times* reporter riding with Mansfield, the general indicated the cannon fire meant the Confederates intended "to resist the further progress of our troops, and that nothing could be done without artillery and a larger force." Mansfield, therefore, did nothing. Nearby, Weber was questioning "some dirty-looking fellows in gray"—probably prisoners from the 24th Virginia Infantry who had not gotten across the bridge before it was set afire. According to Weber, "they were a portion of the garrison of Sewall's Point . . . evacuated by reason of our shelling the previous night."[25]

Viele had enough military experience under his belt to know that delay and confusion signaled an army command in disarray. "The ridiculousness of the situation would have been amusing, if it had not been for the serious aspect that it was gradually assuming," he later observed. "Two regiments of cavalry had been embarked, and two batteries of artillery; yet not a horse or a gun had been sent to the front," fumed the general who had helped capture Savannah's Fort Pulaski. It got worse. "Four regiments of infantry were marching along, uncertain what road to take, and unassigned to any brigade; two brigadier-generals and their staffs, without orders and without commands, were sitting by the road-side, waiting for something to turn up. This," he emphasized, "was the situation, with the enemy firing in front."[26]

24 Viele, "A Trip with Lincoln," 819-20. While the accounts were written as if Chase and Viele had traveled at least seven miles, Chase's and Viele's estimation of distance was, like most other participants, flawed. According to Cram's official campaign map, the distance from the Ocean View Beach to the crossroads was between four and five miles, and from the crossroads to the bridge at Tanner's Creek, another three miles.

25 "The Capture of Norfolk," *New York Times*, May 13, 1862, 1; "Norfolk Repossessed," *Harper's Weekly*, May 24, 1862, 327. The reporter asked the prisoners about the heavy smoke seen during the previous day's shelling. "Youse fellows throw some kind of things that spill fire when they burst, and it just sot every thing in a blaze," the prisoner was quoted as replying, "so we run into the woods and then we all run away."

26 Viele, "A Trip with Lincoln," 820-21. Viele's comment about the regiments not being brigaded contradicts Cram's written report that he spent most of a night earlier in the week working out the assignments of regiments to brigades. No written orders appear in either the

The situation also disgusted Secretary Chase. With no military authority to do so, the cabinet officer ordered Wool to bring up his cavalry and artillery. "This brought the general to the front with two pieces of artillery and some mounted troops," confirmed Viele, though he didn't say how long it took for them to arrive. When Wool finally made his appearance, explained Viele, "Mr. Chase expressed to him in very strong language his astonishment at the conditions of things." In return, Wool speculated that Mansfield may have sensed some "delicacy in assuming command over . . . Weber," while the latter "hesitated to act" with Mansfield close by. Wool's reply further incensed an already angry Chase. "Talk of delicacy," he exclaimed, "with the enemy firing in front! What absurdity! Let General Mansfield go to the rear and bring up reinforcements, and that will settle all questions of delicacy."[27]

The exchange between the treasury secretary and the aging general launched a prolonged discussion between Wool and Mansfield a short distance from the road under the shade of a large sycamore. "Two cackling old hens!" Chase scoffed, bereft of all patience. Turning to Viele, "with a voice and manner that would have become Wellington or Soult," Chase ordered him "in the name of the President of the United States to take command of these troops and march them upon Norfolk."[28]

Chase's directive brought about immediate action. Within minutes an infantry regiment was deployed, its skirmishers out front, and the other regiments "were soon moving rapidly down the Norfolk road." The movement got underway without Wool noticing it. Once he did, however, he brought his horse up next to Chase and demanded an explanation. To Chase's credit, the secretary promptly assumed responsibility for the order. Thereafter, Viele sarcastically observed, everyone "proceeded harmoniously toward our destination." Chase and Viele met up with Mansfield and Weber less than a mile from the burning bridge, where Chase later related they naturally "turned back."[29]

With the short route to Norfolk now impassable, Wool decided—or Chase made the decision for him—to leave a guard at the road and take the longer way,

---

OR or Wool's letter book from the commanding general to either Weber or Mansfield outlining the makeup of brigades.

27 Ibid.

28 Ibid.

29 Ibid.; Chase to "Janet," May 11, 1862, *New York Times*, Sept. 10, 1874, 4; "Evacuation and Occupation of Norfolk," Philadelphia *Press,* May 13, 1862, 1.

skirting the head of the creek and adding another three to five miles to the march. The change involved returning to the intersection at Denby's Church and turning onto the Princess Anne Road. Lt. Col. Cram estimated that those who first marched to the bridge, doubled back to the crossroads, and then went on to Norfolk marched 17 miles that day.[30]

Wool solved the troublesome command issue by sending Mansfield to Newport News to bring over two more of his own regiments. Wool then divided the regiments that had already landed into two brigades, putting Weber in charge of one and Viele the other. "Things now went much better," observed Chase. "The cavalry & Maj. Dodge were in advance. Genl. W. & staff next & then a body of sharpshooting skirmishers—then the main body of V's brigade—& then Weber's."[31]

Historians of both the 10th and the 20th New York claim their regiments led this portion of the march. Both had a claim on the truth. According to the Philadelphia *Press*, the 10th New York received the initial honor of leading the column, but not long thereafter Lt. Col. Weiss, the 20th's commander, approached Gen. Wool with a request. Weiss, wrote a reporter, whose regiment "has done all the hard work of the day, insists that his regiment is not weary, and that as they were the first to advance upon landing, they have the right to be the first in Norfolk." Wool granted Weiss's request. Secretary Chase, who was riding with Wool, inquired as to the identity of that "grotesquely dressed officer." "It is Lieut. Col. Weiss," replied Wool. Chase supposedly disagreed and stated, "No, sir, it is Colonel Weiss. He has earned the title and shall have it."[32]

No matter which regiment was in the vanguard, the march was a hard one. The barracks troops weren't prepared for their first campaign. "Like other inexperienced soldiers, they packed their knapsacks to their upmost capacity,"

30 Cram, "Report," May 31, 1862, Wool Papers, NYSA.

31 Chase to "Nettie," May 11, 1862, in "Diary," Chase Papers, LC.

32 Cowtan, *National Zouaves*, 76; Hewett, ed., *Supplement to the Official Record*, 43/2:272. The reporter for Philadelphia *Press* claimed the 10th New York was initially in front. "Evacuation and Occupation of Norfolk," Philadelphia *Press,* May 13, 1862, 1. Chase may well have described Weiss (whose given name was Chevalier Karl de Unter-Schill) as "grotesquely dressed" if the lieutenant colonel was wearing his old European uniform. Weiss began his long military services as an Austrian officer in the 1830s and became a major in the Hungarian army in 1848 during the revolt against Austria. He changed his name and fled to America after the revolt collapsed. First working as a recruitment agent in Boston for the British army, Weiss was made a major and commander of those recruits during the Crimean War period. Maj. Gen. Wool later presented Weiss with a commission to the rank of colonel, signed by the governor of New York. See Weiss, *Reminiscences*, generally.

recalled Chaplain Murphey, "but before midday the clouds of dust, burning sun, and heated air, confined by the thick pine woods on either side of the road, caused them to loosen their straps and lighten their burdens."[33]

Charles W. Cowtan of the 10th New York described the 15-mile-march as "hot as northern July [that] told severely" on men loaded down with everything from ammunition to a spare uniform. Naturally the troops shed excess weight from knapsacks along the route, unfortunately sometimes with "[c]onsiderable nervous haste . . . blankets, overcoats, extra shoes, underclothes, and even envelopes and postage were left along the road." Only "one or two halting places" afforded the men access to water. As a result, "thirst added its pangs to the heat and fatigue" and the tramping feet stirred massive dust clouds thick enough "to almost stifle the column. To say that the men of our regiment were fatigued by this, their first bona-fide day's march," concluded the New Yorker, "would be poorly expressing the truth."[34]

Men dropped out of line "fainting, pressing their parched lips to the very tussocks of the swamps . . . endeavoring to seek a little moisture," penned a correspondent. "Water is very scarce, each spring as it is found being emptied almost instantly, and the soldiers in their thirst even resort to stagnant pools and ponds." The double-quick pace magnified the suffering. Surgeons galloped up, examined several men fallen on the roadside, and announced "they are sunstruck. They are carried to a shady spot in the woods, but it is impossible for them to recover."[35]

Somewhere up ahead the road cut through a large Confederate defensive position studded with artillery, though whether it was manned and would pose a problem remained to be determined. All along the march "we stopped everybody from [whom] we could obtain information," explained Chase, and it "was not long before we were informed that the intrenched camp . . . had just been evacuated & the barracks were fired." A cavalry detachment rode ahead to reconnoiter and confirm the report. Once he arrived on the scene, Chase described the work as "a very strong one," with 21 guns still in position.[36]

33 Murphey, *Four Years in the War*, 54-55.

34 Cowtan, *National Zouaves*, 78.

35 "Evacuation and Occupation of Norfolk," Philadelphia *Press,* May 13, 1862, 1; Johnson to "Nellie," May 11, 1862, in Eisenberg & Hammerson, eds., *"If I Am Alive,"* 68;

36 Chase to "Nettie," May 11, 1862, in "Diary," Chase Papers, LC.

One of Wool's orderlies turned his horse and raced back down the trudging line of infantry shouting, "Cheer up, boys, you will sleep in Norfolk to-night. The enemy's works are abandoned and the city is evacuated!" The soldiers picked up their pace and the "exultant" 20th New York Germans led the way singing, "We'll hang Jeff Davis on a sour apple tree glory Hallelujah." Wool declined to silence them.[37]

The Federals remained exuberant all the way to the evacuated Confederate defensive works and the encampment on the far side, where the cheering troops "were immediately formed into line for the further march, now only two miles, to Norfolk." Wool later reported that the time was 4:40 p.m. The ringing cheers may have been triggered by the joy of taking the enemy line without having to fight for it, or, as New Yorker Cowtan later suggested, the gleeful shouting may have signified nothing more than the relief of exhausted soldiers glad their march was finally nearing an end.[38]

President Lincoln and Secretary Stanton, meanwhile, were waiting back at Fort Monroe late that afternoon for whatever news they could get regarding what was transpiring across Hampton Roads. For reasons that remain unclear, Wool never updated them on the progress of his advance. Stanton dispatched a couple of telegrams that morning when he and the president returned on the *Baltimore*—one to his assistant secretary, Peter H. Watson, in Washington, and the other to Maj. Gen. McClellan on the Peninsula. The messages notified the bureaucrat and the general that troops had landed to take the city, but "[w]e shall await the result on Norfolk."[39]

And wait they did, "almost overcome" with fearful anxiety at hearing nothing from Wool "[a]ll day long." The men could on occasion hear the sound of firing skipping across the water and even spotted smoke from either the burning bridge spanning Tanner's creek or the fired barracks. "They could not but feel . . . they

37 Evacuation and Occupation of Norfolk," Philadelphia *Press*, May 13, 1862, 1.

38 Chase to "Nettie," May 11, 1862, in "Diary," Chase Papers, LC; Wool to Stanton, May 14, 1862, Letter Book, Wool Papers, NYSA. Also found in "Report of Maj. Gen. John E. Wool, U.S. Army, and congratulations from President Lincoln," May 12, 1862, *OR* 11/1:634-35; Cowtan, *National Zouaves*, 78. Cram's report put the time for Wool's arrival at the entrenched camp at about 5:00 p.m. He also reported that the Confederates had left 30 spiked artillery pieces behind. Cram, "Report," May 31, 1862, Wool Papers, NYSA. The colonel's map depicts the distance from the entrenched artillery line/camp to Norfolk as about five miles.

39 Stanton to P. H. Watson, & to George B. McClellan, both May 10, 1862, U.S. Congress, *Report of the Joint Committee on the Conduct of the War*, 3 vols. (Wilmington, NC, 1998), 1:325.

were in a measure responsible," thought Wool's aide Cannon, "as they had consented to it."[40]

Lincoln did, however, encounter the returning Mansfield, sent back from Ocean's View by Wool to retrieve the additional regiments. According to Col. Joseph Carr, the meeting did not sit well with the exhausted and anxious president.

"While our troops were absent on this expedition," recalled Carr, "General Mansfield and myself were summoned to Fort Monroe by President Lincoln."

"Colonel Carr, where is your command?" asked the president.

"At Camp Hamilton, sir."

"Why are you not on that side at Norfolk?"

"I am awaiting orders."

Lincoln turned to Mansfield. "Why are you here?" he demanded. "Why not on the other side?"

"I am ordered to the fort by General Wool," replied Mansfield.

"With vehement action," recalled Carr, President Lincoln "threw his tall hat on the floor, and, uttering strongly his disapproval and disappointment, he said finally: "Send me some one who can write." When Col. Cannon appeared, "Lincoln dictated an order to General Wool requiring that troops at Camp Hamilton be at once ordered to Norfolk, and that the troops already there be pushed rapidly forward."[41]

Since Mansfield had just returned from Ocean View, it is likely the president asked him other questions about the ongoing operation. The general would have known that the burning of the Indian Pole Bridge had stymied progress, and that Wool was moving his little army by the longer route. Chase later mentioned in passing that "the President had been greatly alarmed for our safety by the report of Genl. Mansfield as he went by to Newport News."[42]

Beyond that, there was no other word.

* * *

40 Cannon, *Personal Reminiscences*, 160.

41 Joseph B. Carr, "Operations of 1861 about Fort Monroe," in *B&L*, 2:152. The 10th New York may have been part of Carr's brigade, but it had already crossed Hampton Roads and was marching on Norfolk. Carr said that later that day he did receive an order to take his troops to Norfolk.

42 Chase to "Nettie," May 11, 1862, in "Diary," Chase Papers, LC.

Confusion and anxiety ran rampant throughout that long day in Norfolk as well. The evacuation continued even as Union soldiers landed at Ocean View. The men of the Norfolk Light Artillery Blues, sent to Norfolk from Sewell's Point the day before, were gathered in their former militia headquarters by 8:00 a.m. The regiment assembled by 11:00 a.m. and proceeded to the Norfolk & Petersburg Railroad depot to board a departing train. An hour later, recalled one of their number, "the whistle blew . . . handkerchiefs waved . . . we gave a parting cheer, and bade farewell to glorious old Norfolk to return! When?"[43]

The Jackson Grays also escaped on a train. After their aborted attempt to check the invading Yankees at the crossroads marked by Denby's church, the Grays marched from Tanner's Creek to Norfolk and then kept marching, right through the city and onto the ferry to cross the Elizabeth River to Portsmouth. "The boat was crowded with soldiers, citizens and women," wrote William Stewart, captain of the Jackson Grays, a part of the 7th Battalion Virginia Reserves. "Two pretty girls with whom I was quite well acquainted, said 'Ar'n't you ashamed to desert us?'" Stewart confessed to being "abashed" about leaving Norfolk's citizens. He recalled his speech earlier in the war when a contingent of young ladies, including these two, presented the Grays with their unit flag. He blamed the retreat on "military orders and . . . superior authority, for really it was a trying ordeal to leave our home and friends with little hope of returning."

Once in Portsmouth, Capt. Stewart described conditions as not much different than those he had found on the other side of the river—excitement and commotion in every direction. At the courthouse, where the company paused to rest, the men assisted in destroying "barrels of ardent spirits to prevent the enemy from getting it, and for a time the gutters on Court Street ran [with whiskey]." The lack of specific orders from a higher command was worrisome and stressful, and left the captain with no choice but "to act upon my own responsibility." His "fagged out" men weren't "capable of a long march to escape the Federal forces," who were expected to arrive via ferry from Norfolk at any time. Stewart convinced "the provost marshal to give us transportation on the last train out of the city, and we rode upon flat cars of this train to Suffolk." The last of the naval stores that could be taken out of the Gosport Navy Yard were also aboard that train. The man in charge of the shipment, William H. Peters, the "naval store keeper" for the yard,

43 Walters, *Norfolk Blues*, 19. The Norfolk & Petersburg Railroad ran south out of Norfolk, crossed the Eastern Branch of the Elizabeth River, and turned west to Suffolk. Northwest of Suffolk, the railroad crossed a trestle bridge over the Blackwater River, which was burned behind it, according to a note by Kenneth Wiley.

continued with the supplies to Charlotte, North Carolina, while the officers proceeded via Weldon to Richmond.[44]

At least Peters, Stewart, and Walters had a train to ride. Louis Merz of the West Point Guards had to walk with his battalion after doing morning drill. The unit got its marching orders at noon and was formed up and on the road in just 30 minutes. Pvt. Merz noted that "some of the sick went ahead of us."

The heat affected the Confederates abandoning the endangered city as much as it did the advancing Federals. Like their counterparts, they also "began to draw off ballast, overcoats, shirts and finally knapsacks went overboard to lighten the fatigued soldiers to march in the middle of the day so hot [and] so unpleasant," recalled Merz. Eventually, the regiment came to a rest stop along with other units gathering around Maj. Gen. Huger and his staff. It was here they learned for the first time that the Federals had reached the outskirts of Norfolk. After a short rest, Merz and his company assumed command of the rear guard of the regiment and continued marching "in the moonshine, while in the direction of Norfolk the horizon seemed to be on fire."[45]

About 4:00 p.m., those left in the city began destroying what could not be carried off. Cotton was burned near the Railroad Depot, and some 250 boxes of tobacco were thrown into the river. The destruction paled in comparison to the blazing light visible in the distant sky just above Portsmouth on the left bank of the Elizabeth River: the Gosport Navy Yard was on fire.[46]

The night before, Lt. William H. Parker, erstwhile commander of a gunboat then under construction, warned yard commander Capt. Sydney S. Lee that the enemy was rapidly approaching. Lee seems not to have heeded his warning. At daybreak, orders were issued to evacuate the yard. "We set fire to the buildings and ships, and tried to blow up the dry dock; in fact destroyed everything we could. I set my vessel on fire with much regret," lamented Parker. "A few more days and she would have been ready to go to Richmond. We continued the work of destruction until we heard the Federal troops were in Norfolk, and then took our departure in

44 Stewart, *A Pair of Blankets*, 64; William H. Peters, "Norfolk Navy Yard: Abandonment by Federal Authorities, April 20, 1861, and same by Confederates on May 10, 1862," Aug. 4, 1891, Hampton Roads Naval Museum, Naval History and Heritage Command (NHHC), 13. Peters was the captain's clerk for the navy yard.

45 Merz, May 10, 1862, in *Diary of Private Louis Merz*, 36.

46 Clipping "The Evacuation and Occupation," Norfolk *Day Book*, May 12, 1862, in "Virginia Gordan Scrapbook," NPL. The *New York Herald* reprinted part of the article in "News from Norfolk and Portsmouth," May 19, 1862, 1; Richmond *Whig*, May 14, 1862, 3.

Alexander Gardner created this photograph of the Gosport Navy Yard ruins in late 1864. Artist Alfred Waud is seated on a stone from the destroyed dry dock. *Library of Congress*

the cars for Weldon where we arrived the same evening at 8 o'clock." The *Norfolk Day Book* later reported the fires started about 10:00 a.m.[47]

As Parker makes clear, the evacuating Confederates focused considerable attention on the navy yard. The dry-dock was mined, much of the machinery that had not been sent off to Richmond was rendered inoperable, and, except for the hospital, most of the buildings were burned. According to a local paper, two or three buildings "near the [yard's] wall" were "not fired through the fear that the flames might be communicated to Gosport."

"An employee in the yard, ever since the war commenced, estimates the loss there at six million [dollars] or more," reported Petersburg's *Daily Express* on May 12. The paper added that the dry dock, valued at five million dollars at the time, was destroyed, but the Richmond *Whig*, which "confidently" expected the repossession

47 Parker, *Recollections*, 279; "The Evacuation and Occupation," Norfolk *Day Book*, May 12, 1862, in "Virginia Gordan Scrapbook," NPL.

of Norfolk, disputed that claim. "The gates were blown off, and the stocks so injured that it would require . . . eighteen months to put it in status quo." However some "very valuable machinery, and some $200,000 worth of copper," had not been destroyed.[48]

Naval personnel rowed out to the little Confederate fleet and set fire to the *William Selden*, *Harmony*, *Kahukee*, *Plymouth*, and *Pilot Boy*, as well as smaller craft such as the new *Escambia* and *Elizabeth*—a total of 15 schooners, a side-wheel steamboat, and a screw steamer. Two of the burning vessels floated dangerously close to Norfolk, threatening to set the city's docks on fire, but firemen successfully towed the flaming ships back into the main channel. The next day, the navy yard was described as nothing but black walls and tall chimneys.[49]

The Petersburg *Daily Express* reported "universal regret" over the loss of the gunboats and their "armaments and stores. . . . These could easily have been carried to Richmond, passing the mouth of James River, under the protection of the *Merrimac*," editorialized the paper. "Four other gunboats, on the stocks, and unfinished, were also consigned to flames. The splendid transport *Wm. Selden* and a number of smaller tugs were all burnt. These too . . . could have been carried to Richmond without risk." The editor was apparently unaware that the Union ironclad *Galena* had already moved up the James River. The newspaperman mocked the Davis administration by adding, "[W]e presume the Confederate government has more money than it well knows what to do with, and desires to give employment to artisans in building new vessels."[50]

Throughout the day William W. Lamb, Norfolk's energetic and resourceful mayor, worked to delay the oncoming Union forces. Norfolk and the surrounding area had been operating under martial law since President Davis' March 5 proclamation. The executive order included, among other provisions, enlisting "the whole male population" for military service, sending women and children as

48 Norfolk *Day Book*, in "News from Norfolk and Portsmouth," *New York Herald*, May 19, 1862, 1; Petersburg *Daily Express*, May 12, 1862, in Richmond *Whig*, May 13, 1862, 2. The destruction of the yard and contents, in 2019 dollars, would be $149,200,000 for the navy yard, $124,400,000 for the dry dock, and almost $5,000,000 for the copper.

49 Thomas J. Wertenbaker, *Norfolk: Historic Southern Port* (Durham, NC, 1931), 239; John W. H. Porter, *A Record of Events in Norfolk County, Virginia, from April 19th, 1861, to May 10th, 1862, with a History of the Soldiers and Sailors of Norfolk County, Norfolk City and Portsmouth Who Served in the Confederate States Army and Navy* (Portsmouth, VA, 1892), 32; William Smith to Louis Goldsborough, May 18, 1862, in Robert M. Browning, Jr., *From Cape Charles to Cape Fear: The North Atlantic Blockading Squadron During the Civil War* (Tuscaloosa, AL, 1993), 52n.

50 Petersburg *Daily Express*, May 12, 1862, in Richmond *Whig*, May 13, 1862, 3.

well as "all merchandise, cotton, tobacco, etc." not needed by the military out of the city, and putting people of questionable loyalty to the Southern cause in prison. Many people remained in Norfolk after the final troops withdrew, so the proclamation's provisions had not been strictly enforced. One reason might have been that the city's mayor was also named as provost marshal to enforce Davis's edict and keep the peace.[51]

The mayor and his two councils reverted to their civil roles when Confederate commander Huger discovered Union forces were landing at Ocean View. The time left for evacuation was almost over, as was the Army's role. Others would need to ensure the safety of the city and its inhabitants from the Yankee invaders. Hence, sometime that morning Huger sent a note to Mayor Lamb advising him that, with the departure of troops, he could no longer defend the city and was turning over Norfolk "to yourself and its Civil officers."

Lamb promptly called for a meeting of the Select and Common Councils. They met that morning, presumably jointly, and agreed to inform the Union commander that the city would be surrendered peacefully. The proclamation read in part that the top two officers of both councils

> hereby appointed a committee to co-operate with the mayor in conferring with the Federal Military commander . . . and assuring him that no resistance can or will be made to the occupation of the city by the United States forces—but that the citizens expect and claim protection to persons and property during such occupation.[52]

Mayor Lamb and the councils' delegates planned to meet with the Union commander before he and his soldiers entered the city. About two hours before the Yankees arrived at the abandoned Confederate encampment, however, Huger, through a commissary officer, informed the mayor that much of the Confederate-owned provisions left in the city would be turned over to the local government.

Maj. W. H. Smith wrote Lamb that he would be handing over all the provisions for distribution to "the poor & needy of our community," especially "our own

51 Jefferson Davis proclamation, Feb. 27, 1862, and Judah P. Benjamin order, March 5, 1862, in James D. Richardson, ed., *A Compilation of the Messages and Papers of the Confederacy Including Diplomatic Correspondence, 1861-1865*, 2 vols. (Nashville, TN, 1904), 1:219. Secretary of War Benjamin suggested Lamb's appointment because he was "a zealous friend of our cause."

52 Benjamin Huger to William W. Lamb & Proclamation of Norfolk Councils, May 10, 1862, both in Wool Papers, NYSA; "The Capture of Norfolk," *New York Times*, May 13, 1862, 1.

absent volunteers." Pressed by time, explained Major Smith, it was impossible to prepare

> an inventory of my stock, but I have several hundred barrels of flour at the Tobacco Warehouse & also at the store of Odom & Clements. At the store of W. D. Reynolds & Co. there is a large quantity of bacon, & in the building occupied by me you will find many articles of need for the needy. All is at your service . . . & I hope you will be able to carry out the wishes of our general.[53]

The implication was clear: the enemy would confiscate any Confederate property still in the warehouses when they arrived. Presumably Lamb organized his councils and other citizens to distribute the valuable stores, which offered another incentive for him to delay the arrival of the Yankees as long as possible.

With Norfolk hanging in the chaotic limbo between the departure of Confederate authorities and the immanent arrival of enemy forces, Mayor Lamb and his council delegation climbed into "two miserable hacks, with lean and horribly groomed horses," one of which had belonged to Maj. Gen. Huger, and rode to the edge of the city to await the commander of the approaching Union forces.[54]

* * *

President Lincoln had had enough of waiting. He thrived on knowing what was happening and could barely tolerate being left in the dark about how the invasion force was faring. Brig. Gen. Mansfield's sketchy report about events on the far side of Hampton Roads was all he had to go on, so the chief executive decided it was time to return to Ocean View and learn firsthand of Wool's progress in taking Norfolk.

Secretary Stanton accompanied Lincoln on the short trip and the pair arrived at the beach about 4:00 pm. Once the president and war secretary went ashore, Lt. Col. Cram met up with them and passed along the information he had, including that "the bridge having been burnt, General Wool was pushing towards the intrenched camp and that I had sent him artillery." The presence of the dignitaries "evidently encouraged and stimulated all to exert every effort for the success of the enterprise," recalled Cram. "Such personal participation as exhibited on this

53 W. H. Smith to Lamb, May 10, 1862, Wool Papers, NYSA.

54 Philadelphia *Press*, "Five Miles from Norfolk," May 13, 1862, 1.

Brig. Gen. Egbert Viele made his headquarters at the government Custom House in Norfolk. The building was completed in 1859 and still stands.

Author

occasion by these high functionaries of the Nation, could not fail to be productive of beneficial results." The engineer could not provide much in the way of updated information, however, so after about an hour with nothing more coming in, "the President and Secretary Stanton returned to Fort Monroe, anxiously waiting the results." On his way back to the fort, Lincoln may have been able to see the *Virginia* in the distance at the upper end of Hampton Roads.[55]

* * *

A missing flag was the first indication to those aboard the *Virginia* that something wasn't right that morning.

The Rebel ironclad had not stirred all day and had remained anchored near Craney Island at the mouth of the Elizabeth River "with steam up" since 8:00 a.m. With little to do, her commander, Josiah Tattnall, awaited Maj. Gen. Huger's promise to signal him (perhaps by firing a gun, or perhaps by some other means) when the city was finally abandoned. Until then, Tattnall remained unaware of what was transpiring in Norfolk.[56]

About ten that morning, someone aboard observed that "the flag was not flying on the Sewell's Point battery and thus it appeared to have been abandoned," was how Tattnall later reported the discovery. "I dispatched Lieutenant J. P. [John

55 Cram, "Report," May 31, 1862, Wool Papers, NYSA.

56 "Abstract Log of the USS *Dacotah*," May 10, 1862, *ORN* 7:334.

Pembroke] Jones, the flag-lieutenant, to Craney Island, where the Confederate flag was still flying, and he there learned that a large force of the enemy had landed on the bay shore and was marching rapidly on Norfolk; that the Sewell's Point battery was abandoned and our troops were retreating." Tattnall sent Jones by rowboat to Norfolk, which was about four miles upstream, "to confer with General Huger and Captain Lee."[57]

The cutter's crew docked first at the navy yard. "The officer [Jones] got out of the boat and went up into the yard," one of the sailors recalled, adding that "very soon he came back and we rowed to Campbell's wharf in Norfolk, where the officer got out and walked to the Custom House, while we rowed around to Town Point; someone standing on the wharf said the enemy was coming into the City and was then on Church street. From Town Point we rowed to Pinners Point and thence to our ship."[58]

Once back aboard the ironclad, Jones reported to an astonished Tattnall that the Gosport Navy Yard was aflame, "and that all its officers had left by railroad." When he reached Norfolk, he continued, he discovered that Maj. Gen. Huger "and all the other Army officers had gone, that the enemy were within a half a mile of the city, and that the mayor was treating for its surrender." Tattnall, his men, and their beloved ship were on their own.[59]

* * *

While Tattnall contemplated his unappealing options off Craney Island, the small column of Union troops with Chase, Viele, and Wool in the lead had marched only a short distance beyond the abandoned Confederate artillery line and camp when they spotted a few church spires and house tops in the dim distance: Norfolk. A short distance ahead was a "small, white frame house" on the side of the road, wrote Viele, "in front of which a man is vigorously waving a white flag." As the brigadier later recalled, "At the extreme limits of the city . . . a large deputation, headed by the mayor and municipal councils, [appeared] with a flag of truce." The group conducted Maj. Gen. Wool and the others, so covered in dust "that their best friends would fail to recognize them," into the house. "The Mayor

57 "Report of Flag-Officer [Josiah] Tattnall, C.S. Navy" to Stephen R. Mallory, May 14, 1862, *ORN* 7:336.

58 Curtis, *Famous Battle*, 16.

59 Tattnall, "Report," May 14, 1862, *ORN* 7:336.

HARPER'S WEEKLY.
A JOURNAL OF CIVILIZATION
NEW YORK, SATURDAY, MAY 24, 1862.

The front cover of *Harper's Weekly* on May 24, 1862, presented five sketches by Theodore Russell Davis relating to Norfolk's surrender.

HarpWeek

and committee of the Councils rise and bow," and after the action was reciprocated, "a general introduction takes place."[60]

A *Harper's Weekly* correspondent with the group described the scene inside as "unique in the extreme." The reporter also took note of the dust-covered and tired officers, with "Mr. Chase's fine features funnily disguised with the pulverized dust." Both Mayor Lamb and the councilmen appeared anxious, while "the proprietor of the shanty 'sans habit,' [stood with his] fists in his pockets and quid in his cheek." Lamb informed Wool that Norfolk had been evacuated and explained that he intended to turn over the city to him.[61]

It was then that the clever Lamb "performed a most skillful ruse to gain time for the Confederates to secure their retreat from the city," observed Viele, who quickly became disgusted by his commander's naivete regarding the mayor's purpose. "The mayor, with all the formality of a medieval warden, appeared with a bunch of rusty keys and formidable roll of papers, which he . . . read with the utmost deliberation [before] delivering the 'keys of the city,'" he explained. "The reading of the documents," he continued,

> which embraced . . . a little of everything that could have the remotest bearing upon the subject and exhaust the longest possible space of time in reading—was protracted until

60 Viele, "A Trip with Lincoln," 821.

61 "Five Miles from Norfolk," Philadelphia *Press*, May 13, 1862, 1; "Norfolk Repossessed," *Harper's Weekly*, May 24, 1862, 327; "The Capture of Norfolk," *New York Times*, May 13, 1862, 1.

> nearly dark. . . . [M]eanwhile the Confederates were hurrying with their artillery and stores over the ferry to Portsmouth, cutting the water-pipes and flooding the public buildings, setting fire to the navy yard, and having their own way generally, while our General was listening in the most innocent and complacent manner to the long rigmarole so ingeniously prepared by the mayor and skillfully interlarded with fulsome personal eulogium upon himself.[62]

Wool, who seems not to have shared with President Lincoln or Secretary Stanton that he fell for a ruse that delayed his entry into the city, related instead that he had accepted the surrender of Norfolk "agreeably to the city's terms . . . so far as related to the civil rights of the citizens."[63]

Once Lamb finished, "a general conversation" ensued amongst the participants. Norfolk's representatives emphasized "that they had discountenanced, in every way possible," all [suggestions] for the destruction of private property," wrote one correspondent, and decried the firing of the Tanner's Creek bridge "as an utterly useless and unauthorized act. The mayor declared his strongest determination to do everything in his power [to preserve] the public peace and social order."[64]

How much time passed is unknown, but it was enough for Secretary Chase, his patience exhausted, to intervene. Chase, recalled Viele, cut to the heart of the matter and "suggested that any further parley was unnecessary, and that we should proceed to the city." The mayor, however, had "another well-devised plan" to delay matters and insisted the Union leaders join him and the other citizens in the carriages for the ride into the city. The troops, meanwhile, would "remain where they were" at the encampment some miles outside town. "Falling readily into this second little trap, the General accepted, and we were driven to the city hall," explained Viele, albeit at a middling pace. Wool rode with Lamb and some members of the deputation, while Viele joined other council members in another carriage. Wool's "body guard" of horsemen accompanied the party.[65]

62 Viele, "A Trip with Lincoln," 821. The "rusty keys" were for the former U.S. Custom House, the post office, and the city jail. "Five Miles from Norfolk," Philadelphia *Press*, May 13, 1862, 1.

63 Wool to Stanton, May 14, 1862, *OR* 11/1:634-35.

64 "The Capture of Norfolk," *New York Times*, May 13, 1862, 1.

65 Viele, "A Trip with Lincoln," 821-22; Chase to "Nettie," May 11, 1862, in "Diary," Chase Papers, LC. So glacial was the pace of the carriages that three reporters preceded them by half a mile and became "the first 'northern men'" to enter the city. "Evacuation and Occupation of

"The inhabitants seemed to be much frightened along the route," wrote the Philadelphia *Press* reporter, with all "doors . . . bolted and barred, and . . . window shutters locked. The families generally had retired to upper stories, and the women leaned out of the windows with their children in their arms" watching the carriages and mounted Union troops move through. "Some few ladies so far forgot themselves as to throw gloves at the troops and spit at them," he continued. "But generally the most excellent order prevailed throughout."[66]

The carriages and horsemen stopped in front of City Hall, where they climbed the granite steps to stand for a short time under the portico. From there, the group proceeded to a large room on the second floor, followed by a group of curious citizens. Mayor Lamb assured Wool that the citizens meant "no harm or obstruction." Turning to the group, he briefly explained "that General Wool and staff must enter alone . . . to draw up the articles by which they were to be protected" and "[afforded] more privileges than even he had hoped for. The crowd cheered," wrote on eyewitness, "and the steps of the building were vacated in an instant, and the party, weary and dusty, entered the chamber accompanied by two or three officials only."[67]

Once inside, Lamb produced more "rusty keys" and made another formal speech. "[S]everal thousand people, some of them in butternut and gray, assembled in front of the building," Viele wrote. While Wool listened to the "high formalities, Mr. Chase . . . wrote an order assigning the command of the city to myself as military governor." Wool had little choice but to sign it.[68]

Wool also issued a general order to guide the Union occupation of the city that "carefully protected rights and civil privileges" of citizens, mandated preservation of order, and prevented soldiers from entering Norfolk except by order or "written permission of his Brigade or Regimental Commander." Any Federal soldier "who

---

Norfolk," Philadelphia *Press*, May 13, 1862, 1. John W. H. Porter, son of the naval constructor of the CSS *Virginia*, claimed many years later that Wool "took particular care not to approach [it] until he was certain that the last Confederate troops had left. . . . Is any better evidence wanted than the fact that it took him from 9 o'clock a.m. to 5:00 p.m. to march [seven miles] from Ocean View to the intrenchments back of Norfolk?" What Porter did not take into consideration was the heat, the condition of the Union soldiers, Wool's long route of march, and his ignorance of whether the city had been evacuated, or whether the enemy was still present and willing to fight. Porter, *Record of Events*, 245.

66 "Five Miles from Norfolk," Philadelphia *Press*, May 13, 1862, 1.

67 Wertenbaker, *Norfolk*, 146; ibid.; "Norfolk Repossessed," *Harper's Weekly*, May 24, 1862, 327. City Hall, built in 1847, still stands as the General Douglas MacArthur Memorial.

68 Viele, "A Trip with Lincoln," 821-22.

may trespass upon the rights of any of the inhabitants" would be summarily punished.[69]

With that, Chase explained, he and Wool climbed back into Huger's former carriage to return, along with their escort (and possibly some of the accompanying reporters) to Ocean View. Brig. Gen. Viele was left in charge or, as he put it, Chase, "bidding me good-bye . . . took the General by the arm and departed, leaving me the solitary occupant of the city hall, without a soldier within two miles, and with not even an aide-de-camp to assist me." Viele rightly adjudged his position as "precarious." In the growing darkness, a "noisy mob surrounded the building, some of the more excitable exhibiting a sort of bravado by firing pistols in the air." The *Virginia's* probable return to a position "off the city," worried Viele, "would certainly complicate matters disagreeably." Occupying the other side of the river "with troops, as speedily as possible" to prevent supplies "from going to the *Merrimac*, and to save the navy-yard from total destruction," he continued, was a matter of no small moment.[70]

By this time a crowd of "some five thousand or more . . . assembled around City Hall. It is a motley group, concluded one reporter, made up of "white men, white women, white children, negroes of all classes, ages, and shades of color, half-breeds, and hosts of small picaninnies." The mob was "very much excited" and Mayor Lamb had little choice but to address the angry citizens.[71]

According to the *New York Times* reporter, Lamb confined himself "mainly to a recital of the incidents of the day, he said that he had had nothing to do with deciding the result; that had been done by the superior authorities." Norfolk's citizens, he continued, "had been deserted by their friends, and all the city authorities could do was to obtain the best terms possible for themselves and their property." The mayor assured them that "in this he had been successful." Gen. Wool, he continued,

> had conceded everything they had asked, and had guaranteed the preservation of order. He enjoined upon the citizens the maintenance of peace and quiet, and exhorted them to abstain from all acts of violence and disorder. If the decision had rested with him he would

69 Cram, "Report," May 31, 1862, Wool Papers, NYSA.

70 Chase to "Nettie," May 11, 1862, in "Diary," Chase Papers, LC; Viele, "A Trip with Lincoln," 822.

71 "Five Miles from Norfolk," Philadelphia *Press*, May 13, 1862, 1.

have defended the city to the last man; but their Government had decided differently, and they must yield to its authority.[72]

After cheering these remarks, the crowd defiantly raised three enthusiastic cheers for Jefferson Davis and, "with less heartiness," three groans for Abraham Lincoln. In his excitement, a city policeman fired off a pistol. To Viele, who had stepped up to a second story window to look at the crowd, it appeared as though the policeman was aiming at the new military governor. After the man apologized for accidently shooting "in a moment of . . . excitement," and explained the gun wasn't loaded, "Viele dismissed him with some good and wholesome advice."[73]

With the crowd having been calmed, Viele appointed the *New York Times* correspondent as his aide and sent him with orders asking that troops be sent to Norfolk as soon as possible. Viele also penned his own proclamation banning the sale of liquor, promising that nothing would be done to disturb private associations and domestic quiet, but that disorder "and disrespect to the Government" would result in "immediate arrest." Occupying soldiers, he assured Norfolk, would protect "the property and individual rights of the citizenry."[74]

Most of the troops who made the march from Ocean View bivouacked at the abandoned Confederate camp. The 10th New York's Charles Cowtan wrote that "guards were thrown out, fires built and coffee and salt pork were soon emitting their savory odors—both officers and men quickly afterwards losing themselves in dreamless sleep on the cool bosom of mother earth."

For some of the Zouaves and men of other regiments, the rest ended much too soon. When Viele's new aide, the unnamed *Times* reporter, arrived with the orders to hurry troops into Norfolk, the 16th Massachusetts fell in and set out for the city and "were the first regiment which entered Norfolk . . . at seven o'clock in the evening without any opposition." Little was said other than "some hearty greetings of the stars and stripes." The 16th's chaplain, Arthur Fuller, claimed the regiment went across the river to Portsmouth that first night, but Company F's captain, Charles Robinson Johnson, recorded that the men assumed guard duty in Norfolk, and crossed over to Portsmouth the following day. Col. Powell T. Wyman, the

72 "The Capture of Norfolk," *New York Times*, May 13, 1862, 1.

73 "Five Miles from Norfolk," Philadelphia *Press*, May 13, 1862, 1.

74 Viele, "A Trip with Lincoln," 822; Thomas P. Kettell, *History of the Great Rebellion* (Hartford, CT, 1865), 257. Viele served as military governor until October 1863.

commander of the 16th Massachusetts, was appointed Portsmouth's military commander.[75]

"Two companies of the Tenth, D and E, Capts. Miner and Patrick, also were ordered forward to the city," recalled Cowtan. Under Maj. Missing's command, they entered about dark, with drums and fifes playing" and established "headquarters . . . at the Custom House. Patrols . . . and details . . . to guard important points" were immediately dispatched. Mayor Lamb turned over "the official transfer of Confederate property" to the acting provost marshal, Capt. Patrick.[76]

Part of the 99th New York also came to Viele's rescue. Lt. Richard Goldwaite of Company B wrote that his company "marched into the city and hoisted the Old Flag." Lt. Col. Weiss claimed in his postwar remembrance that his 20th New York first occupied the Gosport Navy Yard, and encountered "no resistance" marching "through Norfolk to Gosport and [over the river] to the great navy yard of the country." His regiment, he asserted, "has the real claim to the distinction of first entering and occupying the most important and greatest seaport of the government, which gave confidence to the North of final success."[77]

Crossing the river had not been an easy task. Confederates had taken almost all of the boats to the Portsmouth side. It was a "quandary, [b]ut the hardy seamen of the Union Coast guard [the 99th New York] quickly man a barge, and hastening to the river, seize a small flat steam ferry-boat, and bring it to the wharf." The little boat could carry only about 100 soldiers, but it chugged over to the navy yard, where they were greeted "with friendly demonstrations by many ladies and gentlemen—one of the ladies bearing an American flag." The ferry continued back

75 Arthur Buckminster Fuller to unk., May 12, 1862, in Fuller, *Chaplain Fuller*, 250; Charles Johnson to "Nellie," May 13, 1862, in Eisenberg & Hammerson, eds., "*If I Am Alive,*" 69.

76 Cowtan, *National Zouaves*, 77-78; Seville, *Delaware Volunteers*, 41. Cowtan added that some "of the Mounted Rifles [were used] this first night on the environs."

77 F. W. Ritschy, in Corell, *History of the Naval Brigade*, n.p.; Richard Goldwaite & Ellen Goldwaite, *A Handful of Providence: The Civil War Letters of Lt. Richard Goldwaite, New York Volunteers, and Ellen Goldwaite*, Marti Skipper & Jane Taylor, eds. (Jefferson, NC, 2004), 109; Weiss, *Reminiscences*, 118-19. Based on Goldwaite's description, it is uncertain where the 99th's national colors were "hoisted." Samuel P. Bates, in *Pennsylvania Volunteers*, 2:286, wrote that the national flag of the 58th Pennsylvania "was taken to Norfolk, and unfurled upon the Custom House, where it floated in triumph while the regiment remained." The National Zouaves, 10th New York Volunteers, also claimed their regiment's national flag flew over the Custom House, according to that unit's historian Charles W. Cowtan ."The command halted for an instant at the Custom House and saluted with three rousing cheers the National color of the regiment, which had been hoisted on that building by the detachment sent into the city the previous evening." Cowtan, *National Zouaves*, 79.

and forth across the river in the light of the burning yard and ships blazing on the water.[78]

John Nash, Portsmouth's mayor, surrendered the town without incident. Portsmouth's new military governor, Col. Powell Wyman of the 16th Massachusetts, assured its citizens "that the Yankees came not to destroy property, but to restore order; to relieve an oppressed people; and reinstate that g-a-l-r-i-o-u-s flag which had been so long concealed from [their] view," sneered the Richmond *Daily Dispatch*. "Much other gasconade and highfalutin kind of sentiment were indulged in, but we have quoted enough."[79]

Wyman wisely took precautions to keep the peace. Three of the 16th Massachusetts' companies patrolled "the city and suburbs," escorting "every citizen to his house" who was found outside "after nine o'clock." He worried that "some of the desperate secessionist[s]" might try to burn the city or "that the enemy might strike a blow as a parting farewell." His concerns were for naught, and everything remained quiet.[80]

"[B]y the time the troops arrived," wrote a relieved Viele, "the moon had risen, and by its light they were placed in position." The 20th New York had arrived at the navy yard "too late to rescue it from almost complete destruction, but it cut off the *Merrimac* from any supplies from either side of the river."

It was "long after midnight" before Viele had deployed the soldiers around Norfolk, the navy yard, and Portsmouth. By then Norfolk's military governor had secured a room at the city's Atlantic Hotel. The proprietor closed the 200-room establishment since only three boarders remained after the Confederate officers fled the city. The vacant rooms quickly filled with Union officers and newspaper reporters. With everything settling into place, Viele took the time to eat a late supper of steak and chicken with the reporters.[81]

* * *

78 "Five Miles from Norfolk," Philadelphia *Press*, May 13, 1862, 1.

79 "Latest from Norfolk and Portsmouth," Richmond *Daily Dispatch,* May 16, 1862. Portsmouth's mayor, John Nash, had been in office just a month when the Union troops arrived. He was a prominent businessman and civic leader of many years as well as an alderman and city magistrate before and after the war. Edward Pollock, *Sketch Book of Portsmouth, Va: Its People and its Trade* (Portsmouth, VA, 1886), 87.

80 Johnson to "Nellie," May 13, 1862, in *"If I Am Alive,"* 69.

81 Viele, "A Trip with Lincoln," 822; "Five Miles from Norfolk," Philadelphia *Press*, May 13, 1862.

Brig. Gen. Viele need not have worried about the *Virginia* steaming up the Elizabeth to threaten Union-held Norfolk and Portsmouth. That was the last thing on Tattnall's mind. His only concern was how he was going to save his ironclad.

By the time Lt. Jones reported to Tattnall that the *Virginia* (which was still near Sewell's Point) had been deserted by the military without Huger bothering to notify him, the Rebel flag was no longer flying over Craney Island. "[A]ll the other batteries on the river had been abandoned," wrote a disgusted Tattnall. "It was now 7 o'clock in the evening, and this unexpected information rendered prompt measures for the safety of the *Virginia*." "[W]hy [Tattnall] was not 'signalled' I do not know," wrote Lt. W. H. Parker, former commander of the gunboat *Beaufort*.[82]

John Taylor Wood, another lieutenant aboard the *Virginia*, noted that the evacuation of Norfolk left Tattnall with just two options. "We might have run the blockade of the forts and done some damage to the shipping there and at the mouth of the York River," he explained, "provided they did not get out of our way, for, with our great weight and low rate of speed, the enemy's transports would have gone where we could not have followed them." However, the *Monitor* and other warships "would have engaged us with every advantage, playing around us as rabbits around a sloth, and the end would have been the certain loss of the vessel."[83]

Like his predecessor Franklin Buchanan, Tattnall steadfastly resisted that suicidal choice. Soon after taking command of the *Virginia*, Tattnall consulted his friend regarding sailing the ship out to sea, and asked Buchanan about "the character and power of the ship. He expressed the distinct opinion then . . . that she was unseaworthy, and . . . not sufficiently buoyant, and that in a common sea she would founder." Even if the *Virginia* could get around the tip of the Peninsula without being blown out of the water by the guns of Fort Monroe and Fort Wool, she "could not have stood an ordinary storm in Chesapeake Bay," observed ship's gunner Richard Curtis.[84]

That left one other option: The ironclad's safety could only be found up the treacherous and twisting James River. Tattnall decided he would try to get her there, but the *Virginia's* draft would have be reduced by some five feet. "The pilots had assured me that they could take the ship, with a draft of 18 feet, to within 40 miles of Richmond," Tattnall explained in his report. The "chief pilot, Mr.

82 Tattnall, "Report," May 14, 1862, *ORN* 7:336; Parker, *Recollections*, 280.

83 Wood, "First Fight," *B&L*, 1:709.

84 Josiah Tattnall, "Submitted Defense," July 19, 1862, *ORN* 7:793; Curtis, *Famous Battle*, 17.

[William] Parrish, and his chief assistant, Mr. [George] Wright, had asserted [this] again and again; and on the afternoon of the 7th, in my cabin, in the presence of Commodore [George] Hollins and Captain [Isaac] Sterrett, in reply to a question of mine, they emphatically declared their ability to do so."

Based on those assurances, and after consulting his officers, Tattnall "determined to lighten the ship at once and run up the river for the protection of Richmond." At fighting weight, the *Virginia* had a draft of a bit more than 23 feet, which was much too deep to cross the shoals up the James. Her draft, the pilots assured Tattnall, could be reduced by removing some 300 tons of pig-iron ballast and everything else of nonessential value that kept the *Virginia's* bow and stern underwater. It was a laborious challenge, but it would allow the ironclad to make it safely up the James.[85]

Tattnall called all hands on deck, explained what they faced, and informed them of his hope to get up the river before the enemy found out what they were up to. Once safely up the James, the *Virginia* could help defend Richmond. To do this, he continued, "would require all their energy in lightening the ship. They replied with three cheers and went to work at once." The exhausted and ill commander retired to his cabin and left his officers to organize work crews to raise the ship by at least five feet. The men worked until well after dark.[86]

For Eugenius Jack and his 320 or so shipmates aboard the *Virginia*, jettisoning coal, tons of pig iron ballast, and anything else of weight—except cannons, shot, and powder—was backbreaking work. Jack worked deep in the bowels of the ship, cutting out the rivets of the ship's freshwater tanks to drain the crew's drinking water so the pumps could force it outside. The five-hour effort had lightened and raised the ironclad. It was a good start.[87]

85 Alan B. Flanders, "The Man Who Troubled the Waters," *Columbiad* (Fall 1997), 1:119.

86 Tattnall, "Report," May 14, 1862, *ORN* 7:336-37; Curtis, *Famous Battle*, 17. At this point, Union ships *Galena, Aroostook,* and *Port Royal* were still up the James River.

87 Jack, *Memoirs*, 20. The number of sailors and marines aboard the *Virginia* at any one time varied between her commission date on Feb. 17, 1862, and her demise on May 11, 1862. According to the official muster roll, 318 sailors and 55 marines at some point served on the ship. The indefatigable researcher John V. Quarstein, however, in *The CSS Virginia: Sink Before Surrender* (History Press, 2012), 317, identified 431 men assigned to her at some point during her short life, and published a biographical roster in his study. Ibid., 317-434. The general number aboard on her final night varies between 320 and 350, though Tattnall reported the number at 300. The *Richmond Daily Dispatch*, May 22, 1862, put the number at 360. "Muster roll of the C.S.S. Virginia," *ORN*, 1/2:308-11; "Report of Flag-Officer Tattnall, C.S. Navy," May 14, 1862, *ORN* 7:337; "The Finale of the Merrimac," *Richmond Daily Dispatch,* May 22, 1862.

"By midnight the ship had been lightened three feet, when, to our amazement," Wood wrote, "the pilots said it was useless to do more." Although the ship's draft had been reduced to 20.5 feet, and more could be done to lighten her, the pilots now claimed that their goal of 18 feet would not be sufficient. The wind was now blowing from the west (down the James River), they explained, so even at high tide its depth at the shoals was less than 18 feet. "[T]he ship would not go up even to Jamestown Flats," Wood continued. Indeed, the pilots refused to "take the responsibility of taking her up the river at all."[88]

* * *

The Saturday sun was starting to set, but word of Norfolk's and Portsmouth's surrenders had not yet reached Lt. Col. Cram at Ocean View or Lincoln and Stanton at Fort Monroe. About 9:30 p.m., reported Cram, "a negro came and informed me of General Wool's successful entry into Norfolk." The engineering officer immediately told his aide, Capt. Jay, to inform the president, but before a boat could be prepared, "General Wool and Secretary Chase were [spotted] in the lingering glimpses of twilight, approaching on foot through the sand-ridge." Wool and Chase may have ridden back in Huger's former carriage all the way from Norfolk and left it behind the sand dunes. Regardless of how they got there, the pair confirmed the report: Norfolk and its immediate surroundings were in Union hands. Cram cancelled the captain's mission to Lincoln; Chase and Wool would inform him themselves.

Wool, meanwhile, ordered Cram to continue funneling men and supplies to the beach landing site. With the *Virginia* "still in position to dispute the passage by water to Norfolk, and to hold our [naval] squadron in check in Hampton Roads, the route via Ocean View, was the only one by which our troops could be reinforced or supplied," Cram reported. "Accordingly, by about one o'clock a.m. [May 11], some two additional regiments (29th Massachusetts and 20th Indiana), eight wagon loads of provisions, and a section of Howard's battery had been disembarked and ordered forward." Two companies of cavalry and two sections of artillery were yet to leave their ships.[89]

88 Wood, "First Fight," *B&L*, 1:710. Wood never relinquished his belief that the *Virginia* could have been used to save Norfolk if Huger and the Confederate land forces had remained in place.

89 Cram, "Report," May 31, 1862, Wool Papers, NYSA. The two regiments ordered to Norfolk were both from Brig. Gen. Joseph Mansfield's command at Newport News.

Chase and Wool boarded the steamboat *Pioneer* for the return trip to Fort Monroe, stopping along the way to share the good news with Flag Officer Goldsborough, who was visiting the *Susquehanna.* As it turned out, Goldsborough, had already been informed by 10:30 p.m.[90]

By that time Cannon, the aide Wool left behind at Fort Monroe, had persuaded both Lincoln and Stanton to retire for the night. The president wasn't ready for bed. As he later told an interested party, "The night was very warm—the moon shining brightly—and, too restless to sleep, I threw off my clothes and sat for some time by the table reading."[91]

While Lincoln read, Cannon "went outside the fort with Captain Rogers, of the navy, and we went down on to the ordnance wharf" to await further news. After a while "I heard a distant sound of paddle-wheels splashing in the water . . . and finally up came a little gunboat with General Wool and the members of his staff and Secretary Chase on board, and the news that Norfolk was taken. General Huger had run."

The news excited everyone. Cannon left a detailed account about how Wool broke the story to the president:

> General Wool came up into the fort, and as we approached headquarters the sentinel challenged, "Who goes there?" The President heard the challenge, and the next thing we saw was six feet of white nightshirt at the French window.
>
> "What is it?" asked the President.
>
> "General Wool, to present Norfolk to you!" I replied.
>
> "Call up Stanton, and send Wool up here," he said.
>
> I roused up Secretary Stanton, and told him, "General Wool has returned, and we have taken Norfolk."
>
> "My God!" he said, and jumped out of bed, and started up in his night-shirt to the President's room.

The president later related to a friend that Wool had entered his room and blurted "No time for ceremony, Mr. President, Norfolk is ours!"[92]

90 "The Capture of Norfolk," *New York Times*, May 13, 1862, 1; "Abstract Log of the USS *Minnesota*," May 10, 1862, *ORN* 7:334.

91 Francis Bicknell Carpenter, *Six Months at the White House with Abraham Lincoln: The Story of a Picture* (New York, 1866), 104-105.

92 Cannon, *Personal Reminiscences*, 161-63; Carpenter, *Six Months*, 105.

Vanity Fair's illustration from May 31, 1862, depicts the excitement and relief President Lincoln and Secretary Stanton felt upon Maj. Gen. Wool's report of Norfolk's successful capture. *Making of America, University of Michigan Library*

Just then Stanton burst into the room, followed by Cannon. "President Lincoln was sitting on the edge of the bed," recalled Wool's aide. "General Wool was there, in full uniform and all covered with dust, and one or two of his officers were also there. Secretary Stanton rushed impetuously into General Wool's arms in his excitement, and embraced him fervently." The president broke out laughing at seeing a general in full uniform hugging his Secretary of War dressed in his night-shirt clasped in each other's arms. "Look out, Mars! If you don't, the General will throw you,"' quipped Lincoln.

"Stanton with his usual quickness of perception and appreciation" immediately noted the inestimable importance of the capture and urged Lincoln to go to Norfolk "and issue a proclamation on rebel soil." Lincoln postponed such matters till the morning, but that didn't deter his secretary from drafting a presidential proclamation. For his part, a thoroughly tired Chase was just "glad to get to bed."[93]

Stanton wasn't finished. He wired a midnight telegram to the war department announcing the capture of Norfolk, Portsmouth, and the all-important navy yard, and followed that up with a second telegram letting Maj. Gen. McClellan know about the fall of Norfolk.[94]

"The embarkation of the expedition began last night at 4 o'clock," began the *New York Times*, which encapsulated the big story in a few lines:

> It was landed upon a slightly-known shore, without a wharf, early next day. Gen. Wool slept in Fortress Monroe last night—marched with his troops some twenty miles, captured Norfolk, and was in bed again in his own quarters before midnight. The President and Secretary of War were awakened to hear the news, and received *en deshabille*, and with great exultation. They all slept better for it.[95]

93 Cannon, *Personal Reminiscences*, 163; Chase to "Nettie," May 11, 1862, in "Diary," Chase Papers, LC. "Mars" was Lincoln's pet name for Stanton, just as he called his naval secretary Welles "Father Neptune." The president later recalled that "the scene altogether must have been a comical one, though at the time we were all too greatly excited to take much note of mere appearances." Carpenter, *Six Months*, 105.

94 *Baltimore Sun*, May 10, 1862, 1; Stanton to McClellan, May 11, 1862, *OR* 11/3:162-63. Wool also wired a two-sentence message to his wife, passing the news along. Wool to "Sarah," May 10, 1862, Wool Papers, NYSA.

95 "The Capture of Norfolk," *New York Times*, May 13, 1862, 1. *En deshabille* is French for partly dressed in a loose or careless manner.

Chapter 6

Sunday, May 11, 1862

"A shock that shook the city . . . with an ominous sound that could not be mistaken."

— Brig. Gen. Egbert Viele

SOMETIME after 1:00 a.m., Lt. Jones broke the bad news to an infuriated Josiah Tattnall. The pilots, he believed, had deceived him about their ability to push the *Virginia* up the James River and he demanded an explanation from the chief pilot, William Parrish, about what Tattnall called a "palpable deception." Parrish, recorded the disgusted officer, "replied that 18 feet could be carried after the prevalence of easterly winds, but that the wind for the last two days had been westerly."[1]

Speculating later about the pilots' motives, Tattnall concluded that "the only imaginable one is that they wished to avoid going into battle." Her shallower draft now made the *Virginia* "unfit for action, a desperate contest must have ensued with a force against us too great to justify much hope of success." Since battle wasn't their occupation, the pilots "adopted this deceitful course to avoid it." Even this

1 "Report of Flag-Officer [Josiah] Tattnall, C.S. Navy," May 14, 1862, *ORN*, vol. 7, 337. A postwar article in the *New Orleans Times-Democrat* claimed that at least some of the crew—possibly the officers—"contemplated shooting one of the pilots, thinking it would bring the other one to his senses." The article was reprinted as "Interesting Data about the *Merrimac*," *Confederate Veteran* (April 1908), 16:xvii-xix. Another suggestion, even more fanciful, was to leave the ship for the Federals to seize and send Lt. John Taylor Wood to sink her from under the Yankees. Norris, "Confederate States Ship *Virginia*," *SHSP*, 7:223.

conclusion did not sit well with Tattnall, for he "had seen no reason to distrust their good faith to the Confederacy."[2]

With the *Virginia* riding a good three feet higher, part of her wooden hull, as well as a portion of her propeller and rudder, were now exposed above the water line. "I had no time to lose," Tattnall explained. "The ship was not in a condition for battle even with an enemy of equal force, and their force was overwhelming." With Norfolk and the surrounding area in the hands of the enemy, there was no time to add enough weight back to the ship to increase her draft and better protect her. "[H]er shield was then out of the water," Catesby Jones wrote after the war, "and we were not in fighting condition." Dawn was just hours.[3]

John Taylor Wood explained that letting in water to add weight was the only viable way to quickly lower the ship, but that course would drown the ship's steam furnace and flood the magazine. "Never was a commander forced by circumstances over which he had no control into a more painful position than was Commodore Tattnall," lamented the sympathetic lieutenant.[4]

The next decision was Tattnall's alone. "I therefore determined," he explained, "with the concurrence of the first and flag lieutenants, to save the crew for future service by landing them at Craney Island, the only road open to us, and to destroy

2 Tattnall, "Report," May 14, 1862, *ORN* 7:337-38. The commodore was not the only one who doubted the pilots. Franklin Buchanan, the *Virginia's* first commander, in a letter to Catesby Jones on June 19, 1862, *ORN* 7:788-89, wrote: "I have great confidence in my old friend Commodore T[attnall], and can not believe that he acted without reflection, or was governed by any other motives than those his judgment told him were right. As to the pilots, I had no confidence in them, and told him so, and less in the master than in either of the others." However, Richard Curtis, one of Tattnall's gunners, defended the pilots in a postwar account. He said the Richmond authorities "threw the blame on the Pilots, which was a shame to such worthy men." William Parrish, Hezekiah Williams, George Wright, and William T. Clarke—the last being Curtis' cousin—"were all first class Pilots in Va. waters," announced Richard Curtis, "all Virginians by birth, men who stood at the front those two days of heavy fighting and managed that heat heavy draft ship in a narrow channel were no cowards and did not authorize the destruction of the '*Merrimac*,' their memory should be highly praised by all Virginians." The pilots later vigorously defended themselves against Tattnall's suspicions, requesting "a suspension of public opinion as to [the commodore's] statements respecting themselves" until a full investigation was completed. Curtis, *Famous Battle*, Mariner's Museum; "The Destruction of the Virginia," May 22, 1862, Richmond *Whig*, 3.

3 Tattnall, "Report," May 14, 1862, *ORN* 7:337; Jones, "The Services of the 'Virginia,'" *SHSP*, 11:74. Many years after the war, John M. Brooke, the *Virginia's* designer, consulted with John Luke Porter, her builder, about whether she could have been further lifted out of the water and possibly have made it up the James River. Porter believed "the ship could be lightened to even seventeen feet, and would have the stability to that draft in the James River." John M. Brooke, "The *Virginia*, or *Merrimac*: Her Real Projector," *SHSP*, 19:34.

4 Wood, "First Fight," *B&L*, 1:709.

the ship to prevent her falling into the hands of the enemy."Although they hadn't been officially consulted, Tattnall added that "every commissioned officer in the ship" approved of the action.[5]

Once the determination was made to destroy the *Virginia*, Tattnall gave his exhausted crew a short break. "About this time the Boatswain's Mate blew his whistle, saying all hands splice the main brace," recalled gunner Richard Curtis. "[T]his meant two grog tubs, one forward and one aft, the men quickly responded to this call." Normally, the call to "splice the main brace" for a drink of grog —watered-down rum—came after an important shipboard event, such as a victory. In this case, the grog was meant to uplift the crew's spirits as they prepared to destroy their beloved ship.[6]

According to one of the ship's gunners, Tattnall took the opportunity presented by the grog break to offer up a short speech. "Boys, the commodore said: Norfolk has been taken by the Yankees, and our supplies are cut off. Although the vessel has been lightened, the pilot says he cannot get her up the James River, as we had intended to do; therefore, we have concluded to blow her up. You can make your escape in the best way possible." Curtis, the *Virginia's* gunner who memorialized the difficult event, added, "When I had taken my drink I went back to the forward part of the ship, very soon our ship was in motion, she had slipped her cable"[7]

Assistant engineer Jack was working below deck by the light of a swinging lantern when orders arrived to stop popping the water tank rivets. He was instead to take up his regular post at the ship's engine room bells, which the captain used to direct the ship's speed. At first, Jack (who somehow missed the call to "splice the main brace") thought the ironclad was preparing to go into battle. "I took my station thinking that we would soon be in action. Judge, then, my surprise when I saw that we were steaming towards Norfolk. At first I thought that we had started as we headed but would turn when we got underway enough to do so. But as we continued up without changing our course," he continued, "I began to think that

5 Tattnall, "Report," May 14, 1862, *ORN* 7:337.

6 Curtis, *Famous Battle*, 17. The U.S. Navy ended the practice of serving grog (sometimes watered down whiskey rather than rum) on Sept. 1, 1862. The sailors were compensated for losing their grog with an additional daily nickel in their pay. The Confederate Navy continued the practice throughout the war, but captains could offer seamen a 3-cent per day (later raised to 22 cents) bonus pay to forego the drink. James L. Conrad, *Rebel Reefers: The Organization and Midshipmen of the Confederate States Naval Academy* (Cambridge, MA, 2003), 52-53.

7 "The Destruction of the Virginia," Richmond *Whig*, May 22, 1862, 3; Curtis, *Famous Battle*, 17.

we were going to protect the Navy Yard from the enemy. All hopes were soon rudely dispelled by Mr. Jones."[8]

The *Virginia*, remembered one of her crew, soon ran "hard and fast aground in the light of Craney Island." Accounts differ about what followed next. Curtis claimed the men were in a "great confusion" about what to do, and "there was no discipline, no one seemed to have any control and," he added cryptically, "there were many things done that the writer will not speak about." Unfortunately, Curtis was true to his word and did not elaborate further. Lt. Wood mentioned no such confusion in his account and neither did Tattnall, who explained that Catesby Jones supervised "firing the ship and landing the crew, and everything was conducted with the most perfect order."[9]

Engineer Jack described a somber scene as the crew left the ship. Lt. Jones approached him in the engine room, his voice "tremoring," described Jack, as he assigned him "command of a detail of firemen." Jack quoted Jones: "Go muster your men and prepare them to abandon ship. No baggage must be taken into the boats." The engineer moved "to proceed to my new duties with a sad heart and tearful eyes, at the approaching fate of this good ship that had to be ignominiously deserted. I felt that I had rather go down with her . . . in [an] honorable contest with the enemy. But older and wiser heads [believed the *Virginia's* destruction] necessary. . . . Perhaps it was," he added, "but I felt like a coward skulking from the foe."[10]

Despite Jones' order to Jack, some men took baggage with them off the ship. Elsberry V. White, a junior engineer, left his personal effects on board. Gunner Curtis reported that he went down to the berth deck to pick up some of his clothes, and others were told to take their small arms and two day's provisions with them off the boat. With or without their meager baggage, the *Virginia* only carried two

8 Jack, *Memoirs*, 20-21.

9 Curtis, *Famous Battle*, 17; Wood, "First Fight," *B&L*, 1:710; Tattnall, "Report," May 14, 1862, *ORN* 7:337. A later report from a *New York Times* correspondent indicated confusion aboard the doomed ship. According to the paper, there were "two dead bodies floating in the water" when the Yankees came upon the hulk of the *Merrimac*. Tattnall would have never left men behind to be blown up with the ship, and no other independent account exists. Assistant Engineer Jack disputed the claim and other reports of bodies found. "The men were divided into squads and mustered by roll before leaving the ship & mustered again upon reaching the beach, so none could have been overlooked," he explained. See "Later—Destruction of the Merrimac," *New York Times*, May 13, 1862, 1; Jack, *Memoirs*, 21.

10 Jack, *Memoirs*, 21.

small rowboats, so it took about three hours to ferry all the men off the ship and onto shore.[11]

According to crewman John F. Higgins, Tattnall was the first to leave the ironclad. "Nothing was now to be done by the crew but to get to shore," he wrote years later. In the rush to load men onto the boats, someone took down the *Virginia's* flags. When Hardin B. Littlepage, a midshipman, came across the banners, he withdrew clothing from his knapsack, and "carefully folding the old flags" placed them inside to save them.[12]

As the men lined up on the gun deck to climb through a forward gun port and onto a rowboat, Lts. Jones and Wood, with a contingent of eight sailors, prepared the *Virginia* for destruction. Elsberry White, one of the eight, "held the candle for Mr. [Charles B.] Oliver, the gunner, to uncap the powder in the magazine to insure a quick explosion, and, necessarily, was among the last to leave decks." Others in the destruction crew spread powder and flammable materials—including tar, oil, fat, grease, and wood—over the ship's decks and poured powder trails to the open hatches. Her iron sides were already slathered with tallow and fat, and her guns were loaded, but some of the recently installed gun port iron shields were left closed.[13]

When the depressing work was complete and the rest of the men safely on land, the final rowboat stood ready to remove the last ten sailors from the deck of the *Virginia.* Jones and Wood, charged with lighting the powder trains, were the last to step off the doomed ironclad. "Setting her on fire fore and aft, she was soon in a

11 Elsberry V. White, *The First Iron-Clad Naval Engagement in the World: History of Facts of the Great Naval Battle Between the* Merrimac-Virginia, *C.S.N., and the Ericsson* Monitor, *U.S.N., Hampton Roads, March 8 and 9, 1862* (New York, 1906), n.p.; Curtis, *Famous Battle*, 17.

12 John F. Higgins, "Brilliant Career of the *Merrimac*," *Confederate Veteran* (August 1900), 8:357. A capital newspaper reported that Tattnall was so feeble that he had to be carried off the ship on a litter, but no other evidence confirms this. "The Finale of the *Merrimac*," *Richmond Daily Dispatch,* May 22, 1862, 2. Hardin B. Littlepage, "A Midshipman aboard the *Virginia*," pt. 1, *Civil War Times, Illustrated* (April 1974), 11. Littlepage raised those flags at Drewry's Bluff for the May 15 fight, where many of the *Virginia's* crew fought together again by manning some of the guns to drive back the Union ships moving up the James River toward Richmond.

13 White, *First Iron-Clad*, n.p. The ironclad may have had as much as 36,000 pounds of powder aboard. Frank Vandiver, ed., *The Civil War Diary of General Josiah Gorgas,* (Tuscaloosa, AL, 1947), 5. Wertenbaker, *Norfolk*, 240. The *Virginia's* "roof, already covered with tallow and other fatty matter, was saturated with oil, and her decks also received a copious supply of the same material." "The Evacuation of Norfolk and the Burning of the *Merrimac*," *Charleston Mercury*, May 15, 1862, Accessible Archives, accessed June 25, 2009, accessible.com.Dbgateway.Nysed.gov/accessible.

blaze," recalled Lt. Wood, "and by the light of our burning ship we pulled for the shore."[14]

While Jones, Wood, and the other sailors readied the ironclad for destruction, those already ashore prepared for the 22-mile march to Suffolk. "I landed early with my squad of firemen and formed them on the top of a low bank ashore, ready for defence in case the enemy should come upon us," explained Jack. "Other men were placed as outposts with instructions to fire upon any one that advanced without answering a challenge. Our sailors made but sorry soldiers," admitted the engineer, "and were altogether out of our element ashore." Some of those "soldiers" were a little jumpy, continued Jack. "Just before all of the men had landed, a sentry on outpost fired. . . . confused at first . . . my squad nearly crushed me by jumping from the bank against which I was standing. . . . We soon quieted them however & formed behind the bank, expecting a charge, but in short time learned that it was a false alarm."

By the time the last ten sailors landed, the fire aboard the *Virginia* was clearly visible for all to see, the flames rising "from the port holes and hatches." Before the crewmen set off for Suffolk, "her guns began to discharge their charges, some towards us and others towards the Roads; we heard several of the shot whistle past." "[A] more beautiful sight I never beheld than that great ship on fire," realled junior engineer Elsberry White, "flames issuing from the port holes, through the gratings and smokestack—the sight ever to be remembered."[15]

The march to Suffolk occurred without incident, although Jack said the men of the *Virginia* expected to be attacked "at any moment" along their "mournful march for our line." About an hour and a half after tramping away from the shore, the men heard a terrific explosion behind them, the "awful report [of] the magazines of the burning ship" exploding. A sense of loss washed over the men. "Thus the finest fighting ship that ever floated on American waters at that time came to an untimely end at the hands of her friends," lamented Curtis, "with no enemy within 8 or 10 miles of her—a sad finish for such a bright beginning." Tattnall noted the time as "a little before 5 on the morning of the 11th."[16]

14 Wood, "First Fight," *B&L*, 1:710.

15 Jack, *Memoirs*, 20-21; White, *First Iron-Clad*, n.p. While Wood wrote that the last boat landed on the mainland "at daybreak," that time does not agree with numerous other reports from both sides about when the ship could be seen ablaze.

16 Jack, *Memoirs*, 21; Curtis, *Famous Battle*, 17; Tattnall, "Report," May 14, 1862, *ORN* 7:337.

The men marched on. Lt. Jones stopped the sailors for a break when they reached the turnpike linking Norfolk and Suffolk. According to crewman Higgins, Jones "addressed a few encouraging words . . . if any one had a family or friend in Norfolk or Portsmouth," he explained, he would not "blame him for returning home, 'but be men' . . . meaning . . . 'be true to the South.' Only two men stepped out of ranks," added Higgins, "and the crew resumed their march to Suffolk."[17]

The contingent finally made it to Suffolk on the evening of May 11, where the townspeople happily fed the famished crewman. "The good and elegant ladies of this town," recalled one of the men, "prepared for us bountiful tables on both sides of the street, and dispensed gracious and patriotic hospitality . . . accompanied with words of cheer for their hearts." From Suffolk, the former crew of the *Virginia* boarded a train bound for Richmond.[18]

* * *

Northern eyes spotted the burning ironclad shortly after Jones and Wood fired the *Virginia*. George Livingston, on watch aboard the USS *Susquehanna*, told his replacement, Alfred Zerega, "that a big fire raged all during his watch (from midnight to 4 a.m.) in the direction of Norfolk and that a little after 3 a.m. he noticed another quite large fire more to the right and apparently nearer than the first." Intrigued by the news, Zerega used what he called "powerful night glasses"

17 Higgins, "Brilliant Career," 357. Higgins does not name the two men. One named James Thompson, who claimed he had been impressed as a seaman to serve aboard the *Virginia*, asserted that some 200 men from the ship had deserted and made their way to Norfolk. "News from the South By a Refugee," *New York Herald*, May 19, 1862, 8. However, there is no James Thompson listed on the *Virginia's* muster roll, and no corroborating evidence of a mass desertion exists. Another Northern paper reported two *Virginia* officers paroled in Norfolk and "several" of the crew there who had taken the oath of allegiance to the Union. "Our Fortress Monroe Letter," *Philadelphia Inquirer*, May 14, 1862, 4. A Richmond paper expanded on some of the crew having possibly deserted, quoting from the *Inquirer* about two former members who took the oath: seaman and gunner Lemnel Ball, and Master's Mate E. K. McLaughlin, who was reportedly on sick leave and not on board the ship when she was abandoned and destroyed. *Richmond Daily Dispatch*, May 22, 1862, 2. Arthur B. Fuller of the 16th Massachusetts commented in his diary that after the *Virginia* blew up, "deserters from her crew arrived and confirmed her destruction." No names were given, so it is not possible to know how many, if any, "deserters" there may have been. Fuller, *Chaplain Fuller*, 251.

18 Higgins, "Brilliant Career," 357. Only a few days later, the *Virginia*'s crew once against faced off with the *Monitor*, but this time from land. Most of the crew, under the command of Lt. Catesby Jones, helped man the Fort Darling batteries at Drewry's Bluff. On May 15, they successfully held off several Union warships (including the *Monitor*) trying to run the batteries. See reports of the Union naval commanders, May 16, 1862, *ORN* 7:356-65.

The CSS *Virginia* is shown here at the point of her final death explosion in a Currier & Ives illustration. *Naval History & Heritage Command, NH 58723*

to observe the fire, and concluded it was the *Virginia.* The sailor hailed the deck to "call all hands."[19]

The USS *Dacotah's* abstract log confirmed the timing of Zerega's claim. "It was a beautiful sight to us in more senses than one" to see the *Virginia* burn gloated Samuel R. Franklin, *Dacotah's* first lieutenant. Yankee seamen "were glad to have her well out of the way." Franklin spent the rest of that early morning watching the Virginia's immolation. "Gradually the casemate grew hotter and hotter, until finally it became red-hot, so that we could distinctly mark its outlines."[20]

The *Virginia's* death explosion roused almost everyone. According to the *Dacotah's* log, the devastating blast occurred at 4:55 a.m., essentially the same time Secretary Stanton recorded the blast: "2 minutes before 5 o'clock this morning."

19 Zerega, "Last Days," 1:454.

20 "Abstract Log of the USS *Dacotah*," May 11, 1862, *ORN* 7:334; Samuel R. Franklin, *Memoirs of a Rear Admiral: Who Has Served for More than Half a Century in the Navy of the United States* (New York, 1898), 182. Franklin, who had been at Hampton Roads on March 8, 1862, added, "Thus I had seen in a brief space of time the explosion of the magazines of two large ships of war, an event so rare that to see one at all seldom comes within the experience of any one."

The *New York Times* reported the explosion occurred "precisely at 4¾ o'clock [and] made the earth and water tremble for miles around." Norfolk also felt the blast, "an explosion whose concussion shook earth and sea," and cast "a more fearful gloom" on the brows of the town's citizenry. Chaplain Thomas G. Murphey of the 1st Delaware described a massive explosion that lifted the ironclad out of the water: "As it rose the sea trembled, and the earth and houses on shore shook as if by some violent convulsion of nature."[21]

Brig. Gen. Viele, the newly installed military governor, was awake when he experienced "a shock that shook the city . . . with an ominous sound that could not be mistaken." Union troops in the former Rebel entrenchments outside Norfolk also felt and heard the blast, the men "suddenly aroused by a loud explosion . . . the violence of which shook the earth." The men confirmed "a tall column of fire shot into the air in the direction of Craney Island." Some in Suffolk, even though 22 miles away, also claimed to have felt the blow.[22]

The *Charleston Mercury* offered its readers a good, if fanciful, description of the explosion a few days later. The blast "sent her enormous guns and nine hundred tons of iron plating flying in the air to a height of three or four hundred feet. The plates, heated to a cherry red. . . presented an awful but magnificent sight. A moment or two more, the flying fragments fell into the water, and all that remained of the most formidable war vessel ever constructed was her charred and burning hull. We can well imagine," the paper concluded, "the fiendish delight with which our enemies chuckled over this annihilation [and how soundly] Gen. Wool must have slept for the first time since [the *Virginia*] began wreaking her terrible havoc."[23]

Back on the USS *Minnesota*, Flag Officer Goldsborough reported that he witnessed the explosion in the direction of Craney Island. He "inferred immediately that either the works on that island or the *Merrimack* had been blown up." Lt. Franklin from the *Dacotah* confirmed for Goldsborough that the *Virginia* was no more. Goldsborough, who was still in his long nightshirt, was at first

21 "Abstract Log of the USS *Dacotah*," May 11, 1862, *ORN* 7:334; Stanton to P. H. Watson, May 11, 1862, *ORN* 7:341; "News from Fortress Monroe," *New York Times*, May 13, 1862, 8; Murphey, *Four Years in the War*, 54.

22 Viele, "A Trip with Lincoln," *Scribner's Monthly*, Oct. 1878, 822; Seville, *Delaware Volunteers*, 41.

23 "The Evacuation of Norfolk and the Burning of the *Merrimac*," *Charleston Mercury*, May 15, 1862, Accessible Archives, accessed June 25, 2009, accessible.com.dbgateway.nysed.Gov/accessible.

surprised by the news. After ascertaining that Franklin was certain, he ordered, "Then sir, return on board and tell your Captain to get under way and go up to Norfolk."[24]

Just to be sure, however, Goldsborough also ordered his flag lieutenant, Thomas O. Selfridge, to take the tugboat *Zouave* as far above Sewell's Point as he safely could and determine "the real conditions of things." A second tugboat, the *Dragon*, with Commander A. Ludlow Case on board, also headed toward the mouth of the Elizabeth River.[25]

Selfridge confirmed Lt. Franklin's report when he found the *Virginia* "completely destroyed." Commander Case also discovered debris floating on the water near where the *Virginia* exploded. Both men turned their tugs around to race back to report their findings, and "were seen coming on towards the Fortress at full speed, each, apparently, endeavoring to outvie the other," reported one correspondent. Once Case shouted that he had seen parts of the floating wreck, a reassured Goldsborough "at once ordered the entire fleet to proceed up the river, with [Selfridge's] tug in advance to pilot them in."[26]

According to Keeler, the news got a mixed reception aboard the *Monitor*. "Morning came & with it the expected intelligence that our forces were in possession of Norfolk & that the *Merrimac* was blown up. This latter information was not so gratifying to us," he informed his wife, "as we had ever since the fight looked up the 'Big Thing' as our exclusive game & were hoping in a short time to be able to gratify our curiosity by an inspection of her construction & internal arrangement." Now that possibility was gone.[27]

The powerful fleet steaming upriver with the USS *Monitor* included the *E. A. Stevens*, *Susquehanna*, *Dacotah*, *Seminole*, *San Jacinto*, and the Army schooner *Mount Vernon*. Led by Selfridge's tugboat, the vessels slowly approached the mouth of the Elizabeth River. "It was a beautiful sight and attracted throngs of spectators along the whole line of Old Point," reported the *New York Times*, and "as the vessels passed up to Craney Island the excitement became intense." Finally, even the

24 Franklin, *Rear Admiral*, 183.

25 "Report of Flag-Officer Goldsborough, U.S. Navy, Regarding Surrender of Norfolk and Blowing Up of C.S.S. *Virginia* (*Merrimack*)," May 12, 1862, *ORN* 7:342-43.

26 Selfridge, *Finer Tradition*, 66; "News from Fortress Monroe," *New York Times*, May 13, 1862, 8.

27 Keeler to "Anna," May 12, 1862, in Daly, ed., *Aboard the USS* Monitor, 119. On the return trip down the Elizabeth River, Keeler recorded that the *Monitor* passed by the *Virginia's* wreckage, where he picked up a piece of the "Monster" to send to his wife.

diehard skeptics who doubted that the CSS *Virginia* had truly met her end were satisfied she was gone.[28]

Goldsborough sailed to Fort Monroe to carry the news personally to Lincoln, Stanton, and Chase. The treasury secretary rose "at 6 and just before 7 went into the parlor. Commander Goldsborough astonished & gratified us that the rebels had set fire to the *Merrimac* & had blown her up." The president wanted to visit "the point where the suicide had been performed & above the obstructions in the [Elizabeth River] channel if possible," explained Chase, "so as to be sure of the access to Norfolk by water." Lincoln already planned to take the steamship *Baltimore* for the return to Washington.[29]

It had been six days since the president left the capital, and pressing official business awaited his attention. During his absence, his secretaries had sent him reports to read and documents to sign in an effort to keep up with the workload. For example, on May 6, a letter from Pennsylvania's governor arrived requesting that a soldier be promoted. Lincoln wrote out a promotion request himself the next day and asked Stanton to approve it. He also sent a message to McClellan about proposed changes to the organizational structure of the Army of the Potomac, and followed that with a long private letter explaining his reasoning. Lincoln surely had a strong sense of needing to get back to the executive mansion.[30]

First, however, he simply had to see the captured city of Norfolk for himself. The president, cabinet secretaries, Maj. Gen. Wool, Flag Officer Goldsborough, and numerous Navy and Army staff officers boarded the *Baltimore* and steamed toward the far end of Hampton Roads and the Elizabeth River. When breakfast was ready Col. Cannon went looking for Lincoln. "I found he had sought a private place behind the wheel-house, where he was seated reading the Bible," remembered the officer.

The president mulled the significance of the *Virginia's* loss and Norfolk's capture. Both were welcome news, enough so that he could joke about Wool's and Stanton's late night embrace. "Now, Mr. Chase," began the president during breakfast,

> you know we have been solicited by artists to fill the panels at the Capitol with pictures illustrative of this war. I don't think anything has been done on our side until the capture of

28 "News from Fortress Monroe," *New York Times*, May 13, 1862, 8.

29 Chase to "Nettie," May 11, 1862, in "Diary," Chase Papers, LC.

30 Basler, ed., *Collected Works of Abraham Lincoln*, 5:206-209.

> Norfolk worthy of illustration. But now, you can send for artist Leitze [Emanuel G. Leutze], and tell him to illustrate the taking of Norfolk. It should be illustrated by a picture showing the meeting of the Secretary of War and General Wool, on the announcement of the capture.

The joke "was keenly appreciated," recalled Cannon, though he didn't specifically note Stanton's reaction.[31]

While the president and his party steamed to the western end of the Roads, the federal flotilla, behind the little tugboat *Zouave*, and followed closely by the ironclads *Monitor* and *E. A. Stevens*, entered the mouth of the Elizabeth. As the fleet closed on the batteries at Sewell's Point, Selfridge guided his tugboat to the point's wharf, climbed into the battery, and raised the Stars and Stripes where the Confederate flag had recently flown. At Craney Island, however, Rebel flags still waved above the works. "All hands went to quarters as we passed," Keeler wrote. "The cannon peered out at us through casemates & embrasures & over parapets grim & threatening but silent."[32]

Commander Case's *Dragon* returned to Craney Island a little later to haul down the three offending flags, "substituting the 'Pride of America'" in their place, according to a reporter for the *New York Times*. As the *Dragon* approached the shore, Case ordered a gun fired "to test the fact of evacuation." The only response, reported the paper, was "[T]wo negro men" who appeared on the shore. A boat carried the reporter and others, including Case, to the island, where the *Dragon's* captain became "the first loyal man that pressed his foot on the soil of this treasonable stronghold and he immediately raised the 'Old Flag.'"[33]

The *Monitor* and *E. A. Stevens*, trailed by the rest of the fleet, continued up the Elizabeth River. They didn't draw fire, but "found every favourable point on both banks occupied by [formidable] batteries." Land on both sides of the river, noted Keeler, was "dreary & uninviting . . . & covered with a sparse growth of stunted pine." Nearer Norfolk the countryside improved except for the inevitable wartime bruises: "[E]verything looked as if it had been levied on by the recent occupants of the batteries—fields without fences, houses minus doors & windows and pastures without cattle." A double row of obstructions halted the *Monitor* within sight of the

31 Cannon, *Personal Reminiscences*, 167-68.

32 Keeler to "Anna," May 12, 1862, in Daly, ed., *Aboard the USS* Monitor, 120.

33 "News from Fortress Monroe," *New York Times,* May 13, 1862, 8. It is unknown how or why Confederate flags were present at Craney Island when the *Virginia's* crew reported them gone the day before.

city. Keeler took note of the enemy's carelessness. In the narrow opening in the middle of the row, he wrote, was "the hull of the old *United States* frigate positioned to be towed into the opening and sunk to block the channel effectively, and "the traitorous scoundrels had left in such haste that they neglected to do this & we passed up without trouble."[34]

These same obstructions, however, posed a problem for the rest of the fleet. The *Susquehanna's* captain examined the imposing barrier of wooden piles with "their tops being just awash" and decided to crash through it. His ship received little damage save for "the loss of one or two wooden floats of our paddle-wheels, and . . . stripping off a few sheets of copper." According to the *Dacotah's* abstract log, she "scraped over a sunken wreck alongside the frigate *United States*," and the *San Jacinto* "grounded on the obstructions." The latter's captain, William Ronckendorff, likely watched the *Susquehanna* bull her way through and figured his ship could make it as well.[35]

Selfridge was less than impressed with Ronckendorff's decision to run his *San Jacinto* "rather stupidly . . . on the barrier." Once the vessel was stuck fast, he continued, "her captain ordered me to take a line to assist in towing her off." Selfridge did not think he could tow the ship until high tide, and he had no desire to wait there for hours for the water to rise. The lieutenant confessed he was "guilty of a poor piece of seamanship" when he deliberately left too much slack in the line, steamed ahead at full speed, and the line broke. According to Selfridge, he did not hear the captain yell for him to return, so he continued on to Norfolk. The *San Jacinto* worked herself free later that afternoon.[36]

A large crowd of Norfolk citizens gathered at the wharf, and there soon arose a great clamor when a steamer was spotted "coming up the river. . . . They see a little, insignificant wisp of vessel approaching under full steam. It appears to be a round, sheet iron, floating infernal machine or buoy," reported a newspaper. It flew the United States flag. Members of the crowd asked nearby Union soldiers what craft it was. "That?" replied a sergeant of cavalry, "why, I should think you would all know it—that is the Yankee cheese box—the little *Monitor* and [the]one behind her is the

34 Keeler to "Anna," May 12, 1862, in Daly, ed., *Aboard the USS* Monitor, 119-120. A squad of Marines under the command of Lt. Robert S. Kidd was dispatched to take possession of one of the many forts—including Fort Fairfax—erected along the river's approaches to Norfolk. Sullivan, *Marine Corps in the Civil War*, 27.

35 Zerega, "Last Days," 1:456; "Abstract Log of the USS *Dacotah*," May 11, 1862, *ORN* 7:334.

36 Selfridge, *Finer Tradition,* 66.

little *Naugatuck* [*E. A. Stevens*], with her terrible gun that frightened off the *Merrimac* the other day."[37]

Not entirely certain which side controlled Norfolk, the *Monitor* approached with her two guns ready to fire and her crew at their action quarters, "till a bend in the river disclosed the glorious old stars & stripes waving in triumph above the Naval hospital." The hospital, on the north bank a little below Portsmouth, was the first major building visible along the river and, full of local patients, had not been burned by the retreating Confederates. "It was a quiet beautiful Sunday morning," Keeler continued, "the bells ringing for Church as we slowly passed along by warehouses, beautiful residences & finely cultivated gardens & made fast to the *Merrimac's* old moorings."[38]

The *Monitor* made a careful approach and stopped to examine "a large floating sheet-iron buoy, anchored in the stream, no doubt to mark the channel," recorded the Philadelphia *Press*. "In an instant," continued the article,

> a sailor jumps upon it, winking, lest it should be an infernal machine. He opens the sliding-valve, disappears, head and all, within, makes a full examination, jumps out, and reports all correct to commanding officer [Lt. William N. Jeffers]. As the *Monitor* comes to anchor, and her sailors come up on deck, mount the turret, and give a glorious three times three [cheer] for the occupation of Norfolk. The crew of the *Stevens* battery quickly follow suit.[39]

Keeler contrasted the demeanor of the sailors with those of Norfolk's citizens and came away unimpressed. He described them as "a large crowd of rough looking specimens of the genus homo congregated on the docks to witness our arrival. A female could now & then be seen on the verandahs or at the windows of the buildings fronting the river," he added, "but not a handkerchief was waved nor a cheer given to welcome us."

The rest of the fleet came up behind the ironclads and anchored in the harbor, with the last of them settling in as the *Baltimore* arrived. The "little steamer came up with the President, Sec'ys Chase & Staunton, Commodore Goldsborough, & Gen. Wool & Staff," explained Keeler. "The President, as the boat passed us, had his hat

37 "Five Miles from Norfolk," Philadelphia *Press*, May 13, 1862, 1.

38 Keeler to "Anna," May 12, 1862, in Daly, ed., *Aboard the USS* Monitor, 120.

39 "Five Miles from Norfolk," Philadelphia *Press*, May 13, 1862, 1.

This prewar view of Norfolk (left) and Portsmouth (right) depicts the scene President Lincoln would have witnessed as he passed the Marine Hospital point. The burning Gosport Navy Yard would have been in the distance beyond Portsmouth. *Library of Congress*

off bowing, appearing highly pleased at the successful results of *his plans* [emphasis in original]."[40]

The *Baltimore* had briefly stopped off Craney Island at the site of the *Virginia's* demise and, as observed by a reporter for the *New York Herald*, "picked up pieces of the wreck, which were brought up to the city and divided among the friends of the officers. . . . One piece of yellow pine, about eight inches wide and five thick, is supposed to have been a portion of her keel. The wood was eagerly sought after," continued the paper, "and soon all was split up, excepting a fair sized specimen for the navy department and Captain [John A. B.] Dahlgren." The *Baltimore* arrived off Norfolk's wharfs about 10:00 a.m. "The city seemed very quiet. The Navy Yard at Gosport appeared . . . much dilapidated and sadly in want of repair, but she did not go near enough for her passengers to observe the yard particularly."[41]

With Norfolk, Portsmouth, and the navy yard in Union possession, Lincoln wanted to make sure and maximize any momentum offered by the triumph. Lt. Jeffers was summoned to the *Baltimore*, remembered Keeler, and returned with

40 Keeler to "Anna," May 12, 1862, in Daly, ed., *Aboard the USS* Monitor, 120-21.

41 "Effect of the President's Visit to Fortress Monroe," *New York Herald*, May 13, 1862, 7.

orders for the *Monitor* to steam back to Hampton Roads at once and be ready the next morning to ascend the James River for Richmond.[42]

Gideon Welles was of like mind, though clearly conscious of the president's supremacy when it came to military matters. When a telegram arrived in Washington informing him of Norfolk's fall, the naval secretary sent a message to Goldsborough to prepare for an "immediate attack on Fort Caswell" in North Carolina, and to "push all boats up the James River, even to Richmond unless the President directs to the contrary."[43]

When Welles followed up his telegram to Goldsborough the same day with another ordering him to "discharge the ram steamers under charge of the Navy Department," the flag officer informed the naval secretary by return telegram that "the President ordered me not to discharge the ram steamers until I could hear from Washington, after he got there."[44]

Maj. Gen. Wool, meanwhile, went into Norfolk to talk with Brig. Gen. Viele, the new military governor. Goldsborough also disembarked from the *Baltimore* by small boat to board the *Susquehanna*, which he used temporarily as his flagship. Presumably, the various staff members who accompanied the two area service commanders left with their bosses, leaving Lincoln, Stanton, and Chase aboard the *Baltimore*.[45]

42 Keeler to "Anna," May 12, 1862, in Daly, ed., *Aboard the USS* Monitor, 121.

43 Welles to Goldsborough, May 11, 12, 1862, *ORN* 7:341-42. Goldsborough assured Welles the next day that he was already thinking of making Ft. Caswell, which protected Wilmington, his next target, and that Lincoln had ordered the ironclads up the James River to Richmond to "shell the place into a surrender." In the meantime, the only warship he had at Hampton Roads was his own flagship, the *Minnesota*.

44 Goldsborough to Gideon Welles, May 12, 1862, *ORN* 7:342. The steamers named for discharge were the *Arago*, *Illinois*, and the *Ericsson*. Goldsborough added that Lincoln "gave me his reason why he wished those vessels to be longer detained," though Goldsborough did not elaborate on the reason. Lincoln also told Goldsborough "he wished all the guns at the forts and dockyard to be removed to Fortress Monroe, and unless he should think proper to communicate to you otherwise, I presume that I am to have this work done." Goldsborough Report, May 12, 1862, *ORN* 7:343. Lincoln was probably worried the Confederates would attempt to retake the Norfolk area, and he wanted to protect the guns in Union hands. Whether the Navy or Army controlled the captured forts quickly became an issue of contention between the two branches. Maj. Gen. Wool refused to allow Goldsborough's sailors access to the forts without the permission of Lincoln or Stanton. John E. Wool to Goldsborough, May 23, 1862, Wool Papers, NYSA.

45 "Five Miles from Norfolk," Philadelphia *Press*, May 13, 1862, 1. Despite some reports then and later, Lincoln and Stanton did not leave the *Baltimore* to walk or carriage ride through Norfolk and Portsmouth. "News from Fortress Monroe," *New York Times*, May 13, 1862, 8, For false reports on this issue, see Richmond *Whig*, May 21, 1862, 3.

Jammed with political dignitaries, the *Baltimore* steamed briefly around the harbor, probably in order to swing her bow to head back downriver. This allowed the passengers to get a better look at both Norfolk and Portsmouth. Most reports confirm that President Lincoln was in Norfolk's harbor no more than an hour before descending the Elizabeth to glide past some of the Confederate-built forts, especially Fort Norfolk just below the city.[46]

After a quick run across Hampton Roads, the *Baltimore* stopped briefly at the Fort Monroe wharf. There, Lincoln handed off a short telegram for Maj. Gen. Henry W. Halleck, the commander of the Department of the Mississippi. "Norfolk in our possession," Lincoln wrote. "*Merrimac* blown up, & *Monitor* & other boats going up James River to Richmond. Be very sure to sustain no reverse in your Department." Stanton sent a brief telegram at 2:00 p.m. to Maj. Gen. McClellan, who was still making his way up the Peninsula, to alert him that the *Monitor* and several other ships had been ordered "up the James River," and that it would be "executed immediately."[47]

With these administrative details out of the way, the presidential party steamed around Point Comfort and up Chesapeake Bay toward the mouth of the Potomac River and home. The *Baltimore* arrived in the capital on the morning of May 12.[48]

* * *

While Lincoln headed back to Washington, most of the Confederate soldiers who had once defended Norfolk continued their journey toward Richmond. Some lucky ones did so by train, but most were not so fortunate and made the trek on foot.

"At 12 ocl. [midnight] we halted in a certain lane to rest for the night," wrote Pvt. Louis Merz. "Not having blankets or overcoats, we built fires, laid on rails, and covered with the atmosphere. Being most too pleasant to sleep long, we soon got up, when friend Allen cooked some coffee in a cup & a perfect treat it was." Merz and his comrades in Company D (West Point Guards) of the 4th Georgia Infantry heard the *Virginia* explode as they prepared to resume their journey at 5:00 a.m., though of course they had no idea what the blast signified. The men marched for a

46 "Five Miles from Norfolk," Philadelphia *Press*, May 13, 1862, 1.

47 Lincoln to Henry W. Halleck, in Basler, ed., *Collected Works of Abraham Lincoln*, 210; Stanton to McClellan, May 11, 1862, *OR* 11/3:164. Above Lincoln's handwritten message, Stanton crossed out the word "sure" and wrote in "careful."

48 "Effect of the President's Visit to Fortress Monroe," *New York Herald*, May 13, 1862, 7.

couple hours and halted for a rest. They continued at 10 a.m., "passed Suffolk & halted about 2 miles on the other side towards Petersburg."[49]

The Georgians endured a hard march that continued until about 9:30 that evening, when they pitched a meager camp. They had left behind or destroyed "tents, near all our cooking utensils and a good many other things" in Norfolk. Like their Northern counterparts, the Confederates found out that camp life did not prepare them for active campaigning. After "drilling constantly for a year," wrote infantryman Henry Thomas, they thought marching would be easy. Few of them however, "reached their destination without blistered feet or without having straggled at some time during the march."[50]

Another task made the march all that more difficult. Confederates retreating along the rail line from Suffolk to Petersburg and Richmond, acting under the orders of the secretary of war, tore up the rails "on both roads east of Suffolk as far as possible." They were ordered to do the same west of Suffolk as well, "letting the last train take up the iron behind it."[51]

* * *

Back in Norfolk, the Union occupation was a little more than 12 hours old, and its citizens were just beginning to come to grips with the changing circumstances. The fact that it was the Sabbath, and businesses were closed and the city quiet, helped. "The wharves," wrote one eyewitness,

> were crowded with blacks, male and female, and a goodly number of working people, with their wives and children, were strolling about. Soldiers were stationed on the wharves, and picketed through the city, whilst the flag of the Union floated in triumph from the cupola of the Custom House. The houses through the city were generally closed, especially most of those of the wealthier classes.[52]

49 Merz, May 10/11, 1862, *Diary of Private Louis Merz*, CVHS.

50 Henry W. Thomas, *History of the Doles-Cook Brigade of Northern Virginia, C.S.A. . . . by One of Its Own Members* (Atlanta, 1903), 66.

51 George W. Randolph to Huger "or the Officer in Command at Suffolk," May 11, 1862, *OR* 11/3:507. Rail iron was valuable for use as replacement rails, and to cast artillery pieces, fixed ammunition, and as plating for iron ships.

52 *Baltimore American*, May 13, 1862, in Wertenbaker, *Norfolk*, 240-41.

Chaplain Fuller, up early that morning, walked Norfolk's streets and "found the stillness of the Sabbath unbroken, as the soldiers in little squads walked quietly here and there, and the sullen men and women at street corners or behind the blinds of their houses, looked curiously and malignantly at the victors."[53]

Some found occupation more difficult to adjust to than others. According to the *New York Times*, a man in a gray naval uniform stopped Brig. Gen. Viele at the Atlantic Hotel "and wished to know if he would be arrested. The General told him certainly, if he wore that uniform. This morning he made his appearance in the same uniform again, and was arrested." The provost guard also arrested two Confederate soldiers as prisoners of war for wearing their uniforms. The atmosphere was lighter at Viele's headquarters in the Custom House, where another reporter "found that the ladies of Portsmouth (God bless them!) . . . still true to the Union, had presented him with two beautiful bouquets, whose fragrance had scented the whole room."[54]

The *New York Times* correspondent discerned a certain ambivalence in the population. "All the public indications of sentiment in the city thus far have certainly been on the side of secession. Scarcely half a dozen men have ventured to come out boldly as Union men," explained the reporter. "The general tone of conversation," he continued,

> where you succeed in getting any, is dull, discontented and sour. I do not regard this, however, as an infallible indication of settled political sentiment. The people unquestionably feel that they have been abandoned by their friends and conquered by the North. This is never a pleasant feeling, and men must be pardoned for not being able to conquer it on the instant. I saw nothing, during my stay in the city, which was it is true very short, to indicate that spiteful hatred of the Union and its friends which had been manifested in other quarters.[55]

The city's black residents offered a much different response, noted the reporter, and "were out in full force. . . all in their most smiling holiday attire. Whether it was the military show, always so fascinating to the negro mind, or the equally strong passion for something new, or a sanguine perception that all this conquest is for their behoof," he could not say, "but they certainly seemed to be the

53 Fuller, *Chaplin Fuller*, 250-51.

54 "Later—Destruction of the *Merrimac*," *New York Times*, and "Five Miles from Norfolk," Philadelphia *Press*, both May 13, 1862, 1.

55 "Latest from Norfolk," *New York Times*, May 13, 1862, 1.

parties most deeply interested in the pageant of to-day." The same New York reporter noticed "Quite a number of Irishmen . . . in the streets, [who] were mainly quite free to proclaim their satisfaction at the changed aspect of affairs." The "dozen or so of plain, respectable people collected on the wharf" with whom he chatted "deplored the existing state of things, but thought the Abolitionists mainly to blame . . . they were glad no more blood had been shed, because it would only exasperate feelings . . . and it seemed after all that we should be *obliged* to live together again as friends by-and-by [emphasis in the original]."[56]

Chaplain Fuller crossed the Elizabeth River on the ferry to Portsmouth. The water, he observed, was "positively yellow with tobacco and covered with a black scum from burning rebel steamers and gunboats, and the ruined navy-yard." The ships and yard still emitted dense black smoke. Fuller found a different attitude in Portsmouth, and discovered why their ladies might have presented Viele with flowers. Many mechanics had lost their jobs when the Rebels burned the navy yard and were indignant "against their traitorous tyrants. Our troops were welcomed as deliverers [by] almost every woman . . . and half the men." They brought "bouquets of flowers," he marveled, and a pair of citizens "earnestly proffered me a breakfast in an eating-house near."

Fuller accepted the invitation but found the fare less than ample. There was no "beefsteak," he wrote, nor were their eggs, bread, butter, or tea. Indeed, there wasn't "a pound of tea to be bought in all Portsmouth." The chaplain settled for some ham, cornbread, rye coffee, and "excellent oysters." He paid for his breakfast with an American quarter, a coin the hostess was so excited to have that "she exhibited it at once to the admiring crowd, who looked upon it as a mention of their bygone happy days."[57]

Federal soldiers continued to arrive throughout the day. Back at Ocean View, Lt. Col. Cram supervised the disembarkation of two more regiments—the 29th Massachusetts and the 20th Indiana, part of Brig. Gen. Mansfield's brigade—during the early morning. After learning of the *Virginia's* demise, Cram cancelled over-the-beach landings.

56 Ibid.

57 Fuller, *Chaplain Fuller*, 251-54. Fuller stayed with the 16th Massachusetts until just before the Battle of Fredericksburg, when he resigned his chaplaincy. He was discharged on Dec. 10, 1862, and ready to return home, but volunteered to participate with the regiment in the battle the next day and was killed. Jesse F. Stevens, Adjutant General, *Massachusetts Soldiers, Sailors, and Marines in the Civil War*, 8 vols. (Norwood, MA, 1931), 2:224, 225.

Cram had been expecting the weather to worsen and, "Sure enough," at 3:00 a.m. on Sunday May 11, "a sudden blast came sweeping over the sea from the north-east" roiling the waters at Ocean View. The "surf was waging war with the 'wharf of barges' and the schooners and steamer *Nelly Baker* aground there . . . were beating against each other and the barges." He ordered the remaining unloaded ships and transports carrying cavalry units, horses, and supplies back to Fort Monroe.[58]

As the remaining regiments already ashore marched up the Princess Anne Road to the former Confederate artillery line and encampment, those who spent the night there packed up their gear for the march into the city. The 10th New York arrived about noon. Unlike Fuller and the 16th Massachusetts, the reception they received did not impress Charles Cowtan and his comrades. The soldiers were the "objects of curious and eager inspection by the inhabitants . . . evidently . . . led to believe that the Yankee soldiers were semi-barbarous and [uncivilized]. A few women exhibited a rather masculine and vicious spirit in their remarks and actions," he continued, and children "along the streets cheered shrilly for Jeff. Davis" The Zouaves ignored them and continued through the city to take up their new post downriver at Fort Norfolk.[59]

Sailors felt the chill especially from women, who could get away with more "incivility" than could the men. Zerega, aboard the *Susquehanna*, described the large riverfront crowd's reaction to the band on May 11:

> [W]henever it played "Hail, Columbia," "Star-Spangled Banner," etc., the women would show signs of displeasure and walk away, we began to amuse ourselves by having it play selections from the Operas, "Dixie," "My Maryland," etc., and when it became evident that the shore audience was very much interested, the officer of the deck would make a sign to the bandmaster, who would at once break into "Hail, Columbia," etc. The women soon "caught on" and ceased running away, so after a day or two we entertained them with three fine concerts daily, ending, of course, with one of our national airs.[60]

The balance of the 1st Delaware entered Norfolk about the same time as the National Zouaves. "Selected to act as provost-guard in the city," the Delaware regiment established its headquarters "in the offices of the jail." Another soldier

58 Cram, "Report," May 31, 1862, Wool Papers, NYSA.

59 Cowtan, *National Zouaves*, 79.

60 Zerega, "Last Days," 1:457.

considered the provost assignment an "honor" for the regiment, which it accepted after "the earnest solicitations of the citizens." Still, he added, "the duty is very severe, and we are on guard duty every day and night."[61]

The work of the provost-guard, or military police, was vital in keeping order between citizens and the occupying Union soldiers. The Philadelphia *Press's* correspondent praised Brig. Gen. Viele for selecting a worthy provost marshal to head the force. "Capt. Phineas A. Davis, commanding the Richardson Light Battery of Lowell, Mass.," who had been "the efficient and officer-like marshal at Old Point," explained the paper, would "prove as acceptable both to citizens and soldiers."[62]

As the Union soldiers settled into their new duties, Maj. Gen. Wool and Flag Officer Goldsborough set out to survey the occupied cities. Goldsborough took a launch from the *Susquehanna* and made for the destroyed Gosport Navy Yard, which was still burning in many places. The naval officer "went all over it," and filed a report with Secretary Welles. "Nearly everything is destroyed. Of the buildings, the officers' quarters alone remain intact. There are a large number of iron tanks, however," he continued,

> apparently in perfect condition, a good deal of mast and other timber, a number of old, and generally worthless guns, and considerable machinery of one kind or another. The dock gates are all destroyed, and the pier ends, connected with the gates, have been blown up to a partial degree, but otherwise the dock itself seems uninjured.[63]

Following his inspection, the flag officer left the *Susquehanna's* Capt. James L. Lardner—"an officer in whose discretion and good sense I have great confidence"—in charge of the Union ships on the Elizabeth. Goldsborough gave Lardner "full directions" about communications with the shore, but was convinced "matters of importance" would force his return in several days."[64]

Wool also visited the navy yard on the 11th to examine the smoking ruins. At Craney Island, the aging general found 39 large caliber guns, most of them spiked, plus many "shot and shell with about five thousand pounds of provisions." He

61 Seville, *Delaware Volunteers*, 42; "Dido" to "Times," May 11, 1862, in Biggs, *They Fought for the Union*, accessed Aug. 15, 2016, bellicivilis.com.

62 "Five Miles from Norfolk," Philadelphia *Press*, May 13, 1862, 1.

63 Goldsborough to Welles, May 12, 1862, *ORN* 7:342-43.

64 Ibid.

estimated they had captured about 200 cannons, including those at Sewell's Point, a large quantity of shot and shells, and "many other articles of value to the government." In a postscript, Wool asked Stanton to inform him of the president's verbal order to Goldsborough to remove all those cannons. Which service (the Army or the Navy) would take charge of the guns would soon become a bone of contention.[65]

The telegraph wires hummed throughout the day with the news of Norfolk's capture and the *Virginia's* demise, from official notices sent by Secretary Stanton and Maj. Gen. Wool to unofficial descriptions of events filed by various newspaper correspondents. The news electrified a host of cities, two of which the *Philadelphia Inquirer* reported upon. One was West Chester, Pennsylvania, where the "saying that no Sabbath is known in time of revolution was exemplified to-day on the reception of the news of the capture of Norfolk and the destruction of the *Merrimac*," declared the paper. "The bells were rung, cannon were fired, and every demonstration of joy manifested." Even in Baltimore, a city with deeply divided loyalties, there was "intense rejoicing . . . all day over the capture of Norfolk and the destruction of the *Merrimac*. The Secessionists, however, are sorely depressed."[66]

According to the *New York Times*, Philadelphia was "in a furor of excitement—flags are floating in every direction, and the chimes of St. Stephen's Church rang joyful peels this evening." The citizens of Bridgeport, Connecticut, were not content with just chimes, and fired a "salute of one hundred guns . . . in honor of the recent victories."

It was in the nation's capital, however, where the greatest enthusiasm was openly displayed. "Washington has been in a state of tumult all day, growing out of the extraordinary war bulletins that have been posted at the hotels," gushed a New York paper. "People are bewildered," it continued,

> and their joy made grave and inexpressible by the unexpected immensity of the Union triumphs. Willard's Hotel had been crowded, the War Office besieged, and every place of public resort thronged by eager crowds pressing and breathless for news. Extra editions of the Sunday papers were issued, and sold at fabulous prices, until every man, woman and

65 Wool, "Report," May 12, 1862, *OR* 11/1:634-35. Wool was ordered on May 24 to let the Navy take back the navy yard and other property at Gosport. Wool to Goldsborough, May 24, 1862, Wool Papers, NYSA. A battalion of marines "took possession of the navy yard, Major-General Wool having received instructions from the War Department to transfer the public works there to the Navy." A. Ludlow Case to Welles, May 25, 1862, *ORN* 7:427.

66 "The News at West Chester—Great Rejoicing" & "The News at Baltimore—The Sick and Wounded," *Philadelphia Inquirer,* May 12, 1862, 1.

> child of Washington knew the wonderful tidings. . . . the chorus of every congratulation between the people was the same—a paean of enthusiastic praise of the noble General of the Union, who in the unanimous declaration of Congress, has accomplished such great results with such small sacrifice of human life.[67]

The *Times* credited Maj. Gen. Wool—"the noble General of the Union"—rather than President Lincoln, for the victory. At least Wool had a direct hand in the result. When he learned of Norfolk's fall, Maj. Gen. McClellan, camped with his army "19 miles from Williamsburg" and closing in on Richmond, wrote his wife, "Norfolk is in our possession, the result of my movements." A *New York Times* reporter partially endorsed McClellan's interpretation when it claimed Norfolk's fall was "a direct and inevitable result of the surrender of Yorktown and the retreat of the great rebel army. After that event the fall of Norfolk was simply a question of time."[68]

* * *

Southern reaction was decidedly sour. "We have sustained a great calamity in the loss of the Navy Yard and the evacuation of the city of Norfolk," exclaimed the editor of the *Lynchburg Virginian* to his readers. "It would have been better had Savannah, Charleston, Pensacola, and every other city in the Gulf States been abandoned, than that Norfolk should have been given to the enemy." In a weak attempt to dispel the gloom, the editor added that the city's fall "releases a large army to operate elsewhere and may add to the security of the Capital." The "large garrison of Yankees" required to hold Norfolk "will thus be kept from active operations, and furnish food for wasting disease this summer. Norfolk will be a grave yard of thousands of Hessians."[69]

It was the loss of the *Virginia*, however, and not the fall of Norfolk, that caused the most lamentation. Varina Davis wrote in her memoir that her husband's "consternation was great when her loss was known—coming as it did so fast upon

67 "The News in Washington," *New York Times*, May 12, 1862, 1.

68 George B. McClellan, *McClellan's Own Story: The War for the Union, the Soldiers Who Fought It, the Civilians Who Directed It and His Relations to It and to Them* (New York, 1887), 355; "News from Fortress Monroe," *New York Times*, May 13, 1862, 8.

69 Clipping, "The Evacuation of Norfolk," in "Virginia Gordan Scrapbook," Sargeant Memorial Collection, n.d., NPL. The reference to Hessians, who were hired by the British to fight in America during the Revolutionary War, was intended as a slur against invading Union soldiers.

the heels of her triumph over the Federal fleet." Robert E. Lee told his wife, Mary, that "the loss of the *Virginia* has produced such profound sensation that all personal considerations are smothered." Col. Josiah Gorgas, chief of ordnance for the Confederate War Department, told his diary that "no one event of the war, not even the disaster of Fort Donelson, created such a profound sensation as the destruction of this noble ship." John M. Brooke, the navy lieutenant who had so much to do with the *Virginia's* creation, blamed mid-level officials of the government for the loss of the ship. When he learned of the ironclad's destruction, Brooke, surely recalling how hard it was to acquire all the necessary materials and supplies needed to build her, warned that "[if] the cause of the Confederacy is in danger, it is in consequence of execrable management, not on the part of executives but on the part of directors who act without concert."[70]

The loss of their ironclad champion also affected a host of civilians. "The destruction of the *Virginia* was the most unexpected and distressing of this series of disasters which came upon us so rapidly at this period of the war," wrote Richmond resident Sallie Brock Putnam. "This invincible iron-clad had become, from her brilliant achievements in the naval engagement in Hampton Roads, the pride of the South. Her loss to us is said to have been of greater importance than if ten thousand men had perished on the field of battle."[71]

Richmond's *Daily Dispatch* described the *Virginia's* loss as "exceedingly painful to this community. That vessel had achieved so much and given such proof of power, that the public relied upon her in the exigency of the day. She was looked to with the deepest interest," continued the paper. "When . . . Norfolk was occupied by the enemy, all asked with breathless anxiety, 'What of the *Virginia*?' The answer came slowly, but terribly." Another Richmond paper, the *Richmond Examiner*, flatly claimed that the fall of New Orleans in April wasn't as bad a shock to the South's cause as the loss of the *Virginia*.[72]

The people of Norfolk, Portsmouth, and the surrounding area faced an uncertain future. "The business of the place is evidently ruined," pronounced the

70 Varina Davis, *Jefferson Davis*, 2:220-21; R. E. Lee to wife, *Wartime Papers*, 1:172; Vandiver, ed., *Diary of General Josiah Gorgas*, 4; John M. Brooke, May 12, 1862, in George M. Brooke Jr., ed., *Ironclads and Big Guns of the Confederacy: The Journal and Letters of John M. Brooke* (Columbia, SC, 2002), 90.

71 Sallie Brock Putnam, *Richmond During the War: Four Years of Personal Observation* (New York, 1867), 127.

72 "The Virginia," Richmond *Daily Dispatch*, May 13, 1862, 2; Richmond *Examiner*, May 13, 1862, in Lucille M. Stephens, "Historic Norfolk: 'A Child of Mars,'" M.A. thesis, Southern Methodist University, Aug. 1948, 40.

New York Times rather prematurely on May 13: "Grass is literally growing in what were once some of the busiest and most bustling commercial streets." The Army had stimulated "certain limited kinds of business, but nothing upon which the prosperity of a great community can be based." The citizens' pockets were full of Confederate scrip, which many believed would be redeemed to the last dollar, continued the paper. "But this was rather an attempt to bolster their own faith in the only kind of money they had, than an indication of confidence in its substantial value."[73]

73 "Latest from Norfolk," *New York Times*, May 13, 1862, 8.

Chapter 7

Monday, May 12, 1862

"So ended a brilliant week's campaign of the President."

— *Treasury Secretary Salmon P. Chase*

PRESIDENT Lincoln arrived at the Washington Navy Yard aboard the USS *Baltimore* on the morning of May 12. With word of the capture of Norfolk and the destruction of the CSS *Virginia* preceding him, the nation's capital greeted the president as a conquering hero. The president appeared "in high spirits, and greatly refreshed and invigorated by his sojourn to the seat of war," the *New York Times* reported. "He was received with enthusiastic demonstration of delight by all classes, plainly showing that in the new character of General and Commander he has added immeasurably to his popularity."[1]

In the same issue, the reporter for the *Times* who had covered the momentous Hampton Roads events credited Lincoln with the victory. "His visit here has been of the most unostentatious," he began,

> but certainly of the most useful sort. He has given his personal attention and care to every department of operations here, and has brought a very excellent and safe judgment to bear upon matters which required something more than mere professional knowledge and skill

1 "The Return of the President," *New York Times*, May 13, 1862, 4.

> for their solution. And I do no injustice to others in saying that much of the vigor and success of the recent operation here is due to the stimulus of his presence.[2]

Accolades for the president's leadership abounded. *Harper's Weekly* of May 24 acknowledged what others were saying: "the expedition against Norfolk was mainly planned by President Lincoln." Another newspaper praised Lincoln's military ability and wished it had gone further:

> The President is entitled to all the honors of a successful campaign, and to the bestowment of the formal title of full General as the result of his visit to Fortress Monroe. A week's operations under his own eye, and the energy of his Secretary of War, were enough to destroy the *Merrimac*, the terror of the nation, and reduce Norfolk and its surrounding fortifications to the just authority of the United States. . . . The general wish here is, that he had gone to the headquarters of his army now in front of Richmond, for it is believed that the power of his presence would have driven Jeff. Davis headlong from his capital, and made the way smooth for our victorious forces.[3]

The capital's *Evening Star* noted how Lincoln's actions at Hampton Roads had also impressed the sailors on the *Baltimore*, who united "in saying he is 'a trump,' and they express a belief that he has some time served an apprenticeship on board ship, so much at home there did he seem. They also express the opinion," continued the editorial, "that the success of the movement is due to the energy infused into it by 'Uncle Abe.'"[4]

Even Secretary Chase, whose objections to some of Lincoln's policies would lead him to consider a challenge for the party's nomination in 1864, described the taking of Norfolk as the president's triumph. "So ended a brilliant week's campaign of the President," Chase wrote to his daughter from the *Baltimore*. Chase was "quite certain that if he [Lincoln] had not come down, Norfolk would still have been in

2 "Effect of the President's Visit to Fortress Monroe," ibid.

3 "Norfolk Repossessed," *Harper's Weekly*, May 24, 1862, 327; Clipping, Wool Papers, NYSA.

4 "Direct from Norfolk," Washington *Evening Star*, May 12, 1862, 2. By the spring of 1862, Lincoln had already taken some short excursions on the Potomac River. His previous sailing experience began at the age of 19 when he was commissioned to take a flat-bottomed boatload of goods to sell in New Orleans. Along with the son of the owner of the goods, Lincoln successfully steered the flatboat down the Ohio and Mississippi rivers and completed the transactions. The future president made a second trip to New Orleans three years later. As a freshman congressman in 1848, Lincoln took a boat for part of the trip from Washington City back to Illinois.

the possession of the enemy & the *Merrimac* as grim & defiant & as much a terror as ever."[5]

Lincoln was also pleased with his own efforts, so much so that on the day after he returned to the Executive Mansion, he told the entire story to one of his friends, Illinois Senator Orville Browning. While Browning obviously misunderstood parts of the story, the senator clearly caught the president's enthusiasm. "He gave me all the details and particulars of this trip and what he did," wrote the senator. "He sent Commodore Rodgers up the James River with a fleet after having had a struggle with Goldsborough on the subject. He also devised and Caused to be executed the March upon York Town [Norfolk] under Wool which resulted in its Capture—having, himself, the day before explored the Coast and found a landing place for the troops."[6]

Not surprisingly, the two top military commanders who carried out the president's orders overlooked Lincoln's direct involvement. On the same day the president returned to Washington, Maj. Gen. Wool penned a short message to his wife that failed to mention the president: "I telegraphed you yesterday & day before that I had taken Norfolk."[7]

Nor did Louis Goldsborough's testimony before the Joint Committee on the Conduct of the War almost a year later credit Lincoln's role in the fall of the city. By then a rear admiral, Goldsborough seemed to support McClellan's argument and conveniently omitted Lincoln's orders to both he and Wool to take action. "The landing of McClellan's army on the peninsula, and their advance to Yorktown and beyond towards Richmond," testified the admiral, "undoubtedly caused the fall of Norfolk and the self-destruction of the *Merrimack*." Goldsborough continued:

5 Chase to "Nettie," May 11, 1862, in "Diary," Chase Papers, LC.

6 Pease & Randall, eds., *Orville Hickman Browning*, 1:545. Lincoln apparently also told the story to then-Congressman and future president James A. Garfield, whose rendition of events was considerably garbled. Noah Brooks, *Abraham Lincoln: the Nation's Leader in the Great Struggle Through Which was Maintained the Existence of the United States* (New York, 1888), 336-37. Not everyone credited Lincoln with the victory. McClellan, for example, claimed that Norfolk's capture occurred because of the Army of the Potomac's movement up the Virginia Peninsula.

7 Wool to Sarah Wool, May 13, 1862, Wool Papers, NYSA. After the war, Wool maintained his primacy in Norfolk's capture and blamed McClellan and the administration for not allowing him to take the city earlier. Wool claimed that his capture of Norfolk and destruction of the *Virginia* "was no less fortunate for the Country than for the Army of the Potomac." He maintained that the move saved McClellan's army by opening up the James River for its eventual retreat after the Seven Days' Battles, while also allowing those soldiers to be on hand to block Gen. Robert E. Lee's army from taking Washington. Wool to Benson J. Lossing, Dec. 10, 1865, accessed Sept. 13, 2016, www.sethkaller.com/item/437-General-Wool-Takes-Shot-at-McClellan.

All the troops of the enemy, in consequence of that movement, were withdrawn from Norfolk. As soon as that was known a small force landed at Willoughby's Point, and marched up, and the civil authorities came out and gave up the place to General Wool. We had been informed by a deserter of their condition, and knew that a small force would be sufficient to induce a surrender.[8]

* * *

Some Confederate officials spun the events to depict the evacuation as a strategic move by Jefferson Davis and others. Richmond's *Daily Dispatch*, for example, editorialized that the withdrawal from Norfolk was all part of a plan to draw Northern forces toward Richmond and away from their base of supplies. "The authorities had well considered that question before Norfolk was abandoned," claimed the paper's editor. "That evacuation was made with the utmost deliberation, and in pursuance of the system of concentration to which the Government is now fairly committed. It was well and thoroughly considered."[9]

Others saw the loss as but a temporary setback and urged the government to retake Norfolk as soon as possible. J. B. Gladney, a prominent citizen of Jackson, Mississippi, wrote Davis a lengthy letter on August 2, 1862, that the South's best strategy would be to secure the border states before driving northward to the Great Lakes while "holding . . . Charleston, Savannah, and Mobile, and [recapturing] Norfolk and New Orleans." What Davis thought of the fantastical plan passed unremarked.[10]

What was clear was that the loss of Norfolk and Portsmouth, coupled with Gen. Joseph E. Johnston's methodical retrograde up the Peninsula ever closer to Richmond raised doubts in the Confederate president's mind about whether even

8 Goldsborough testimony, Apr. 1, 1863, *Report of the Joint Committee*, 1:633-34. Note Goldsborough said Willoughby's Point, when he meant Ocean View.

9 "The War," Richmond *Daily Dispatch,* May 12, 1862, 2. The *Daily Dispatch* took a particular interest in Norfolk, Portsmouth, and the people of that part of the state. For the rest of the war and long after the port cities were the scene of important action, the paper published tidbits and news gleaned from those who evaded Union patrols to visit Richmond or smuggled letters into the Confederacy.

10 J. B. Gladney to Davis, Aug. 6, 1862, *OR* 2/4:40. Rumors persisted in Norfolk that the Confederate Army and/or Navy would sweep down from Richmond as liberators. See, for example, "The Rebel *Merrimac*, No. 2," Richmond *Daily Dispatch*, Aug. 5, 1862, 1. Lt. Gen. James Longstreet tried unsuccessfully to capture Suffolk the following spring while on a massive supply-gathering operation for the Army of Northern Virginia. The Confederates would not come any closer to Norfolk for the rest of the war.

the capital of the Confederacy could be held against McClellan's large and well-equipped army. "If the withdrawal from the Peninsula and Norfolk had been with due preparation and desirable deliberation," he wrote his wife and confidant Varina on May 13, "I should be more sanguine of a successful defense of this city."[11]

Secretary of the Navy Stephen Mallory also viewed the recent events as a catastrophe for the struggling Confederacy. "The abandonment of Norfolk stripped us not only of a vast amount of valuable property and building material," he reported forthrightly to President Davis on on August 16, "but deprived us of our only drydock and of tools which are not found and cannot be replaced or made in the Confederacy."[12]

* * *

While Davis, Mallory, and other insightful Southerners recognized the abandonment of Norfolk and loss of the CSS *Virginia* as disastrous, but not fatal, to the cause of Southern independence, some Northerners believed President Lincoln's expedition would soon achieve the ultimate goal of ending the war and reunifying the country. "We believe this to be the beginning of the end; and there will be small delay in its consumption," editorialized the *Philadelphia Inquirer* on May 12. "Follow [the Rebels] with alacrity," it argued,

> leave them no time or means to rally, enclose them, on all sides, in the mountains, and the end itself is very near. Their military power being destroyed, the political fabric will crumble to dust; for the former is the foundation on which the latter is built. Iron battering rams and mail-clad monsters could not save them. The *Manassas* [below New Orleans] lies a mass of timber and iron at the bottom of the Mississippi, and the far-famed *Merrimac* has gone into pieces to keep company with her noble victim, the glorious *Cumberland*.[13]

Five days later, *The Christian Recorder*, an African-American newspaper in Philadelphia, echoed the *Inquirer's* optimism:

> Whole volumes would not minutely record the events of the last week, and one of the grandest themes of the future historians of our country will be the evacuation of

11 Varina Davis, *Jefferson Davis*, 2:265; Davis to Varina Davis, May 13, 1862, in Crist, et al., *Papers of Jefferson Davis*, 8:174.

12 Report, Mallory to Davis, Aug. 16, 1862, *ORN* 2/2:243.

13 "Glorious News—The General Breaking Up," *Philadelphia Inquirer*, May 12, 1862, 4.

> Yorktown, the battles of Williamsburg and West Point, the hot pursuit of the Secessionists by Gen. McClellan's victorious army, the terrific attack made on Sewall's Point by our fleet, under the eye of the President, the capture of Norfolk, and the grand denouement of the destruction of the *Merrimac.*[14]

Predictions that the end of the war was in sight proved woefully premature, but Lincoln's week at Hampton Roads was without doubt a remarkable success. In what can fairly be described as his own Norfolk Campaign, Lincoln proved to himself and others that his judgment on military matters was sound, and in some ways better, than the Army and Navy professionals around him. West Point generals and Annapolis naval officers often lacked Lincoln's focus on grand strategy and perceived only the problems directly in front of them while failing to see how those issues fit into the larger solution of bringing the war to an end.

The president grasped the larger national picture, and he was beginning to gain confidence in his ability to sift through the smaller pieces to achieve the whole. Others close to Lincoln appreciated his vision. After the war, Robert L. Wilson, the president's friend, fellow attorney, and politician, explained to William Herndon, Lincoln's former law partner in Illinois, how the president ability to rise to the occasion, even when it came to complex military matters:

> In 1862, after Gen. McClellan fell back on the Potomac, and the prospects were very dark, and uncertain; and Mr. Lincoln's letters urging McClellan to strike and advance and take Richmond, I was that Summer with the Army under Buell and Halleck. The matter of placing Mr. Lincoln at the head of the Army in the field, was generally advocated outside the Regular Army influence. It was conceded that he was not a military man. But he had proved to the world that he was equal to the exigencies of the times, and no man in the army appeared to be. That was the great trait of his character, all through his life. Whatever the exigency might be, he was equal to it, not only disappointing his friends, but also, I have no doubt, himself often.[15]

Before the war, Lincoln would have shuddered at the idea of any president commanding armies in the field. As early as 1848, he expressed his view that the Constitution granted Congress, not the executive, the power to make war, for the

14 "Character of the War in Virginia," Philadelphia *Christian Recorder*, May 17, 1862, Accessible Archives, accessed Aug. 28, 2009, accessible.com.dbgateway.nysed.gov/accessible.

15 Robert L. Wilson to William H. Herndon, Feb. 10, 1866, Herndon-Weik Collection of Lincolniana, LC.

good reason that in experience of the Founding Fathers, absolute monarchs had always wielded that power in Europe, "involving and impoverishing their people in wars pretending generally, if not always, that the good of the people was the object." The framers of the Constitution "understood [this] to be the most oppressive of all Kingly oppressions." A president leading an army was one step closer to tyranny.[16]

Before Norfolk, Lincoln had never led a military operation. George Washington could have done so as president during the Whiskey Rebellion of 1794, but chose instead to place the troops under the command of Virginia's governor, Henry "Light-horse Harry" Lee. In 1814, on the battlefield at Bladensburg, President James Madison declined to assume military command. He left the movement and disposition of the American soldiers, with one small exception, to his designated general and a reluctant secretary of war. As soon as the British forces opened the battle, Madison withdrew from the field to leave the fighting to the "military functionaries."[17]

Despite his rising confidence after the Norfolk campaign, Lincoln still had much to learn, and he made many mistakes in the weeks and months following his triumph. Within two weeks of his return to Washington, his meddling and tinkering with various forces in the Shenandoah Valley allowed Confederate Maj. Gen. Thomas J. "Stonewall" Jackson to demonstrate that the president still hadn't grasped the difficulties of maneuvering armies in the field.

The problems began when Lincoln decided to organize a response to Jackson's small army marching down (north) the Shenandoah Valley toward the Potomac River, driving Maj. Gen. Nathaniel P. Banks' small Union army before them. From the confines of the war department's telegraph room, the president, acting as his own general in chief of the Army, studied the maps, sought information, and sent out orders to cut off Jackson's eventual retreat south back up the valley. Through a series of telegrams on May 24, he ordered Maj. Gen. John C. Frémont, commander of the Virginia Mountain District, to move his little army east from Franklin in the Allegheny Mountains to Harrisonburg in the southern reaches of the Shenandoah. "This movement must be made immediately," Lincoln ordered. Shortly thereafter,

16 Lincoln to Herndon, Feb. 15, 1848, in Basler, ed., *Collected Works*, 1:451-52.

17 Leland D. Baldwin, "The Watermelon Army Marches," in *Whiskey Rebels: The Story of a Frontier Uprising* (Pittsburgh, 1967), 220. See also, Robert S. Kyff, "The Whiskey Rebellion," *American History* (July/August 1994), 29:36; Peter Snow, *When Britain Burned the White House: The 1814 Invasion of Washington* (New York, 2013), 80. Henry "Light-horse Harry" Lee was Robert E. Lee's father.

the president reemphasized the need for speed: "Much—perhaps all—depends upon the celerity with which you can execute [the movement]. Put the utmost speed into it. Do not lose a minute."[18]

Lincoln also ordered Maj. Gen. Irvin McDowell, the I Corps commander east of the Shenandoah, to move two divisions under Brig. Gen. James Shields west toward Strasburg. Like Frémont, McDowell replied that the order would be carried out. "I am highly gratified by your alacrity in obeying my order," Lincoln replied. "Everything now depends upon the celerity and vigor of your movements."[19]

With both forces sitting on Jackson's line of retreat up the valley, Lincoln believed he had trapped him. To Lincoln it all seemed rather simple. The maps hanging in the telegraph room denoted the distances Frémont and Jackson would have to travel. The former had the shorter march. McDowell's forces had farther to go. What the maps did not show, and the military men tried to explain to him, were the types and state of the roads, the condition of the soldiers, the amount of food and supplies they had on hand or that would be available, and when and how the weather might affect the movements.

McDowell tried to explain these variables to Lincoln. "I obeyed your order immediately, for it was positive and urgent," he reported back, "and perhaps as a subordinate I ought to stop." But he pressed on. "I beg to say that co-operation between General Frémont and myself to cut Jackson and [Maj. Gen. Richard S.] Ewell there is not to be counted upon, even if it is not a practical impossibility." He added that he could not help Banks, who would eventually cross the Potomac to get away from Jackson. Just getting to the Shenandoah from his base at Fredericksburg, he explained, would take "a week or ten days . . . by the route which will give it food and forage, and by that time the enemy will have retired."[20]

Frémont did not even try to explain the reality of the situation to Lincoln. He merely reinterpreted the president's order, reporting that the short road to Harrisonburg the president could see on the map was nothing more than a narrow dirt path. Three days later Lincoln sent Frémont a terse message: "I see you are at Moorefield," which was north of Frémont's starting point, not east. "You were expressly ordered to march to Harrisonburg. What does this mean?" Frémont

18 Lincoln to John C. Frémont, May 24, 1862, in Basler, ed., *Collected Works*, 5:230, 231. For a good sketch of Lincoln's long-distance generalship during this campaign, see Mark Grimsley, "Lincoln as Commander in Chief: Forays into Generalship," in Stephen D. Engle, ed., *The War Worth Fighting: Abraham Lincoln's Presidency and Civil War America* (Gainesville, FL, 2015), 62-84.

19 Lincoln to McDowell, May 24, 1862, in Basler, ed., *Collected Works of Abraham Lincoln*, 5:231.

20 *OR* 12/3:220.

explained the next day. "My troops were not in condition to execute your order—otherwise than has been done," he replied. "They have marched day & night to do it. The men had had so little to eat that many were weak from want of food. . . . In executing any order rec'd," he added, "I take it for granted that I am to exercise discretion concerning its literal execution according to circumstances."[21]

Despite the liberties taken with his orders and the resulting setbacks, Lincoln still hoped his plan would work. Later on May 28 he wired McDowell: "It is, for you a question of legs. Put all the speed you can. I have told Frémont as much, and directed him to drive at [the Confederates] as fast as possible."[22]

The plan did not work. Jackson's troops retreated south up the Valley on a macadamized (crushed stone) road. Frémont's and Shields' soldiers were confronted with roads little better than wide dirt paths. Jackson easily slipped past the Northern troops, which gave him the chance to confront Frémont's small army first, and then Shields' forces before the two could come together.

By July, Lincoln realized some of his own weaknesses and that he could not simultaneously run the war effort and perform his presidential duties. On July 23, he called Maj. Gen. Henry W. Halleck to Washington from the Western Theater and designated him General in Chief of the Army. Halleck's job was to coordinate the various commands and run the war. Alas, such a large responsibility was was not his forte. Lincoln, along with Secretary Stanton, continued to set overall military policy while Halleck exercised his organizational strengths. As the conflict dragged on, Lincoln took bolder steps to control the Northern war effort, using the telegraph to gather information and to direct far-flung action in broad strokes. He also continued to hunt for a military leader who shared his vision.

Two months after the Norfolk campaign, the president passed through Hampton Roads on his way to confer with Maj. Gen. McClellan on the James River. He wanted to see for himself what, if anything, could be done to resurrect McClellan's Peninsula Campaign that had failed just outside Richmond. Gen. Robert E. Lee (who replaced Gen. Joseph E. Johnston in command after Johnston was severely wounded at Seven Pines/Fair Oaks on May 31), had transferred Jackson's men east to Richmond from the Shenandoah Valley and, during the final week of June and first day of July, attacked McClellan's Army of the Potomac in a bloody series of combats known as the Seven Days' Battles. The assaults drove the

21 Lincoln to Frémont, & Frémont to Lincoln, May 27, 28, 1862 in Basler, ed., *Collected Works of Abraham Lincoln*, 5:243, 244.

22 Lincoln to McDowell, May 28, 1862, ibid., 246.

Union army away from Richmond and back to the James River and the protection of the gunboats. The defeat was a heartbreaking setback for Lincoln and Northern morale and signaled the ascendency of Lee's star. McClellan's failure prompted Lincoln to summon Maj. Gen. John Pope from the Western Theater to command the new Army of Virginia composed of troops from the Shenandoah and other parts of northern Virginia. McClellan's troops, meanwhile, were shipped north by water and some were assigned to Pope.

When Pope was thrashed by Lee at Second Bull Run at the end of August 1862, Lincoln had little choice but to call upon McClellan's organizational ability to put the army back together, especially since Lee moved his own victorious Army of Northern Virginia north of the Potomac River in early September in what would be his first invasion of the North. McClellan did as ordered and moved westward more quickly than Lee anticipated, scored a significant strategic and tactical victory in the gaps at South Mountain on September 14, and waged a day-long bloody battle at Antietam three days later on September 17 that forced Lee to retreat south of the Potomac. McClellan's failure to follow up his victory as quickly as Lincoln demanded led to his eventual sacking in early November.

Lincoln continued to cycle through generals. In the East, he replaced McClellan with Maj. Gen. Ambrose Burnside, then Burnside with Maj. Gen. Joseph Hooker, and, during the middle of the Gettysburg Campaign in late June 1863, accepted Hooker's proffer of resignation and elevated V Corps commander Maj. Gen. George Meade to lead the Army of the Potomac. Meade would defeat Lee at Gettysburg and lead his army through the end of the war.

Lincoln, however, still needed a general who understood how to organize offensives and win the war. Maj. Gen. Ulysses S. Grant had been doing that in the Western Theater since his capture of Forts Henry and Donelson in February 1862. He followed that with a decisive win at Shiloh that April, captured Vicksburg the following July, and crushed the Confederate army laying a quasi- siege to Chattanooga, Tennessee, that November. Lincoln promoted Grant to lieutenant general in the spring of 1864 and gave him command of all the Union armies, a move that effectively displaced Halleck as general in chief (leaving the latter to act as chief of staff). On the sea and inland waterways, Lincoln came to rely on Rear Admiral David Farragut and David Dixon Porter, soon to be an acting rear admiral.

Although he never again directly orchestrated a campaign in the field, the week he spent at Fort Monroe in May 1862 provided the foundation Abraham Lincoln needed to develop the confidence and vision he would need to fight the long war ahead and bring it to a successful end.

Chapter 8

Aftermath

"The most influential citizens, if they refuse to bow the knee to the Lincoln ape, are hurried off to cells in distant forts; even women are thrown into prison."

— *Richmond Daily Dispatch*

PORTSMOUTH shoppers quickly learned on May 12, 1862, what military occupation meant when no meat was available at Monday's open-air market. Earlier that morning, a U.S. Army wagon pulled up to the market-house and "swept every pound of beef from the butchers' stalls," reported a Richmond paper. "Upon being told that the citizens desired to live, the [Union army] Commissary replied that the citizens must dispense with beef for the present, as he desired it for the soldiers." The paper added, however, that the stall keepers "were promptly paid to the last cent in gold and silver."[1]

Across the Elizabeth River in the quiet streets of Norfolk, the citizens didn't venture out on the first business day of the week. While most stores were closed, the *New York Times* reported, they were expected to "open in a day or two" unless the owners had left with the Confederate army. "[S]ome excitement still prevails,"

1 "Latest From Norfolk and Portsmouth," Richmond *Daily Dispatch*, May 16, 1862, 2.

the reporter continued, "but it is supposed in a few days, when communication is fully opened with the Northern ports, confidence will be completely restored."[2]

As the situation in Portsmouth illustrated, the area's population, black and white, struggled with shortages of food and other necessities. Prices for basic goods, already high due to the inflation of Confederate notes, spiked again after the Union takeover. "The prices of almost everything are astonishingly high," wrote a Washington *Evening Post* reporter on May 12. "Candles, for instance, of a miserable quality, 60 cents per pound; common brown wrapping paper and envelopes 50 cents per package; brown sugar 29 cents per pound."[3]

Like the *Times* reporter, many people thought the occupation would ease the shortages. Maj. Gen. Wool allowed some necessities to be landed at Norfolk's harbor, especially for Northern merchants setting up new shops. The *New York Herald* on May 14 reported that in Norfolk, "many stores have been opened, and some of the establishments are resuming operations. The market is better supplied than on Monday and yesterday," it continued, "and the people generally whom we meet in the streets seem more sociable and cheerful. . . .The stores," continued the paper, "it must be confessed, do not present a very attractive appearance; the stocks are meager and prices very uncertain as yet." A few "days of patience and forbearance," suggested the reporter, "will settle matters satisfactorily all round."[4]

A large number of new stores were preparing to open, but according to Washington's *National Republican*, local shopkeepers would not be allowed to buy new goods to sell without taking the oath of allegiance to the United States. Requiring an oath of allegiance was just one more reminder that the people were under an occupation. During the week, many more soldiers crossed Hampton Roads from Fort Monroe to settle into camps in and around Norfolk and Portsmouth, increasing the stress on the local residents. On May 15, a delegation of government officials, including Lincoln's secretaries of state and the navy, the attorney general, and other "ladies and gentlemen," sailed into Norfolk's harbor aboard the *Baltimore*.[5]

2 "News from Norfolk," *New York Times*, May 14, 1862, 8.

3 "Latest from Norfolk, Business Reopening Here," Washington *Evening Star*, May 13, 1862, 3. The equivalent costs in 2019 dollars: almost $15.00 for candles, $12.44 for paper and envelopes, and more than $7.21/lb. for brown sugar.

4 "From General Viele's Division," *New York Herald*, May 16, 1862, 1.

5 "From Norfolk," *Evening Star*, May 15, 1862, & "Affairs in Norfolk," *The National Republican*, June 26, 1862, both Washington, DC, 2.

Norfolk and her citizens were on display, at least at the wharf. In town, however, as Capt. John A. B. Dahlgren told his diary, "[P]eople kept their houses shut, and themselves inside. I am sorry for them, for I fear their town is ruined." The next day, the party of dignitaries toured the destruction at the navy yard and stopped to see the heavy fortifications on Craney Island before heading back to Washington. "In coming away, we paused over the wreck of the *Merrimac*, added the captain, "from which only a large timber showed itself above the full tide."[6]

The *Day Book*, Norfolk's local newspaper, now under the purview of the Northern military, agreed with Dahlgren that the city was remarkably quiet, with "the streets presenting day by day much the appearance of one prolonged Sabbath." Small groups of citizens gathered on street corners to discuss the situation and speculate about the future, explained the paper, but "the most perfect order reigns throughout the entire community, and we are glad to be able to chronicle the fact that the people have respected themselves and the city too much to engage in any acts which might have gotten them in trouble, without being of a practical benefit to any one."[7]

Residents bristling under Union occupation, however, found ways to convey their opinion about the intruders. Some women knew just how to signal their disgust. Years after the war, Alfred L. B. Zerega, a sailor from the USS *Susquehanna*, recalled one such scene. "When we first went on shore the ladies did not receive us very cordially," he explained. The women crossed the street to avoid the approaching seamen, "at the same time drawing their skirts to one side so as not to be contaminated by contact with a 'Yank.' Some would put on an extra veil." The actions triggered friendly, though mocking, responses from the sailors. "All this was fun for us, and we got into the habit of drawing our coat-tails on one side on

6 M. Dahlgren, ed., *John A. Dahlgren*, 367.

7 Norfolk *Day Book*, quoted in "From Norfolk," Richmond *Daily Dispatch*, May 31, 1862, 2. The *Day Book*, operated by editor John R. Hathaway and Norfolk's only daily paper at the time, was allowed to continue publishing but was closely monitored by the federal authorities to be "respectful in its tone." It was also switched from a morning to an afternoon paper. The *Day Book's* ability to publish would be short, however. Ongoing threats of shutdown, especially after complaints following the publication of a column unfavorable to the North, pushed the paper out of business by late June. The *Norfolk Union*, which replaced it, "was a lively and outspoken Union paper," according to the *National Republican*, but "a miserable, lying little sheet," according to the *Daily Dispatch*. "Latest from Norfolk, Business Reopening Here," Washington *Evening Star*, May 13, 1862, 3; "News from Norfolk," *New York Times*, May 14, 1862, 8; "From Fortress Monroe," & "The Feeling in Norfolk," Richmond *Daily Dispatch*, June 2 & 17, 1862; "Visit of Gen. Burnside to Gen. McClellan's Camp," Washington *National Republican*, June 12, 1862, 2.

meeting ladies who made any motion to switch their skirts, and if they attempted to put on an extra veil we would all stop, put on eye glasses and stare at them."[8]

Some women deliberately marched into the street to avoid coming upon a Union soldier on the sidewalk, and others spit from second story windows on officers passing below, observed the *New York Daily Tribune* the following month. "I know how difficult it is to deal with such Rebels who forget their sex, and with it forget decency itself; but if they forget that they ever were ladies, can they complain if occasionally we forget it likewise?"[9]

Not every Norfolk resident was offended by the Yankee presence. "Speaking of the Union sentiment among the men, I must [also] allude to the devotion of the ladies to the good cause," a correspondent wrote. "On Saturday evening [May 10], as the Commanding General was passing through the streets, attending to the disposition of his troops, several ladies expressed their delight at the appearance of Union soldiers by waving their handkerchiefs and saying in the most musical of voices, 'We are very glad to see you sir.' As affairs grow more calm," continued the reporter, "the influence of the Union women of Norfolk will be made more and more apparent."[10]

Outside of Norfolk, relations between residents and the occupying forces also gave reason to hope that the situation would settle down. While at a rural encampment, Frederick W. Ritschy of the 99th New York wrote that although a "Mr. Hendren" was a farmer and "a staunch Confederate," he possessed "humane feelings." Hendren, along with his wife and daughters, "did what lay in their power to add to the comfort of the officers and men." Later, at another camp, this one along Tanner's Creek outside Norfolk, Ritschy thought "the monotony of the camp life was somewhat relaxed during our stay at Camp Greble, and at this time it is no flattery to say that the farmers of the vicinity were very friendly to our boys, and no complaint was ever recorded showing that our boys, although a rough and ready lot, committed any act, however remote, to cast any reflection on the regiment."[11]

Back in Norfolk, a number of soldiers hoped that their overtures would win a change of heart among hostile residents. Through parades, snappy drills, and music, some thought that the hostility, if not the suspicion, was gradually thawing.

8 Zerega, "Last Days," 1:457.

9 "From Gen. Dix's Army," *New York Daily Tribune,* June 11, 1862, 3.

10 "From General Viele's Division," *New York Herald*, May 16, 1862, 1.

11 Manuscript, Ritschy, "Naval Brigade," NYSA, n.p.

William P. Seville, captain and historian of the 1st Delaware, observed a change. "The citizens kept themselves secluded for a few days, and acted spitefully for a time," he explained, "but gradually they appeared in the streets and opened their houses as they found that their fears of the Yankees were groundless, and that the hated foe were nothing of a more formidable character than well-behaved and tolerably handsome soldier boys." Regular parades helped greatly:

> The practice of holding dress-parades in the public square, which was commenced about a week after the occupation, entirely broke the shyness and reserve of the citizens, who gathered in great numbers, a majority of whom were ladies, to witness our military displays and listen to the excellent music our band always furnished. Indeed, before the regiment was relieved from provost duty in Norfolk the men had grown to be great favorites with many of the citizens, and when they departed they left many sore hearts and sad faces behind them, and not a few matrimonial engagements.[12]

Some Northerners optimistically believed Norfolk and Portsmouth had many silent Union sympathizers who could be coaxed to show their support. Reporters even speculated on when Norfolk would begin its own Union meetings. "Efforts are making to get up a meeting [for] the Union men of the city . . . to express their sentiments," the *New York Herald* reported. As soon as the city administration allowed it, "a large [such] assemblage can be gathered. . . . Some are for pressing the matter immediately, but the more judicious are for waiting a short time," not because they doubted Federal ability to maintain supremacy, "but because they believe that a greater number of wavering men [would stiffen up] as the beneficent polity of the authorities is more fully demonstrated."

The reluctance of the city's "Union men"—even "very sensible" ones—to come forth stemmed from a fear that the Confederates might recapture Norfolk, thought the *Herald* reporter. The recent change had so dazzled the loyal citizens "that they cannot yet determine whether the intensity of the previous darkness or brilliancy of the present light blinds them." Confidence may have grown slowly

12 Seville, *Delaware Volunteers*, 42. Charles Cowtan of the 10th New York (National Zouaves) also credited his regiment's parades with easing at least some of the tension. "The dress parades of the regiment at its camp became a feature, and were witnessed by numbers of the citizens each afternoon," he wrote in a post-war regimental history. "The splendid appearance of the command and the exactness of its evolutions forc[ed] encomiums from the sometimes not very friendly observers of both sexes." Cowtan, *National Zouaves*, 80.

because "the love of the Union here has been so oppressed—so nearly crushed out—that it dares hardly raise its head from the dust."[13]

Another newspaper, the *Evening Star*, reported closet Union supporters who might be silent in public, "but take every opportunity when not observed by the local tyrants of the rebellion to exchange friendly words and assurances of their loyalty with the soldiers." That would change in time, the writer predicted. "So soon as Richmond falls they will speak out boldly and defy the traitors amongst them." The year-long "subjection [they were] compelled to submit to has almost unmanned them," but as soon as they learned "their real strength and consult together it will be found that the Union sentiment of Norfolk is still formidable." *Harper's Weekly* reported a "Union meeting" later in the month at Portsmouth that drew "not less than eight hundred persons, including many from Norfolk." Maj. Gen. Wool gave such residents "ample assurance of protection."[14]

Southern newspapers scoffed at such assurances. Under the headline "Yankee Falsehood," the *Edgefield Advertiser* in South Carolina ridiculed a report that 1,800 Norfolk townspeople had taken the oath. "In the day of her greatest prosperity, Norfolk never pulled one thousand votes," scoffed the editor, "and it is palpably a falsehood that, while a large number of her citizens are absent in the army and as refugees, so many could be there to act as traitors." The Richmond *Daily Dispatch* concurred regarding another Union meeting that claimed "all the Union men in Norfolk . . . were there," about 20 people total. "The rest of the audience was made up of Yankee soldiers."[15]

Both sides recognized propaganda value in these claims, but Union occupiers in Norfolk knew the real story. "The glowing descriptions, given by newspaper correspondents, of the Union sentiment found in the city, were, to any honest and candid observer, whose wish was not father to the thought, simply false," exclaimed Chaplain Murphey after the war. Whatever support the Union had, he realized that the more affluent class hoped Southern troops would once more rout the Yankees and bring the cities back into the Confederacy. "The Unionists were

13 "From General Viele's Division," *New York Herald*, May 16, 1862, 1.

14 "From Norfolk," Washington *Evening Star*, May 15, 1862, 2; "Norfolk Still Sulky," *Harper's Weekly*, June 7, 1862, 355.

15 "Yankee Falsehood," *Edgefield* (SC) *Advertiser*, June 18, 1862, 2; "The Feeling in Norfolk," Richmond *Daily Dispatch*, June 17, 1862, 3. The next day, the paper revised its estimate of Union men upward to "not above thirty." "From Norfolk," Richmond *Daily Dispatch*, June 18, 1862, 1.

powerless," continued Murphey. "The wealthy and more influential classes were, almost to a man, so far as we could learn, Secessionists."[16]

Maj. Gen. Wool, who may have shared Murphey's feelings about the Virginians, decided to force the issue. Shortly after solidifying Federal control, Wool asked Norfolk's governmental leaders whether they considered themselves to be citizens of the United States, the Confederacy, neutral, or "a conquered people." The general later told Chase and Stanton that he had queried only "with the Kindest feelings towards the citizens of Norfolk, and for no other reason than to promote their prosperity and to encourage them in their well being and to return to their allegiance to the United States and with reference to opening the ports."[17]

Following a joint meeting of Norfolk's select and common councils, the leaders initially demurred in answering the question. A unanimous resolution ordered the councils to inform Wool that they had "no power or means by which to furnish a fair answer to his questions." Wool, however, continued pressing the matter until the councils decided that the city's citizens were a conquered people. The city had been given up "to superior force," they said. Force had been employed to overpower the people [and] "to overpower the people is to conquer them, and to conquer them is . . . to subject them to the rule of the conqueror. Thus the status of Norfolk is plain." Wool urged Mayor Lamb and other city leaders to take the oath of allegiance, but they refused. Their resistance prompted Wool to write Stanton and Chase on May 23 that their response could be nothing but a "determination to adhere to the traitorous Government of the South." He therefore pursued the only course remaining for him, explained the general, and that was to "leave the citizens in the position in which we found them when the authorities surrendered the city to the United States." In other words, there would be no trade even with Norfolk and Portsmouth under Union control.

The Lincoln administration agreed with Wool's stance: No ships would be allowed to bring merchandise into or out of the ports. Initially, only ships under Navy or Army contract carrying in supplies for the U.S. military were allowed. Wool indicated to Stanton and Chase that he thought the blockade wouldn't last long. "[M]any of the citizens are beginning to see the folly of the course they are

16 Murphey, *Four Years in the War*, 57.

17 Ludwell A. Johnson, III, "Blockade or Trade Monopoly? John A. Dix and the Union Occupation of Norfolk," *The Virginia Magazine of History and Biography* (Jan. 1985), 55-78.

pursuing," he believed, "and probably will soon take steps to divert public opinion in the right way."[18]

The leaders of the two cities "continued in the sulks," was how one Brooklyn newspaper put it, "so that [Wool] now refuses all intercourse with the people of Norfolk and Portsmouth. Even the little business they have been doing in . . . strawberries and peas is now stopped." If people were ill-clothed and ill-fed, Wool's solution was simple: Take the oath. In "another proclamation," he told "the people that the matter is entirely in their own hands; that by acknowledging the supremacy of the Government they can enjoy its fostering care, and the advantages of trade and commerce."[19]

The order, issued May 15, limited supplies to the military only and nothing of any other kind, no matter the owner, would "be allowed to pass through any other channel" unless approved in writing by the commanding general. Wool amplified his decision four days later with another order barring any vessel except those required by the military entry into Norfolk. The latest orders would kill off the city's trading life blood, wrote the *Daily Dispatch*, "together with the fact that the stock of provisions has not been considerably augmented keeps all kinds of eatables up to enormous prices, and causes those on hand to move off slowly, as no one is buying more than necessity compels."[20]

Soon, even the trickle of trade goods the people had received ran out. The residents now had no choice but to depend upon whatever produce local farmers could supply and goods that might be smuggled in from elsewhere. As was quickly apparent, Wool's strict adherence to the blockade punished not only recalcitrant

18 Resolution of the Norfolk Joint Councils, May 16, 1862, Wool Papers, NYSA; *New Regime*, Mar. 11, 1864, in Wertenbaker, *Norfolk*, 242; Wool to Chase and Stanton, [n.d.], Wool Papers, Letter Book, NYSA.

19 "From Fortress Monroe," *Brooklyn Daily Eagle*, May 24, 1862, 3; "Norfolk Still Sulky," *Harper's Weekly*, June 7, 1862, 335. The oath of allegiance to the national government continued to be an issue into the summer of 1862. The city's officers once again refused to take the oath of allegiance on June 23, so Brig. Gen. Viele canceled the scheduled city elections, dismissed some council members, and imposed martial law. Maj. Gen. Dix, Viele's immediate superior, supported the move. One newspaper claimed it was the result of the "consequence of numerous petty disturbances between the Union men and Secessionists," while another wrote an election delay was warranted, but to wait until after McClellan's Army of the Potomac took Richmond. "Norfolk Under Martial Law," *The* [NY] *Sun*, June 26, 1862; "Affairs in Norfolk," *National Republican*, June 26, 1862.

20 Wool, General Orders Nos. 43 & 48, May 15 & May 19, 1862, Wool Papers, NYSA; "From Norfolk," Richmond *Daily Dispatch*, May 31, 1862, 2.

Rebels but also Union supporters, hardening attitudes of even those who may have been open to the change in governance.

Just a few weeks after Wool's proclamation, a visitor described Norfolk as "a city of the dead, almost all the stores being closed, grass growing in the streets, and few residents to be seen." While some foods were scarce, area farmers did bring to market strawberries, vegetables, chickens, and eggs. But the market prices were out of reach for many citizens. "The scarcity of provisions and necessaries of life are so great and prices so high that the poorer classes have to live almost entirely on fish and oysters," reported the Brooklyn *Daily Eagle*. "The secessionists are nearly all wealthy people, who can stand high prices and have laid in their stock long ago." Wool's decision added "to the real suffering among the poorer classes," which had "suffered beyond endurance for a year past," and had expected "speedy relief from their privations" when the Federals captured the town.[21]

Albert Bärenreuth, a German immigrant private in the 20th New York, noticed the shortage of foodstuffs and hoped the blockade would be lifted so more produce could reach the stores. Although "we soldiers are pretty well provided for," he wrote, they still needed "dried produce—beans, peas, lentils, etc." What he most missed was kommisbrot, a stout German rye bread that he had not eaten "since Camp Hamilton. There just isn't any rye flour."[22]

According to the *Daily Eagle*, Unionists at the May meeting with Wool in Portsmouth also criticized his policy. Wool seemed to have relented somewhat, possibly recognizing the Union support expressed at the Portsmouth meeting or because of the strong criticism of his edict. The general informed Military Governor Viele on May 21 that a limited amount of supplies was coming for Portsmouth's citizens only—Norfolk's population didn't receive any help. He had permitted a "Mr. Whitehurst" to land and offer for sale "certain articles of provisions, viz, beef, bacon, cheese, butter, &c.," Wool said. But the commander restricted the shipment. As he told Viele, "please see that Mr. Whitehurst does not exceed his invoices" of $1,300 to $1,400 worth of goods. Wool's small softening of the heart for the plight of the Southern citizens proved fleeting. "This is not to be

21 "Virginia Gordan Scrapbook" article in Wertenbaker, *Norfolk,* 241; "From Fortress Monroe," *Brooklyn Daily Eagle*, May 24, 1862, 3.

22 Albert Bärenreuth to his mother, May 20, 1862, Army Military History Institute (AMHI), accessed Mar. 17, 2010, http://bit.ly/2LT4HwM.

regarded as an example for others who may come with similar applications," he admonished.[23]

By May 28, Wool sent his provost marshal, Maj. M. P. Jones, to Norfolk to ensure that no one was selling goods to citizens [and] ascertain whether there are any Sutlers in [Norfolk, Portsmouth, and Gosport] "with goods or articles for sale, . . . under the pretext of supplying the several regiments with supplies." If he found "any such persons," Jones was to close down their operations, "place them under arrest and send them to these Head Quarters." Moreover, "[n]o strangers or Sutlers will be allowed to open stores or shops [to sell] goods" to the citizens. The merchants could, however, sell to U.S. military personnel. Wool particularly enjoined Jones to check on a clerk from "McAlpins Store" who appeared to be selling goods to the populace "contrary to orders in Norfolk."[24]

No trade restrictions are air tight, and this one was no exception. Some Northerners tried to turn a quick buck by selling goods, albeit at inflated prices, to the people of Norfolk and Portsmouth. Wool reinforced his original orders on May 28. "Hereafter no vessel, not employed by the Army or Navy," read his General Order 51,

> will be permitted to go to Norfolk, Portsmouth or Gosport, or any other place on either side of the Roads, not occupied by the troops of the United States, except by express authority of the Commanding General, communicated by him or through the appropriate Staff Department. Any violation of this order will subject the vessels and property to seizure and confiscation, and the persons who may be the cause, directly or indirectly, will be severely punished.[25]

While food and other necessities greatly concerned the area's citizens, the status of the once-enslaved blacks also stirred sometimes heated comment, especially since Union commanders refused to be drawn into the "negro question." That position only provoked contempt and further eroded the Union's moral authority. The black population of the occupied cities, many of whom had walked away from their slave masters, had welcomed the Yankees as liberators. The military commanders in these cities, however, took no responsibility for feeding or

23 "From Fortress Monroe," *Brooklyn Daily Eagle*, May 24, 1862, 3; Wool to Viele, May 21, 1862, Letter Book, Wool Papers, NYSA.

24 Wool to M. P. Jones, two messages, May 28, 1862, Letter Book, Wool Papers, NYSA.

25 Wool, General Order No. 51, May 28, 1862, ibid.; "From Gen. Wool's Department," *New York Daily Tribune*, May 30, 1862, 1.

housing them. They were looked upon as simply contraband—personal property seized from the Rebels.

Nor was the Northern press sympathetic. "The irrepressible negro begins to become troublesome hereabout," the *New York Herald* reported a week after the cities fell. These "insolent" and "worthless [black] servants" were "hanging around the streets to the annoyance and disgust of everybody but themselves." At suppertime, the paper continued, many returned to their former masters demanding to be fed. Military commanders addressed these complaints by declaring that a black person could not expect to receive food if he didn't go back to work either in the home or shop of the former master. Viele, however, refused to involve his soldiers in hunting down runaway slaves. He could not "spare valuable time to bother about insubordinate and unreasonable personal property."[26]

Tensions involving Northern soldiers and blacks spawned a "riotous and bloody affair" on May 27, just a little more than two weeks after the occupation began. A group of soldiers from the 99th New York led by Cpl. John Hogan entered the city from their camp a couple of miles away. As soldiers are wont to do, they "got hold of some liquor, in which they indulged rather freely," reported the *Philadelphia Inquirer*. "While under its influence they accidentally met a colored man named Zeke, a servant in the employ of Lieut. [Isaac] Van Trump, Co. I, First Delaware, with whom the corporal had, on some previous occasion, had some difficulty." Hogan allegedly threatened Zeke, who took off running to Van Trump's tent. "Here [Zeke] picked up a loaded revolver, and turning, shot Hogan through the body, inflicting a wound from which he latter died in a short time. The colored man was promptly arrested and lodged in jail."[27]

Cpl. Hogan's friends returned to their camp and told others about the shooting. "An hour or two later," continued the paper,

> a crowd of them came into the city, armed only with bayonets and clubs, and as they passed through the streets, sought to obtain satisfaction by attacking, in a murderous manner, every colored person . . . so unfortunate as to come in their way. In this manner a large number of blacks were wounded, and two so severely that they have since died . . . of their injuries.[28]

26 "From General Viele's Division," *New York Herald*, May 16, 1862, 1.

27 No other information on the fate of "Zeke" could could located.

28 "Our Norfolk Letter, The Riot in Norfolk—Its Origin and Results," *Philadelphia Inquirer*, May 30, 1862, 1.

Other reports said as many as six had been killed. The Provost Marshal, along with a company from the 1st Delaware, arrested 18 members of the 99th New York. Half a dozen of them were later held as ringleaders. "The whole affair was disgraceful in the extreme," announced the *Inquirer*, "and a deep stain upon the fair fame which the Union soldiers have heretofore enjoyed." Still, added the paper, "Some of the citizens profess to be glad that the colored population, which has been grossly independent rapidly since the arrival of our forces, has received so salutary a lesson."[29]

Southern newspapers quickly realized the propaganda value of the slayings. "[T]he Yankees say they have long since ceased to regard the negroes of the South as anything else but a most intolerable nuisance and one which they intend to abate by the sword, if necessary," exclaimed Petersburg's *Daily Express*. On June 13, Richmond's *Daily Dispatch* reported that the affair was triggered by the killing of an officer, causing the men to be "so exasperated . . . that they determined to seek their revenge upon the innocent negroes of Norfolk. This indiscriminate slaughter," continued the paper, "was continued until over 100 of the unoffending creatures had been violently cut and maimed." A day later, another paper gave a different twist to the story when it claimed that "ten valuable negroes were shot down in the streets of Norfolk last week because they refused to leave their owners."[30]

Maj. Gen. Wool once again sent his provost marshal, Maj. Jones, from Fort Monroe to Norfolk "to investigate the circumstances attending the riot." Wool did his best to tamp down the news, despite the Philadelphia paper's widely read report. The *Daily Dispatch* claimed that Norfolk's *Day Book* "received orders from the military governor of Norfolk, that under no circumstances was the massacre to be hinted at in . . . that paper, and the correspondents of all Yankee journals in the

29 Ibid. The *New York Daily Tribune* of May 30 reported the same incident twice in the same paper giving two slightly different short versions. In one, the corporal's name is John Burke, and in the other, John Hogan. Hogan (or Burke) "lingered twelve hours" before dying in the hospital, reported the paper. In the resulting rampage lasting about a half hour, "five or six [blacks] were mortally wounded and many others badly beaten." The paper concluded: "This is the only serious disturbance that has taken place since our troops occupied the city, and is not of a character greatly to disturb its quiet or create apprehension." "Six Negroes Shot, Quiet Restored," *New York Daily Tribune*, May 30, 1862, 1. The *New York Herald* gave the "disturbance" two paragraphs and also reported the dead corporal as John Burke. "Important Arrest at Norfolk," *New York Herald*, May 30, 1862, 7. Regimental historian, Capt. Seville, wrote after the war that Lt. Van Trump resigned his commission the following month. Seville, *Delaware Volunteers*, 42.

30 "From Norfolk," North Carolina *Southerner*, June 14, 1862, 2; "Interesting from Norfolk—Slaughter of Negroes," Richmond *Daily Dispatch*, June 13, 1862, 2.

city were positively prohibited from making any reference to the butchery in their letters."[31]

The brutal attack only diverted white Southerners for a short while. The stress and shortages imposed by the blockade caused them far more grief. Having to rely solely on locally produced food was unpleasant, as was the inability to acquire other goods, from cloth and needles, to thread, tools, and even nails. Any sense of normalcy vanished with the Confederate troops, as had any good feeling about the Union's intent.

Whatever trifling Union sentiment once lingered in Portsmouth had disappeared. "I find more Secesh than at its occupation" declared a reporter. "When here before I met none but declared Unionists; to-day several avowed themselves . . . to be Secessionists." He discovered the same to be true in Suffolk. "Patriotism and loyalty are almost dead, except as they live in the hearts of our soldiers." Capt. Charles R. Johnson also discovered this sentiment there when the 16th Massachusetts occupied the city. "There does not appear to be [a] union man in town," he wrote, "the people keeping themselves in door and out of sight. One company on picket is insulted by three cheers for Bull Run and another by secession flags being repeatedly thrust out of windows."[32]

Southern newspapers continued using Norfolk as an example of what could happen across the South if Northern armies moved in. The *Richmond Enquirer* described Wool's actions as "the savage barbarity and demon cruelty of this hoary headed old man!" The editor continued: "To every cry of distress, to every appeal for the observance of ordinary humanities, to every demand for the usages of civilized war, this old man, with one foot in the grave and the other on the brink, has but one answer. Take the oath of allegiance or starve!"[33]

Richmond's *Daily Dispatch* blasted Wool's policy that same day. "Suffer or Submit" shouted a headline on June 6, with the accompanying text claiming that if the people refused to become loyal citizens of the United States, they "will have to taste the sweets of martial law" until the end of the war:

31 Wool to Jones, May 28, 1862, Letter Book, Wool Papers, NYSA; "Interesting from Norfolk—Slaughter of Negroes," Richmond *Daily Dispatch*, June 13, 1862. With but few exceptions, Viele's admonishment to the "Yankee journals" to not report the affair was generally followed. The military report does not appear in the *Official Records*, and it is possible Maj. Jones never prepared a formal report for Wool.

32 "From Gen. Dix's Army," *New York Daily Tribune*, June 11, 1862, 3; Johnson to "Nellie," May [18?], 1862, in Eisenberg & Hammerson, eds., "*If I Am Alive*," 70.

33 "Gen. Wool," *Richmond Enquirer*, June 6, 1862, 4.

> The policy of the Yankees in . . . [occupied] towns is now well understood. At first, they come with the blandest professions of fair dealing, toleration, and humanity, but as soon as they become firmly seated in the saddles, their real purposes are disclosed. Their course in Alexandria, Nashville, New Orleans and other captured cities is precisely the same. As soon as they are sure of their hold, their affectation of moderation vanishes, and reign of brutal tyranny is inaugurated. The most influential citizens, if they refuse to bow the knee to the Lincoln ape, are hurried off to cells in distant forts; even women are thrown into prison. . . . Submission, entire and abject . . . is the only condition of deliverance. . . . Such are terms proclaimed to a proud people by the scum of Northern sewers. We have drunk deeply of the cup of suffering already, but its bitterest dregs would be nectar and ambrosia compared with submission to these Pariahs of modern civilization.[34]

In the same issue, the *Dispatch* illustrated its editorial position by quoting three sentences from the *Philadelphia Inquirer* under the title "Barbarianism." "The Rebels still hold out, and refuse to submit and take the oath of allegiance. For their obstinacy General Wool maintains the blockade. If they desire starvation in preference to Yankee notions and the protection of Government offers, the General has no objection to allowing them time to repent." All this brought a sneer from the *Dispatch's* editor: "[S]tarvation is an exceedingly humane manner of driving people into reverence for the 'old flag.'"[35]

Whether Washington recognized the damage being done by Wool's policies, or it had other plans for the aging general, by June 2 Maj. Gen, John A. Dix had replaced Wool in command of the Department of Virginia. Dix, who had been in charge in Baltimore, knew some of what was happening around Hampton Roads and held a different view of the "conquered" inhabitants of Norfolk and Portsmouth. The new commander believed they should be helped both on humanitarian grounds and as a way to gain their loyalty, and came up with a way to do so through trade permits.[36]

34 "Suffer or Submit," Richmond *Daily Dispatch*, June 6, 1862, 2.

35 Ibid. *The Daily Dispatch* first reported the *Inquirer's* statements on June 2, 1862, "Affairs in Norfolk—A Good Batch of Munchausens," 2.

36 Wool and Dix essentially switched commands with the essential difference being that Dix reported to Maj. Gen. McClellan while Wool did not. The pattern repeated itself on July 15, 1863, during the draft riots in New York City when Dix was again ordered to replace Wool, this time as commander of the Department of the East. Dix took over on July 18, 1863. A.G.'s Office to Wool, John A. Dix, & McClellan, War Department, June 1, 1862, & War Department General Order No. 217, July 15, 1863, Wool Papers, NYSA. On August 1, 1863, Lincoln ordered the 79-year-old Wool to retire after 51 years in the U.S. Army. Wool launched a

Maj Gen. John A. Dix

Library of Congress

One of Dix's first acts after taking command was to alert Secretary of War Stanton to "the destitute condition of the 20,000 people of Norfolk, arising from the interruption of their commercial intercourse while the rebels [held] the city, and the system of exclusion . . . adopted after it was captured. . . . I recommended a total change of regimen on grounds of humanity as well as policy."[37]

Stanton, in turn, contacted Chase, who informed four treasury collectors on June 5 that "Much suffering exists in Norfolk" before asking them to send provisions to relieve the inhabitants. The tariff officials—in Boston, New York City, Philadelphia, and Baltimore—were tasked with finding "any reliable and loyal person" to dispatch one or two ships of provisions, clothing, and materials for making clothing.[38]

---

letter-writing campaigning to be reinstated that began with Lincoln and passed through the Andrew Johnson and into U. S. Grant administrations, to no avail. He died in 1869.

37 Dix to Stanton, Sept. 4, 1862, *OR* 18:382. Dix referred to the 20,000 people living in Norfolk, but the occupation area also included Portsmouth, Suffolk, and some smaller villages. The trade policy affected up to some 40,000 people, although many citizens fled before the occupation. See, for example, Richmond *Daily Dispatch*, July 14, 1862, 1, quoting the Petersburg *Daily Express*, which reported "several hundred" people from Norfolk and Portsmouth staying in Charlotte, NC.

38 Chase circular No. 42 to his collectors, June 4, 1862, *Report of the Joint Committee*, 3:595. Since Norfolk was subject to the Union naval blockade, the relief effort "could only be done as a military measure" at Stanton's request. The shipment also required a list of the articles being shipped for Stanton's approval and a "statement of military necessity and request."

Some people misinterpreted this permission to allow a few shipments as a complete resumption of trade. Dix has relaxed "all restrictions upon trade with Norfolk," announced the *New York Daily Tribune* on June 5. "After this date, provisions of all kinds may be taken to Norfolk and Portsmouth by any parties on exhibiting a manifest of cargo and receiving a permit here, the only condition being that the articles shall be sold at the market prices here and at Baltimore." The paper added, "Hundreds of loyal citizens of the two cities" would be overjoyed.[39]

These reports quickly filtered south. On June 7, the *Daily Dispatch* reported Norfolk's opening as well as Wool's replacement. "The people are now receiving supplies from Baltimore and other cities of the North," explained the Richmond paper. "Wool's determination to starve the people of that city, unless they took the oath of allegiance to the Government of Abe Lincoln, it seems did not suit the Washington dynasty. They thought . . . that the people should be lured into the old Union by clement measures, and not by starvation—and therefore they have annulled Wool's policy and removed Norfolk from [his] department."[40]

No matter the reason, the citizens of the occupied cities—staunch Southerners and secret Unionists both—couldn't resist the lure of fresh merchandise. "Since Friday last, heavy amounts of goods have arrived at these ports, consisting principally of groceries, miller's stores, and [other greatly needed] goods," confirmed a New York paper. "In every direction are seen housekeepers wending their way to the Yankee stores, over anxious to enjoy the long wished for luxury of sugar, coffee, butter, &c. It is a perfect day of rejoicing; it resembles the breaking up of a famine."[41]

However humane, because Dix's recommendations were adopted only to a limited extent, few ships were allowed into Norfolk's harbor. The British and French objected to even this limited arrangement. Their concern was that under international law, a port is either under blockade—which permitted no trade of any kind—or it was not being blockaded—which allowed in all shipping, including British and French merchants. The British Consul in Norfolk moved in immediately to halt the unloading of goods from the first Northern ship to arrive. At Sewell's Point, a French frigate "overhauled" another provision-laden Yankee

39 "Fortress Monroe, Wednesday, June 4, 1862," *New York Daily Tribune*, June 5, 1862, 5.

40 "Affairs at Norfolk," Richmond *Daily Dispatch*, June 7, 1862, 2.

41 "From Norfolk, Re-opening of the Port," *Brooklyn Daily Eagle*, June 12, 1862, 3.

vessel and sent a message to President Lincoln that "if the Federal Government could not enforce the blockade, France would help him."[42]

Despite foreign protests, the supplies on those ships were eventually unloaded at Norfolk when the Lincoln administration designated the shipments a "military necessity." The supplies did not last long, and Chase agreed that more could be sent in, provided (in keeping with the declaration of military needs) that each shipment included a federal permit issued by either himself, Stanton, or Welles. The attempt at a thin legal cover soon broke down, since more important war-related matters occupied the cabinet secretaries. Authority for issuing shipping permits devolved to Maj. Gen. Dix, and both he and some of his subordinates issued them quite freely. Dix's soldiers bought many supplies, but so did the people of Norfolk and Portsmouth. Although Chase agreed that permits were required to provide for "the sustenance of people within military jurisdiction," no products were shipped out of the city.[43]

For those residents with little or no money to pay for the goods coming in, the shipments did little or nothing to ease their hardships. "Business in every department is dead; no store is selling five dollars per day," reported Petersburg's *Daily Express*. "Many Yankee stores have been opened, but they have now pretty well gathered in all the gold and silver in circulation."[44]

Many local citizens possessed only Confederate-issued paper dollars; hard currency—silver or especially gold coins—was a rarity. The *Daily Dispatch* speculated, "Perhaps the real cause of the delay [of commerce in the city] is the scarcity of money, excepting Confederate notes, which are refused in many cases." The scarcity of Union-recognized money might cause "some suffering," admitted the editor, but in that case, the federal government would "probably be compelled to forward assistance."[45]

42 "Affairs at Norfolk," Richmond *Daily Dispatch*, June 7, 1862, 2. Besides having observer ships outside several Southern ports, some foreign governments, mostly Great Britain and France, also had consuls or vice-consuls at most of ports and in a few interior cities such as Richmond, even though none of these countries recognized the Confederacy as a separate country.

43 Chase to H. W. Hoffman, June 23, 1862, "Letters Sent by the Secretary of the Treasury Relating to Restricted Commercial Intercourse, 1861-1887," NA.

44 "A Letter in the Petersburg *Daily Express*," Richmond *Daily Dispatch*, July 14, 1862, 1.

45 "Affairs at Norfolk," Richmond *Daily Dispatch*, May 27, 1862, 2. "The Confederate notes are refused in many instances. Gold and silver are welcomed with enthusiasm by all classes of the population, many of whom have not seen either for many months." "Latest from Norfolk, Business Reopening Here," Washington *Evening Star*, May 13, 1862, 3.

To make up for the paper shortage, the cities of Norfolk and Portsmouth, as well as savings institutions, banks, and insurance corporations, printed their own paper scrip that was "readily" accepted. "The paper money from other places and issues of irresponsible individuals are thrown out of circulation, but the amount" was insignificant, only a minor inconvenience, wrote the *New York Herald.* While scrip worked, what the public really wanted was specie. "Silver change is still a novelty to the people," continued the paper, "and is grasped with the greatest avidity . . . one would almost be inclined to believe that the inhabitants here have for a long time regarded a five cent piece as something about as large as a cart wheel, and very nearly as heavy."[46]

With few goods available, how much or how little money someone had did not really matter. No one could make money without permission to ship and sell products in the North. As a result, Norfolk's economy continued to struggle. "[T[he dull and almost insupportable monotony of our city has undergone no change," explained one resident, "but everything . . . wear[s] the blighting aspect of war. The houses begin to look rusty; the wharves are going to decay; the streets are deserted. Our citizens . . . look care worn and depressed." Even the "Federal rulers" refuse to put a smile "on their Puritanic faces. . . . Norfolk is now a city of gloom."[47]

As their suffering continued, the open hostility of the citizens toward the occupiers increased. Some townsmen accused soldiers of robbing merchants of their stores and destroying books and papers. Others complained that people who came into town only to see a doctor were detained until they took the oath of allegiance. The Yankees were relying on coercion to extract loyalty from the populace, groused the papers. "No person is allowed to leave the city without taking the oath of allegiance," complained the *Daily Dispatch* in mid-June. "One day a gentleman requested to bury a child in a cemetery beyond the lines. The picket refused to allow him to pass unless he returned and take the oath." When the citizen refused, the funeral was interrupted. The following month several locals were forced to take the oath "to secure the privilege of selling their farm and garden products in the market." After another month, the *Dispatch* reported that only 150 people in Norfolk had "manifested any submission to the Yankees, or returned to their loyalty to the 'old flag.'" A couple of months later, the paper revised that

46 "From General Viele's Division," *New York Herald*, May 16, 1862, 1.

47 Petersburg *Daily Express*, July 19, 1862, in "Virginia Gordan Scrapbook," NPL."

number down to about 50 and labeled them as mostly Confederate deserters of no "respectability or influence."[48]

To Southern loyalists, people freely taking the oath were to be treated as traitors and cowards. One resident vented his anger in a July letter smuggled out of Norfolk. "Our Union men are growing daily more malignant and devilish," he complained. "They are either employed spies, or act as spies 'pro bono publico.'" After naming four Union supporters, he urged his fellow Southerners to hold them "in holy remembrance." Generally, according to one report, "no person of any respectability holds any intercourse whatever with the Yankees. They will not even look at them, and our contempt for them cuts. . . . They tried in every way to overcome this hatred, but finding it impossible, at length have given up the attempt."[49]

Union soldiers felt their scorn. Pvt. Albert Bärenreuth of the 20th New York reported to his mother that the citizens are "not particularly friends towards us." A soldier of the 1st Delaware told his hometown paper that Norfolk's ladies "are proof against the charms of brass buttons. They care nothing for sash or sword. You may get yourself up exquisitely and they wont deign you a look, except through the blinds."[50]

Papers reported some serious acts of defiance, including the possible murder of a Northern officer—only one of "several attempts . . . to assassinate Union soldiers," alleged Boston's *The Liberator.* The paper cited the specific example of the "death" of Col. William L. Brown, the commander of the 20th Indiana that was then occupying Portsmouth. Word of Brown's demise spread when his wounded and riderless horse returned shortly after the colonel rode away on May 22. A day later the *Daily Dispatch* added, "it was feared the Colonel had been killed or captured." The report proved false, for Brown was very much alive when the regiment transferred from Portsmouth to the Army of the Potomac on June 8, 1862.[51]

48 "From Norfolk," Richmond *Daily Dispatch*, June 18, July 12 & 31, Sept. 3, & "From Princess Ann and Norfolk Counties," Sept. 5, 1862, with quotes from June 18 & July 12, 1862.

49 Clippings, Petersburg *Daily Express*, July 19, 1862, & "Inquirer," Norfolk *Day Book*, n.d., both in "Virginia Gordan Scrapbook," NPL; Wertenbaker, *Norfolk*, 241.

50 Bärenreuth to his mother, May 20, 1862, AMHI; *Delaware State Journal and Statesman*, June 17, 1862, quoted in Wertenbaker, *Norfolk,* 241.

51 "Repulse of the Federal Gunboats," Boston *Liberator*, May 23, 1862, 3; "Accounts from Fortress Monroe," Richmond *Daily Dispatch*, May 25, 1862, 1; Report, John C. Robinson, Aug. 31, 1862, *OR* 12/2:422. Brown was killed on August 30, 1862 at Second Bull Run.

It also was rumored that Confederates were carrying on a quiet campaign of terror against townspeople who had befriended the Union forces. The Richmond *Whig*—the only newspaper in central Virginia that had opposed secession—reported unsubstantiated claims "by an hundred or more persons" that a West India fruit dealer had been hanged "by order of the [underground] military authorities for his outspoken sympathy with the Lincoln cause; and that a man recently employed in the Navy Yard named Mahone was shot through the head for a similar offence."[52]

By the end of June, the lack of local loyalty to the Union had become a serious issue for Brig. Gen. Viele, Norfolk's military governor. On June 28, he banned people from gathering in the streets for "purposes of political discussions" because it was "provocative of the civil disturbance." He also prohibited "the exhibition of badges and flags . . . of disloyal sentiments." Finally, Viele decreed that "parents will be held responsible for the conduct of their children in this particular," an indication of the daily torrent of abuse being inflicted upon his troops by even the youngest denizens of the occupied cities.[53]

To Viele's displeasure, Norfolk's Confederate supporters devised other ways to display their loyalty. The *Dispatch* ran a story of the funeral of a North Carolina soldier injured in battle outside of Richmond, captured, and sent to Fort Monroe, where he died a few weeks later. His body was shipped to Norfolk for burial. With the date and time of the internment generally known, between 3,000 and as many as 5,000 people attended. "The procession to the cemetery was of vast length, and as men, women, and children . . . hundreds of the most respectable citizens of Norfolk, moved with silent tread behind the hearse, the scene was one of most affecting solemnity." This march, attested the paper, took place "surrounded by Federal bayonets," but the people "were not to be deterred from testifying their respect to . . . one who had fallen in defence of Southern rights." The bold Rebel demonstration "greatly exasperated" the Union occupiers, and Viele ordered that no more dead Southern soldiers would be sent to Norfolk for burial.[54]

52 "Latest from Norfolk and Portsmouth," *Daily Richmond Whig*, May 14, 1862, 3. No evidence has been found to support those claims.

53 "Despotism in Norfolk," Richmond *Daily Dispatch*, July 4, 1862, 1.

54 "Burial of a Confederate Soldier in Norfolk," Richmond *Daily Dispatch*, July 19, 1862, 2. The regulation was only lightly enforced. A mid-September funeral attracted 4,000 mourners to bury an 18-year-old Alabama soldier. "Young ladies threw wreaths and garlands into the grave," reported a newspaper, "and it was then filled up by our most prominent citizens."

The military governor also sought to ease the desperate problem of feeding the population. His solution was to permit the shipment of goods to leave the ports as payment for what came in. Secretary Chase agreed to allow this for ships leaving Norfolk because of "military necessity." Maj. Gen. Dix, the military commander, was tasked with enforcing the regulation of the outbound cargoes since the treasury department lacked jurisdiction.[55]

With Flag Officer Goldsborough in command of the North Atlantic Blockading Squadron, the U.S. Navy appeared to care little about trade between Norfolk and the rest of the Union. However, on August 3, Goldsborough forwarded a copy of Navy department instructions to Dix about purportedly excessive permits. "I have reason to believe that vessels under our own flag, and perhaps even some [with permission] to trade with the Army and Navy, have traded with the enemy at different points along the rivers," wrote the naval officer. Some of that trade, he continued, included "salt, shoes, quinine, liquors, etc." He requested Dix to order his staff to withhold any permits that had not been approved by the treasury, war, or navy departments, and sought help in examining each merchant vessel that arrived at Hampton Roads.[56]

The accusation from a rival branch officer did not sit well with Dix, who responded that no permits had been granted without the proper approvals, and that his command had, in fact, been examining ships. "Attempts to smuggle whisky and other contraband articles are exposed almost every day," he shot back, "and the vessels and cargoes of the transgressors are seized and sent to Baltimore." He was sparing no effort "to suppress this illicit traffic."[57]

To clarify the issue, Secretary Chase—doubtless with Lincoln's blessing—issued a new set of trade regulations on August 28. Article III stated: "No clearance or permit whatsoever will be granted for any shipment to any port, place or section affected by the existing blockade, except for military purposes, and upon the

---

"Affairs in Norfolk—Correspondence of the Richmond *Dispatch*," Richmond *Daily Dispatch*, Sept. 20, 1862, 1.

55 Chase to C. B. Dibble, July 24, 1862, "Letters Sent by the Secretary of the Treasury," NA.

56 Goldsborough to Dix, Aug. 3, 1862, *ORN* 7:621. Although Dix visited Goldsborough on June 4 right after replacing Wool as area commander, the two men exchanged little correspondence. Only two messages between them relate to trade with Norfolk. Goldsborough's replacement, however, carried on an extensive correspondence with Dix on that subject. Goldsborough to Gustavus V. Fox, June 4, 1862, in Thompson & Wainwright, eds., *Confidential Correspondence*, 1:284.

57 Dix to Goldsborough, Aug. 7, 1862, *ORN* 7:635.

certificate and request of the Department of War or the Department of the Navy." Article VI forbade permits for shipping merchandise from any blockaded location. However, Chase's regulations allowed his treasury officials—collectors and surveyors of custom—to issue permits, unlike the previous assumption that only the cabinet secretaries could do so.[58]

While the war of permits was underway, Viele grew more concerned about the hungry poor. Even under Dix's liberal permit system, not enough supplies arrived to feed them. Two questions concerning administration of civil affairs in Norfolk and Portsmouth had "become a source of embarrassment," Viele informed Dix on September 2. The first was "procurement of supplies for those who have the means," and the other, getting provisions to those that didn't. Essentially, the United States was holding 20,000 people "in custody. We must either let them feed themselves or we must feed them," he announced.[59]

Widening trade was "a measure of necessity" to save the federal government. "Food must be allowed to come in or the people will starve," explained the frustrated military governor. "If food is allowed to come in the products of the surrounding country must be allowed to go out to pay for it." Those with neither means nor friends, which he described as "helpless women and children . . . begging daily at my headquarters for food," should be allowed to go elsewhere, even into Confederate-controlled areas. Taxing those with some financial means could support the poor and indigent," he continued, alluding obliquely to the threat of trouble if nothing was done to relieve the suffering. "I have always considered that the only point to be attained here was perfect tranquility. This has been secured so far; in order to continue it the steps I have referred to appear to be necessary."[60]

Dix, who was keenly aware of the problem, supported Viele's request in a long letter to Secretary Stanton. His own less onerous suggestions on the trade issue had been "adopted only to a limited extent," he complained, while the citizens of Norfolk and the surrounding area "are even more destitute than they were when they came under our dominion." Dix argued that the "suspension of business" had forced people to live on savings "instead of their daily earnings, which are for the most part cut off." Spending savings only made them "less able to pay high prices." In fact, suspension of commercial intercourse had emptied the city "of many of the

58 Isaac Smith Homans, "Internal and Coastwise Commercial Intercourse," *The Merchant's Magazine and Commercial Review*, July-Dec. 1862, 575, 576.

59 Viele to Dix, Sept. 2, 1862, *OR* 18:384.

60 Ibid.

Acting Rear Admiral Samuel P. Lee

Naval History & Heritage Command, NH 48279

essential articles of subsistence," which couldn't "be had at any price. This infliction, and it is a serious one," he continued, "has fallen on the loyal as well as the disloyal, and it is certainly not calculated to add to the number of our friends or diminish the number of our enemies."[61]

The general continued by requesting that he be allowed to issue trade permits for ships "to go to Norfolk with such supplies as I deem indispensable to save the inhabitants from suffering by hunger and cold, and that Rear Admiral Goldsborough be directed to respect the permits thus granted by me." To the dismay of Dix (and no doubt Viele), on September 4 acting Rear Admiral Samuel P. Lee replaced Goldsborough as squadron commander. Lee was even more of a stickler than Goldsborough, a strictly by-the-book naval officer.[62]

Dix's request to expand trade quickly clashed with Lee's strict interpretation of his orders from Secretary Welles. The new squadron commander first confronted the issue in mid-September when the president of the Norfolk Gas Company asked the military to allow a shipment of roofing shingles to leave Norfolk. The shingles were intended to pay for a load of coal that would come into the city. Lee, who was bereft of any files about trade in the papers Goldsborough had left behind,

61 Dix to Stanton, Sept. 4, ibid., 383-84.

62 Welles upgraded Lee's rank to acting rear admiral and ordered him to replace Goldsborough on Sept. 2, 1862. "Order of the Secretary of the Navy to Captain Lee," Sept. 2, 1862, *ORN* 7:695. The new commander of the NABS was a member of the Lee family of Virginia (Robert E Lee's third cousin) who had remained in the U.S. military. The word "Virginia," he said, was not in his naval commissioning papers.

appealed to Welles for instructions. His answer came quickly: No traffic in goods of any kind was "permitted in the region blockaded."[63]

Welles expanded on the government's policy the following day by making it clear that "no favoritism or license for trade" would be given to any U.S. citizen "to traffic within the blockaded region, or to import or export merchandise. That would be . . . evasion of the blockade and in bad faith." No military officer "is authorized to grant permits, and you will seize all vessels . . . engaged in illegal traffic."[64]

That same day, Adm. Lee informed Dix that he had ordered his patrol ships in Hampton Roads to prevent any vessels to pass unless on Army or Navy business and they carried an official certificate. This protocol triggered a series of back-and-forth arguments between the local commanders and their Washington superiors that eventually landed on Lincoln's desk. The positions of Army and Naval commanders in Norfolk had reversed. Wool had objected to Goldsborough's silent acquiescence to the trade. Now, however, Dix accepted controlled trade, while Secretary Welles and Adm. Lee opposed it.

Allowing trade with a blockaded port courted international repercussions and opened the possibility of profiteering or diverting some of Norfolk's aid to Richmond to help the Confederate Army. Dix turned this argument around on September 21 in a letter to Chase by recounting that he had given a permit to "shippers to bring certain enumerated articles for the people at Back River and the vicinity." The treasury collector in Baltimore, however, allowed other items not on the permit to ship. These included "3,000 percussion caps[,] . . . 84 gross of matches—12,096 boxes," which cost $75 in Baltimore, but in Richmond could be worth 75 cents a box, or $9,072. Obviously, these goods were meant for trade on the fabulously profitable black market.

While he ordered items without a permit confiscated, Dix told Chase that he also should be allowed to issue the trade permits to prevent such smuggling meant for both Rebels and profits. "Through my provost marshals and other[s]" he could "ascertain the wants of every neighborhood . . . and family," and ensure a supply limited "to their reasonable wants. Collectors at a distance have no such

63 Samuel P. Lee to Welles, Sept. 14 & 16, 1862, *ORN* 8:19-20; Welles to Lee, Sept. 17, 1862, *ORN* 8:20.

64 "Order of the Secretary of the Navy to Acting Rear-Admiral Lee," Sept. 18, 1862, *ORN* 8:20.

knowledge," thus "a privilege intended to meet real necessities may be perverted . . . to purposes of traffic with [the enemy.]"[65]

The following week, one of Admiral Lee's guard ships seized the merchant vessel *Marblehead* as she left Norfolk with a load of "staves and headings." The ship originally had sailed to Hampton Roads to deliver bricks for the ongoing construction of Fort Wool on the Rip Raps. *Marblehead's* owner, Churchill H. Cutting, appealed to Secretary Chase to free his ship and cargo. The secretary's reply only served to muddy the water. First, he stated, the treasury department could only issue permits with war or naval department authority—Treasury's customs officials could not. Next, a ship's clearance from a blockaded port was "entirely within the discretion of the military authorities in command at such point, and this Department has no jurisdiction in regard to such clearances."[66]

Chase's reply left the matter to Dix, formerly a New York attorney, and Admiral Lee to interpret what Chase meant. Lee thought that the *Marblehead* could only "be cleared without a cargo of merchandise." Dix's conclusion and proposed course, Lee argued, "seem to me to be clearly in conflict with my orders." Dix replied that he would "do all in my power . . . in preventing any commercial intercourse with Norfolk except such as is permitted by the Secretary of the Treasury, under special permit, granted in conformity to the printed regulations concerning internal and coastwise intercourse."[67]

The arguing continued into October. Both men repeatedly appealed their positions to their respective department heads. Lee followed Welles's strict instructions ("supplies may be conveyed to the troops but not to the people of Norfolk and Virginia") while Dix sought from both Stanton and then General-in-Chief Henry W. Halleck a less narrow interpretation. Dix argued that the Navy department's instructions were "so broad" that he had sought Lee's interpretation of circumstances in which trade could take place. Did no trade include merchandise cleared by regulations or permits for Norfolk? Was a ship with return cargo and a treasury permit allowed?[68]

65 Dix to Chase, Sept. 21, 1862, *OR* 18:398-99. In 2019, a $75 investment would be more than $1,865, while profit of 75 cents a box ($18.66) would be almost $225,662.

66 Chase to C. H. Cutting, Sept. 27, 1862, *ORN* 8:27.

67 Lee to Dix, Oct, 2, 1862, ibid., 28; Dix to Lee, Oct. 6, 1862, *OR* 18:418.

68 Dix to Lee, Oct. 1 & 6, 1862 & Lee to Dix, Oct. 6, 1862, *OR* 18:412, 417-18; Lee to Welles, Oct. 2, 1862, *ORN* 8:26.

The issue finally became so heated that it was brought up in a cabinet meeting on October 10 with President Lincoln. "We were told the people [of Norfolk] are in great distress and trouble, cannot get subsistence nor make sale of anything by reason of the blockade," Welles told his diary. Chase "thought it very hard" and he "was disposed to open the port or relax the blockade." Stanton, however, "opposed both," saying "Norfolk was hot with rebellion, and aid to Norfolk would relieve Richmond." Lincoln, Welles added, "in the kindness of his heart, was at first inclined to grant relief."

Welles admitted that he had ordered his Navy to rigidly enforce the blockade, and would continue to do so until the president changed the policy. "That to strictly maintain the blockade caused suffering I had no doubt; that was the chief object of the blockade." He had told Lincoln and the rest of the cabinet, "I was doing all in my power to make rebellion unpopular, and as a means, I would cause the whole insurrectionary region to suffer until they laid down their arms and became loyal. The case was not one of sympathy," he added, "but of duty."

When Chase urged that some trade be allowed to ease the suffering, Welles, quoting himself: "Then, raise the blockade. Act in good faith with all; let us have no favoritism. That is my policy. You must not use the blockade for domestic traffic or to enrich a few." It was at that point that Lincoln admitted he had not "sufficiently considered" these matters, and asked Chase and Secretary of State William H. Seward to "see what could be done."

In addition to the point of international law, Welles suspected some of the Army officers in Norfolk, and others were using the permit system to enrich themselves. "There is, I can see," he began, "a scheme for permits, special favors, Treasury agents, and improper management in all this; not that Chase is to receive any pecuniary benefit himself." Gen. Dix is, presumed Welles, "as clear of pecuniary gain as Chase, but he has on his staff and around him a set of bloodsuckers who propose to make use of the blockade as a machine to enrich themselves. A few favorites design to monopolize the trade of Norfolk," he continued,

> and the Government is to be at the expense of giving them this monopoly by absolute non-intercourse, enforced by naval vessels to all but themselves. As we have absolute possession of Norfolk and its vicinity, there is no substantial reason for continuing the blockade, and it can benefit none but Army and Treasury favorites. General Dix has, I regret to see, lax notions. Admiral Lee holds him in check; he appeals to Chase, who is very

> severe towards the Rebels, except in certain matters of trade and Treasury patronage carrying with them political influence.[69]

Just five days later Dix was in Washington lobbying for his position. Of course, he called on Secretary Welles. Admiral Lee, he complained, "is extremely rigid, allows no traffic; that the people of Norfolk are suffering, though in his opinion one half the people are loyal." Ever the lawyer, Dix laid out his arguments for a more liberal trade policy. "[Dix] [t]ells me [he] has been reading on the question," Welles continued. "I told him if Norfolk was not, and could not be, a blockaded port, I should be glad to be informed of the fact." He explained to the general that Lincoln had declared a blockade of the Southern coast, that Congress agreed to the blockade, and also gave the president the power to open Union-occupied ports. Norfolk was not one of them. "If he was disposed to raise the blockade of that port, I should not oppose it but be glad of it," Welles went on, adding that the opposition came from Stanton. If the war secretary should change his mind, he would agree. "There was no substantial reason for continuing the blockade," he continued, and "that not only humanity towards the people but good policy on the part of the Administration required we should extend and promote commercial intercourse. Commerce promotes friendship. It induces the people in other localities to seek the same privileges by sustaining the Union cause."

The discussion continued for another week without resolution. Dix claimed people suffered under the trade restrictions, but he didn't want to open trade completely. His goal was to allow more trade, under permits he granted. Welles insisted on either a blockade with tight restrictions or no blockade with open trade for all. Of Dix's plan, he wrote that "shame, demoralization, and wrong" would result from creating a measure of this kind to cover favoritism."

Dix, Welles confided to his diary, may not have been selling permits for trade, but "the scoundrels who surround him are." The general had to know this was taking place. "The gang of rotten officers on his staff have sent him here," believed Welles. "One of the worst has his special confidence . . . and Dix is under the influence of this cunning, bad man. He has plundering thieves about him." The identity of the "cunning, bad man" remained unstated.[70]

The following day, October 18, Dix appeared to have more confidence in his position and believed that Stanton and the war department finally supported him.

69 E. Welles, ed., *Diary of Gideon Welles*, 1:165-66.

70 Ibid., 1:172-73, 174-75, 177.

Back at his headquarters in Fort Monroe, the general wrote Admiral Lee that he did not see how he could "properly refuse" permits for ships with return cargoes from Norfolk if they bore the proper dispositions from the secretary of the treasury. With that, he washed his hands of the matter. "If you deem it your duty under the instructions from the Secretary of the Navy to seize a vessel having such a permit I can have no possible objection. It is a conflict between two Departments of the Government, for which neither of us is responsible."[71]

Exactly when on the 18th Dix wrote Lee is unclear, but that morning he had received a wire from Stanton authorizing him to clear ship passages. The cabinet had decided the day before "that the Norfolk trade should be placed under your personal direction." The treasury department would grant the clearances for admission into the port, and the navy would allow "exports permitted by you" to pass.[72]

The news surprised Admiral Lee, who knew of no such decision. Welles had not notified Lee of any change in policy because, to his knowledge, there had been no such change. No official decision had been made at the October 17 cabinet meeting. The secretary of war had simply decided the matter for himself and conveyed his decision to Dix.[73]

Welles found out about Stanton's message at the next cabinet meeting on October 24. Stanton claimed that he thought Welles "had consented to traffic under permits by Dix," scribbled Welles in his diary. He had not done so, Welles announced, nor could Stanton have had any "such thought from anything I had said or done." Welles once more stated that he was "opposed to traffic through any blockaded ports and to return cargoes even in army transports, or vessels carrying army supplies."[74]

Before that cabinet meeting, Welles had engaged in some lobbying of his own with Secretary Chase. Although Chase agreed the port should remain either blockaded or opened to all trade, at the meeting "Chase flinched, as he often does, and he did not sustain me," penned the frustrated naval secretary, "though he did not oppose me—said nothing."[75]

71 Dix to Lee, Oct. 18, 1862, *OR* 18:431.

72 Stanton to Dix, ibid., 433.

73 Lee to Dix, Oct. 20, 1862, ibid., 433.

74 Welles, *Diary of Gideon Welles,* 1:178.

75 Ibid., 177.

For the next couple of weeks everyone remained confused. Lee told Dix he had not received anything from Welles about Stanton's notice of opening trade. Dix told Stanton that Lee had no notice of the cabinet's supposed decision. The general had given Lee a copy of Stanton's "dispatch of the 18th, but he has directions from the Navy Department as late as the 22d which seem to be in conflict with it."[76]

On October 28, Stanton wired Dix to return to Washington so Secretary of State Seward could talk to him about Norfolk trade. Suspend the issuance of any trade permits for the time being, Stanton ordered. Before leaving for the capital, Dix told Lee that he realized the issue had to be resolved in Washington because the admiral was just carrying out Navy department orders. Lee agreed.[77]

In a follow-up message on this latest Washington visit, Dix informed Chase that the situation was indeed dire. "The Government owes it to me, to itself, and to the people of Norfolk, who are starving with hunger and cold, to do something," he pleaded. "I am willing to give any certificate which will insure these people food, fuel, and clothing. The loyal portion of the people of Norfolk and the Government employees not in the army are all suffering. Even the officers, who do not draw rations, are paying enormous prices for all the necessaries of life."[78]

Welles admitted in his diary that further persuasion by Dix, his officers, and unnamed members of the war and treasury departments had their desired effect. "There has been a good deal of maneuvering, much backing and filling," Welles wrote after November 11. "The prize is great. . . . men of political influence" were interested. "Dix has made three distinct visits to Washington on the subject. Some of his staff and Treasury agents were urgent."[79]

Welles, however, remained adamantly opposed to allowing Dix to issue the permits without the president's approval of the policy change, and Lincoln requested both Chase and Stanton to write out an order for him to sign. The cabinet adopted Stanton's version on November 11 and Lincoln signed it the next day.[80]

The order read as follows:

76 Dix to Stanton, Oct. 25, 1862, *OR* 18:440.

77 Stanton to Dix, Oct. 28, 1862; Dix to Lee, Oct. 29, 1862; Lee to Dix, Oct. 31, 1862, ibid. 443-44, 447-48.

78 Dix to Chase, Nov. 7, 1862, *OR* 18:451.

79 Welles, *Diary of Gideon Welles*, 1:183.

80 *OR* 18:452.

> 1st. That clearances issued by the Treasury Department for vessels or merchandise bound for the port of Norfolk for the military necessities of the Department, certified by the military commandant of Fort Monroe, shall be allowed to enter said port.
>
> 2d. That vessels and domestic produce from Norfolk permitted by the military commandant at Fort Monroe, for the military purpose of his command, shall, on his permit, be allowed to pass from said port to its destination to any port not blockaded by the United States.[81]

While Dix appeared to have carried the day, the dispute still was not over. Once again, more trade applications than he could possibly satisfy piled up in the general's office. Two days after Lincoln signed the order, Stanton's assistant, Peter H. Watson, informed Dix that the trade would be limited. With the "aggregate amount of goods embraced in the schedules . . . (almost if not quite enough to supply Richmond as well as Norfolk and neighborhood), the Secretary of War deems it proper to suggest that in acting upon applications for licenses to ship goods to those places care should be taken to scale them down so as to limit the supplies imported to the actual necessities of the inhabitants." This was the very argument Dix put to Chase weeks earlier to justify his issuance of permits, rather than some far-off customs agent doing so.[82]

The Navy also wanted to prevent Dix and his staff from issuing unlimited trade permits, so the navy department put a strict interpretation on the president's order. It issued instructions "to recognize the signature of Major-General Dix only and not that of persons signing, or professing to sign, for him."[83]

Even that didn't end the trade issue. Welles complained to his diary twice during 1863 that his worst fears had been realized. On January 23, 1863, he wrote that "continued and increasing abuses and much illicit traffic are going on under the Army permits issued by General Dix to pass the blockade." He again complained about Dix more than four months later, confessing his surprise at Dix's "loose and improper management . . . in regard to the blockade and traffic in the Rebel region. Admiral Lee has sent me, yesterday and to-day, some strange

81 P. H. Watson to Dix, Nov. 13, 1862, *OR* 18:452-53.

82 Ibid.

83 Thomas Turner to Welles, Nov. 13, 1862; Fox to Turner, Nov. 18, 1862, *ORN* 8:67.

permits for trade signed by Dix, wholly unauthorized and which cannot in sincerity and good faith be allowed."[84]

Finally, on November 19, 1864, more than a year after Dix had been reassigned, President Lincoln officially proclaimed that the blockade in Norfolk, and by implication, Portsmouth, would end on December 1. In doing so, he said "commercial intercourse . . . except as to persons, things and information contraband of war, may, from that time, be carried on" subject to the laws and regulations of the United States and the treasury department.[85]

With more normalized trade allowed and the advancement of the Union army on the outskirts of Richmond and Petersburg, the citizens of Norfolk, Portsmouth, and Suffolk could live in the war's wings and not on its main stage.

Their part was done.

84 Welles, *Diary of Gideon Welles,* 1:226-27, 318. The smuggling of contraband goods from occupied Norfolk and Portsmouth into the Confederacy continued to be an issue throughout the war. Norfolk's Confederate supporters came up with clever ways to move goods, including in coffins. Smuggling through Dix's department helped feed the Confederate Army in early 1863. Some estimates suggest about eight million pounds of northern bacon crossed the lines to feed the Army of Northern Virginia that winter. Johnson, "Blockade or Trade Monopoly?" 76.

85 Proclamation, Nov. 19, 1864, in Basler, ed., *Collected Works*, 8:115.

Appendix 1

Dramatis Personae

Joseph Nicholson Barney (1818-1899)

Born in Baltimore, Barney attended the U.S. Naval Academy, graduated first in the class of 1841, became a master in 1847, and was promoted to lieutenant a few months later. He resigned his commission on June 4, 1861 to serve in the Confederacy. He commanded the gunboat CSS *Jamestown* and successfully supported the CSS *Virginia* during the battle of Hampton Roads on March 8-9, 1862, and on a naval raid the next month, and escaped with his ship up the James River before Norfolk fell. Barney was promoted to commander the following year. He was sent to Brest, France, to command the raider CSS *Florida* after replacing the ailing John Newland Maffit. Barney suffered from bouts of ill health, however, and was replaced on January 9, 1864, before he could take his ship out to sea. He continued serving the Confederacy as an agent in Europe until the end of the war, returned to the Unites States, and eventually settled in Fredericksburg, Virginia. He died there on June 10, 1899.[1]

John Mercer Brooke (1826-1906)

Best known for his role in the creation of the CSS *Virginia*, the former U.S. naval officer spent most of the war as chief of the Confederate Bureau of Ordnance and Hydrography. Brooke designed and successfully cast a large number of rifled cannons that

1 Naval History Division, *Chronology*, II:20, II:47, IV:5; Spencer C. Tucker, "Joseph Nicholson Barney," Spencer Tucker, Paul G. Pierpaoli, & William E. White, eds., *The Civil War Naval Encyclopedia*, 2 vols., (Santa Barbara, CA, 2011), 1:51; Joseph N. Barney, "Log and Diary," SHC, Wilson Library, UNC.

bear his name. After the war he joined fellow former Confederate officers Robert D. Minor and Catesby ap R. Jones in a business venture called the "Civil Bureau of Supply" to sell ordnance, supplies, and machinery to foreign governments. That venture, and a subsequent effort, failed. In 1871, Brooke began what would be a 35-year teaching career at the Virginia Military Institute in Lexington.[2]

Le Grand Bouton Cannon (1815-1906)

A prominent New Yorker before the war, Cannon and his family had been active in the iron rolling industry in Troy, N.Y., which he expanded into a shipping business. When war came, Cannon helped organize New York City's Union Defence Committee and was a member of the upper-crust elite who provided financial aid to help the war effort. Shortly thereafter, he became aide-de-camp to John E. Wool, the Department of the East commander based in New York.

Cannon accompanied Wool when he was reassigned to command Fort Monroe in late 1861, and he played a prominent role as a staff officer during the Norfolk campaign. Lincoln asked the newly minted colonel to head a committee looking into the plight of the former slaves who had flocked to the Hampton Roads area after Union occupation. Cannon recommended putting the "contrabands" to work for wages, cleaning up their camps, offer schooling for both children and adults, and a police force to protect the camp's residents. Near the end of the war, Lincoln asked Cannon to serve as military governor of Virginia, but he declined due to ill health.

After the war Cannon returned to business life in New York City and became a gentleman farmer on a Vermont estate where he bred horses and cattle. He also participated in New York's Army and Navy Club and the Loyal Legion and wrote *Personal Reminiscences of the Rebellion, 1861-1866* (published in 1895) that provides key insights into many of the various personalities who served during the Norfolk Campaign.[3]

Salmon Portland Chase (1808-1873)

A politically ambitious man, Lincoln's treasury secretary was also one of the president's constant critics. New Hampshire-born Chase was raised by his uncle, an

2 Naval History Division, *Chronology,* I-10, III-159, IV-17, IV-56; Tucker, "John Mercer Brooke," in Tucker, et al., eds., *Naval Encyclopedia*, 1:79; J. Brooke, in G. Brooke Jr., ed., *Ironclads and Big Guns*, 299-310, 319-20.

3 "Colonel Cannon Dead," *New York Daily Tribune*, Nov. 4, 1906, 9; Richard F. Miller, ed., *States at War, A Reference Guide for New York in the Civil War*, 6 vols. (Hanover, NH, 2014), 2:401.

Episcopalian religious leader, and strongly supported the abolitionist cause. After graduation from Dartmouth and a short stint as a school headmaster, Chase studied law, set up a practice in Cincinnati, and entered politics. He was elected to the U.S. Senate in 1849 as a Liberty Party member and later became the first Republican governor of Ohio in the mid-1850s. Lincoln frustrated his ambitions to become the Republican nominee for president in 1860, but the new president named Chase to his cabinet over William Seward's objections.

As the head of the treasury, Chase provided the government with a strong banking system, created "greenback" paper money, collected taxes—by helping to create the Bureau of Internal Revenue—and set up the sale of government bonds. Chase and Lincoln continued to differ over various issues, especially when the secretary strayed into military matters that were not within his area of responsibility. Chase often offered his resignation. The president rejected each until after the 1864 nominating convention when, to Chase's amazement, Lincoln allowed him to resign.

With the death of Supreme Court Chief Justice Roger Taney in October 1864, Lincoln offered the post to Chase to placate the radical Republicans in Congress. As chief justice, Chase upheld many of Lincoln's initiatives on black emancipation and political participation and presided over the impeachment trial of President Andrew Johnson in 1868. Chase served as chief justice until his death in 1873.

Chase's participation letters written during the Norfolk Campaign provide many private details not to be found elsewhere.[4]

Philip Corell (1847-1935)

On March 2, 1861, 14-year-old Corell enlisted as a drummer boy for three years in Company B, 99th New York Infantry (known as the Union Coast Guard, or Bartlett's Naval Brigade). The unit was sent to Fort Monroe and reorganized as a standard infantry regiment. Corell participated in Maj. Gen. Ambrose Burnside's Roanoke Island campaign on the North Carolina coast in early 1862. The fragmented regiment went on to see varied service, with parts of it involved in skirmishes in North Carolina, the taking of Norfolk, the siege of Suffolk, and duty on Virginia's Peninsula.

By the time the original members of the 99th reached the end of their enlistment, Corell was a veteran. He was discharged on December 3, 1864, but reenlisted for a $300

4 David H. Donald, *Lincoln*, (New York, 1995), 236, 264, 281, 352, 478-79, 507-508; Donald, ed., *Inside Lincoln's Cabinet*, 74-87; Merrill D. Peterson, *Lincoln in American Memory* (New York, 1994), 91.

bounty on March 10, 1865, as a private in the 5th U.S. Veteran Volunteers. He was discharged a month later.

The former drummer boy became a piano maker in New York City, married, raised a family and was active in veterans' organizations including his regiment's Infantry Association, where he served as both secretary and regimental historian. He published a history of the regiment in 1905 that contributed to our knowledge of the Norfolk operation. His name continued to appear in census records through 1930. The drum he carried during the war resides today at the New York Historical Society.[5]

Charles W. Cowtan (1841-1928)

Like many young men in New York City, Cowtan responded to Lincoln's call for volunteers, joining the "Union Volunteers," which became the nucleus of the 10th Regiment of New York Volunteer Infantry. To revive their flagging enthusiasm, the young recruits hit upon the idea of becoming a Zouave unit patterned after Elmer E. Ellsworth's Zouaves. The fancy French North African-inspired uniform attracted enough recruits to flesh out a regiment with the help of volunteer companies from other areas of the state.

The two-year private in Company A, with the rest of the 10th New York (dubbed the National Zouaves), enlisted into federal service on April 26, 1861, trained in New York, and was posted to Fort Monroe, where it was held in reserve during the battle of Big Bethel. The New Yorkers performed various guard and garrison duties until participating in the Ocean View landing and march on Norfolk on May 10, 1862. The 10th was needed on the Peninsula and did not stay long in Norfolk. The regiment went on to fight in the Seven Days' Battles, Second Bull Run, Antietam, and Fredericksburg. Cowtan was promoted to sergeant.

As the two-year enlistments expired the 10th regiment was reorganized into veteran companies with new recruits to beef up its numbers. In February 1863, Cowtan was commissioned a second lieutenant in the newly created Company K and was promoted to first lieutenant at the end of the war and soon thereafter mustered out of service. The *New York Times* reported the remaining men of the regiment returned to the city on July 1, 1865. The *Times* listed the 10th's battles and took note of the "very great" losses it had suffered. Some years after the war, the surviving veterans decided they needed a regimental history

5 Philip Corell, "Biographical note," Philip Corell Papers, NYSL; "Phil and Fred Hold Reunion of the '99th,'" *New York Times*, June 1, 1913, 10; Frederick Phisterer, *New York in the War of the Rebellion* (Albany, NY, 1890), 51, 454; *The Union Army: A History of Military Affairs in the Loyal States, 1861-65—Records of the Regiments in the Union Army—Cyclopedia of Battles—Memoirs of Commanders and Soldiers*, 8 vols. (Madison, WI, 1908), 2:121.

and chose Cowtan to write it. His work offers key insights into the Norfolk Campaign from the perspective of infantrymen.[6]

Thomas Jefferson Cram (1804-1883)

A native of New Hampshire, Cram graduated fourth out of 41 cadets in his 1826 class at the U.S. Military Academy and his first assignment was as assistant professor of mathematics. He held that post until 1829, when he switched to teach natural and experimental philosophy. After the 1836 academic year, Cram resigned his commission to enter the business world, becoming an assistant engineer on railroads in Maryland and Pennsylvania. He missed the service, however, and just two years later was reappointed captain and served as a topographical engineer performing surveying work on the frontier for the next 20 years.

While in Arizona in 1858, Cram wrote a short pamphlet on behalf of business interests advocating that the U.S. follow up the Gadsden Purchase of 1854 by also buying the Mexican state of Sonora and possibly Baja California. Perhaps because of the looming secession crisis and then the outbreak of war, no action was taken on his recommendation.

Cram was called east and promoted to major in August 1861 and lieutenant colonel (a rank he would retain until the end of the war) the following month. He worked as a topographical engineer under Maj. Gen. John E. Wool. Cram's reports and other writings are invaluable in understanding the roles played by Lincoln, Wool, and others in the May 1862 Norfolk Campaign.

Cram later served as part of the Army Corps of Engineers and was promoted to colonel in 1865 after the end of the war and breveted twice to brigadier general and major general. He retired from the service in 1869 and died in Philadelphia.[7]

6 Cowtan, *National Zouaves*, 5, 12-14; National Museum of American History (NMAH), "First Lieutenant Charles W. Cowtan," accessed Dec. 8, 2016, americanhistory.si.edu/collections/search/object/nmah_1411120; "The Homeward March," *New York Times*, July 3, 1865.

7 James G. Wilson & John Fiske, eds., *Appleton's Cyclopaedia of American Biography,* 7 vols. (New York, 1900), 1:767; H. H. Metcalf, "Acworth Matters and Men: People and Affairs of a New Hampshire Hill Town," *A Granite Monthly: A New Hampshire Magazine Devoted to History*, Aug.-Sep., 1913, 270; Thomas J. Cram, *Memoir Showing How to Bring the Lead, Copper, Silver and Gold of Arizona into the Marts of the World, and Project of a Railroad Through Sonora to Connect with the Pacific Railroad in Arizona* (Washington, DC, 1858).

John Adolph B. Dahlgren (1809-1870)

Dahlgren's reputation rests mostly on his development of the Dahlgren smoothbores, a series of reliable and widely used artillery pieces. As the commander of the Washington Navy Yard, he also was a confidant of Abraham Lincoln.

Born in Philadelphia, the son of the Swedish consul longed to join the U. S. Navy from a young age and finally did so in 1826 at 17. He was a lieutenant by 1837 and aided in surveying the U.S. coast, a difficult operation that affected Dahlgren's eyesight. He was on a leave of absence until 1842, when he returned to service. His mathematical ability propelled him toward ordnance duty in Washington rather than sea duty during the Mexican War. In 1850 Dahlgren created his first "soda bottle" shaped gun, large at the breach with a diminished circumference toward the muzzle. The new guns of various caliber were cast solid of iron and bored (with the 9- and 11-inch guns the best known). He also developed a line of less successful rifled cannon. Both sides during the Civil War heavily relied on his guns. Many of the cannons aboard the ships in Hampton Roads that May were Dahlgrens, including the USS *Monitor's* two 11-inch smoothbores in her rotating turret.

Dahlgren's efforts were recognized when he was named as chief of ordnance July 1862 and promoted to rear admiral in February 1863. That summer he commanded the South Atlantic Blockading Squadron and held that position until the end of the war. He later headed the U.S. Pacific Squadron and would once again serve as chief of ordnance and commander of the Washington Navy Yard.[8]

John Adams Dix (1798-1879)

Unlike most political generals, Dix had previous military experience before the Civil War in 1812 as a teenager and later as a civilian became active in New York City politics, holding various offices including adjutant general and secretary of state. He was an attorney when he was elected to the U.S. Senate (1845 to 1849) and operated railroad companies.

President James Buchanan named Dix secretary of the treasury to fill the vacant position until Lincoln's inauguration, when the new president replaced him with Salmon Chase and Dix returned to his businesses. Once Fort Sumter was shelled Dix helped organize and later chaired New York City's Union Defence Committee, which raised funds and created regiments for the war effort. He was appointed a major general on May 8, 1861, and because of his age sent to command the military district in the pro-secession city of

8 Wilson & Fiske, *Appleton's Cyclopaedia,* 2:53-54.

Baltimore. That September, acting on Lincoln's instructions, Dix arrested disloyal Maryland legislative members before they could vote to have Maryland secede. The following year Dix commanded the district containing Fort Monroe and Norfolk and played a major role in trade issues after Union forces occupied Norfolk. Dix would again replace Wool, this time in New York City during the 1863 draft riots. After the war he served as U.S. minister to France, and in 1872 was elected to a single term as governor of New York.[9]

Charles Cleveland Dodge (1841-1910)

Dodge raised a battalion of "mounted rifles" that eventually became part of the 1st New York Mounted Rifles (also known as the 7th New York Volunteer Cavalry) and was commissioned captain. As major, he was active in the Norfolk operations, took part in the Ocean View landing, and pushed inland to discover that the Confederate artillery position at the head of Tanner's Creek was abandoned. Following the capture of Norfolk and Portsmouth, Dodge was ordered to push his mounted battalion on to Suffolk, where the town's mayor surrendered to him on May 13, 1862. Dodge promoted to colonel that August, and brigadier general that November.

Although praised for his "natural characteristics," "spirit," and "good judgment," he didn't get along with Maj. Gen. John A. Dix, who during the siege of Suffolk in 1863 vowed "that General Dodge shall not command the cavalry . . . at Suffolk." When an older (though junior in rank) cavalry commander was appointed, Dodge resigned his commission and moved back to his native New York City, where he helped quell the city's draft riots. Dodge spent the rest of his life in various business pursuits there until his death in 1910.[10]

Louis Malesherbes Goldsborough (1805-1877)

After the fall of Norfolk, Goldsborough suspected his tenure as commander of the North Atlantic Blockading Squadron was nearing its end. He generally despised newspaper reporters, but when his decision-making was questioned, he declared that as long as President Lincoln and Secretary of Navy approved his actions, "this is all I care for." He added that if he were incapable or had not "faithfully & honestly served the nation, the

9 John W. Leonard, *History of the City of New York: 1609-1890* (New York, 1910), 368, 369, 372; Warner, *Generals in Blue*, 125-26; Various correspondence, *OR*, 1/2:679-89.

10 "From General Viele's Division," *New York Herald*, May 14, 1862, 1; Warner, *Generals in Blue*, 126-27.

sooner I am thrown aside the better." Goldsborough would lose his command that September, and the rear admiral would hold administrative positions for the rest of the war.

Goldsborough's naval career as a midshipman began in 1816, but he officially joined the navy in 1812 at the young age of 7. He became a lieutenant in 1825 and participated in the fight against the Barbary pirates. After suggesting the Navy should start an office to collect charts and logbooks in a central facility, Goldsborough was named its commander. He left that post to command a mounted volunteer company during the Second Seminole War, saw action during the Mexican War, explored the California and Oregon coasts, served as superintendent of the U.S. Naval Academy (1853–57), and was in command of the Brazil Squadron when the the Civil War began.

In early 1862, Goldsborough supported Brig. Gen. Ambrose Burnside's capture of Roanoke Island on the North Carolina coast. He was not in Hampton Roads on March 8–9 when the CSS *Virginia* launched it stunning and deadly attack, an event that left him wary of facing off against the ironclad and drained the squadron commander of his aggression. The event was a turning point in his long career. On more than one occasion and to the frustration of the president and naval secretary, Goldsborough demurred when asked to provide ships to support Maj. Gen. George B. McClellan's Peninsula Campaign. Even with the *Monitor* present, the flag officer's concern remained focused on the *Virginia*, and he wanted the bulk of his ships kept at Hampton Roads, not away helping McClellan. Only the president's personal presence in early May prompted Goldsborough to become more active. Comments critical of the Navy and other issues damaged his career, and he asked to be relieved. Lincoln promoted him to rear admiral in August, and he lost his command the next month. He spent the balance of his time performing administrative duties.

Despite being shuffled to a desk job, the rear admiral enjoyed a successful postwar career. In July 1865, he was sent to Europe to command the reconstituted U.S. Navy presence from the North Sea to the Canary Islands, and from 1868 to 1873 oversaw the Washington Navy Yard.[11]

Benjamin Huger (1805-1877)

"A singular, silent and proud figure [Huger] dimly appears through the years," wrote the Pulitzer Prize-winning Confederate historian Douglas Southall Freeman. Benjamin

11 Goldsborough to Gustavus V. Fox, June 4, 1862, in Thompson & Wainwright, eds., *Confidential Correspondence*, 1:283-84; Navy History Division, *Chronology*, I:27, II:6-7, II:42, II:83, II:95 V:120; Timothy Neeno, "Louis M. Goldsborough," in Tucker, et al., eds., *Naval Encyclopedia*, 1:263-64; *Harper's Weekly*, May 24, 1862, 327.

Huger, he concluded, was unable to adjust from the routine of a peacetime army to active field command "for which he had no aptitude."

The South Carolina native graduated in 1825 from West Point, was commissioned into the artillery, and soon took up duties as a topographical engineer. He was promoted to captain and commanded at Fort Monroe twice, from 1832 to 1839 and again from 1841 to 1846. He found his true calling as a little more than a bureaucrat on the Army's ordnance board. He turned in an able performance during the Mexican War as Gen. Winfield Scott's chief of ordnance in charge of the siege train at Vera Cruz, and was brevetted three times. By 1855 he was a major in the Regular Army, and commanded once more at Fort Monroe, the arsenals in Harpers Ferry, Pikesville, Maryland, and Charleston. When the war began, Huger resigned from the U.S. Army to serve the Confederacy and was commissioned brigadier general.

Huger came in for some criticism soon after his appointment as the Norfolk area commander, where his indecisive nature proved he was not up to the difficult task of running an important front-line department. His mismanagement of the evacuation cost the Confederacy dearly in guns and supplies and the Confederate Congress launched an investigation into his actions. Gen. Joseph Johnston called Huger to the Peninsula for service as a division commander later that May. He was unjustly condemned for being slow at the terribly mismanaged Battle of Seven Pines, and performed so poorly during Gen. Robert E. Lee's Seven Days' Battles that he was reassigned to a familiar role: first as inspector of artillery and ordnance in Virginia, and then to perform administrative duties in the Trans-Mississippi Theater. After the war Huger farmed in North Carolina and Virginia and died in his hometown of Charleston.[12]

William Nicholson Jeffers (1824-1883)

The United States almost went to war with Paraguay in 1858 because three years earlier William Jeffers had refused to move his ship. Lieutenant Jeffers first joined the U. S. Navy in 1840 as a midshipman. After he graduated from the naval academy he was second in command aboard the steamer USS *Water Witch* on a survey expedition of South American waters. There, the vessel's commander was drawn into a trade dispute between Paraguay's president and the U.S. consul that resulted in the president banning the *Water Witch* from approaching the land-locked country up the Paraña River. A few months later Jeffers was ordered to survey the river, which the United States considered neutral territory because it

12 Douglas S. Freeman, *Lee's Lieutenants: A Study in Command,* 3 vols. (New York, 1949), 1:613; Wilson & Fiske, *Appleton's Cyclopaedia*, 3:302.

was an international boundary between Paraguay and Argentina. The river split into two channels, one for international traffic and the other closer to Paraguay. Jeffers sailed up the latter—a move that agitated the commander of a nearby fort. Jeffers ignored a letter in Spanish demanding he use the central channel because he could not read it. When the fort's guns opened fire on the *Water Witch* and killed one sailor, Jeffers returned fire. President James Buchanan ordered a fleet of mostly chartered merchant vessels to sail to South America and punish Paraguay, but that country conceded, paid the family of the dead seaman, ratified a commercial treaty, and avoided a war.

Jeffers was home on sick leave during the secession crisis of early 1861, but quickly returned to service. His first wartime posting was as an ordnance officer at the Gosport Navy Yard in Norfolk. In April and May of 1861 he commanded a ship on the Potomac River and took part in operations at Roanoke Island and Elizabeth city. When the commander of the USS *Monitor* was wounded on March 9, 1862, Jeffers was given command. He participated in all the events covered in this book, as well as the move up the James River and attack at Drewry's Bluff on May 15.

Jeffers was not well liked by his crew, but had the longest tenure of any captain of the ironclad. He was promoted to lieutenant commander while in charge of the *Monitor*, and was a commander by war's end. In 1873 Jeffers was named Chief of Naval Ordnance. He died in Washington.[13]

Catesby ap Roger Jones (1821-1877)

Jones had the remarkably good fortune to be serving as the executive officer aboard the CSS *Virginia*, the South's first ironclad, when its commander, Franklin Buchanan, was wounded on March 8, 1862, in a battle against wooden ships. Jones took the helm and steamed out the next day into Hampton Roads and into history, fighting the first ironclad-to-ironclad engagement against the USS *Monitor*. Two months later he was in command of the Virginia's gunners on Drewry's Bluff who stopped a small U.S. fleet from ascending the James River to shell Richmond. Jones' desire was to command another Confederate fighting ship and the war was still young.

Jones had been preparing for a military career since childhood. His father, Roger ap Catesby Jones, was adjutant general in the U.S. Army and his uncle, Commodore Thomas

13 John H. Williams, *The Rise and Fall of the Paraguayan Republic, 1800-1870* (Austin, TX, 2014), np; Wilson & Fiske, *Appleton's Cyclopaedia,* 3:414.

ap Catesby Jones, was a hero of the War of 1812.[14] Young Jones signed up for the U.S. Navy as a midshipman in 1836 and by 1849 was a lieutenant. He spent most of those years as an ordnance officer under the inventive Capt. John Dahlgren, who sent his trusted lieutenant on the first voyage of a ship carrying his eponymous guns to observe and report on their effectiveness.

When the Civil War began, Jones, a native of Virginia and 25-year veteran of the U.S. Navy, offered his services and expertise to the South. His first assignment included the supervision and preparation of the CSS *Virginia* for duty, and he worked closely with John M. Brooke to test the ship's iron siding. Jones' handling of the ironclad during the battle with the *Monitor* only increased his standing within naval circles and among his fellow Southerners. When Flag officer Josiah Tattnall was put in command of the defense of Virginia's waterways, he made the *Virginia* his flagship and Jones was once more its executive officer. In that capacity Jones was present throughout the Norfolk operations and assisted in the destruction of the ironclad off Craney Island.

Despite Jones' desire to fight on the water, Secretary of the Navy Stephen Mallory put him in charge of the Naval Gun Foundry and Ordnance Works in Selma, Alabama, in May 1863. Jones spent the rest of the war struggling to produce guns, ironclads, wooden gunboats, and other essential iron parts—all in the face of a desperate shortage of skilled workers, supplies, and iron. Jones let the naval secretary know of his preference to fight, but Mallory was convinced the appointment was "not less valuable to its best interests than those which . . . [have been] rendered by any other Naval officer."

Jones struggled to earn a living after the war. He joined former officers Brooke and Minor in a business that failed, traveled to South America to offer his ordnance expertise to various countries with scant success, and finally returned to Selma, where he married well and started a family.

Jones met an unfortunate end when he was shot and killed by an irate neighbor while attempting to mitigate a dispute between their children. He died the next day, June 20, 1877. The *New York Tribune* underscored the irony of it all: "It was certainly a strange fate

14 The use of the term "ap" was traditional in the Jones family's Welsh heritage. After England conquered Wales, parliament ordered the inhabitants to adopt surnames. Since John was a common name among them, they called themselves "John ap John" or John son of John. The English would alter these into such surnames as Johnson, Jones, and Johns. But the use of the "ap" as "son of" continued in some families, among them immigrants to America. Lyon G. Tyler, ed., *Men of Mark in Virginia: Ideals of American Life; a Collection of Biographies of the Leading Men in the State*, 5 vols. (Washington, DC, 1909), 5:238.

that the gallant sailor who commanded the *Merrimac* in her second day's fight should be shot down like a dog for playing the part of peacemaker in a child's quarrel."[15]

William Frederick Keeler (1821-1886)

A prolific writer with an adventurous streak, Keeler served as paymaster aboard the USS *Monitor*, where both aspects sharpened his understanding of the remarkable ironclad ship and the remarkable events of her history.

Keeler was born in Utica, New York, the oldest of five children. By the 1830s he and his family were living in Illinois, but he was in Connecticut in 1846 seeking the hand of Anna Elizabeth Dutton, daughter of a state legislator and later governor. Described by one of his sons as a father with "a roving disposition," Keeler wanted something more than a simple married life. He left his family to sail around Cape Horn to California in 1849 to seek gold, and when that didn't pan out, he crossed the Pacific to China and returned via the Cape of Good Hope—an experience that would later help him secure a navy commission. Back home in Illinois in 1853, Keeler bought property for business ventures and worked as a merchant of dry goods from watches and jewelry to guns, toys, and fishing tackle. He also became a senior partner in an iron works and steam engine manufacturing plant.

Keeler enlisted in the U. S. Navy and, with help from his congressman, secured the position of acting assistant paymaster and clerk assigned to the newly built USS *Monitor.* He remained onboard and survived her sinking on December 31, 1862 off Cape Hatteras. In 1864, while serving on the USS *Florida*, Keeler sustained a wound from a shore battery.

The restless Keeler moved to Florida after the war, where he grew oranges, wrote a weekly column about local community events, and kept a detailed diary. His daily wartime letters to his wife, Anna, are an invaluable resource for understanding a wide variety of events that unfolded during the Norfolk Campaign.[16]

William Wilson Lamb (1804-1874)

When the Confederates evacuated Norfolk on May 10, 1862, William Lamb, the city's mayor, first elected in 1858 and a strong supporter of the Confederate cause, faced the

15 Ethel Ames, *The Story of Coal and Iron in Alabama* (Birmingham, AL, 1910), 141; William S. Mabry, *Brief Sketch of the Career of Captain Catesby ap R. Jones* (Selma, AL, 1912); "Captain Catesby Jones: Particulars of His Murder in Selma, Alabama," Memphis *Public Ledger*, June 30, 1877, 2.

16 Robert W. Daly, "Introduction," in Daly, ed., *Aboard the USS* Monitor, 11-17.

challenge of leading an occupied city. His actions in the immediate wake of the city's fall allowed the transfer of power to take place without violence.

Lamb's relationship with Brig. Gen. Egbert L. Viele, the commander of the occupying Union force, wasn't always a smooth one. At one point Viele had Lamb arrested and confined at Fort Monroe. Lamb's daughter-in-law (a native of Providence, Rhode Island), married his son William, a Confederate officer who would later command Fort Fisher in North Carolina. When she gave birth to her third child during the occupation, Lamb counseled her to return to her parents. "A city under military occupation," he cautioned, "was no place for a nursing mother with two other small children." She took his advice. Lamb served as mayor until 1863.[17]

Samuel Phillips Lee (1812-1897)

Although a member of the famous Lee family line of Virginia, Samuel P. Lee did not stay with his state upon secession. Instead, the third cousin of Sydney S. Lee and Robert E. Lee remained in the U.S. Navy, where he played a key role in defeating the Confederacy.

Samuel entered the navy in 1825 and had a long and distinguished career. During the secession crisis Lee captained the sloop *Vandalia* as part of the East India Squadron and, when the civil war broke out, was sailing back to the United States and captured a blockade-runner along the way. Lee was in command of the USS *Oneida*, and sailed with David Farragut's fleet when it bypassed the forts south of New Orleans and captured that city. Lee and his ship continued up the Mississippi River to Vicksburg, where he presented Farragut's initial demand for the city's surrender. In September 1862, Lee was promoted to acting rear admiral and ordered to Hampton Roads to replace Louis Goldsborough as commander of the North Atlantic Blockading Squadron. His stance regarding trade with occupied Norfolk clashed with that taken by Army commander John Dix.

Lee's post-Norfolk career proved he was an innovative commander. After the loss of two of his ships to Confederate torpedoes (mines) in the James River, he created a "torpedo and picket division." The division's ships patrolled the river, checked for enemy gun positions, and regularly dragged the water to find new torpedoes. In July 1864, Lee supported Lt. William Cushing's plan to use a light craft and a spar torpedo to successfully attack and sink the Confederate ironclad *Albemarle*. He tried to capture the illusive raider CSS *Florida* by ordering one of his ships to disguise itself as a merchant to "entice" the Florida to come alongside.

17 H. W. Burton, *The History of Norfolk, Virginia* (Norfolk, VA, 1877), 234; Robert Carse, *Blockade: The Civil War at Sea* (New York, 1958), 107-108.

Despite the conflict with Maj. Gen. John A. Dix over trade issues, Lee supported him with several naval vessels during the siege of Suffolk, and supported small-scale, joint Army-Navy expeditions. His blockading fleet performed superbly. "Nine steamers have been lost to the rebels in a short time, all due to the 'fine spirit' of our people engaged in the blockade," Lee wrote to his squadron in November 1863. "Jeff Davis pays us a higher compliment than our own people when he declares . . . [only] one port in 3,500 miles" is open to receive supplies.

Lee took command of the Mississippi Squadron in September 1864, a role he held until after the war. The end of the war saw Lee revert back to captain, but he was promoted a year later to commodore, and then rear admiral in 1870. He retired in 1873.[18]

Sydney Smith Lee (1802-1869)

The third child of Henry "Light Horse Harry" Lee is not nearly as famous as his younger brother Robert Edward. He appears in few history books, but was a longtime officer in the U.S. Navy during the antebellum years. As a Confederate naval officer, he spent most of the war behind a desk in Richmond.

Whereas Robert E. Lee went into the U.S. Army, Sydney Smith Lee (his family called him Smith) joined the U.S. Navy in 1820. By 1828 he was a lieutenant and served on numerous ships until the war with Mexico. Both Sydney and Robert participated in the landing at Vera Cruz, where Sydney commanded a 64-pounder on land removed from his ship, the USS *Mississippi*. Promoted to commander, Sydney took charge of the *Mississippi*, which Matthew Perry had used as a flagship when he opened Japan to foreign trade. Lee also served as commandant at the U.S. Naval Academy and commanded the Philadelphia Navy Yard.

Both Lees followed Virginia out of the Union. The secretary of the navy rejected Sydney's resignation and he was dismissed on April 22, 1861. He briefly served in the Virginia state navy until it was absorbed into the Confederate Navy, where he was commissioned as a commander. He was assigned to the Bureau of Ordnance and Hydrography and spent many days at the Gosport Navy Yard preparing the CSS *Virginia* for duty. There, members of Norfolk's city council visited with Lee to plead that the yard not be set afire as the Yankees had done a year earlier when they abandoned Gosport.

After Norfolk and the navy yard fell, Lee commanded naval personnel—many from the CSS *Virginia*—at Drewry's Bluff on the James River. He missed the battle on May 15,

18 Tucker, "Samuel Phillips Lee," in Tucker, et al., eds., *Naval Encyclopedia*, 1:345-46; Naval History Division, *Chronology*, III:156-57, IV:59, IV:86-87; Wilson & Fiske, *Appleton's Cyclopaedia*, 3:668.

but expanded and improved the bluff's defenses in anticipation of further Union attempts to pass upriver to Richmond. Lee was promoted to captain later in the year and ended the war as the chief of the navy's Bureau of Orders and Details.[19]

Stephen Russell Mallory (1813-1873)

Mallory had no actual naval experience when President Jefferson Davis appointed him in 1861 to serve as Confederate secretary of the navy. But for all practical purposes, the Confederacy did not have a navy over which Mallory could preside.

Born in Trinidad, West Indies to American parents, Mallory spent most of his childhood in Key West, Florida, and completed his education in Alabama and Pennsylvania. President Andrew Jackson appointed 19-year-old Mallory as the Key West customs inspector, which allowed him time to study law. His successful practice led to a couple of judgeships and, while still young, Mallory volunteered to fight in the Second Seminole War. He was later elected as one of Florida's senators in 1851, and was re-elected in 1857.

As chairman of the Senate's naval affairs committee, Mallory knew how the navy department under President James Buchanan was responding to the secession crisis. One of his main concerns was Fort Pickens near Pensacola, Florida. The fort's commander had refused to surrender to Florida authorities, and the Federal Army and Navy were planning to send reinforcements. Mallory put out a message "calculated to alarm the President and induce him to countermand the order," he explained a couple months later. The reinforcements were not sent, but the fort remained in Union hands throughout the coming war.

When Florida left the Union on January 21, 1861, Mallory resigned from the Senate and intended to return home. Jefferson Davis, the new Confederate president, had other plans. Mallory demurred when first offered the cabinet post, telling Davis (whom he knew from the Senate) that he would freely give any advice Davis requested, but he wanted to remain a private citizen. Unbeknownst to Mallory, Davis had already submitted his name to the Confederate Congress. Mallory resolved not to accept it, but when he learned two members of Florida's delegation were opposing his nomination, he found himself unable "withdraw in the face of unknown opposition." Mallory would be the only original Confederate cabinet member to hold his position throughout the war.

19 Tucker, "Sidney Smith Lee," in Tucker, et al., eds., *Naval Encyclopedia*, 1:347-48; Caroline Davis, "The Less Famous Lee," in "Emerging Civil War," accessed Jan. 13, 2017, emergingcivilwar.com/2014/01/11/the-less-famous-lee.

Mallory knew he could not build enough ships to compete with the Union navy, and resolved instead to construct ironclads across the South and purchase ships abroad. His full support of this strategy resulted in the speedy creation of the CSS *Virginia*, her successful attack in Hampton Roads on March 8, 1862, and the historic duel of the ironclads the following day. Despite limited resources, Mallory created a respectable brown water and harbor-based naval presence out of practically nothing, and powerful ocean raiders that crippled American overseas shipping. Mallory's effort helped keep parts of the Confederacy in Southern hands for longer than they otherwise would have been.

Mallory was confined for ten months at Fort Lafayette in New York harbor after the war. Once paroled, he moved to Pensacola and resumed the practice of law. Mallory enjoyed an insider's role from beginning to the end, but died relatively young and without leaving any substantial body of papers or recollections behind for posterity.[20]

Joseph King Fenno Mansfield (1803-1862)

Joseph K. F. Mansfield was Regular Army through and through. The Connecticut native entered the military academy in his early teens and graduated five years later, second in the class of 1822. As an engineer officer, Mansfield supervised construction projects along the southern coast until the Mexican War and served as Gen. Zachary Taylor's chief engineer and commanded troops in combat. He was brevetted three times up to colonel in the Regular Army, and was made a full colonel in 1853 with his appointment to the Inspector General's Office by Secretary of War Jefferson Davis.

Mansfield was elevated to brigadier general in the Regular Army in May 1861 and helped organize and create the Washington defenses. In March of 1862, he was sent to Hampton Roads under Maj. Gen. John E. Wool's command and put in charge of Camp Butler at Newport News. His first combat experience during the Civil War was during the Norfolk operation, where Mansfield's failure to take control of the command situation with Brig. Gen. Max Weber after landing at Ocean View could not have instilled confidence in Mansfield's superiors.

After the fall of Norfolk, Mansfield led a division guarding Suffolk until September 8, when he was called to the Army of the Potomac and put in command of the XII Corps just two days before he would lead it at Antietam on September 17. Mansfield was positioning his regiments near the East Woods when members of the 10th Maine exchanged fire with the enemy. Mansfield's horse was hit first, and another round found the general. When

20 Mallory to "some friends in Florida," Mar. 22, 1861, in "Early Journal Content on JSTOR," accessed Feb. 8, 2012, http://bit.ly/2Wecg5T; Wilson & Fiske, *Appleton's Cyclopaedia*, 4:183-84.

Mansfield dismounted to help his horse, staff members saw blood on the front of his uniform. He was unable to mount another horse, and collapsed and was carried off the field. He died the next day. Mansfield received a posthumous promotion to major general the following March.[21]

Louis Merz (1833-1862)

Merz (sometimes spelled "Mertz") was born in Durkheim, Bavaria and moved to the United States with his family in 1845, settling in West Point, Georgia. On April 26, 1861, Merz enlisted in Troup County, Georgia, as a private in the "West Point Guards," which became Company D of the 4th Georgia Infantry. The Georgians were sent to the Norfolk area near the end of 1861 to help defend against a possible Union invasion, and were posted at Camp Jackson near the James River. It was there Merz became a dutiful diarist. He wrote nearly every day, although his entries were often short. His diary is especially valuable because there are few primary sources from within the Confederate ranks during the Norfolk operations.

Once Norfolk fell in May of 1862, the 4th Georgia was put together with three other regiments (one from Georgia and two from North Carolina) to form a brigade under Brig. Gen. Roswell Ripley. The brigade suffered heavy losses during the Seven Days' Battles at the end of June and first day of July outside Richmond. Merz's last entry was made on July 9 near the July 1 Malvern Hill battlefield. Merz marched with Robert E. Lee's Army of Northern Virginia into Maryland and participated and survived the critical battle to hold the gaps in South Mountain on September 14, but was killed three days later at Sharpsburg somewhere east of the Smoketown Road on or near the Mumma farm.[22]

William Harwar Parker (1826-1896)

Parker, whose father and brother were navy men, entered the service in 1841 at age 14. He spent the first few months of his career aboard the USS *North Carolina* learning to be a sailor and remained at sea for several years. During the Mexican War Parker served aboard the USS *Potomac* as a midshipman, and during the siege of Vera Cruz helped move a

21 Warner, *Generals in Blue,* 309; Boatner, *Civil War Dictionary*, 508; John M. Gould, "What Confederate Troops Fought the 10th in East Woods?" Washington *National Tribune*, Aug. 25, 1892, 4; John M. Gould, "Maj. Gould's Reply to Lieut. Dunegan about the Death of Gen. Mansfield," Washington *National Tribune*, Nov. 17, 1892, 4.

22 William H. Davidson, "A Word about the Diary," in *Diary of Private Louis Merz*, 16.

32-pounder from the *Potomac* to a land-based naval battery that included a gun from the USS *Mississippi* under Sydney Smith Lee's command.

Once the war ended Parker attended the Naval Academy at Annapolis and began his education in 1847. As a passed midshipman, Parker was assigned to various ships, most of which policed the slave trade off Africa. He also served on the USS *Merrimack*, which would one day be transitioned into the CSS *Virginia.* Parker wrote the textbook *Naval Light Artillery* (adopted by the Naval Academy) during his 26-month voyage on the *Merrimack* and served as an instructor of seamanship and naval tactics at the Academy. He was still in that position during the secession crisis of 1860-1861. When Virginia seceded Parker resigned his commission and the governor of Virginia appointed him as a lieutenant. Later, when the Confederate government took over naval operations, Parker was given command of the gunboat *Beaufort.*

Parker's primary service for the rest of the war was as superintendent of the Confederate States Naval Academy aboard the CSS *Patrick Henry.* During the Norfolk operations, Parker was waiting for his new ship, the gunboat CSS *Dixie*, to be finished. His postwar memoirs of his time there, observations of events, and interactions with Maj. Gen. Benjamin Huger, are enlightening. Later, after Norfolk's fall and while stationed on the James River, Parker was sometimes called away for other duty, such as his brief stint as assumed temporary commander of the ironclad CSS *Richmond* in May and June 1864. The following year, with the end of the Confederacy at hand, Parker and his students guarded the government archives and treasury during the flight through North Carolina and Georgia to South Carolina. At one point, the academy students formed the escort of Varina Davis, wife of the fleeing Confederate president.

After the war, Parker wrote textbooks on naval tactics and seamanship and captained ships in the Pacific Mail Steamship Company. In the early 1880s he was wounded in the head by an Apache bullet and lost the use of one eye. The bullet was so close to his brain doctors did not want to operate, and he carried it the rest of his life. Later, Parker became a serious alcoholic and one naval acquaintance called him a "hopeless drunkard." Despite his fondness for the bottle, he was appointed resident minister and consul general to Korea, a position he held for a short dozen weeks. He died in 1896 at the age of 70.[23]

23 Parker, *Recollections*, 215-17; Craig L. Symonds, "Introduction," in Parker, *Recollections*, ix-x, xii-xv, xvii-xxi; Naval History Division, *Chronology*, III:151, IV:63, 82, 131; V:76, 81, 89, 96; J. Thomas Scharf, *History of the Confederate States Navy From Its Organization to the Surrender of Its Last Vessel* (New York, 1887), 773; Office of the Historian, "Chiefs of Mission for Korea," U.S. Department of State, accessed Jan. 13, 2017, history.state.gov/departmenthistory/people/chiefsofmission/korea.

Frederick William Ritschy (ca. 1846-1920)

Ritschy was 15 when, along with Philip Corell, he enlisted on Dec. 4, 1861, in the 99th New York Volunteer Regiment. The young boys became drummers, with Ritschy joining Company F. His recollections, together with Corell's history of the regiment, offer a unique perspective from within the Union ranks of the operations around Norfolk in May 1862. Later, after the city was captured, Ritschy served as an orderly for Maj. Gen. John James Peck, who commanded the Union troops defending Suffolk during a quasi-siege conducted by two divisions under of Lt. Gen. James Longstreet in early 1863.

Ritschy was discharged on December 9, 1864. He later moved to New Jersey, where he worked for an express company well into his old age. Like Corell, Ritschy remained active in veteran associations. They were the only two who attended the 1913 reunion of the 99th because the remaining 23 old volunteers were too feeble to make the trip. Ritschy and Corell elected each other to the association's leadership posts.[24]

John Rodgers (1812-1882)

The son of a commodore entered the U.S. Navy in 1828 and spent his first four years as a midshipman aboard the USS *Constellation.* After attending naval school at Norfolk for two years he graduated as a passed midshipman and took a year's leave of absence to attend the University of Virginia. His experience and education sped his rise in the peacetime navy's ranks. He was promoted to lieutenant in 1840 and commanded his own ship off the Florida Keys doing survey work, sailed the Pacific as far north as the Arctic Ocean, and as far west as the waters off China. By 1855 Rodgers had attained the rank of commander.

His first assignment after the outbreak of the Civil War was to superintend the construction of ironclads on the Ohio and Mississippi rivers, though he was sent back east in November 1861 to take part in the Port Royal expedition. Rodgers was in command of the ironclad USS *Galena* at Hampton Roads when Lincoln arrived and moved up the James River to threaten Richmond. His letters and reports are important in helping to understand naval matters during these important days. During the duel with the Confederate shore batteries at Drewry's Bluff on May 15, 1862, the *Galena* lost a dozen crewmen and was heavily damaged by 129 direct hits. The ungainly iron-sided *Galena* and the other ships of

24 Frederick W. Ritschy, "Reminiscences of Camp Hamilton and Norfolk, Va.," in "History of the Naval Brigade: 99th N. Y. Volunteers, Union Coast Guard, 1861-1865," manuscript notes (New York, 1905), NYSL, n.p.; "Adams Express Company Employee's Benevolent Association," *Express Gazette*, 47 vols. (Mar., 1903), 28:78; "Phil and Fred Hold Reunion of the 99th," *New York Times*, June 1, 1913, 10.

Rodgers' little fleet helped secure the James River and thus assisted Maj. Gen. George B. McClellan's Army of the Potomac operating on the Peninsula. Perhaps buoyed by McClellan's approbation, Rodgers was promoted to captain the following July.

Rodgers's next ship was the monitor-class USS *Weehawken*. On June 17, 1863, his ironclad came upon and captured the grounded and exposed Confederate ironclad *Atlanta* off Savannah in the Wilmington tidal river. Rodgers fired only five shots and the first missed. The other four, however, inflicted structural and human damage to the ship sufficient to convince her captain to surrender. Congress adopted a resolution of "thanks" for the captain's "eminent zeal and ability" and promoted Rodgers to commodore. He finished the war as commander of the Navy's largest monitor, the USS *Dictator*.

After the war Rodgers steamed the double-turreted monitor USS *Monadnock* through the Straits of Magellan to San Francisco, was in charge of the Boston Navy Yard, earned a promotion to rear admiral with command of the Asiatic fleet, and superintended the U.S. Naval Observatory from 1877 until his death.[25]

William Penn Seville (1833-1913)

Pennsylvania-born Seville spent many prewar years in the U.S. Corps of Engineers. He participated in the 1858 long march from Fort Leavenworth, Kansas to Fort Bridger, Utah to re-establish federal control over the Mormons and wrote a book years later based on the diary he kept during that march.

Following the firing on Fort Sumter, Seville received permission to raise a company of Pennsylvania volunteers, but before they could be sworn into service he was sent to Wilmington, Delaware, to help organize a 90-day regiment that would become the 1st Delaware Volunteer Infantry. Because of his previous military experience, Seville became the unit's adjutant general with the rank of lieutenant. Just before its 90-day enlistment expired, the 1st Delaware was reorganized into a three-year regiment with Seville serving as the regimental adjutant by mid-1862.

The 1st Delaware was first sent to Fort Monroe, and served in the Ocean View landing and march to Norfolk. Thereafter it was transferred to the Army of the Potomac and went on to fight in the battles of Antietam, Fredericksburg, and Chancellorsville, after which brigade commander Col. Charles Albright recommended Seville for promotion. Later that year, Seville assumed the rank of captain and given command of the regiment's Company

25 Wilson & Fiske, *Appleton's Cyclopaedia*, 5:297-98; Naval History Division, *Chronology*, II:75, III:95-96.

E, which he led (and thereafter Company K) until the end of his three-year enlistment on October 30, 1864.

After the war Seville worked as a clerk in the U.S. Pension Office in Washington and was active in veterans' organizations. At the request of his former Delaware comrades, he wrote a history of the regiment, which he completed in 1884. In it, he details many aspects of the Norfolk operation that would have otherwise been lost to history.[26]

Edwin McMasters Stanton (1814-1869)

"A long-armed ape." That was how Stanton described Lincoln after meeting him for the first time. Put off by the lanky country-style lawyer, Stanton objected to his participation as an associate attorney in 1855 on a patent infringement case. Lincoln was no longer needed when the matter was moved to Cincinnati, but he prepared for it nonetheless and attended. Stanton refused to allow him to participate. Thus, President Lincoln's selection of Stanton to head the war department in January 1862 was looked upon by many as a strange choice. Stanton, explained his aide, was not chosen "for his politics, but for his patriotism and power."

At the time of his appointment Stanton had been a prosecutor and a successful litigation attorney, arguing more than 300 cases before the U.S. Supreme Court, and served as attorney general during the last months of the James Buchanan administration. The former Jacksonian Democrat held a strong anti-slavery position qualified "by his view of the obligations imposed by the Federal constitution." His goal was "saving the Union whether the constitution was saved or not." As he stated, to save the constitution at the expense of the Union would only result in the destruction of both.

Following Lincoln's death, Stanton stayed on as secretary of war, though he increasingly came into conflict with President Andrew Johnson over what he saw as leniency in Johnson's policies toward the former Confederate states and citizens. Twice Johnson tried to fire Stanton, and twice the secretary's congressional allies saved him. The second attempt spurred Johnson's impeachment. Stanton resigned. In 1869, President Ulysses Grant, appointed Stanton to an open seat on the Supreme Court, to which he was quickly confirmed, but he died four days later.

Charles A. Dana, one of Stanton's war department assistant secretaries, summed up his boss thusly: "impulsive, warm-blooded, very quick in execution, perhaps not always infallible in judgment. I never knew a man who could do so much work in a given time. . . . a nervous man . . . of imagination, . . . utterly absorbed in the idea of the republic one and

26 Miller, ed., *States at War*, 4:212n; Seville, *Delaware Volunteers*, 23, 47, 94, 134; *OR* 21:306.

indivisible; and he lived for it, wore himself out in the service, and shortly after he ceased to serve in that office he passed into another world, entirely exhausted, consumed by his devotion to public duties."

Stanton played an important, if subordinate, role during the Norfolk operations during that critical week in May of 1862, and his correspondence and actions add significant insight into how the affairs unfolded, and why.[27]

Josiah Tattnall Jr. (1795-1871)

Tattnall served in a variety of assignments in the U.S. Navy since 1812, but resigned his commission on February 21, 1861, after his native Georgia seceded. He was promptly commissioned as senior flag officer in Georgia's state navy, and in late March received his commission as a captain in the Confederate States Navy in charge of defending the Georgia and South Carolina coasts. In early March 1862, he was put in command of the defense of Virginia's waters and used the CSS *Virginia* as his flagship. Tattnall, by then a flag officer, directed the CSS *Jamestown* and other warships in their capture of Federal merchantmen off Sewell's Point in April 1862.

Tattnall was present throughout the Norfolk operations covered in this study, and his report filed immediately after he lost the *Virginia* is a key piece of primary information about what was transpiring aboard ship and throws light on the relations between the Army (Gen. Huger) and the Confederate Navy. On May 11, 1862, when it became apparent that the *Virginia* had no way to escape from the Federal forces advancing on Norfolk, it was Tattnall who ordered the ironclad destroyed. Some, including members of the Davis administration, criticized him for the loss of the *Virginia* and he was court-martialed, but Tattnall offered a spirited defense and he was justly acquitted of all charges stemming from his decision to destroy the *Virginia.*

Tattnall returned to the command of Georgia's coastal defense on May 29, 1862, and retained it until March 31, 1863, when he was replaced to concentrate on Savannah's shore defenses. He was captured in December 1864 when the city fell from an inland attack by Maj. Gen. William T. Sherman.

27 Wilson & Fiske, *Appleton's Cyclopaedia,* 5:648-49; Albert E. H. Johnson, "Reminiscences of the Hon. Edwin M. Stanton, Secretary of War," *Records of the Columbia Historical Society, Washington, D.C.* (1910): 69-97, accessed Dec. 12, 2016, jstor.org/stable/40067012; Lamon, *Recollections of Abraham Lincoln,* Teillard, ed., 236-37; Charles A. Dana, *Lincoln and His Cabinet: A Lecture Delivered Before the New Haven Colony Historical Society, Tuesday, March 10, 1896* (New York, 1899), 27.

The naval officer was paroled on May 9, 1865, and eventually returned to Savannah, where he served as the city's port inspector until his death.[28]

Egbert Ludovicus Viele (1825-1902)

Viele's (pronounced "Vee-lee") is famous today not for anything he did during the Civil War as a brigadier general or as military governor of Norfolk, but for what he created before the war, and then returned to in 1863. The native of Waterford, New York, drew a map of Manhattan Island and later expanded to include the Bronx. Without Viele's map, the skyline of New York City would probably be completely different today.

As he stated in 1859, "The Sanitary condition of any city or district or country is intimately connected with its proper drainage, any inquiry into causes or remedies for sanitary evils . . . shall be based upon a thorough knowledge of the topography of the island." As a result, the civil engineer surveyed and mapped the many waterways once flowing through the island that had long since been covered. He had noticed that people who lived near these covered former waterways were more likely to become sick, and he wanted to provide a means for the city's sanitary department to understand the connection. Viele also sketched former marshlands, ponds, areas filled in to create new land, meadows, and the island's high points—all superimposed over the present-day street grid and sewer lines. (Viele's work began before the Civil War when he surveyed as a civil engineer the land that would become Central Park. His plan for the park was rejected in favor of the one submitted by Frederick Law Olmsted.)

It quickly became apparent, though, that Viele's map could be used for another purpose. From the late 1800s and through the heyday of New York's skyscraper building phase until the present, it has been a construction aid for architects and engineers. The map was useful, for example, in the placement and design of the Empire State Building.

Viele graduated from West Point in 1847 and returned to the ranks when the Civil War began. He helped construct the defenses around Washington, and, after promotion to brigadier general, was posted to the expedition to capture Fort Pulaski, which protected one of the approaches to Savannah, Georgia. His active military career essentially ended after that expedition. Ordered to Hampton Roads, Viele took part in the Norfolk Campaign overseen by President Lincoln and was installed as military governor of the Norfolk area. Rumors circulated that he had been involved in kidnapping and selling free blacks into slavery across enemy lines and accusations of embezzlement plagued the officer. Although the allegations were never investigated, Viele abruptly requested a 30-day

28 Wilson & Fiske, *Appleton's Cyclopaedia,* 6:38-39.

leave of absence in early 1863 and was eventually reassigned as a draft officer in Ohio. He resigned from the U.S. Army that fall and returned to his former position in New York.

Viele would later become commissioner of New York's parks, a one-term member of Congress, and president of a home building company. His time in Norfolk in May of 1862, followed by his writing on the subject, remain invaluable.[29]

Gideon Welles (1802-1878)

Although Welles had a reputation as "an old fogy," he was anything but. Despite his peculiarities, recorded Assistant Secretary of War Charles A. Dana, Welles "was a very wise, strong man. There was nothing decorative about him; there was no noise in the street when he went along; but he understood his duty, and did it efficiently, continually, and unvaryingly. . . . [H]e was patient, laborious, and intelligent at his task." One of the secretary's best attributes as a cabinet member was his lack of political ambition. Unlike many who surrounded Lincoln, Welles had no desire to be president. He did not always agree with Lincoln, and he often tangled with Stanton, but he supported the Union cause wholeheartedly.

The younger Welles worked toward a law degree but succumbed to the call of the written word to become part owner and editor of the *Hartford* (Connecticut) *Times*, a staunchly Democratic pro-Andrew Jackson newspaper. Unlike some, Welles did not just talk about politics; he became Connecticut's youngest legislator in 1827 and served in that capacity until 1835. The future naval secretary was appointed and then elected as state comptroller, and later became Hartford's postmaster. President James K. Polk appointed him chief of the U.S. Navy's Bureau of Provisions and Clothing in Washington during the war with Mexico—a position that later brought him to the attention of Lincoln. Strongly anti-slavery, Welles bolted the Democratic Party for the new Republican Party and ran unsuccessfully for Connecticut governor on that party's ticket in 1856.

Welles brought to his job as Lincoln's secretary of the navy the energy and vision the national crisis demanded. During the war's first four months he expanded the Navy's ship complement from 42 effective vessels to 82. Within a few months more, through purchase, conversion, and construction, the count topped 500. The department's personnel grew to 1,500 officers and 7,600 enlisted men. Although he had some initial reluctance to the idea, Welles soon embraced the innovation of iron ships. The correspondence and reports to

29 Wilson & Fiske, *Appleton's Cyclopaedia,* 6:291; Johnson, "Blockade or Trade Monopoly?", 55-78; Warner, *Generals in Blue*, 526-27; "Viele's Famous Topographical Atlas of the City of New York," in "Treasures of the New York Public Library," accessed Dec. 6, 2016, exhibitions.nypl.org/treasures/items/show/35.

and from Welles during the period under study in this book offer important information from the command level of operations down to the minutia of naval affairs.

Welles remained in place after Lincoln was slain through Andrew Johnson's administration. When he finally retired, he returned to his first love: writing and commenting about politics and current events, which now included the late war he had experienced from such a unique perspective.[30]

John Ellis Wool (1784-1869)

Both President Lincoln and Secretary of War Stanton publicly praised Wool after the capture of Norfolk. In acknowledgment of the honor, the general promised his superiors that neither would ever regret "so generously" bestowing praise upon him. He spoke too soon, for Lincoln and Stanton did come to lament their praise for the aging general and eventually moved him out of Fort Monroe. Wool had made a habit over the decades of coming into conflict with the government's civilian authorities.

If it had not been for the War of 1812, Wool may never have entered the Army. He was orphaned at a young age, raised by his grandfather in Troy, New York, and at the age of 12 began working in the local stores. He continued to do so for the next 16 years and during that period studied law. With the advent of war, Wool organized a company of volunteers and became their captain. His actions at the battles of Queenstown Heights, where he was severely wounded, and Plattsburg attracted Winfield Scott's notice and earned the new officer a promotion to major as well as a brevet to lieutenant colonel. Delighted with military life, Wool remained in the Army and was assigned (with the rank of colonel), as one of the Army's two inspectors general.

His assignments stirred controversy. Wool clashed with local civil authorities in 1836 during the removal of the Cherokees from their homeland in Georgia, Tennessee, and the Carolinas to Indian Territory. While marching through Alabama, Wool allegedly seized private property to feed and provide for his own soldiers as well as the Cherokees. He was recalled and later exonerated by a board of inquiry. So cleared, Wool was sent to the Canadian border to ensure American neutrality during the Lower Canadian Rebellion, a difficult assignment that pitted his soldiers against other Americans intent on seizing Canada for the United States. Wool was a brigadier general by the start of the Mexican War, and commanded troops under Gen. Zachary Taylor at Buena Vista in 1847. His honors

30 Charles A. Dana, *Recollections of the Civil War With the Leaders at Washington and in the Field in the Sixties* (New York, 1898), 170; Wilson & Fiske, *Appleton's Cyclopaedia,* 6:427.

included a Congressional Sword, a resolution of "thanks," and a bump in rank to brevet major general.

His next assignment, the command of the Pacific Department, almost sparked an international incident when he accused the French consul in San Francisco of working to provoke an American takeover of Mexico. President Franklin Pierce stepped in to repudiate the charge in order to satisfy the French government. A dispute between Indian tribes and white settlers in the Oregon and Washington territories led to his being relieved of command.

Despite his age, Wool was active during the early years of the Civil War. He served as the commander of the Middle District of Pennsylvania, Delaware, Maryland, and Western Virginia and was based in Baltimore. The city was populated with Southern sympathizers who did not appreciate his efforts "The most infamous falsehoods have been engendered and palmed upon the President and the public" in an effort to have him removed, complained Wool in a letter to a New York newspaper. In an effort to calm the city, Wool was given command of the Department of Virginia and he took steps to make sure Fort Monroe, at the tip of the Virginia Peninsula, remained in Union hands. John A. Dix took his place in Baltimore.

At Fort Monroe, of course, Wool played an integral role in the affairs of Hampton Roads, clashed at times with naval officers, and (in words that surely warmed Lincoln's heart), openly complained that Maj. Gen. George McClellan was not moving aggressively enough up the Peninsula toward Richmond.

Maj. Gen. Dix again replaced Wool at Fort Monroe shortly after Norfolk was captured. Louis M. Goldsborough, the Navy's commanding officer at Hampton Roads, aptly characterized the two army commanders: "[H]ow unlike [Dix] is that inflated fool Wool, whose logic is so very ridiculous." Wool was sent to New York City in command of the Eastern District. A year later, when the summer draft riots were out of hand, Lincoln dispatched Dix to take Wool's place for a third time. The 79-year-old major general returned to Troy to await new orders that never came.[31]

Alfred Lubaugh Bernier Zerega (1838-1920)

A long-time sailor, Zerega became an acting ship's master during the war. As a French naval officer, he had commanded one of his father's ships during the Crimean War

31 Wool to Stanton, May 17, 1862, Letter Book, Wool Papers, NYSA; Wool, "Biographical Note," Wool Papers, NYSA; Wool to [editor], Oct. 31, 1862, Wool Papers, NYSA; Louis M. Goldsborough to Gustavus V. Fox, June 4, 1862, *Confidential Correspondence*, Thompson & Wainwright, eds., 1:284; Wilson & Fiske, *Appleton's Cyclopaedia*, 6:609.

(1853-56). He returned to his native New York and when the war began, volunteered for the U.S. Navy and received his appointment on July 24, 1861.

In 1863, Zerega was given command of the USS *Antona*, a blockade ship operating off the Texas coast. Within a few days he captured the *Mary Ann*, a schooner with a cargo of cotton out of Sabine, Texas. His second prize was the British schooner *Exchange*, spotted coming up from Mexico with a cargo of liquor. Zerega didn't believe her captain's protestations of being bound for New Orleans and he seized the alcohol.

Following the war, Zerega spoke and wrote about his experiences. He gave speeches before various local chapters of the Military Order of Loyal Legion, including "The Last Days of the Rebel Iron-Clad Merrimac and Occupation of Norfolk," and "The Expedition for the Capture of the Forts at Port Royal, November 7, 1861"—both "as seen from the U.S.S. *Susquehanna*." His eyewitness accounts offer keen insights into naval affairs during that fascinating week of the war.[32]

32 *Register of Commissioned and Warrant Officers of the United States Navy and Marine Corps and Reserve Officers on Active Duty* (Washington, DC, 1865), 135; Arthur Wyllie, *The Union Navy* (Morrisville, NC, 2007), 48. Zerega's name is sometimes given as Di Zerega.

Appendix 2

Ship Directory

Adelaide, US

Built in 1854, the side-wheel passenger and freight steamer made regular runs through the Chesapeake Bay between Baltimore and Norfolk, with other stops in between. The trip was cut short to end at Fort Monroe when Virginia seceded. The U.S. Navy chartered the ship to serve as a transport for the Atlantic Blockading Squadron during the expedition to the Carolina coasts, after which she was returned to her owners to resume her previous occupation. On May 9, 1862, the *Adelaide* was once more commandeered into service to transport soldiers from Fort Monroe to the beach landing at Ocean View.[1]

A. H. Schultz, CSS

This New York-built 164-ton side-wheel steamer started the war on the James River, appropriated first by the state of Virginia and then by the Confederacy. She acted as a flag-of-truce ship between Richmond and Union-held Fort Monroe mostly delivering and picking up exchanged prisoners of war after the events discussed in this book. (Despite her role, she may have been armed.) She had just delivered more than 400 Union prisoners and was returning to Richmond on February 19, 1865, when she struck a Rebel torpedo (mine) that had broken loose near Chaffin's Bluff on the James River and sank. A clerical error that had prevented Southern prisoners from boarding for the return trip saved countless lives.[2]

1 Arthur Wyllie, *The Union Navy* (Morrisville, NC, 2007), 11.

2 Naval History Division, *Chronology*, V:46, VI:299.

Arago, US

The side-wheel steamer joined the Union war effort after USS *Monitor* and CSS *Virginia* fought in Hampton Roads. Along with other large merchant ships (*Ericsson*, *Cornelius Vanderbilt*, and *Illinois*), her role was to ram the *Virginia* if she ventured far enough out into Hampton Roads. Like the other "rams," the *Arago* had a mostly civilian crew which spurned a combat role and quit the ship. Capt. Henry A. Gadsden appealed to Flag Officer Louis Goldsborough for 44 replacements, from officers and engineers to seamen and coal passers, to fill in until another crew could be recruited up North. Other crewmembers were needed immediately, and among those who volunteered were recent runaway slaves who worked as coal haulers.

With the *Virginia's* destruction on May 11, 1862, the Navy eventually dismissed the rams. Thereafter, the U.S. Army chartered the *Arago* as a transport ship for runs along the southern Atlantic coast. A year later, she captured the Confederate blockade-runner *Emma* outside Charleston.[3]

Aroostook, USS

A double-masted and screw steamship, the *Aroostook* was one of the "90-day gun boats" built in 1861 as the U.S. Navy expanded for war. Contractors used unseasoned timber to complete the vessels within three months, which hampered their sailing abilities. The *Aroostook* rolled heavily in anything but calm seas. In May 1862, under President Lincoln's orders, the *Aroostook* took part—together with the ironclad USS *Galena* and the USS *Port Royal*—in an expedition up the James River. On May 15, along with the USS *Monitor* and the USS *E. A. Stevens*, the *Aroostook* supported the unsuccessful attempt to reduce the Confederate river defenses at Drewry's Bluff, during which the *Galena* was badly pummelled.

The *Aroostook* later served on the Gulf Blockading Squadron and spent most of her time stationed off the Texas coast. The *Aroostook* captured five vessels and destroyed one. After the war, she was part of the U.S. Asiatic Squadron until sold at Hong Kong in October 1869.[4]

3 Gibson & Gibson, *Dictionary*, 20; "Runaway Slaves Bolster Crew of *Arago*; Replace Sailors Who Refused Orders," *Washington Times*, March 6, 2004.

4 Paul H. Silverstone, *Warships of the Civil War Navies* (Annapolis, MD, 1989), 49-51; James L. Mooney, ed., *Dictionary of American Naval Fighting Ships*, 8 vols. (Washington, DC, 1959), 1:64.

Baltic, US

The steamship was another heavy merchant ship designated to ram the CSS *Virginia* if the opportunity arose. The ship's war record is somewhat murky. The U.S. Navy chartered her for the attempt to relieve Fort Sumter during the early secession period. Two more chartered Army transport ships moved soldiers to Port Royal Sound in November 1861, then sailed to Fort Pickens, Florida. The *Baltic* is mentioned in a March 10, 1862, dispatch as towing a stone ship to Hampton Roads to be sunk at the entrance to the Elizabeth River to prevent the *Virginia* from coming out again (the plan was aborted). Following the *Virginia's* destruction, the *Baltic* again came under Army charter and carried supplies to Ship Island in the Gulf of Mexico and other places. She continued under various charters until the end of the war, including a stint as a hospital ship transporting injured soldiers.[5]

Baltimore, USS

A side-wheel steamship armed with two guns, the *Baltimore* was mainly used for ordnance transport and communication, first between Washington and locations along the Potomac and later between the capital and Fort Monroe. She transported President Lincoln and two of his cabinet secretaries (Chase and Stanton) back to Washington following Norfolk's capture. Commissioned by the U. S. Navy, she was sold into private hands at the end of the war.[6]

Beaufort, CSS

Formerly called the *Caledonia*, the *Beaufort* was described by one source as "a small iron propeller, built for service on the [Albemarle canal]." She was commissioned into Confederate service in July of 1861. Under Capt. William H. Parker and his 35-man crew, the *Beaufort* participated in the failed defense of Roanoke Island and Elizabeth City, North Carolina, then fled north through the Dismal Swamp Canal to Norfolk , where she became part of the CSS *Virginia's* support fleet. The *Beaufort* escaped a second time, on this occasion up the James River, and remained with the James River fleet until her capture in April of

5 Gibson & Gibson, *Dictionary*, 28.

6 Ibid.; Osbon, ed., *Hand Book*, 17; Mooney, ed., *Naval Fighting Ships*, 1:88.

1865. After the war she became a small merchant ship called the *Roanoke* before being converted into a barge.[7]

Cambridge, USS

The U.S. Navy purchased the *Cambridge* at Boston and commissioned her into the service in August 1861. The armed steamer, built in 1860, was part of the North Atlantic Blockading Squadron until October 1864, and then served with the South Atlantic Squadron until the end of the war. She spent most of her time cruising along the Atlantic coast interdicting blockade-runners, where she took 11 prizes and chased several others onto sandbars or shoals. She was decommissioned in June 1865.[8]

Cayuga, USS

Part of the West Gulf Coast Blockading Squadron, *Cayuga* participated in running the Mississippi River forts below New Orleans in April 1862. She successfully avoided a confrontation with the CSS *Governor Moore* when that Confederate ship came upon the rest of the Union fleet. Following a trip to Hampton Roads and Washington in May to deliver the official dispatches on the capture of New Orleans, the *Cayuga* returned to the Mississippi to take part in the bombardment of Baton Rouge and the engagement with the Confederate ironclad CSS *Arkansas* in August. She continued patrolling the Mississippi and the western Gulf area, capturing a number of blockade-runners. She was decommissioned in July 1865 and sold later that year.[9]

Columbia, USS

This powerful United States sailing ship was built in 1838. She carried ten 8-inch guns and 40 32-pound guns. *Columbia* was sister ship to the *Cumberland*, *Raritan*, and *St. Lawrence*, among others, she had sat unused at the Gosport Navy Yard since 1855. U.S. Navy forces

7 Parker, *Recollections*, 225, 232; Silverstone, *Warships*, 243; Mooney, ed., *Naval Fighting Ships*, 2:503.

8 Mooney, ed., *Naval Fighting Ships*, 2:20.

9 Silverstone, *Warships*, 51; Kevin J. Dougherty, *Ships of the Civil War, 1861-1865* (New York, 2013), 124.

scuttled and burned the ship on April 20, 1861, to prevent her capture by Virginia state forces.[10]

Columbus, USS

Though her construction was authorized by Congress during the War of 1812, the *Columbus* wasn't started until 1816. Considered a good vessel for her time, the ship of the line wasn't able to carry all of the 74 guns intended for her. When fully loaded for sea duty, her bottom gun deck was too low to be useful. She was destroyed at the Gosport Navy Yard to prevent her capture by Virginia state forces in April 1861.[11]

Congress, USS

Launched at Portsmouth, New Hampshire, in 1841, by the beginning of the Civil War the *Congress*—the fourth navy ship so named—already had a long service record in the Mediterranean, southern Atlantic, and in the Pacific during the Mexican War. Twice decommissioned, she was back at sea and ordered to Hampton Roads in September 1861. Confederate Flag Officer Franklin Buchanan considered the *Congress* the lesser threat of the U.S. Navy's two major ships stationed off Newport News in March 1862. The frigate's 50 guns proved no match for the CSS *Virginia,* and in a windless sea the *Congress* was completely at the ironclad's mercy. After the *Cumberland* sank, the *Congress* was towed into shallower water, where the *Virginia's* hotshot set her ablaze. She eventually exploded when fire reached her magazine. After the war what was left of the wreck was raised, taken to the Gosport Navy Yard, and sold for scrap.[12]

Cornelius Vanderbilt, US

The *Cornelius Vanderbilt,* named after her owner, was a massive side-wheel steamer boasting two masts. In her 1857 maiden voyage she crossed the Atlantic in record time. With the coming of the war, Vanderbilt unsuccessfully offered his ship to the U.S. Navy.

10 Howard I. Chapelle, *The History of the American Sailing Navy: The Ships and Their Development* (New York, 1949), 535; Silverstone, *Warships*, 127.

11 Chapelle, *Sailing Navy*, 309-310, 315.

12 Mooney, ed., *Naval Fighting Ships*, 2:163-64; Osbon, *Hand Book*, 33.

The Army chartered her as a troop transport for use against Port Royal, South Carolina. She may have acted under the command of the U. S. Navy as one of the ships designated to ram and sink the CSS *Virginia* at Hampton Roads during the spring of 1862, but other records indicate she remained under Army charter as an armed vessel protecting transports. Later, the *Vanderbilt* came under complete Navy control, though Secretary of the Navy Welles did not want the ship and her expensive operating costs. Armed with a battery of 15 guns, she conducted a fruitless hunt for the CSS *Alabama* in the Caribbean, off Brazil, South Africa, and up the African coast to Spain, but did capture other ships during this patrol. Following a refit, the *Vanderbilt* participated in the attacks on Fort Fisher.

After the war, she remained in the U.S. Navy for a couple of years as a receiving ship at the Portsmouth Navy Yard in New Hampshire and saw service in the Pacific before being decommissioned in May 1867. Sold in 1873, she became a merchant ship, converted to a full-sailed vessel. By 1885 she was hauling coal at Gibraltar and was scrapped in 1929.[13]

Cumberland, USS

The sailing frigate was launched in 1842 at the Boston Navy Yard and over the course of numerous assignments during the next 20 years served as a flagship both in foreign waters and with the Home Squadron. The *Cumberland* was at the Gosport Navy Yard awaiting refitting and reassignment when Virginia seceded. She was towed out of the yard on April 20, 1861, and thus escaped the destruction suffered by other vessels there, including the USS *Merrimack*. The ironclad *Virginia's* incursion into Hampton Roads, however, spelled her doom. Confederate Flag Officer Franklin Buchanan considered the *Cumberland's* 32- pound smoothbores and ten 8-inch rifled guns the most dangerous ship opposed to him, and decided to ram the frigate before turning to fight the USS *Congress*. Although the *Virginia's* iron ram may have broken off inside the *Cumberland*, the three-masted frigate quickly sank with a great loss of life.[14]

Dacotah, USS

The steam sloop was commissioned out of the Gosport Navy Yard in 1860 and traveled around the Cape of Good Hope to Hong Kong to join the East Indian Squadron.

13 Silverstone, *Warships*, 77-78; Gibson & Gibson, *Dictionary*, 46; Osbon, *Hand Book*, 260-61; Mooney, ed., *Naval Fighting Ships*, 7:463-65.

14 Mooney, ed., *Naval Fighting Ships*, 2:214-15; Osbon, *Hand Book*, 37.

The outbreak of war brought her back to the United States, where she refitted at the New York Navy Yard before steaming for Hampton Roads on March 9, 1862. On May 8, under orders from President Lincoln, she participated in the engagement against the Confederate batteries at Sewell's Point. Except for a couple of trips to New Orleans carrying dispatches, the *Dacotah* spent most of 1862 either in Hampton Roads or up the James River skirmishing with land-based batteries. Part of her crew of 147 sailors and marines landed twice to destroy batteries at Harden's Bluff and Day's Point. She spent most of the balance of the war chasing Confederate privateers and on blockade duty. After the war, the *Dacotah's* engines were removed to convert her to a pure sailing ship, and she again entered the Pacific Ocean to sail along the coast of the Americas. She was inactive after 1869 and sold in 1873.[15]

Delaware, USS

The sister ship to the *New York* was launched in 1820 at the Gosport Navy Yard in Virginia. The impressive ship of the line was destroyed by the U.S. Navy in April 1861 in the very place of her creation to prevent her capture by Virginia state forces.[16]

Dolphin, USS

The sailing brigantine *Dolphin* (the third with that name) was launched in 1836 and was one of the fastest sailing vessels in the Navy, matching the best British ships of the same class. She successfully carried out operations off the coast of Africa to stem the slave trade. The Navy destroyed her at the Gosport Navy Yard to prevent her capture by Virginia state forces in April 1861.[17]

Dragon, USS

The U.S. Navy bought the screw steamer in December 1861. Outfitted with one 30-pound muzzle-loading rifled gun, one 24-pound smoothbore gun, and a crew of 42, the *Dragon* sailed to Hampton Roads to join the North Atlantic Blockading Squadron. Along

15 Silverstone, *Warships*, 40-41; Osbon, ed., *Hand Book*, 38-39; Mooney, ed., *Naval Fighting Ships*, 2:230.

16 Chapelle, *Sailing Navy*, 314.

17 Ibid., 393.

with the *Zouave*, the *Dragon* acted as a tender for the frigates *Cumberland* and *Congress* in case of an attack by the CSS *Virginia*. When that attack came, neither *Dragon* nor *Zouave* could do anything to prevent disaster. With her primary assignments sunk or burned, the *Dragon* tried to assist the stuck USS *Minnesota* from the shallow "middle ground" of Hampton Roads. She was still there when the USS *Monitor* and the *Virginia* fought their famous battle on March 9. One of the *Virginia's* errant shots at the *Minnesota* struck and exploded in *Dragon's* boiler, killing and wounding several men and inflicting significant damage. Towed to Baltimore for repairs, she returned to Hampton Roads on April 22, 1862, and remained there until transferred to the Potomac Flotilla in August, when she began patrolling the Potomac and Rappahannock rivers. The *Dragon* was decommissioned in May 1865 and sold two months later.[18]

E. A. Stevens, USRC

The Stevens brothers, Edwin A. and Robert, proposed a ship to the Navy Department in 1841 driven by steam-powered screw propellers and protected by 4 ½ inches of iron plating. When experiments by John Ericsson proved the plating would not be sufficient, the proposal died. The brothers built a smaller version to demonstrate its practicality. The *Naugatuck* was impressive and accepted by the Treasury Department in early 1862. Secretary Salmon P. Chase insisted the name be changed to *E. A. Stevens* in honor of her designer and loaned her to the U. S. Navy.

The iron-hulled *Stevens* featured several innovations. Though originally powered by a steam-driven single screw, a second engine and propeller were added to allow her to turn around on her center. Her main armament was a single 100-pound rifled gun mounted below the main deck, where it could be loaded and raised to fire. A reporter for the Philadelphia *Press* was less than impressed: "Externally, she looks like an ordinary towboat." The *Stevens* participated in the May 8 bombardment of the Sewell's Point batteries and in the May 15 attack on Drewry's Bluff. Her lone gun exploded, ending her usefulness. The ship was sold in 1889.[19]

18 Mooney, ed., *Naval Fighting Ships*, 2:298.

19 Chase to "Janet," May 8, 1862, "The Life of Chase. His Account of the Capture of Norfolk," *New York Times*, Sept. 10, 1874, 4; Silverstone, *Warships*, 105, 187; Osbon, ed., *Hand Book*, 147; "Letter from Fortress Monroe," Philadelphia *Press*, Apr. 10, 1862, 1.

Elizabeth, CSS

The small gunboat was constructed at the Gosport Navy Yard by the Confederate Navy and burned by the retreating Rebels soon after she was completed on May 10, 1862.[20]

Ericsson, US

Contrary to popular belief, the wooden steamer was not named after John Ericsson, the designer of the USS *Monitor.* This craft was chartered by the Army from fall 1861 to early March 1862 for the expedition to Port Royal Sound, and re-chartered from March 21 until January 1863. Some reports claim she was part of the ramming fleet arrayed against the CSS *Virginia.* The *Ericsson* continued under additional charters to the end of the war.[21]

Escambia, CSS

Like her sister ship *Elizabeth*, the *Escambia* had just been completed at the Gosport Navy Yard when she was burned on May 10, 1862, to avoid capture by Union forces.[22]

Galena, USS

Designed by Samuel H. Pook for Cornelius Bushnell, the *Galena* was the last of the three ironclad ships authorized by the Iron-Clad Board in the fall of 1861. Earlier, the board had raised concerns about the *Galena's* stability, prompting Bushnell to consult with John Ericsson. The inventor assured Bushnell of the *Galena's* seaworthiness, prompting Bushnell to go ahead with the project. The consultation also resulted in the board's consideration of Ericsson's "monitor" design. The *Galena* was considered a "corvette" with an armor of interlocking horizontal iron bars. In addition to having a steam-powered screw, she also had two masts.

Her first major assignment, ordered by President Lincoln, was to ascend the James River in early May 1862, knock out Confederate batteries, and attack Richmond. Her only accomplishment was to became stuck on the river bottom. After Norfolk fell and the

20 Porter, *Record of Events*, 32.

21 Gibson & Gibson, *Dictionary*, 106.

22 Porter, *Record of Events*, 32.

Galena was released, Lincoln added the *Monitor* and *E. A. Stevens* to the fleet upriver, only to have them stopped on May 15 by the artillery at Drewry's Bluff. *Galena's* side armor proved of little use against the plunging fire, and 12 crewmen were killed and 15 wounded. Despite the damage, the *Galena* continued active service on the James River, supporting the Army of the Potomac until it was withdrawn.

In May 1863, *Galena* underwent extensive repairs and conversion to lose her armor to become a three-masted screw sloop. Recommissioned on February 15, 1864, she participated in the battle of Mobile Bay that August. The *Galena* was decommissioned on June 17, 1865, and condemned in 1870. The once-unique ironclad was broken up in 1872 at the Gosport Navy Yard.[23]

Gassendi, HIMS

The French frigate *Gassendi* acted as a neutral naval observer during the Civil War. Unlike the British *Rinaldo,* however, the *Gassendi,* under Capt. Jules Gautier, was at Hampton Roads to witness the battles of March 8 and 9, 1862. The following month, the ship—described as a "French paddle sloop" or "coaling ship"; she was not a frigate as many claimed—left Hampton Roads for Washington, D.C. French ambassador Henri Mercier invited President Lincoln to visit the ship on April 26. Frederick Seward, son of and assistant to Secretary of State William Seward, thought it "a graceful suggestion [tending] to promote international friendship."

Lincoln accepted and he, both Sewards, and Capt. John A. Dahlgren attended and enjoyed a champagne reception and tour of the warship. When the visit finished, Lincoln and his party returned to a rowboat for the trip back to shore. Lincoln, however, asked to be taken around the ship's bow. The French officers did not notice the small rowboat had altered course and began a 21-gun salute to honor the U.S. leader. "Several sudden flashes and racket of a cannon, just over [the] heads" of the presidential party's rowboat spurred its swift retreat from the ship, wrote the younger Seward. The *Gassendi's* guns were not shotted, but the wadding caught fire and dropped to the water when the guns fired. "Whether Mr. Lincoln realized the danger or not, I never knew. He sat impassively through it, and made no reference to it afterwards."[24]

23 Silverstone, *Warships*, 16; Mooney, ed., *Naval Fighting Ships*, 3:6-7.

24 "News from Washington," *New York Herald*, Apr. 27, 1862, 4; Frederick William Seward, *Reminiscences of a War-Time Statesman and Diplomat, 1830-1915* (New York, 1916), 173-75.

George Washington, US

The steam-driven tugboat was chartered and used by the Army as a gunboat in 1862. She assisted U.S. Navy ships following the two-day battle at Hampton Roads in early March and transported soldiers along the Atlantic coast. In April 1863, the *George Washington* ran aground and came under Confederate fire during an expedition up the Coosaw River in South Carolina. The gunboat was badly damaged, and some sources claim she was destroyed.[25]

Germantown, USS

The *Germantown* was constructed between 1843 and 1846 at the Philadelphia Navy Yard. The fast first-class corvette carried 20 guns and a crew of 210. She was undergoing a refit at the Gosport Navy Yard when war broke out in April 1861. The U.S. Navy burned her to prevent her capture by Virginia state forces. Once the Union reoccupied the yard, the ship's hulk was raised and sold in 1863.[26]

Hampton, CSS

The wooden *Hampton* was built at the Gosport Navy Yard. She was the first of a proposed class of 100 such gunboats. She weighed 171 tons and carried two guns, a 9-inch cannon forward and a 32-pounder aft. Despite their grand plans, the Confederates were only able to complete one other similar gunboat (the *Nansemond*). Others in that *Hampton* class, such as the unfinished *Norfolk* and the *Portsmouth*, were burned on May 10, 1862, when Norfolk was evacuated. The *Hampton* and *Nansemond* escaped that fate by eluding Union picket boats at the entrance to the James River and steaming up to Richmond.

The *Hampton's* war service included battles at Dutch Gap, Fort Harrison, and Chaffin's Bluff, all in 1864. She was burned on April 3, 1865, during the Confederate evacuation of Richmond.[27]

25 Gibson & Gibson, *Dictionary*, 132.

26 Chapelle, *Sailing Navy*, 440, 444, 541.

27 Mooney, ed., *Naval Fighting Ships*, 2:532-33; Silverstone, *Warships*, 218.

Harmony, CSS

The small steam tugboat acted as the official vessel of the inspector general of naval ordnance at the Gosport Navy Yard. She transported ordnance supplies to the various Confederate ships anchored in the James River and to the fortified batteries along the river's bank. Flag Officer French Forrest, the yard's first commander after the Union evacuation in 1861, praised her work as "indispensable." *Harmony* took on additional duties in August 1861 when she was armed with a pair of 32-pound rifled guns. The small gunboat took a position outside the range of the Union sloop-of-war *Savannah* anchored off Newport News and hit the Union ship several times, inflicting heavy damage. *Harmony* continued as an ordnance boat until May 10, 1862, when she was burned to keep her from falling into Union hands.[28]

Illinois, US

After initial service as a transport, the Army chartered the *Illinois* as one of four large vessels the Navy intended to use for ramming the CSS *Virginia.* Her civilian crewmen, however, objected to going into combat and quit. Only five members of the crew, including her captain and chief engineer, stayed with the *Illinois.* The ship's owner, Marshall O. Roberts, assisted by New York businessman Moses Taylor, eventually recruited a new crew. The *Illinois* never sailed against the *Virginia* because the Confederate ironclad was destroyed by her own crew. The *Illinois* reverted to her previous role as an Army transport for most of the rest of war.[29]

Jamestown, CSS (*Thomas Jefferson*)

The *Jamestown's* service in the Confederate Navy lasted less than a year, but during that time she participated in the battles at Hampton Roads in March 1862 and the subsequent capture of three Union transport ships a month later. The ship was built in 1853 and originally intended to carry passengers and cargo between Richmond and New York City. With Virginia's secession, she entered Confederate service in April 1861 and her name was

28 Mooney, ed., *Naval Fighting Ships*, 2:533-34; Parker, *Recollections*, 207.

29 Gibson & Gibson, *Dictionary*, 158; "Runaway Slaves Bolster Crew of Arago; Replace Sailors Who Refused Orders," *Washington Times*, March 6, 2004; D. B. Barton (*Illinois*' captain) to Goldsborough, Mar. 20, 1862, *ORN*, 7:145.

changed to the *Thomas Jefferson* (which no one, even her own crew, ever called her). The demise of the *Jamestown* came on May 15, 1862, as the small Union fleet, led by the USS *Galena* and the USS *Monitor*, sailed up the James River and approached Drewry's Bluff. The *Jamestown*, with her guns removed, steamed into the middle of the river where her crew scuttled her to help block the channel.[30]

Jamestown, USS

The sailing sloop-of-war *Jamestown* had a long career with the U.S. Navy. Built and commissioned at the Gosport Navy Yard in 1844, her assignments included interdicting the slave trade off the coast of Africa, delivering badly needed food to Ireland during the potato famine, and protecting American interests in the Mediterranean. During the Civil War, the *Jamestown* helped protect American commerce from Confederate privateers and blockaded Southern ports. In nearly a year's time, she captured, burned, or sank five blockade-runners as part of the North Atlantic Blockading Squadron. Thereafter she sailed through the Straits of Magellan into the Pacific Ocean, where she spent the rest of the war and many subsequent years. Her final assignments in the 1890s included training apprentices and acting as a Marine hospital ship. The *Jamestown* was burned at the renamed Norfolk Navy Yard in 1913.[31]

John B. White, CS (US)

Before the war, the *John B. White*—a small steam tugboat owned by a company in Erie, Pennsylvania, was involved in a construction project on the Albemarle Canal south of Norfolk. Virginia authorities seized the tug when the state seceded. Her crew remained with her. She made a dramatic escape into Union lines on May 8, 1862, after which the war department employed the tug in the Hampton Roads area. She struck a torpedo and sank on January 1, 1864.[32]

30 Silverstone, *Warships*, 242; Robert Wright, "Sinking of the *Jamestown*," *Richmond Times*, July 16, 1899).

31 Mooney, ed., *Naval Fighting Ships*, 3:501-502.

32 "Our Fortress Monroe Correspondence, A Boat From the Enemy," *New York Times,* May 10, 1862, 1; Mooney, ed., *Naval Fighting Ships*, 2:540; Silverstone, *Warships*, 243.

Kahukee, CSS

At the start of the war the *Kahukee* was a Confederate army screw tugboat employed on the Elizabeth River around Norfolk. Sometimes called the *Kakakee* or the *Kahuha*, the tug was purchased by the Confederate Navy in July 1861 and was later sent down the Dismal Swamp Canal to New Berne, North Carolina. She participated in the failed attempt to drive off Union forces at Hatteras Inlet in August 1861, and returned to Norfolk, where she was burned on May 10, 1862, during the Confederate evacuation.[33]

Marblehead, US

The schooner was commissioned in March 1862 as a merchant ship and co-owned by Churchill H. Cutting. Samuel Philips Lee's squadron in Hampton Roads seized the *Marblehead* in September 1862 for illegally bringing out "staves and headings" from Norfolk.[34]

Marcus, US (CSS)

The small sailing brig was chartered by the U.S. Army on March 6, 1862, to transport supplies. She was at the Newport News wharf on April 12 when the CSS *Virginia* and two consorts sailed into Hampton Roads. As the *Virginia* defiantly enticed the rest of the Union fleet into battle, the CSS *Jamestown's* crew captured the *Marcus* and towed her up the Elizabeth River to Norfolk. As a Confederate ship, she escaped destruction the next month by ascending the James River, but was burned in June 1863.[35]

Merrimack, USS

The wooden frigate USS *Merrimack* was commissioned in 1856. As a class, she and her sister ships were considered some of the best naval vessels in the world. Primarily a sailing ship, the *Merrimack* carried 40 smoothbore guns, an auxiliary steam engine, and a crew of 519. She sailed on the waters near Europe, and was part of the Pacific Squadron until 1860.

33 Mooney, ed., *Naval Fighting Ships*, 2:540-41.

34 Silverstone, *Warships*, 49.

35 Gibson & Gibson, *Dictionary*, 212.

By early 1861, she was ordered to the Gosport Navy Yard near Norfolk, to refit her underpowered, unreliable engine. She was both burned and scuttled by U.S. naval forces there on April 20, 1861, to prevent her capture by rebellious Virginians. The Confederates hauled the hulk of the *Merrimack* off the James River bottom and converted her into the ironclad CSS *Virginia*. Both sides continued to call the new ironclad by her original name though it was often spelled without the "k" at the end.[36]

Miami, USS

Built along the River Clyde in England, the *Miami* began life as the *Lady Le Marchant* in 1853. She was sold to the U.S. Treasury Department in February 1862 and converted into a revenue cutter carrying three guns. Secretary Salmon P. Chase had the cutter further upgraded to carry Washington dignitaries, including the president, to and from the capital. The *Miami* participated in the landing of Union troops at Ocean View, Virginia, in May 1862, though an engine problem prevented her from returning the president to Washington. Thereafter she escorted the captured Confederate steamer *Chesapeake* from Nova Scotia to New York. She remained in service through the war, worked out of Delaware thereafter, and was sold in 1871.[37]

Minnesota, USS

A sister ship to the USS *Merrimack*, the wooden steam frigate *Minnesota*—named after the Minnesota River, not the state—was commissioned in May 1857. Her complement consisted of 646 men, and 37 smoothbore and 5 rifled guns, one of which fired a 200-pound shell. After completing her prewar assignment with the East India Squadron, she returned home in 1859 and was decommissioned. With the outbreak of the war, the *Minnesota* was recommissioned and joined the North Atlantic Blockading Squadron as the flagship based at Hampton Roads. In August 1861, the *Minnesota* participated in the capture of Hatteras Inlet, North Carolina. Back at Hampton Roads, she ran aground in her haste to protect the *Cumberland* and *Congress* during the CSS *Virginia's* attack on March 8, 1862. She sustained damage that day and the next, the worst being a rifled shell from the *Virginia* that crashed through the chief engineer's stateroom and the engineer's mess room before

36 Silverstone, *Warships*, 27; Osbon, *Hand Book*, 127.

37 Kern, "President Lincoln on Board Cutter *Miami*," in *Revenue Cutters*, chap. 10; Silverstone, *Warships*, 187.

exploding in the boatswain's room. Confederate forces attempted to sink the *Minnesota* two years later during an attack by the torpedo boat *Squib*, which exploded a large powder charge alongside that failed to do much damage. The *Minnesota* was decommissioned before the war's end, but was brought back into service in 1867 for a midshipmen's cruise to Europe, and again in 1875 as a training ship. After lying in ordinary (out of service for any one of many reasons) for 20 years, she was loaned to the Massachusetts Naval Militia, which held onto her until 1901. The steam frigate was later sold and burned.[38]

Monitor, USS

The most famous of the three experimental ironclads approved by the Navy's Iron-Clad Board in 1861, the *Monitor* almost wasn't built. Her inventor, John Ericsson, had a distaste for the U.S. Navy and many of the service's officers did not trust Ericsson. They continued to blame the Swedish engineer for the 1844 deaths of six people, including the secretaries of state and the navy, as well as the U. S. Navy's chief of construction, when a cannon Ericsson designed but someone else had cast exploded aboard the USS *Princeton.*

The board reluctantly approved Ericsson's unusual ironclad design, and her construction proceeded quickly. Her keel was laid on October 25, 1861, she was launched on January 30, 1862, and commissioned 26 days later. Though almost lost on her maiden voyage from New York City to Hampton Roads, she saved the Union fleet on March 9 by fighting the CSS *Virginia* to a stalemate. The *Monitor* later shelled enemy shore batteries, but, to the chagrin of her crew, the ironclads never fought again.

In preparation for a planned assault on Wilmington, North Carolina, the *Monitor* was ordered to make the voyage south to Beaufort, South Carolina, in late December. She was being towed along the Atlantic coast on December 31, 1862, when she foundered in a gale off Cape Hatteras and went down with 16 members of her crew. Ten years later, Alban C. Stimers, the *Monitor's* original chief engineer, maintained that the iron ship sank because of the long hot summer at Hampton Roads. The heat, he argued, dried out and shrank the green wood backing up the iron deck and hull, causing a gap through which seawater poured into the ship.[39]

38 Silverstone, *Warships*, 29; Osbon, *Hand Book*, 132-33; Mooney, ed., *Naval Fighting Ships*, 4:372-74.

39 Silverstone, *Warships*, 4; Alban C. Stimers to Gustavus V. Fox, Oct. 18, 1875, Fox Papers, NYHSL; Osbon, *Hand Book*, 135-39.

Mount Vernon, USS

Although used as an Army transport, the wooden screw ship *Mount Vernon* (five guns, crew of 50) participated in a daring raid on a Rebel vessel in December 1861. Two groups of her sailors attacked and destroyed a light craft being converted into a warship off Frying Pan Shoals, North Carolina. She was in Hampton Roads when the CSS *Virginia* sank, and joined a small fleet of ships (including the USS *Monitor*) that sailed into the mouth of the Elizabeth River. In August 1863, she took part in the capture of the blockade-runner *Kate* from under a protective Rebel battery. The *Mount Vernon's* war record included the capture of 13 other vessels. She was sold at the end of the war and became a merchant ship.[40]

Nansemond, CSS

The *Nansemond* was the second of the *Hampton* class of proposed Confederate gunboats. Of the 100 planned, only the *Nansemond* and *Hampton* were finished and entered service. Both escaped from Norfolk up the James River on May 4, 1862, before President Lincoln arrived and the effort to capture the city and the Gosport Navy Yard got underway. With two 8-inch guns, the *Nansemond* took part in the 1864 engagements along the river at Dutch Gap and Fort Harrison, and in the battle at Trent's Reach on January 23-25, 1865. The *Nansemond* was burned on April 3, 1865, during the evacuation of Richmond.[41]

Naugatuck, USS

See entry for the *E. A. Stevens*, USS.

New York, USS

The *New York* was begun in 1818 at the Gosport Navy Yard, but was unfinished in April 1861. She was set afire when United States forces evacuated the yard.[42]

40 Osbon, *Hand Book*, 144-45; Silverstone, *Warships*, 93.

41 Mooney, ed., *Naval Fighting Ships*, 2:551; Silverstone, *Warships*, 218.

42 Chapelle, *Sailing Navy*, 314, 324. Another ship by the same name was chartered during the war, stationed at Hampton Roads, and used as a prisoner exchange ship and mail carrier.

Norfolk, CSS

Another of the *Hampton* class of gunboats under construction at the Confederate Gosport Navy Yard. The *Norfolk* was burned in May 1862 to prevent her capture by Union forces.[43]

Patrick Henry, CSS (*Yorktown*)

After Virginia seceded, the state seized this 1853 side-wheel steam ship *Yorktown* and renamed her the *Patrick Henry*. The addition of 1-inch iron plates bolted onto her hull to protect her engine and boilers converted her from a fast passenger and freight ship into a warship with the James River fleet. She also received 10 guns, eight of them rifled, and a crew of 150 men. During the war, the *Patrick Henry* fought off Union gunboats near Newport News in September and December 1861, and on March 8, 1862, helped the CSS *Virginia* in her attack against the USS *Cumberland* and *Congress*. When the latter struck her colors and the *Patrick Henry* approached to remove prisoners, other ships, such as the USS *Zouave*, together with Union shore batteries, drove the *Patrick Henry* off with heavy fire. One shot exploded the ship's steam chest and killed four of her crew. The *Patrick Henry* had to be towed out of the action. With quick repairs, she was ready for action the next day (March 9), but was held back during the fight between the ironclads and only fired an occasional shot at the USS *Monitor*. The *Patrick Henry* served as the home of the Confederate Naval Academy from 1863 until April 1865, and was burned when Richmond was evacuated.[44]

Pennsylvania, USS

After the War of 1812, the *Pennsylvania* was one of the vessels authorized to be built to replenish the American fleet. Construction began in 1822, but wasn't completed until 1837. The large and powerful ship was built to break any blockade of U.S. ports. Armed with 120 guns, she was the largest sailing man-of-war built by the United States during the sailing age, and was very expensive to operate. For most of her useful life she remained in ordinary (out

43 Silverstone, *Warships*, 218.

44 Parker, *Recollections*, 223-24; Silverstone, *Warships*, 242; James Lee Conrad, *Rebel Reefers: The Organization and Midshipmen of the Confederate States Naval Academy* (Cambridge, MA, 2003), 89; Mooney, ed., *Naval Fighting Ships*, 2:555.

of service). Stuck at the Gosport Navy Yard during the crisis in April 1861, the *Pennsylvania* was destroyed by the U.S. Navy to prevent her capture by Virginia state forces.[45]

Portsmouth, CSS

Another of the *Hampton* class of gunboats under construction at the Gosport Navy Yard, the *Portsmouth* was burned by the Confederates in May 1862 to prevent her capture by Union forces when Norfolk was evacuated.[46]

Plymouth, USS (CSS)

The *Plymouth* first entered U.S. service in 1843. The sloop-of-war made several cruises to various ports around the world, including an initial assignment to the Mediterranean Sea. By 1859 she had become the practice ship for Naval Academy's midshipmen. In April 1861, the *Plymouth* was at anchor near the Gosport Navy Yard when Union forces abandoned the yard. She was scuttled and partially burned. The Confederates raised the *Plymouth's* hulk with plans to rebuild her, but she was burned a second time on May 10, 1862, just before Union forces occupied Norfolk and the navy yard.[47]

Port Royal, USS

As a double-ender, the side-wheel *Port Royal* could sail in either direction without having to turn around in tight river channels. Commissioned in April 1862, she had a complement of 131 men and carried eight guns. She steamed up the James River on May 8 with the USS *Galena* in a failed attempt to reach Richmond. In July 1863, she participated in the bombardment of Battery Wagner off Charleston. In August 1864, she was part of the fleet that ran past Forts Gaines and Morgan into Mobile Bay.

The *Port Royal* was decommissioned and sold after the war, and later became a merchant ship. She disappears from the shipping rolls after 1886.[48]

45 Chapelle, *Sailing Navy*, 338-39, 372; Silverstone, *Warships*, 127.

46 Silverstone, *Warships*, 218.

47 Mooney, ed., *Naval Fighting Ships*, 2:558.

48 Silverstone, *Warships*, 60; Mooney, ed., *Naval Fighting Ships*, 5:355.

Raleigh, CSS (*Roanoke*)

The first of two Confederate Navy vessels to carry that name, the *Raleigh* was a small iron-hulled screw steamer working on the Albemarle and Chesapeake Canal when North Carolina seceded. The state government seized the ship, but she was soon transferred to the Confederate Navy. From August 1861 to February 1862, the *Raleigh* attempted to help keep Union forces out of North Carolina's inlets. When that failed, she made her way up the Dismal Swamp Canal to Norfolk to join the James River Fleet. She took part in the March 8-9 battles at Hampton Roads, but with Northern forces expected to capture Norfolk, the *Raleigh* fled up the James. Plagued by a lack of personnel, she was used mostly for flag-of-truce trips and river patrols. Toward the end of the war she was renamed *Roanoke* and destroyed on April 4, 1865, when Richmond was evacuated.[49]

Rancocas, US

A steamer, *Rancocas* was under charter from December 18, 1861 to April 12, 1862. The ship was reportedly used to tow barges to the landing at Ocean View on May 10, 1862.[50]

Raritan, USS

Commissioned in 1848, the *Raritan* carried eight 8-inch guns and forty-two 32-pound guns. Laid up in ordinary (out of service) at the Gosport Navy Yard, she was burned by the U.S. Navy when the shipyard was evacuated in April 1861.[51]

Richmond, CSS

The unfinished ironclad *Richmond* and the nearly finished wooden gunboats *Hampton* and *Nansemond* were the only Confederate ships moved out of harm's way before the Union occupation of Norfolk on May 10, 1862. John L. Porter, the ironclad's constructor, designed the *Richmond* to be a casemated ironclad with a barn-roof gun deck just above the

49 Mooney, ed., *Naval Fighting Ships*, 2:559; Silverstone, *Warships*, 241. There was also a previous *Roanoke*, which the Confederate government chartered for use in the Nansemond River near Hampton Roads and later in North Carolina. Silverstone, *Warships*, 243.

50 Gibson & Gibson, *Dictionary*, 267; Cram, "Report," in Wool Papers, NYSA.

51 Silverstone, *Warships*, 127.

water line very similar to the CSS *Virginia.* She had 22 inches of yellow pine and oak wood covered by four inches of iron. Private citizens from Virginia provided the money and scrap iron to build the ship. Though her construction was completed along the James River at Rocketts Navy Yard in Richmond, she would not see any action for more than a year. In 1864, the *Richmond* took part in fights at Dutch Gap, Fort Harrison, and Chapin's Bluff, and played a key role (and suffered a heavy fire without sustaining damage) at Trent's Reach on January 23-25, 1865, during a failed effort to move downriver and raid City Point.

The *Richmond's* end, like many other ships, came with the evacuation of the Confederate capital in April 1865 when she was destroyed by Southern torches. The *Richmond* has erroneously been called by other names, including *Young Virginia* and the *Virginia II* (the ironclad *Virginia II* was built at Rocketts in 1863 and was part of the same James River Squadron as the *Richmond*). Northerners sometimes referred to the *Richmond* as the *Merrimack No. 2* or the *New Merrimack.*[52]

Rinaldo, HMS

The British ship *Rinaldo,* a screw-sloop under William N. W. Hewett, was observing Union activities off the coast of South Carolina when news arrived of the CSS *Virginia's* succssful attack on Union ships at Hampton Roads on March 8, 1862. The British and the French had developed ironclad vessels in the late 1850s with varying degrees of success, but no iron ship had yet been tested in battle. The opportunity to observe such a clash prompted Hewett to immediately sail his ship north. He arrived at Hampton Roads on March 10. The French ship *Gassendi* was already there also hoping to see a second battle between the *Virginia* and the USS *Monitor.* The foreign observers were beset by disappointment because there would never be a second battle of the ironclads. After the Union occupation of Norfolk, the *Rinaldo* ascended the Elizabeth River and docked at the city for several days.

The British sloop had played a small role in the international Trent Affair at the end of 1861 when she picked up Confederate commissioners James Mason and John Slidell in Massachusetts and carried them to St. Thomas in the West Indies.[53]

52 Mooney, ed., *Naval Fighting Ships,* 2:561-62.

53 Dougherty, *Ships,* 194; *Rinaldo* ship's log, Mar. 8-10, May 14-27, 1862, BNA.

Sabine Saboah, US

The U.S. Army chartered the sailing brig *Sabine Saboah* to transport supplies. She was caught at the Newport News wharf on April 12, 1862, when the CSS *Virginia* and other ships of the James River Fleet emerged hoping to engage the Union fleet. The *Sabine Saboah*, along with the *Marcus* and an unnamed transport ship, was captured and taken to Norfolk.[54]

San Jacinto, USS

Built in 1850, the *San Jacinto*, with a dozen guns and a crew of 235, was one of the earliest U.S. Navy's screw warships. The frigate also had sails, but her propeller shaft was off center and she suffered throughout her career from engine and other mechanical problems. Nevertheless she was well traveled and her prewar assignments included the West and East Indies, the Far East, and Africa. She is best known as the ship that stopped the British steamer *Trent* in November 1861, which was carrying Southern envoys James Mason and John Slidell and their families to Britain and France in an attempt to gain foreign recognition for the Confederacy. The seizure of Mason and Slidell by Charles Wilkes, commander of the *San Jacinto*, caused a diplomatic embarrassment for Lincoln, who released them to avoid a potential conflict with the England. Following repairs and refitting, the *San Jacinto* was ordered to the Gulf of Mexico, but she was sent to the Hampton Roads area after the emergence of the CSS *Virginia* and took part in shelling Confederate batteries at Sewell's Point. After the destruction of the Confederate ironclad, the *San Jacinto* went out to search for the raiders CSS *Alabama* and *Tallahassee*, and also took part in the blockade of Mobile Bay. Her crew suffered through two yellow fever epidemics. The *San Jacinto* was wrecked off a Bahamian island in January 1865, and is today a popular dive site.[55]

Seminole, USS

A small screw sloop-of-war, the *Seminole* carried only nine guns and a crew of 120. She was commissioned out of the Pensacola Navy Yard in 1860 and sent to Brazil but recalled

54 Gibson & Gibson, *Dictionary*, 281.

55 Silverstone, *Warships*, 26; Osbon, *Hand Book*, 238-39; Mooney, ed., *Naval Fighting Ships*, 6: 295-97.

when the Civil War began. Her first war assignment was off Savannah and then the Potomac River to engage Confederate shore batteries. After taking part in the capture of Port Royal, South Carolina, the *Seminole* was dispatched to Hampton Roads to bolster the fleet guarding against another appearance of the CSS *Virginia.* She took part in the bombardment of Sewell's Point on May 8, 1862, and in the fleet's ascent of the Elizabeth River to the newly captured Norfolk. After repairs at the New York Navy Yard, the *Seminole* joined the East Gulf Blockading Squadron and sailed into Mobile Bay as part of David Farragut's fleet. She patrolled the Texas coast until the end of the war, was decommissioned in August 1865, and sold five years later.[56]

St. Lawrence, USS

The St. Lawrence was one of the Navy's older sailing frigates. Her keel was laid down at the Gosport Navy Yard in 1826, but she wasn't commissioned until 1848. Despite her age and lack of a steam engine, the St. Lawrence carried 52 guns. She almost became a victim of the CSS *Virginia* on March 8, 1862, when she was sent to replace the USS *Congress* at Newport News. Her attempt to the aid the doomed ships ended when she grounded in shallow water, as did the *Minnesota.* The *Virginia* and *St. Lawrence* exchanged shots at about 900 yards, with the latter's bouncing harmlessly off the ironclad. One of the *Virginia's* shots, however, hit just above the waterline and did considerable damage inside the ship. Once she was again underway she retired to Fort Monroe, where from her decks the crewmen watched the USS *Monitor* and *Virginia* battle the following day.

The frigate was sent north to the Potomac to protect the capital against a possible naval invasion and returned to the Hampton Roads in late April. While Lincoln was visiting the Roads, the *St. Lawrence* departed to become the flagship of the East Gulf Coast Squadron. By 1864, she was back at the Roads as the North Atlantic Squadron's ordnance ship.[57]

Susquehanna, USS

The U.S. Navy commissioned the triple-masted side-wheel steamer *Susquehanna,* with a crew of 300 men and 18 guns, in 1850. She was part of Matthew Perry's fleet when Japan was opened to American trade in 1853 and also served in the Mediterranean. Her early

56 Osbon, *Hand Book*, 243; Mooney, ed., *Naval Fighting Ships*, 6:435-36.

57 Osbon, *Hand Book*, 248; www.history.navy.mil/research/histories/ship-histories/danfs/s /st-lawrence.html.

wartime assignments included helping to capture Hatteras Inlet and Port Royal and stopping blockade-runners. The *Susquehanna* was posted to Hampton Roads in April 1862 to strengthen the effort to contain the CSS *Virginia*, and she took part in the bombardment of Sewell's Point. Her reliable paddle wheels were removed during an attempted conversion to screw propulsion. This work took the ship out of commission from May 1863 to July 1864. Back in action late in the war, she took part in the attacks on Fort Fisher. During the second attempt to take the fort, her 150-pound rifled cannon burst. Following repairs and the end of the war, the *Susquehanna* was sent to the South Atlantic. She was decommissioned in 1868 and sold for scrap in 1883.[58]

Teaser, CSS (USS)

Sometimes spelled *Teazer*, this steam-paddle tugboat served both sides during the war. The state of Virginia bought the old tugboat *York River* early in the war and reassigned her to the Confederate Navy. She played an active role under Lt. William A. Webb in the fighting in Hampton Roads on March 8-9, 1862, as a tender to the CSS *Virginia* and received the thanks of the Confederate Congress for her service there. She escaped up the James River before the fall of Norfolk.

After the demise of the *Virginia*, the *Teaser* served mainly as a "minelayer," setting and servicing Confederate torpedoes in the James and acted as the launching pad for the Confederate hydrogen balloon *Gazelle*. Under the command of Lt. Hunter Davidson, a former commander of one section of the *Virginia's* broadside guns, the *Teaser* sailed down the James River to get close enough to the action of the Seven Days' battles so the *Gazelle* could be sent aloft to observe the battle lines. However, the *Teaser* grounded along the riverbank on July 4, 1862. The USS *Maratanza* spotted her. Armed with only two small guns, the *Teaser* was not prepared to fight and when an enemy shell exploded her boiler, her crew abandoned ship. An attempt to blow her up failed, and she was captured. As a Union gunboat, the *Teaser* sailed with the Potomac River Flotilla and operated in the Nansemond River, interdicting small-scale Confederate smuggling operations. The *Teaser* was decommissioned shortly after the war and auctioned off. She reverted back to her original name and occupation as the merchant boat *York River*.[59]

58 Silverstone, *Warships*, 23; Osbon, *Hand Book*, 252-53; Mooney, ed., *Naval Fighting Ships*, 6: 685-86.

59 Charles M. Evans, *The War of the Aeronauts: A History of Ballooning During the Civil War* (Mechanicsburg, PA, 2002), 206-07, 214, 241-43; Silverstone, *Warships*, 106; Mooney, ed., *Naval Fighting Ships*, 2:573, 7:76-77.

Thomas Jefferson, CSS

See the entry on the *Jamestown*, CSS.

United States, USS (CSS)

The sailing frigate *United States* was one of the oldest ships in the U.S. Navy. Launched in 1797, she was the first of the 44-gun ships authorized by the new nation. The frigate served in the War of 1812 and other conflicts, was decommissioned in 1849 at the Gosport Navy Yard. She was considered worthless by the beginning of the Civil War and no attempt was made to destroy her during the April 1861 evacuation. The Confederate Navy, which sometimes called the old ship the *Confederate States*, placed a few cannons on her as a floating gun platform and she was used as a receiving ship for naval personnel awaiting orders. With the expected invasion by Union forces, the *United States* was moved out and sunk to partially block the Elizabeth River channel to Norfolk. After the reoccupation, the ship was re-floated and broken up.[60]

Virginia, CSS

Unable to confront the U.S. Navy ship-to-ship, Confederate Secretary of the Navy Stephen Mallory decided to build ironclads and purchase ships overseas. John M. Brooke, who worked in the Navy Department, sketched out a design for one such vessel, but he was unable to create the necessary detailed drawings. John L. Porter, a naval constructor at the Gosport Navy Yard, performed that work (though the two men spent the rest of their lives arguing about who did exactly what). Construction from scratch was not practical at that point in the war, so the burned and sunken USS *Merrimack*, recently raised and in the Gosport dry dock, was converted into an ironclad. After cutting the former steam-and-sail frigate to the waterline, Porter created the iron-covered "barn roof" to create the ship's gun platform at water level. From inside to outside, the shield consisted of 14 inches of yellow pine, four inches of pine, four inches of oak, two inches of horizontal rolled iron plates, and two inches of vertical rolled iron plates for a total of 22 inches of wood and four inches of iron. Porter also added an iron ram to the ship's prow. Though a formidable fighter, the *Virginia* was plagued by her deep draft, her slow speed, and her unreliable engines.

60 Chapelle, *Sailing Navy*, 127; Francis W. Dawson, *Reminiscences of Confederate Service, 1861-1865*, Bell I. Wiley, ed. (Baton Rouge, LA, 1980), 37.

The *Virginia's* foray into Hampton Roads on March 8, 1862, resulted in the most important and spectacular Southern naval victory of the entire war. Unable to escape out of Hampton Roads up the James River because she drew too much water, she was destroyed by her crew off Craney Island on May 11, 1862.[61]

Whitehall, USS

On March 9, 1862, the *Whitehall* assisted in moving the USS *Minnesota* off the bottom of Hampton Roads. The former ferryboat, which had been converted into a gunboat, may have been damaged by a shot from the *Virginia* during the fighting the previous day. The next day, while back at anchorage near Fort Monroe, the *Whitehall* caught fire and was destroyed after her guns and ammunition exploded.[62]

Yorktown, USS

See the entry for the *Patrick Henry*, CSS.

Zouave, USS

When black smoke drifted down the Elizabeth River toward Hampton Roads on March 8, 1862, the screw tugboat *Zouave* was sent to investigate. Before the little boat, which carried a 30-pound rifled gun forward and a smaller howitzer aft, crossed the mouth of the James River, it was plain the smoke was coming from the new Confederate ironclad *Virginia*, which the Union knew had been built but had not yet been seen in the Roads. Under the command of Acting Master Henry Reaney, the *Zouave* fired six rounds with no effect. A signal from the USS *Cumberland* recalled the tug. The *Zouave's* main job when the *Virginia* appeared was to maneuver the sailing ships *Cumberland* and *Congress*. Unable to prevent the sinking of the *Cumberland*, the tug moved the *Congress* into shallower water while under fire from the *Virginia's* escort ships *Patrick Henry* and *Jamestown*, as well as occasional poorly aimed shots from the U.S. Army batteries at Newport News. When the *Congress*

61 Silverstone, *Warships*, 202; Porter, *Record of Events*, 335.

62 Joseph G. Fiveash, Virginia (Merrimac)-Monitor *Engagement* (Norfolk, VA, 1907), 22; Cowtan, *National Zouaves*, 71; Henry Reaney, "The *Monitor* and *Merrimac*," Nov. 7, 1897, *War Papers Read Before the Michigan Commandery of the Military Order of the Loyal Legion of the United States*, 60 vols. (Wilmington, NC, 1993), 2:167.

showed the white flag, the *Zouave* cut loose the connecting hawser to continue fighting. Despite severe damage to her rudder and propeller, she next made her way to the grounded USS *Minnesota* and remained by the big frigate's side all night and the next day as the *Monitor* and *Virginia* fought on March 9. The *Zouave* was later towed to Baltimore for repairs and returned to Hampton Roads in time for President Lincoln's visit in May.

For the most part, the *Zouave* remained in the Hampton Roads-James River area for the rest of the war performing picket duty, towing ships, and guarding against torpedo boat attacks. She was decommissioned in June 1865, sold, and worked as a small merchant ship until 1918.[63]

63 James L. Mooney & Richard T. Speer, eds., *Naval Fighting Ships*, 8 vols. (Washington, DC, 1981), 8:569-70; Silverstone, *Warships*, 122; Henry Reaney, "How the Gun-Boat 'Zouave' Aided the 'Congress,'" Johnson & Buel, eds., in *B&L*, 714-15.

Bibliography

Newspapers

Atlanta *Southern Confederacy*
Baltimore *American*
Baltimore *Sun*
Boston *Liberator*
Brooklyn *Daily Eagle*
Charleston *Mercury*
Columbus *Daily Enquirer*
Delaware *State Journal and Statesman*
Edgecombe County (North Carolina) *Southerner*
Edgefield (South Carolina) *Advertiser*
Harper's Weekly
Illustrated London News
Memphis *Public Ledger*
Mobile *Register*
New York *Daily Tribune*
New York *Herald*
New York *Home Journal*
New York *Sun*
New York Times
Norfolk *Day Book*
Petersburg *Daily Express*
Philadelphia *Christian Recorder*
Philadelphia Inquirer
Philadelphia *Press*
Pickens Court House (South Carolina) *Keowee Courier*
Richmond *Daily Dispatch*

Richmond *Enquirer*
Richmond *Whig*
Shreveport *South-Western*
Washington *Evening Star*
Washington *National Republican*
Washington *National Tribune*
Washington *Times*

Government Sources

Kennedy, Joseph C. G. *Population of the United States in 1860; Compiled from the Original Returns of the Eighth Census.* Bureau of the Census. Washington, DC: U.S. Government Printing Office, 1864.

Lull, Edward P. *History of the United States Navy-Yard at Gosport, Virginia.* Washington, DC: Government Printing Office, 1874.

Naval History Division. *Civil War Naval Chronology, 1861-1865.* Washington, DC: Navy Department, 1971.

Official Records of the Union and Confederate Navies in the War of the Rebellion. 30 Vols. Washington, DC: Government Printing Office, 1894-1922.

"Register of Commissioned and Warrant Officers of the United States Navy and Marine Corps and Reserve Officers on Active Duty." Washington, DC: Government Printing Office, 1865.

U.S. Congress. *Congressional Globe.* 37th Cong., 2nd sess., 1862.

U.S. Congress. *Journal of the Congress of the Confederate States of America, 1861-1865.* Vols. 5 and 6. U.S. Senate Document no. 234, 58th Cong., 2nd sess., 1904. American Memory, Library of Congress. memory.loc.gov/ammem. Accessed Apr. 20, 2015.

War of the Rebellion: A Compilation of the Official Records of the Union and Confederate Armies. 128 Vols. Washington, DC: Government Printing Office, 1880-1901.

Archival Sources and Manuscripts

American Swedish Historical Museum, Philadelphia
Ericsson, John. Papers

[British] National Archives, Kew, United Kingdom
HMS *Rinaldo* ship's log. January-September 1862

Casemate Museum. Fort Monroe, VA
"Abraham Lincoln's Campaign Against the Merrimack." No. 9. Tales of Old Fort Monroe, n.d.

"Fort Monroe in the Civil War." No. 6. Tales of Old Fort Monroe, n.d.

"Is It a Fort or a Fortress?" No. 5. Tales of Old Fort Monroe, n.d.

Chattahoochee Valley Historical Society, Valley, AL

Merz, Louis. Diary of Private Louis Merz

Historical Society of Pennsylvania, Philadelphia

Thompson, Samuel S. "Some Personal Experiences at Fortress Monroe in 1862"

Library of Congress, Washington, DC

Chase, Salmon P. Papers

Herndon-Weik Collection of Lincolniana

National Archives, Washington, DC

Record Group 56

Letters Sent by the Secretary of the Treasury

Naval History & Heritage Command (Hampton Roads Naval Museum), Norfolk, VA

Peters, William H. "Norfolk Navy Yard: Abandonment by Federal Authorities, Apr. 20, 1861, and same by Confederates on May 10, 1862"

New York Historical Society Library, New York City

Fox, Gustavus V. Papers

New York State Archives, Albany, NY

Corell, Philip, ed. "History of the Naval Brigade, 99th N.Y. Volunteers, Union Coast Guard, 1861-1865"

Cram, Thomas J. "Report of T. J. Cram." Wool Papers

Ritschy, Frederick W. "Reminiscences of Camp Hamilton and Norfolk, Va."

Shurtleff, R. M., & Mendenhall, J. B. "Formation of Naval Brigade"

Wool, John E. Papers

Norfolk Public Library, Norfolk, VA

Gordan, Virginia. "Virginia Gordan Scrapbook"

Southern Historical Collection, University of North Carolina, Chapel Hill, NC

Barney, Joseph Nicholson. Log & Diary

Virginia Historical Society, Richmond, VA

Whitlock, Philip. Recollections, 1843-1913

Primary Published Sources

Basler, Roy P., ed. *The Collected Works of Abraham Lincoln.* 9 Vols. New Brunswick, NJ: Rutgers University Press, 1953.

Brooke, George M., Jr., ed. *Ironclads and Big Guns of the Confederacy: The Journal and Letters of John M. Brooke.* Columbia, SC: University of South Carolina Press, 2002.

Brooke, John M. "The *Virginia*, or *Merrimac*: Her Real Projector," in *Southern Historical Society Papers*, 52 vols. (January 1891), vol. 19, 3-34.

Burnside, Ambrose E. "The Burnside Expedition," in Johnson, Robert Underwood & Buel, Clarence Clough, eds., *Battles and Leaders of the Civil War*, 4 vols. New York: Castle Books, 1956, vol. 1, 660-69.

Cannon, Le Grand B. *Personal Reminiscences of the Rebellion, 1861-1866.* New York: Burr Printing House, 1895.

Carpenter, Francis Bicknell. *Six Months at the White House with Abraham Lincoln: The Story of a Picture.* New York: Hurd and Houghton, 1866.

Carr, Joseph B. "Operations of 1861 About Fort Monroe," in Johnson, Robert Underwood & Buel, Clarence Clough, eds., *Battles and Leaders of the Civil War*, 4 vols. New York: Castle Books, 1956, vol. 2, 144-52.

Cowtan, Charles W. *Services of the Tenth New York Volunteers, National Zouaves, in the War of the Rebellion.* New York: Charles H. Ludwig, Publisher, 1882.

Cram, Thomas J. *Memoir Showing How to Bring the Lead, Copper, Silver and Gold of Arizona into the Marts of the World, and Project of a Railroad Through Sonora to Connect with the Pacific Railroad in Arizona.* Washington, DC: Henry Polkinhorn, Printer, 1858.

Crist, Lynda Lasswell, et al., eds. *The Papers of Jefferson Davis.* 14 Vols. Baton Rouge, LA: Louisiana State University Press, 1995.

Dahlgren, Madeleine Vinton, ed. *Memoir of John A. Dahlgren, Rear Admiral, U.S.N.* Boston: J. R. Osgood and Co., 1882.

Daly, Robert W., ed. *Aboard the USS Monitor: 1862, The Letters of Acting Paymaster William Frederick Keeler, U.S. Navy to his Wife, Anna.* Annapolis, MD: United States Naval Institute, 1964.

Dana, Charles A. *Lincoln and His Cabinet: A Lecture Delivered Before the New Haven Colony Historical Society, Tuesday, March 10, 1896.* New York: D. Appleton and Co., 1899.

——. *Recollections of the Civil War with the Leaders at Washington and in the Field in the Sixties.* New York: D. Appleton and Co., 1898.

Davis, Varina. *Jefferson Davis, ex-President of the Confederate States of America: A Memoir.* 2 Vols. New York: Bedford Co., 1890.

Dawson, Francis W. *Reminiscences of Confederate Service, 1861-1865*, Bell I. Wiley, ed. Baton Rouge, LA: Louisiana State University Press, 1980.

Donald, David, ed. *Inside Lincoln's Cabinet: The Civil War Diaries of Salmon P. Chase.* New York: Longmans, Green and Co., 1954.

Eisenberg, Albert C. & Hammerson, Michael, eds. *"If I Am Alive Next Summer": The Civil War Letters of Captain Charles Robinson Johnson of the 16th Massachusetts Infantry, "The Iron Sixteenth."* Berwyn Heights, MD: Heritage Books Inc., 2015.

Ericsson, John. "The Building of the 'Monitor,'" in Johnson, Robert Underwood & Buel, Clarence Clough, eds., *Battles and Leaders of the Civil War*, 4 vols. New York: Castle Books, 1956, vol. 1, 730-44.

Flanders, Alan B. & Westfall, Neale O., eds. *Memoirs of E. A. Jack, Steam Engineer, CSS Virginia.* White Stone, VA: Brandylane Publishers, 1998.

Franklin, Samuel Rhoades. *Memoirs of a Rear Admiral: Who has Served for More than Half a Century in the Navy of the United States.* New York: Harper & Brothers, 1898.

Fuller, Richard F. *Chaplin Fuller: Being a Life Sketch of a New England Clergyman and Army Chaplain.* Boston: Walker, Wise, and Co., 1863.

Goldwaite, Richard and Goldwaite, Ellen. *A Handful of Providence: The Civil War Letters of Lt. Richard Goldwaite, New York Volunteers*, Marti Skipper and Jane Taylor, eds. Jefferson, NC: McFarland & Co., 2004.

Hawkins, Rush C. "Early Coast Operations in North Carolina," in Johnson, Robert Underwood & Buel, Clarence Clough, eds., *Battles and Leaders of the Civil War*, 4 vols. New York: Castle Books, 1956, vol. 1, 232-59.

Hewett, Janet B., ed. *Supplement to the Official Record of the Union and Confederate Armies.* 80 Vols. Wilmington, NC: Broadfoot Publishing Co., 1997.

Higgins, John F. "Brilliant Career of the Merrimac." *Confederate Veteran* (August 1900), vol. 8, 356-57.

Homans, Isaac Smith. "Internal and Coastwise Commercial Intercourse." *The Merchant's Magazine and Commercial Review*, July-December 1862, 575-76.

"Interesting Data About the Merrimac." *Confederate Veteran* (April 1908), 16, xvii-xix.

Jones, Catesby ap Roger. "Services of the 'Virginia' (Merrimac)," in *Southern Historical Society Papers* (February-March 1883), vol. 11, 65-75.

Jones, John Beauchamp. *A Rebel War Clerk's Diary at the Confederate States Capital.* 2 Vols. Philadelphia: J. B. Lippincott and Co., 1866.

Lamon, Ward Hill. *Recollections of Abraham Lincoln, 1847-1865*, Dorothy Lamon Teillard. ed. Washington, DC: Published by Editor, 1911.

Lee, Robert E. *The Wartime Papers of R. E. Lee*, 2 Vols. New York: Collectors Reprints Inc., 1996.

Littlepage, Hardin Beverly. "A Midshipman Aboard the Virginia." Part 1. *Civil War Times Illustrated* (April 1974), 4-6, 8, 10-11, 42-47.

Martin, Isabella D. & Avary, Myrta Lockett, eds. *A Diary from Dixie, as Written by Mary Boykin Chesnut.* New York: D. Appleton and Co., 1905.

Marvel, William, ed. *The Monitor Chronicles: One Sailor's Account.* New York: Simon & Schuster, 2000.

McClellan, George B. *McClellan's Own Story: The War for the Union, the Soldiers Who Fought It, the Civilians Who Directed It and His Relations to It and to Them.* New York: Charles L. Webster & Co., 1887.

McGuire, Judith Brockenbrough. *Diary of a Southern Refugee during the War.* New York: E. J. Hale & Son, 1868.

Moore, Frank, ed. *The Rebellion Record: A Diary of American Events, with Documents, Narratives, Illustrative Incidents, Poetry, etc.* 11 Vols. New York: G. P. Putnam, 1862.

Morgan, James Morris. *Recollections of a Rebel Reefer.* Boston: Houghton Mifflin Co., 1917.

Murphey, Thomas G. *Four Years in the War: The History of the First Regiment of Delaware Veteran Volunteers.* Philadelphia: James S. Claxton, 1866.

Nicolay, John G., & Hay, John. *Abraham Lincoln: A History.* 10 Vols. New York: Century Co., 1890.

Norris, William. "The Story of the Confederate States Ship *Virginia* (Once *Merrimac*): Her Victory over the *Monitor*," in *Southern Historical Society Papers*, 52 vols. (October 1917), vol. 42, 204-33.

O'Brien, John Emmet. *Telegraphing in Battle: Reminiscences of the Civil War.* Scranton, PA: Raeder Press, 1910.

Osbon, Bradley S., ed. *Hand Book of the United States Navy: Being a Compilation of All the Principal Events in the History of Every Vessel of the United States Navy from April, 1861, to May, 1864.* New York: D. Van Nostrand, 1864.

Paine, Albert Bigelow, ed. *A Sailor of Fortune: Personal Memoirs of Captain B. S. Osbon.* London: McClure, Phillips & Co., 1906.

Parker, William Harwar. *Recollections of a Naval Officer, 1841-1865.* New York: Charles Scribners' Sons, 1883.

Pease, Theodore Calvin & Randall, James G., eds. *The Diary of Orville Hickman Browning.* 2 Vols. Springfield, IL: Illinois State Historical Library, 1925.

Porter, John W. H. *A Record of Events in Norfolk County, Virginia, from April 19th, 1861, to May 10th, 1862, with a History of the Soldiers and Sailors of Norfolk County, Norfolk City and Portsmouth Who Served in the Confederate States Army and Navy.* Portsmouth, VA: W. A. Fiske, 1892.

——. "Origin of an Ironclad: How the Merrimac Came to Be Transformed." *Confederate Veteran* (May 1915), 23:219-21.

Putnam, Sallie Brock. *Richmond During the War: Four Years of Personal Observation.* New York: G. W. Carleton & Co., 1867.

Reaney, Henry. "How the Gun-Boat 'Zouave' Aided the 'Congress'," in Johnson, Robert Underwood & Buel, Clarence Clough, eds., *Battles and Leaders of the Civil War*, 4 vols. New York: Castle Books, 1956, vol. 1, 714-15.

——. "The *Monitor* and *Merrimac*," Nov. 7, 1897, *War Papers Read Before the Michigan Commandery of the Military Order of the Loyal Legion of the United States*, 60 vols. Wilmington, NC: Broadfoot Publishing Co., 1993.

Richardson, James D. *A Compilation of the Messages and Papers of the Confederacy Including Diplomatic Correspondence, 1861-1865.* 2 Vols. Nashville, TN: United States Publishing Co., 1904.

Selfridge, Thomas O., Jr. *What Finer Tradition: The Memoirs of Thomas O. Selfridge Jr., Rear Admiral, U.S.N.* Columbia, SC: University of South Carolina Press, 1987.

Seville, William P. *History of the First Regiment, Delaware Volunteers: From the Commencement of the Three Months Service to the Final Muster-Out at the Close of the Rebellion.* Wilmington, DE: The Historical Society of Delaware, 1884.

Seward, Frederick William. *Reminiscences of a War-Time Statesman and Diplomat, 1830-1915.* New York: G. P. Putnam's Sons, 1916.

Stewart, William H. *A Pair of Blankets: War-Time History in Letters to the Young People of the South*, Benjamin H. Trask, ed. Wilmington, NC: Broadfoot Publishing Co., 1990.

Thomas, Henry Walter. *History of the Doles-Cook Brigade of Northern Virginia, C.S.A., Containing Muster Roles of Each Company of the Fourth, Twelfth, Twenty-first and Forty-fourth Georgia Regiments, with a Short Sketch of the Services of Each Member, and a Complete History of Each Regiment, by One of Its Own Members.* Atlanta: Franklin Printing and Publishing Co., 1903.

Thompson, Robert Means & Wainwright, Richard, eds. *Confidential Correspondence of Gustavus Vasa Fox, Assistant Secretary of the Navy, 1861-1865.* 2 Vols. New York: Naval History Society, 1918.

U.S. Congress. *Report of the Joint Committee on the Conduct of the War.* 9 Vols. Wilmington, NC: Broadfoot Publishing Co., 1998.

Vandiver, Frank, ed. *The Civil War Diary of General Josiah Gorgas.* Tuscaloosa, AL: University of Alabama Press, 1947.

Viele, Egbert Ludovicus. "A Trip with Lincoln, Chase and Stanton," in *Scribner's Monthly: An Illustrated Magazine for the People* (October 1878), 813-22.

Walters, John. *Norfolk Blues: The Civil War Diary of the Norfolk Light Artillery Blues*, Kenneth Wiley, ed. Shippensburg, PA: Burd Street Press, 1997.

Weiss, Francis. *Reminiscences of Chevalier Karl de Unter-Schill, Later Known as Colonel Francis Weiss.* Troy, NY: Edward H. Lisk, 1903.

Welles, Edgar T., ed. *Diary of Gideon Welles: Secretary of the Navy Under Lincoln and Johnson.* 3 Vols. Boston: Houghton Mifflin Co., 1911.

Welles, Gideon. "The First Iron-Clad Monitor," in *Annals of the War by Leading Participants North and South*, Alexander Kelley McClure, ed. Philadelphia: Times Publishing Co., 1879.

Wells, William S., ed. *The Original United States Warship* Monitor*: Copies of Correspondence Between the Late Cornelius S. Bushnell, Captain John Ericsson and Gideon Welles.* New Haven, CT: The Cornelius S. Bushnell National Memorial Association, 1899.

White, Elsberry Valentine. *The First Iron-Clad Naval Engagement in the World: History of Facts of the Great Naval Battle Between the* Merrimac-Virginia*, C.S.N., and the Ericsson* Monitor*, U.S.N., Hampton Roads, March 8 and 9, 1862.* New York: J. S. Ogilvie Publishing Co., 1906.

Wood, John Taylor. "The First Fight of Iron-Clads," in Johnson, Robert Underwood & Buel, Clarence Clough, eds., *Battles and Leaders of the Civil War*, 4 vols. New York: Castle Books, 1956, vol. 1, 692-711.

Wright, Robert. "Sinking of the *Jamestown*," in *Southern Historical Society Papers*, 52 vols. (January-December 1901), vol. 29, 371-72.

Zerega, Alfred L. B. "The Last Days of the Rebel Iron-Clad *Merrimac* and Occupation of Norfolk, as Seen from the U.S.S. *Susquehanna*." Feb. 1897, in *War Papers: Being Papers Read Before the Commandery of the District of Columbia, Military Order of the Loyal Legion of the United States*. 70 Vols. Wilmington, NC: Broadfoot Publishing Co., 1993.

Published Secondary Sources

Ames, Ethel. *The Story of Coal and Iron in Alabama*. Birmingham, AL: Chamber of Commerce, 1910.

Baldwin, Leland D. "The Watermelon Army Marches," in *Whisky Rebels: The Story of a Frontier Uprising*. Pittsburgh: University of Pittsburgh Press, 1967.

Barthell, Edward E., Jr. *The Mystery of the Merrimack*. Muskegon, MI: Danna Printing Co., 1959.

Bates, Samuel. *History of Pennsylvania Volunteers, 1861-5*. 5 Vols. Harrisburg, PA: B. Singerly, State Printer, 1869.

Boatner, Mark M., III. *The Civil War Dictionary*. New York: Vintage Books, 1988.

Brewer, James. *The Confederate Negro: Virginia's Craftsman and Military Laborers, 1861-1865*. Durham, NC: Duke University Press, 1969.

Brooks, Noah. *Abraham Lincoln: The Nation's Leader in the Great Struggle Through Which Was Maintained the Existence of the United States*. New York: G. P. Putnam's Sons, 1888.

Browning, Robert M., Jr. *From Cape Charles to Cape Fear: The North Atlantic Blockading Squadron During the Civil War*. Tuscaloosa, AL: The University of Alabama Press, 1993.

Burton, H. W. *The History of Norfolk, Virginia*. Norfolk, VA: Norfolk Virginia Job Printer, 1877.

Cahin, Joan E. *First Lady of the Confederacy: Varina Davis' Civil War*. Cambridge, MA: The Belknap Press, 2006.

Carse, Robert. *Blockade: The Civil War at Sea*. New York: Rinehart & Co., 1958.

Chapelle, Howard I. *The History of the American Sailing Navy: The Ships and Their Development*. New York: W. W. Norton & Co., 1949.

Cobb, J. Michael. *Fort Wool: Star-Spangled Banner Rising*. Charleston, SC: History Press, 2009.

Collum, Richard S. *The Description of the Fight Between the* Monitor *and* Merrimac *on 9th of March, 1862*. Philadelphia: Pennsylvania Commandery, Naval Order of the United States, 1898.

Conrad, James Lee. *Rebel Reefers: The Organization and Midshipmen of the Confederate States Naval Academy*. Cambridge, MA: Da Capo Press, 2003.

Coski, John M. *Capital Navy: The Men, Ships, and Operations of the James River Squadron*. Campbell, CA: Savas Woodbury Publishers, 1996.

Davidson, William H. "A Word About the Diary," in "Diary of Private Louis Merz." Chattahoochee Valley Historical Society, Valley, AL.

Davis, George B., Perry, Leslie J. & Kirkley, Joseph W., eds. *Atlas to Accompany the Official Records of the Union and Confederate Armies, 1891-1895.* New York: Barnes & Noble Books, 2003.

Donald, David H. *Lincoln.* New York: Simon & Schuster, 1995.

Dorr, Eben P. *A Brief Sketch of the First Monitor and Its Inventor.* Buffalo, NY: Buffalo Historical Society, 1874.

Dougherty, Kevin J. *Ships of the Civil War, 1861-1865.* New York: Metro Books, 2013.

Egnal, Marc. *Clash of Extremes: The Economic Origins of the Civil War.* New York: Hill & Wang, 2009.

Evans, Charles M. *The War of the Aeronauts: A History of Ballooning During the Civil War.* Mechanicsburg, PA: Stackpole Books, 2002.

Fiveash, Joseph G. Virginia (Merrimac)–Monitor *Engagement.* Norfolk, VA: Fiveash Publishing Corp., 1907.

Freeman, Douglas Southall. *Lee's Lieutenants: A Study in Command.* 3 Vols. New York: Charles Scribner's Sons, 1949.

Gibson, Charles Dana & E. Kay. *Assault and Logistics: Union Army Coastal and River Operations, 1861-1866.* The Army's Navy Series. 2 Vols. Camden, ME: Ensign Press, 1995.

——. *Dictionary of Transports and Combatant Vessels, Steam and Sail, Employed by the Union Army, 1861-1868.* The Army's Navy Series. Camden, ME: Ensign Press, 1995.

Grimsley, Mark. "Lincoln as Commander in Chief: Forays into Generalship," in *The War Worth Fighting: Abraham Lincoln's Presidency and Civil War America*, Stephen D. Engle, ed. Gainesville, FL: University Press of Florida, 2015.

Hansen, Harry. *The Civil War: A History.* New York: New American Library, 1961.

Heilder, David S. & Heilder, Jeanne T., eds. *Encyclopedia of the American Civil War: A Political, Social, and Military History.* New York: W. W. Norton & Co., 2000.

Hoole, William Stanley & Hoole, Addie Shirley. *Confederate Norfolk: The Letters of a Virginia Lady to the Mobile* Register, *1861-1862.* Tuscaloosa, AL: Confederate Publishing Co., 1984.

Kern, Florence. "President Lincoln on Board Cutter Miami," in *The United States Revenue Cutters in the Civil War.* Bethesda, MD: Alised Enterprises, 2010.

Kettell, Thomas P. *History of the Great Rebellion.* Hartford, CT: L. Stebbins, 1865.

Leonard, John William. *History of the City of New York: 1609-1890.* New York: The Journal of Commerce and Commercial Bulletin, 1910.

Long, Armistead Lindsay. *Memoirs of Robert E. Lee: His Military and Personal History.* New York: J. M. Stoddart & Co., 1886.

Mabry, William S. *Brief Sketch of the Career of Captain Catesby ap R. Jones.* Selma, AL: privately printed, 1912.

Marvel, William. *Lincoln's Autocrat: The Life of Edwin Stanton.* Chapel Hill, NC: University of North Carolina Press, 2015.

Miller, Richard F., ed. *States at War: A Reference Guide for New York in the Civil War.* 6 Vols. Hanover, NH: University Press of New England, 2014.

Mooney, James L., ed. *Dictionary of American Naval Fighting Ships.* 8 Vols. Washington, DC: Naval Historical Center, 1959-1981.

Neeno, Timothy. "Louis M. Goldsborough," in *The Civil War Naval Encyclopedia*, Spencer Tucker, Paul G. Pierpaoli & William E. White, eds. Santa Barbara, CA: ABC-CLIO, 2011.

Nelson, James L. *Reign of Iron: The Story of the First Battling Ironclads, the Monitor and the Merrimack.* New York: HarperCollins, 2004.

Park, Carl D. *Ironclad Down: The USS* Merrimack-CSS Virginia *From Construction to Destruction.* Annapolis, MD: Naval Institute Press, 2007.

Peterson, Merrill D. *Lincoln in American Memory.* New York: Oxford Press, 1994.

Phisterer, Frederick. *New York in the War of the Rebellion, 1861-1865.* Albany, NY: Weed, Parsons & Co., 1890.

Pollock, Edward. *Sketch Book of Portsmouth, Va.: Its People and its Trade.* Portsmouth, VA: G. W. Purdie & Co., 1886.

Quarstein, John. *Sink Before Surrender: The CSS* Virginia. The History Press, 2012.

Salter, William. *The Life of James W. Grimes, Governor of Iowa, 1854-1858; a Senator of the United States, 1859-1869.* New York: D. Appleton & Co., 1876.

Scharf, J. Thomas. *History of the Confederate States Navy From Its Organization to the Surrender of Its Last Vessel.* New York: Rogers & Sherwood, 1887.

Silverstone, Paul H. *Warships of the Civil War Navies.* Annapolis, MD: Naval Institute Press, 1989.

Snow, Peter. *When Britain Burned the White House: The 1814 Invasion of Washington.* New York: Thomas Dunne Books, 2013.

Stevens, Jesse F. *Massachusetts Soldiers, Sailors, and Marines in the Civil War.* 8 Vols. Norwood, MA: Norwood Press, 1931.

Still, William N., Jr. *The Confederate Navy: The Ships, Men and Organization, 1861-65.* London: Conway Maritime Press, 1997.

Sullivan, David M. *The United States Marine Corps in the Civil War—The Second Year.* Shippensburg, PA: White Mane Publishing Co., 1997.

Tucker, Spencer C. "Joseph Nicholson Barney," in *The Civil War Naval Encyclopedia*, Spencer Tucker, Paul G. Pierpaoli & William E. White, eds. Santa Barbara, CA: ABC-CLIO, 2011.

Tucker, Spencer, Pierpaoli, Paul G., and White, William E., eds., *The Civil War Naval Encyclopedia.* Santa Barbara, CA: ABC-CLIO, 2011.

Tyler, Lyon G., ed. *Men of Mark in Virginia: Ideals of American Life: A Collection of Biographies of the Leading Men in the State.* 5 Vols. Washington, DC: Men of Mark Publishing Co., 1909.

Union Army, The: A History of Military Affairs in the Loyal States, 1861-65—Records of the Regiments in the Union Army—Cyclopedia of Battles—Memoirs of Commanders and Soldiers. 8 Vols. Madison, WI: Federal Publishing Co., 1908.

Warner, Ezra J. *Generals in Blue: Lives of the Union Commanders.* Baton Rouge, LA: Louisiana State University Press, 1964.

——. *Generals in Gray: Lives of the Confederate Commanders.* Baton Rouge: LA: Louisiana State University Press, 1959.

Wertenbaker, Thomas J. *Norfolk: Historic Southern Port.* Durham, NC: Duke University Press, 1931.

Wheeler, Tom. *Mr. Lincoln's T-Mails: How Abraham Lincoln Used the Telegraph to Win the Civil War.* New York: HarperCollins, 2006.

Williams, John Hoyt. *The Rise and Fall of the Paraguayan Republic, 1800-1870.* Austin, TX: University of Texas Press, 2014.

Wilson, James Grant, & Fiske, John, eds. *Appleton's Cyclopaedia of American Biography.* 7 Vols. Rev. ed. New York: D. Appleton and Co., 1900.

Wyllie, Arthur. *The Union Navy.* Morrisville, NC: Lulu Press, 2007.

Articles

"Adams Express Company Employee's Benevolent Association." *The Express Gazette,* March 1903, 78.

Flanders, Alan B. "The Man Who Troubled the Waters," *Columbiad,* No. 3, 1:108-26.

Johnson, Ludwell H., III. "Blockade or Trade Monopoly? John A. Dix and the Union Occupation of Norfolk." *The Virginia Magazine of History and Biography,* 1985, 55-78.

Kyff, Robert. "The Whiskey Rebellion." *American History,* July-Aug. 1994, 36-43, 65-66.

Metcalf, Henry Harrison. "Acworth Matters and Men: People and Affairs of a New Hampshire Hill Town." *A Granite Monthly: A New Hampshire Magazine Devoted to History.* Aug.-Sept. 1913, 257-81.

Internet Sources

Bärenreuth, Albert. Letter to his mother. http://bit.ly/2LT4HwM. Accessed January 5, 2011.

Biggs, Jeffrey R. "They Fought for the Union: A History of the First Delaware Volunteers in the Army of the Potomac." First Delaware Infantry Regiment letters. Belli Civilis Press, 2016. bellicivilis.com/letters-from-camp-hamilton. Accessed Aug. 15, 2016.

Curtis, Richard. *History of the Famous Battle Between the Iron-Clad Merrimac, C.S.N., and the Iron-Clad Monitor and the Cumberland and Congress, of the U.S. Navy,* 1907. Catalogs.marinersmuseum.org/search?query="Richard Curtis." Accessed May 5, 2019.

Davis, Caroline. "The Less Famous Lee." Emerging Civil War. Emergingcivil war.com/2014/01/11/the-less-famous-lee. Accessed Jan. 13, 2017.

"First Lieutenant Charles W. Cowtan." Collections. http://americanhistory.si.edu/ collections/search/object/nmah_1411120. Accessed Dec. 8, 2016.

Edling, Richard. "Fort Wool, Hampton, Virginia." Civil War Album. www.civil waralbum.com/misc7/fort_wool1.htm. Accessed July 6, 2007.

"Fort Monroe History." Hampton.gov/fort_monroe/history.html. Accessed May 20, 2013.

Goodwin, Eugene. "Diary." Transcript. Louise Goodwin McKlveen. www.ioweb. com/civilwar/goodwin_diary/. Accessed June 5, 2011.

Hatfield, Egon. "War of 1812 Bicentennial: Battle of Craney Island," Research, Development and Engineering Command History Office, June 6, 2013. www.army.mil/article/104909/war_of_1812_bicentennial_battle_of_craney_island. Accessed on Feb. 5, 2019.

"Intelligence in the Civil War." Washington, DC, n.d. Fas.org/irp/cia/product/ civilwar.pdf. Accessed Jan. 20, 2019.

Johnson, Albert E. H. "Reminiscences of the Hon. Edwin M. Stanton, Secretary of War." Society Records (1910). 13. www.jstor.org/stable/40067012. Accessed Dec. 12, 2016.

Lancaster, William. Letter to his wife, Maggie, May 8, 1862. home.comcast.net/~captancaster/theCivilWarLetters.htm. Accessed Aug. 12, 2004.

Lincoln Papers. Memory.loc.gov/cgibin/query/rammem/mal:@field(DOCID+@lit (d1535700). Accessed May 6, 2009.

Mallory, Stephen R. Letter to [??]. March 22, 1861. In "Early Journal Content on JSTOR." http://bit.ly/2Wecg5T. Accessed Feb. 8, 2012.

Office of the Historian. "Chiefs of Mission for Korea." U.S. Department of State. history.state.gov/departmenthistory/people/chiefsofmission/korea. Accessed Jan. 13, 2017.

"Viele's Famous Topographical Atlas of the City of New York." Treasures of the New York Public Library. http://exhibitions.nypl.org/treasures/items /show/35. Accessed Dec. 6, 2016.

Wool, John E. Letter, Dec. 10, 1865. www.sethkaller.com/item/437-General-Wool-Takes-Shot-at-McClellan. Accessed Sept. 13, 2016.

Theses

Stephens, Lucille Madora. "Historic Norfolk: 'A Child of Mars'." M.A. thesis, Southern Methodist University, August 1948.

Index

About the Author